PERSONAL MEMOIRS

OF

U. S. GRANT.

VOL. II.

PERSONAL MEMOIRS

OF

U. S. GRANT.

IN TWO VOLUMES.

VOL. II.

NEW YORK:
CHARLES L. WEBSTER & COMPANY,
1886

PERSONAL MEMOIRS OF
U.S. GRANT

By Ulysses S. Grant

Originally Published in 1885 by J. J. Little and Co.

VOLUME 2

Library of Congress Control Number: 2018953769

The Library of Congress has established a
Catalog-In-Publication for this title.

Hardcover ISBN Volumes 1 & 2   9781582188591
Hardcover ISBN Volumes 1   9781582188577
Hardcover ISBN Volumes 2   9781582188584

*River-
Moor
Books*

WWW.RiverMoorBooks.Com
Scituate, MA 02066

Rivermoor Books is an imprint of Digital Scanning Inc., reproducing Large
Print Editions of significantly relevant titles pertaining to United States
History.

TABLE of CONTENTS

VOLUME II

CHAPTER LXII

SHERMAN'S MARCH NORTH-SHERIDAN ORDERED TO
LYNCHBURG - CANBY ORDERED TO MOVE AGAINST MOBILE
- MOVEMENTS OF SCHOFIELD AND THOMAS
- CAPTURE OF COLUMBIA SOUTH CAROLINA
- SHERMAN IN THE CAROLINAS

CHAPTER LXIII

ARRIVAL OF THE PEACE COMMISSIONERS - LINCOLN AND
THE PEACE COMMISSIONERS - AN ANECDOTE OF
LINCOLN - THE WINTER BEFORE PETERSBURG
- SHERIDAN DESTROYS THE RAILROAD - GORDON CARRIES
THE PICKET LINE - PARKE RECAPTURES THE LINE
- THE BATTLE OF WHITE OAK ROAD

CHAPTER LXIV

INTERVIEW WITH SHERIDAN - GRAND MOVEMENT OF THE
ARMY OF THE POTOMAC - SHERIDAN'S ADVANCE ON FIVE
FORKS - BATTLE OF FIVE FORKS - PARKE AND WRIGHT
STORM THE ENEMY'S LINE - BATTLES BEFORE PETERSBURG

CHAPTER LXV

THE CAPTURE OF PETERSBURG - MEETING PRESIDENT
LINCOLN IN PETERSBURG THE CAPTURE OF RICHMOND -
PURSUING THE ENEMY - VISIT TO SHERIDAN AND MEADE

CHAPTER LXVI

BATTLE OF SAILOR'S CREEK - ENGAGEMENT AT FARMVILLE
- CORRESPONDENCE WITH GENERAL LEE
- SHERIDAN INTERCEPTS THE ENEMY

MAPS AND ILLUSTRATIONS

VOLUME II

PERSONAL MEMOIRS

OF

U.S. GRANT VOLUME II

CHAPTER XL

FIRST MEETING WITH SECRETARY STANTON - GENERAL ROSECRANS - COMMANDING MILITARY DIVISION OF MISSISSIPPI - ANDREW JOHNSON'S ADDRESS - ARRIVAL AT CHATTANOOGA.

THE reply (to my telegram of October 16, 1863, from Cairo, announcing my arrival at that point) came on the morning of the 17th, directing me to proceed immediately to the Galt House, Louisville, where I would meet an officer of the War Department with my instructions. I left Cairo within an hour or two after the receipt of this dispatch, going by rail via Indianapolis. Just as the train I was on was starting out of the depot at Indianapolis a messenger came running up to stop it, saying the Secretary of War was coming into the station and wanted to see me.

I had never met Mr. Stanton up to that time, though we had held frequent conversations over the wires the year before, when I was in Tennessee. Occasionally at night he would order the wires between the War Department and my headquarters to be connected, and we would hold a conversation for an hour or two. On this occasion the Secretary was accompanied by Governor Brough of Ohio, whom I had never met, though he and my father had been old acquaintances. Mr. Stanton dismissed the special train that had brought him to Indianapolis, and accompanied me to Louisville.

Up to this time no hint had been given me of what was wanted after I left Vicksburg, except the suggestion in one of Halleck's dispatches that I had better go to Nashville and superintend the operation of troops sent to relieve Rosecrans. Soon after we started the Secretary handed me two orders, saying that I might take my choice of them. The two were identical in all but one particular. Both created the "Military Division of the Mississippi," (giving me the command) composed of the Departments of the Ohio, the Cumberland, and the Tennessee and all the territory from the Alleghenies to the Mississippi River north of Banks' command in the southwest. One order left the department commanders as they were, while the other relieved Rosecrans and assigned Thomas to his place. I accepted the latter. We reached Louisville after night and, if I remember rightly, in a cold, drizzling rain. The Secretary of War told me afterwards that he caught a cold on that occasion from which he never expected to recover. He never did.

A day was spent in Louisville, the Secretary giving me the military news at the capital and talking about the disappointment at the results of some of the campaigns. By the evening of the day after our arrival all matters of discussion seemed exhausted, and I left the hotel to spend the evening away, both Mrs. Grant (who was with me) and myself having relatives living in Louisville. In the course of the evening Mr. Stanton received a dispatch from Mr. C.A. Dana, then in Chattanooga, informing him that unless prevented Rosecrans would retreat, and advising peremptory orders against his doing so.

As stated before, after the fall of Vicksburg I urged strongly upon the government the propriety of a movement against Mobile. General Rosecrans had been at Murfreesboro', Tennessee, with a large and well equipped army from early in the year 1863, with Bragg confronting him with a force quite equal to his own at first, considering it was on the defensive. But after the investment of Vicksburg Bragg's army was largely depleted to strengthen Johnston, in Mississippi, who was being reinforced to raise the siege. I frequently wrote General Halleck suggesting that Rosecrans should move against Bragg. By so doing he would either detain the latter's troops where they were or lay Chattanooga open to capture. General Halleck strongly approved the suggestion, and finally wrote me that he had repeatedly ordered Rosecrans to advance, but that the latter had constantly failed to comply with the order, and at last, after having held a council of war, had replied in effect that it was a military maxim "not to fight two decisive battles at the same time." If true, the maxim was not applicable in this case. It would be bad to be defeated in two decisive battles fought the same day, but it would not be bad to win them. I, however, was fighting no battle, and the siege of Vicksburg had drawn from Rosecrans' front so many of the enemy that his chances of victory were much greater than they would be if he waited until the siege was over, when these troops could be returned. Rosecrans was ordered to move against the army that was detaching troops to raise the siege. Finally he did move, on the 24th of June, but ten days afterwards Vicksburg surrendered, and the troops sent from Bragg were free to return.

It was at this time that I recommended to the general-in-chief the movement against Mobile. I knew the peril the Army of the Cumberland was in, being depleted continually, not only by ordinary casualties, but also by having to detach troops to hold its constantly extending line over which to draw supplies, while the enemy in front was as constantly being strengthened. Mobile was important to the enemy, and in the absence of a threatening force was guarded by little else than artillery. If threatened by land and from the water at the same time the prize would fall easily, or troops would have to be sent to its defense. Those troops would necessarily come from Bragg. My judgment was overruled, and the troops under my command were dissipated over other parts of the country where it was thought they could render the most service.

Soon it was discovered in Washington that Rosecrans was in trouble and required assistance. The emergency was now too immediate to allow us to give this assistance by making an attack in rear of Bragg upon Mobile. It was therefore necessary to reinforce directly, and troops were sent from every available point.

Rosecrans had very skillfully maneuvered Bragg south of the Tennessee River, and through and beyond Chattanooga. If he had stopped and intrenched, and made himself strong there, all would have been right and the mistake of not moving earlier partially compensated. But he pushed on, with his forces very much scattered, until Bragg's troops from Mississippi began to join him. Then Bragg took the initiative. Rosecrans had to fall back in turn, and was able to get his army together at Chickamauga, some miles southeast of Chattanooga, before the main battle was brought on. The battle was fought on the 19th and 20th of September, and Rosecrans was badly defeated, with a heavy loss in artillery and some sixteen thousand men killed, wounded and captured. The corps under Major General George H. Thomas stood its ground, while Rosecrans, with Crittenden and McCook, returned to Chattanooga. Thomas returned also, but later, and with his troops in good order. Bragg followed and took possession of Missionary Ridge, overlooking Chattanooga. He also occupied Lookout Mountain, west of the town, which Rosecrans had abandoned, and with it his control of the river and the river road as far back as Bridgeport. The National troops were now strongly intrenched in Chattanooga Valley, with the Tennessee River behind them and the enemy occupying commanding heights to the east and west, with a strong line across the valley from mountain to mountain, and with Chattanooga Creek, for a large part of the way, in front of their line.

On the 29th Halleck telegraphed me the above results, and directed all the forces that could be spared from my department to be sent to Rosecrans. Long before this dispatch was received Sherman was on his way, and McPherson was moving east with most of the garrison of Vicksburg.

A retreat at that time would have been a terrible disaster. It would not only have been the loss of a most important strategic position to us, but it would have been attended with the loss of all the artillery still left with the Army of the Cumberland and the annihilation of that army itself, either by capture or demoralization.

All supplies for Rosecrans had to be brought from Nashville. The railroad between this base and the army was in possession of the government up to Bridgeport, the point at which the road crosses to the south side of the Tennessee River; but Bragg, holding Lookout and Raccoon mountains west of Chattanooga, commanded the railroad, the river and the shortest and best wagon roads, both south and north of the Tennessee, between Chattanooga and Bridgeport. The distance between these two places is but twenty-six miles by rail; but owing to the position of Bragg, all supplies for Rosecrans had to be hauled by a circuitous route north of the river and over a mountainous country, increasing the distance to over sixty miles.

This country afforded but little food for his animals, nearly ten thousand of which had already starved, and not enough were left to draw a single piece of artillery or even the ambulances to convey the sick. The men had been on half rations of hard bread for a considerable time, with but few other supplies except beef driven from Nashville across the country. The region along the road became so exhausted of food for the cattle that by the time they reached Chattanooga they were much in the condition of the few animals left alive there "on the lift." Indeed, the beef was so poor that the soldiers were in the habit of saying, with a faint facetiousness, that they were living on *"half rations of hard bread and beef dried on the hoof."*

Nothing could be transported but food, and the troops were without sufficient shoes or other clothing suitable for the advancing season. What they had was well worn. The fuel within the Federal lines was exhausted, even to the stumps of trees. There were no teams to draw it from the opposite bank, where it was abundant. The only way of supplying fuel, for some time before my arrival, had been to cut trees on the north bank of the river at a considerable distance up the stream, form rafts of it and float it down with the current, effecting a landing on the south side within our lines by the use of paddles or poles. It would then be carried on the shoulders of the men to their camps.

If a retreat had occurred at this time it is not probable that any of the army would have reached the railroad as an organized body, if followed by the enemy.

On the receipt of Mr. Dana's dispatch Mr. Stanton sent for me. Finding that I was out he became nervous and excited, inquiring of every person he met, including guests of the house, whether they knew where I was, and bidding them find me and send me to him at once. About eleven o'clock I returned to the hotel, and on my way, when near the house, every person met was a messenger from the Secretary, apparently partaking of his impatience to see me. I hastened to the room of the Secretary and found him pacing the floor rapidly in his dressing gown. Saying that the retreat must be prevented, he showed me the dispatch. I immediately wrote an order assuming command of the Military Division of the Mississippi, and telegraphed it to General Rosecrans. I then telegraphed to him the order from Washington assigning Thomas to the command of the Army of the Cumberland; and to Thomas that he must hold Chattanooga at all hazards, informing him at the same time that I would be at the front as soon as possible. A prompt reply was received from Thomas, saying, "We will hold the town till we starve." I appreciated the force of this dispatch later when I witnessed the condition of affairs which prompted it. It looked, indeed, as if but two courses were open one to starve, the other to surrender or be captured.

On the morning of the 20th of October I started, with my staff, and proceeded as far as Nashville. At that time it was not prudent to travel beyond that point by night, so I remained in Nashville until the next morning. Here I met for the first time Andrew Johnson, Military Governor of Tennessee. He delivered a speech of welcome; His composure showed that it was by no means his maiden effort. It was long, and I was in torture while he was delivering it, fearing something would be expected from me in response. I was relieved; however, the people assembled having apparently heard enough. At all events they commenced a general handshaking, which, although trying where there is so much of it, was a great relief to me in this emergency.

From Nashville I telegraphed to Burnside, who was then at Knoxville, that important points in his department ought to be fortified, so that they could be held with the least number of men ; to Admiral

Porter at Cairti, that Sherman's advance had passed Eastport, Mississippi, that rations were probably on their way from St. Louis by boat for supplying his army, and requesting him to send a gunboat to convoy them; and to Thomas, suggesting that large parties should be put at work on the wagon-road then in use back to Bridgeport.

On the morning of the 21st we took the train for the front, reaching Stevenson, Alabama, after dark. Rosecrans was there on his way north. He came into my car and we held a brief interview, in which he described very clearly the situation at Chattanooga, and made some excellent suggestions as to what should be done. My only wonder was that he had not carried them out. We then proceeded to Bridgeport, where we stopped for the night. From here we took horses and made our way by Jasper and over Waldron's Ridge to Chattanooga. There had been much rain, and the roads were almost impassable from mud, knee deep in places, and from washouts on the mountain sides. I had been on crutches since the time of my fall in New Orleans, and had to be carried over places where it was not safe to cross on horseback. The roads were strewn with the debris of broken wagons and the carcasses of thousands of starved mules and horses, At Jasper, some ten or twelve miles from Bridgeport, there was a halt. General O.O. Howard had his headquarters there. From this point I telegraphed Burnside to make every effort to secure five hundred rounds of ammunition for his artillery and small arms. We stopped for the night at a little hamlet some ten or twelve miles farther on. The next day we reached Chattanooga a little before dark. I went directly to General Thomas's headquarters, and remaining there a few days, until I could establish my own.

During the evening most of the general officers called in to pay their respects and to talk about the condition of affairs. They pointed out on the map the line, marked with a red or blue pencil, which Rosecrans had contemplated falling back upon. If any of them had approved the move they did not say so to me. I found General W.F. Smith occupying the position of chief engineer of the Army of the Cumberland. I had known Smith as a cadet at West Point, but had no recollection of having met him after my graduation, in 1843, up to this time. He explained the situation of the two armies and the topography of the country so plainly that I could see it without an inspection. I found that he had established a sawmill on the banks of the river, by utilizing an old engine found in the neighborhood; and, by rafting logs from the north side of the river above, had got out the lumber and completed pontoons and roadway plank for a second bridge, one flying bridge being there already. He was also rapidly getting out the materials and constructing the boats for a third bridge. In addition to this he had far under way a steamer for plying between Chattanooga and Bridgeport whenever we might get possession of the river. This boat consisted of a scow, made of the plank sawed out at the mill, housed in, and a stern wheel attached which was propelled by a second engine taken from some shop or factory.

I telegraphed to Washington this night, notifying General Halleck of my arrival, and asking to have General Sherman assigned to the command of the Army of the Tennessee, headquarters in the field. The request was at once complied with.

CHAPTER XLI

ASSUMING THE COMMAND AT CHATTANOOGA - OPENING A LINE OF SUPPLIES - BATTLE OF WAUHATCHIE -ON THE PICKET LINE

THE next day, the 9th, I started out to make a personal inspection, taking Thomas and Smith with me, besides most of the members of my personal staff. We crossed to the north side of the river, and, moving to the north of detached spurs of hills, reached the Tennessee at Brown's Ferry, some three miles below Lookout Mountain, unobserved by the enemy. Here we left our horses back from the river and approached the water on foot. There was a picket station of the enemy on the opposite side, of about twenty men, in full view, and we were within easy range. They did not fire upon us nor seem to be disturbed by our presence. They must have seen that we were all commissioned officers. But, I suppose, they looked upon the garrison of Chattanooga as prisoners of war, feeding or starving themselves, and thought it would be inhuman to kill any of them except in self defense.

That night I issued orders for opening the route to Bridgeport, a cracker line, as the soldiers appropriately termed it. They had been so long on short rations that my first thought was the establishment of a line over which food might reach them.

Chattanooga is on the south bank of the Tennessee, where that river runs nearly due west. It is at the northern end of a valley five or six miles in width, through which Chattanooga Creek runs. To the east of the valley is Missionary Ridge, rising from five to eight hundred feet above the creek and terminating somewhat abruptly a half mile or more before reaching the Tennessee. On the west of the valley is Lookout Mountain, twenty-two hundred feet above tide water. Just below the town the Tennessee makes a turn to the south and runs to the base of Lookout Mountain, leaving no level ground between the mountain and river. The Memphis and Charleston Railroad passes this point, where the

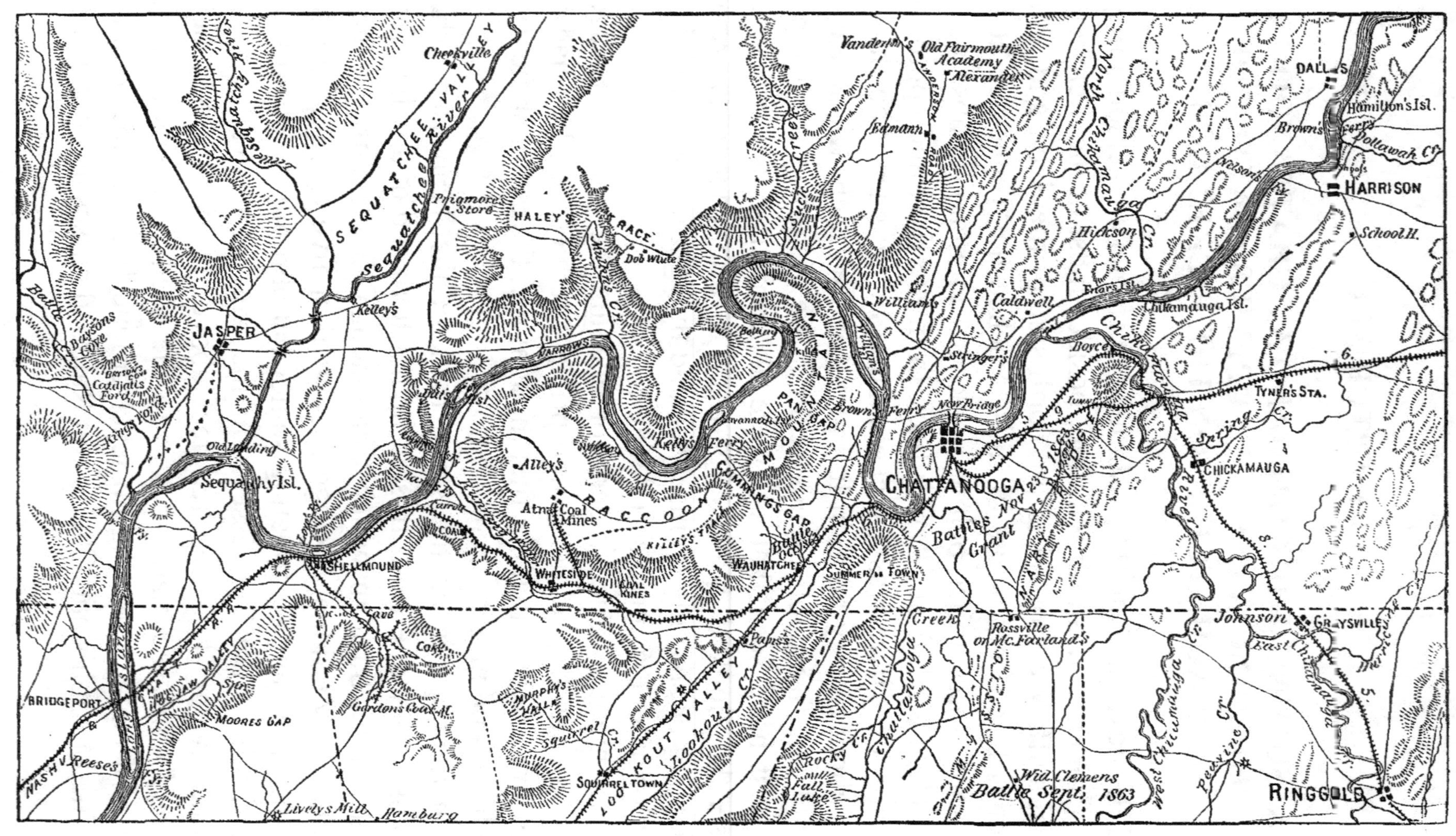

HARRISON
DALLAS
RINGGOLD
CHATTANOOGA
CHICKAMAUGA
TYNERS STA.
GRAYSVILLE
JASPER
BRIDGEPORT
SHELLMOUND
WHITESIDE
WAUHATCHEE
SQUIRREL TOWN
RACCOON MOUNTAIN
LOOKOUT VALLEY
SEQUATCHEE VALLEY
Sequatchee River
Cheekville
Kelley's
Sequatchy Isl.
Old Landing
Atna Coal Mines
Coal Mines
Phigmore's Store
HALEY'S
RACE
Dob White
Alley's
Cummings Gap
Pan Gap
Summer Town
Brown's Ferry
New Bridge
Battles Nov Grant
Battle Sept. 1863
Wid. Clemens Battle Sept. 1863
Vanderen's Old Fairmouth Academy Alexander
Edmann
Hickson
School H.
Williams
Caldwell
Friars Isl.
Chickamauga Isl.
Hamilton's Isl.
Brown's Ferry
Pottawah Cr.
North Chickamauga Cr.
Chickamauga River
West Chickamauga Cr.
East Chickamauga
Johnson
Boyce
Stringer's
Spring Cr.
Rossville on Mc.Farland's
Chattanooga Creek
Rocky Cr.
Fall Lake
Murray's Valley
Gordon's Coal M.
Moores Gap
Lively's Mill
Hamburg
Nash. V. Reese's
Chat. View Valley
Coal
Killey's
Barsons Cove
Catdjats Ford
Kings Road
Battle
Nittles
Kelly's Ferry
Savannah
Narrows
Dallas
Tuck Creek Cr.
Peevine Cr.
Hurricane Cr.

mountain stands nearly perpendicular. East of Missionary Ridge flows the South Chickamauga River; west of Lookout Mountain is Lookout Creek; and west of that, Raccoon Mountains. Lookout Mountain, at its northern end, rises almost perpendicularly for some distance, then breaks off in a gentle slope of cultivated fields to near the summit, where it ends in a palisade thirty or more feet in height. On the gently sloping ground, between the upper and lower palisades, there is a single farmhouse, which is reached by a wagon-road from the valley east.

The intrenched line of the enemy commenced on the north end of Missionary Ridge and extended along the crest for some distance south, thence across Chattanooga valley to Lookout Mountain. Lookout Mountain was also fortified and held by the enemy, who also kept troops in Lookout valley west, and on Raccoon Mountain, with pickets extending down the river so as to command the road on the north bank and render it useless to us. In addition to this there was an intrenched line in Chattanooga valley extending from the river east of the town to Lookout Mountain, to make the investment complete. Besides the fortifications on Mission Ridge, there was a line at the base of the hill, with occasional spurs of rifle-pits halfway up the front. The enemy's pickets extended out into the valley towards the town, so far that the pickets of the two armies could converse. At one point they were separated only by the narrow creek which gives its name to the valley and town, and from which both sides drew water. The Union lines were shorter than those of the enemy.

Thus the enemy, with a vastly superior force, was strongly fortified to the east, south, and west, and commanded the river below. Practically, the Army of the Cumberland was besieged. The enemy had stopped with his cavalry north of the river the passing of a train loaded with ammunition and medical supplies. The Union army was short of both, not having ammunition enough for a day's fighting.

General Halleck had, long before my coming into this new field, ordered parts of the 11th and 12th corps, commanded respectively by Generals Howard and Slocum, Hooker in command of the whole, from the Army of the Potomac to reinforce Rosencrans. It would have been folly to send them to Chattanooga to help eat up the few rations left there. They were consequently left on the railroad, where supplies could be brought to them. Before my arrival, Thomas ordered their concentration at Bridgeport.

General W.F. Smith had been so instrumental in preparing for the move which I was now about to make, and so clear in his judgment about the manner of making it, that I deemed it but just to him that he should have command of the troops detailed to execute the design, although he was then acting as a staff officer and was not in command of troops.

On the 24th of October, after my return to Chattanooga, the following details were made: General Hooker, who was now at Bridgeport, was ordered to cross to the south side of the Tennessee and march up by Whitesides and Wauhatchie to Brown's Ferry. General Palmer, with a division of the 14th corps, Army of the Cumberland, was ordered to move down the river on the north side, by a back road, until opposite Whitesides, then cross and hold the road in Hooker's rear after he had passed. Four thousand men were at the same time detailed to act under General Smith directly from Chattanooga. Eighteen hundred of them, under General Hazen, were to take sixty pontoon boats, and under cover of night float by the pickets of the enemy at the north base of Lookout, down to Brown's Ferry, then land on the south side and capture or drive away the pickets at that point. Smith was to march with the remainder of the detail, also under cover of night, by the north bank of the river to Brown's Ferry, taking with him all the material for laying the bridge as soon as the crossing was secured.

On the 26th, Hooker crossed the river at Bridgeport and commenced his eastward march. At three o'clock on the morning of the 27th, Hazen moved into the stream with his sixty pontoons and eighteen hundred brave and well equipped men. Smith started enough in advance to be near the river when Hazen should arrive. There are a number of detached spurs of hills north of the river at Chattanooga, back of which is a good road parallel to the stream, sheltered from the view from the top of Lookout. It was over this road Smith marched. At five o'clock Hazen landed at Brown's Ferry, surprised the picket guard, and captured most of it. By seven o'clock the whole of Smith's force was ferried over and in possession of a height commanding the ferry. This was speedily fortified, while a detail was laying the pontoon bridge. By ten o'clock the bridge was laid, and our extreme right, now in Lookout valley, was fortified and connected with the rest of the army. The two bridges over the Tennessee River, a flying one at Chattanooga and the new one at Brown's Ferry, with the road north of the river, covered from both the fire and the view of the enemy, made the connection complete. Hooker found but slight obstacles in his way, and on the afternoon of the 28th emerged into Lookout valley at Wauhatchie. Howard marched on to Brown's Ferry, while Geary, who commanded a division in the 12th corps, stopped three miles south. The pickets of the enemy on the river below were now cut off, and soon came in and surrendered.

The river was now opened to us from Lookout valley to Bridgeport. Between Brown's Ferry and Kelly's Ferry the Tennessee runs through a narrow gorge in the mountains, which contracts the stream so much as to increase the current beyond the capacity of an ordinary steamer to stem it. To get up these rapids, steamers must be cordelled; that is, pulled up by ropes from the shore. But there is no difficulty in navigating the stream from Bridgeport to Kelly's Ferry. The latter point is only eight miles from Chattanooga and connected with it by a good wagon road, which runs through a low pass in the Raccoon Mountains on the south side of the river to Brown's Ferry, thence on the north side to the river opposite Chattanooga. There were several steamers at Bridgeport, and abundance of forage, clothing and provisions.

On the way to Chattanooga I had telegraphed back to Nashville for a good supply of vegetables and small rations, which the troops had been so long deprived of. Hooker had brought with him from the east a full supply of land transportation. His animals had not been subjected to hard work on bad roads without forage, but were in good condition. In five days from my arrival in Chattanooga the way was open to Bridgeport and, with the aid of steamers and Hooker's teams, in a week the troops were receiving full rations. It is hard for any one not an eyewitness to realize the relief this brought. The men were soon re-clothed and also well fed; an abundance of ammunition was brought up, and a cheerfulness prevailed not before enjoyed in many weeks. Neither officers nor men looked upon themselves any longer as doomed. The weak and languid appearance of the troops, so visible before, disappeared at once. I do not know what the effect was on the other side, but assume it must have been correspondingly depressing. Mr. Davis had visited Bragg but a short time before, and must have perceived our condition to be about as Bragg described it in his subsequent report. "These dispositions," he said, "faithfully sustained, insured the enemy's speedy evacuation of Chattanooga for want of food and forage. Possessed of the shortest route to his depot, and the one by which reinforcements must reach him, we held him at our mercy, and his destruction was only a question of time." But the dispositions were not "faithfully sustained," and I doubt not but thousands of men engaged in trying to "sustain" them now rejoice that they were not. There was no time during the rebellion when I did not think, and often say, that the South was more to be benefited by its defeat than the North. The latter had the people, the institutions, and the territory to make a great and prosperous nation. The former was burdened with an institution abhorrent to all civilized people not brought up under it, and one which degraded labor, kept it in ignorance, and enervated the governing class. With the outside world at war with this institution, they could not have extended their territory. The labor of the country was not skilled, nor allowed to become so. The whites could not toil without becoming degraded, and those who did were denominated "poor white trash." The system of labor would have soon exhausted the soil and left the people poor. The non-slaveholders would have left the country, and the small slaveholder must have sold out to his more fortunate neighbor. Soon the slaves would have outnumbered the masters, and, not being in sympathy with them, would have risen in their might and exterminated them. The war was expensive to the South as well as to the North, both in blood and treasure, but it was worth all it cost.

The enemy was surprised by the movements which secured to us a line of supplies. He appreciated its importance, and hastened to try to recover the line from us. His strength on Lookout Mountain was not equal to Hooker's command in the valley below. From Missionary Ridge he had to march twice the distance we had from Chattanooga, in order to reach Lookout Valley; but on the night of the 28th and 29th an attack was made on Geary at Wauhatchie by Longstreet's corps. When the battle commenced, Hooker ordered Howard up from Brown's Ferry. He had three miles to march to reach Geary. On his way he was fired upon by rebel troops from a foothill to the left of the road and from which the road was commanded. Howard turned to the left, charged up the hill and captured it before the enemy had time to intrench, taking many prisoners. Leaving sufficient men to hold this height, he pushed on to reinforce Geary. Before he got up, Geary had been engaged for about three hours against a vastly superior force. The night was so dark that the men could not distinguish one from another except by the light of the flashes of their muskets. In the darkness and uproar, Hooker's teamsters became frightened and deserted their teams. The mules also became frightened, and breaking loose from their fastenings stampeded directly towards the enemy. The latter, no doubt, took this for a charge, and stampeded in turn. By four o'clock in the morning the battle had entirely ceased, and our "cracker line" was never afterward disturbed.

In securing possession of Lookout Valley, Smith lost one man killed and four or five wounded. The enemy lost most of his pickets at the ferry, captured. In the night engagement of the 28th-9th Hooker lost 416 killed and wounded. I never knew the loss of the enemy, but our troops buried over one hundred and fifty of his dead and captured more than a hundred.

After we had secured the opening of a line over which to bring our supplies to the army, I made a personal inspection to see the situation of the pickets of the two armies. As I have stated, Chattanooga Creek comes down the centre of the valley to within a mile or such a matter of the town of Chattanooga, then bears off westerly, then north westerly, and enters the Tennessee River at the foot of Lookout Mountain. This creek, from its mouth up to where it bears off west, lay between the two lines of pickets, and the guards of both armies drew their water from the same stream. As I would be under short range fire and in an open country, I took nobody with me, except, I believe, a bugler, who stayed some distance to the rear. I rode from our right around to our left. When I came to the camp of the picket guard of our side, I heard the call, "Turn out the guard for the commanding general." I replied, "Never mind the guard," and they were dismissed and went back to their tents. Just back of these, and about equally distant from the creek, were the guards of the Confederate pickets. The sentinel on their post called out in like manner, "Turn out the guard for the commanding general," and, I believe, added, "General Grant." Their line in a moment front-faced to the north, facing me, and gave a salute, which I returned.

The most friendly relations seemed to exist between the pickets of the two armies. At one place there was a tree which had fallen across the stream, and which was used by the soldiers of both armies in drawing water for their camps. General Longstreet's corps was stationed there at the time, and wore blue of a little different shade from our uniform. Seeing a soldier in blue on this log, I rode up to him, commenced conversing with him, and asked whose corps he belonged to. He was very polite, and, touching his hat to me, said he belonged to General Longstreet's corps. I asked him a few questions -but not with a view of gaining any particular information- all of which he answered, and I rode off.

CHAPTER XLII

CONDITION OF THE ARMY - REBUILDING THE RAIL-ROAD - GENERAL BURNSIDESS SITUATION - ORDERS FOR BATTLE-PLANS FOR THE ATTACK - HOOKERS POSITION - SHERMAN'S MOVEMENTS

HAVING got the Army of the Cumberland in a comfortable position, I now began to look after the remainder of my new command. Burnside was in about as desperate a condition as the Army of the Cumberland had been, only he was not yet besieged. He was a hundred miles from the nearest possible base, Big South Fork of the Cumberland River, and much farther from any railroad we had possession of. The roads back were over mountains, and all supplies along the line had long since been exhausted. His animals, too, had been starved, and their carcasses lined the road from Cumberland Gap, and far back towards Lexington, Ky. East Tennessee still furnished supplies of beef, bread and forage, but it did not supply ammunition, clothing, medical supplies, or small rations, such as coffee, sugar, salt and rice.

Sherman had started from Memphis for Corinth on the 11th of October. His instructions required him to repair the road in his rear in order to bring up supplies. The distance was about three hundred and thirty miles through a hostile country. His entire command could not have maintained the road if it had been completed. The bridges had all been destroyed by the enemy, and much other damage done. A hostile community lived along the road; guerilla bands infested the country, and more or less of the cavalry of the enemy was still in the West. Often Sherman's work was destroyed as soon as completed, and he only a short distance away.

The Memphis and Charleston Railroad strikes the Tennessee River at Eastport, Mississippi. Knowing the difficulty Sherman would have to supply himself from Memphis, I had previously ordered supplies sent from St. Louis on small steamers, to be convoyed by the navy, to meet him at Eastport. These he got. I now ordered him to discontinue his work of repairing roads and to move on with his whole force to Stevenson, Alabama, without delay. This order was borne to Sherman by a messenger, who paddled down the Tennessee in a canoe and floated over Muscle Shoals; it was delivered at Iuka on the 27th. In this Sherman was notified that the rebels were moving a force towards Cleveland, East Tennessee, and might be going to Nashville, in which event his troops were in the best position to beat them there. Sherman, with his characteristic promptness, abandoned the work he was engaged upon and pushed on at once. On the 1st of November he crossed the Tennessee at Eastport, and that day was in Florence, Alabama, with the head of column, while his troops were still crossing at Eastport, with Blair bringing up the rear.

Sherman's force made an additional army, with cavalry, artillery, and trains, all to be supplied by the single track road from Nashville. All indications pointed also to the probable necessity of supplying Burnside's command in East Tennessee, twenty-five thousand more, by the same route. A single track could not do this. I gave, therefore, an order to Sherman to halt General G.M. Dodge's command, of about eight thousand men, at Athens, and subsequently directed the latter to arrange his troops along the railroad from Decatur north towards Nashville, and to rebuild that road. The road from Nashville to Decatur passes over a broken country, cut up with innumerable streams, many of them of considerable width, and with valleys far below the road-bed. All the bridges over these had been destroyed, and the rails taken up and twisted by the enemy. All the cars and locomotives not carried off had been destroyed as effectually as they knew how to destroy them. All bridges and culverts had been destroyed between Nashville and Decatur, and thence to Stevenson, where the Memphis and Charleston and the Nashville and Chattanooga roads unite. The rebuilding of this road would give us two roads as far as Stevenson over which to supply the army. From Bridgeport, a short distance farther east, the river supplements the road.

General Dodge, besides being a most capable soldier, was an experienced railroad builder. He had no tools to work with except those of the pioneers-axes, picks, and spades. With these he was able to intrench his men and protect them against surprises by small parties of the enemy. As he had no base of supplies until the road could be completed back to Nashville, the first matter to consider after protecting his men was the getting in of food and forage from the surrounding country. He had his men and teams bring in all the grain they could find, or all they needed, and all the cattle for beef, and such other food as could be found. Millers were detailed from the ranks to run the mills along the line of the army. When these were not near enough to the troops for protection they were taken down and moved up to the line of the road. Blacksmith shops, with all the iron and steel found in them, were moved up in like manner. Blacksmiths were detailed and set to work making the tools necessary in railroad and bridge building. Axemen were put to work getting out timber for bridges and cutting fuel for locomotives when the road should be completed. Car builders were set to work repairing the locomotives and cars. Thus every branch of railroad building, making tools to work with, and supplying the workmen with food, was all going on at once, and without the aid of a mechanic or laborer except what the command itself furnished. But rails and cars the men could not make without material, and there was not enough rolling stock to keep the road we already had worked to its full capacity. There were no rails except those in use. To supply these deficiencies I ordered eight of the ten engines General McPherson had at Vicksburg to be sent to Nashville, and all the cars he had except ten. I also ordered the troops in West Tennessee to points on the river and on the Memphis and Charleston road, and ordered the cars, locomotives and rails from all the railroads except the Memphis and Charleston to Nashville. The military manager of railroads also was directed to furnish more rolling stock and, as far as he could, bridge material. General Dodge had the work assigned him finished within forty days after receiving his orders. The number of bridges to rebuild was one hundred and eighty-two, many of them over deep and wide chasms; the length of road repaired was one hundred and two miles.

The enemy's troops, which it was thought were either moving against Burnside or were going to Nashville, went no farther than Cleveland. Their presence there, however, alarmed the authorities at Washington, and, on account of our helpless condition at Chattanooga, caused me much uneasiness. Dispatches were constantly coming, urging me to do something for Burnside's relief; calling attention to the importance of holding East Tennessee; saying the President was much concerned for the protection of the loyal people in that section, etc. We had not at Chattanooga animals to pull a single piece of artillery, much less a supply train. Reinforcements could not help Burnside, because he had neither supplies nor ammunition sufficient for them; hardly, indeed, bread and meat for the men he had. There was no relief possible for him except by expelling the enemy from Missionary Ridge and about Chattanooga.

On the 4th of November Longstreet left our front with about fifteen thousand troops, besides Wheeler's cavalry, five thousand more, to go against Burnside. The situation seemed desperate, and was more aggravating because nothing could be done until Sherman should get up. The authorities at Washington were now more than ever anxious for the safety of Burnside's army, and plied me with dispatches faster than ever, urging that something should be done for his relief. On the 7th, before Longstreet could possibly have reached Knoxville, I ordered Thomas peremptorily to attack the enemy's right, so as to force the return of the troops that had gone up the valley. I directed him to take mules, officers' horses, or animals wherever he could get them: to move the necessary artillery. But he persisted in the declaration that he could not move a single piece of artillery, and could not see how he could possibly comply with the order. Nothing was left to be done but to answer Washington dispatches as best I could; urge Sherman forward, although he was making every effort to get forward, and encourage Burnside to hold on, assuring him that in a short time he should be relieved. All of Burnside's dispatches showed the greatest confidence in his ability to hold his position as long as his ammunition held out. He even suggested the propriety of abandoning the territory he held south and west of Knoxville, so as to draw the enemy farther from his base and make it more difficult for him to get back to Chattanooga when the battle should begin.

Longstreet had a railroad as far as Loudon; but from there to Knoxville he had to rely on wagon trains. Burnside's suggestion, therefore, was a good one, and it was adopted. On the 14th I telegraphed him:

"Sherman's advance has reached Bridgeport. His whole force will be ready to move from there by Tuesday at farthest. If you can hold Longstreet in check until he gets up, or by skirmishing and falling back can avoid serious loss to yourself and gain time, I will be able to force the enemy back from here and place a force between Longstreet and Bragg that must inevitably make the former take to the mountain passes by every available road, to get to his supplies. Sherman would have been here before this but for high water in Elk River driving him some thirty miles up that river to cross."

And again later in the day, indicating my plans for his relief, as follows:

"Your dispatch and Dana's just received. Being there, you can tell better how to resist Longstreet's attack than I can direct. With your showing you had better give up Kingston at the last moment and save the most productive part of your possessions. Every arrangement is now made to throw Sherman's force across the river, just at and below the mouth of Chickamauga Creek, as soon as it arrives. Thomas will attack on his left at the same time, and together it is expected to carry Missionary Ridge, and from there push a force on to the railroad between Cleveland and Dalton. Hooker will at the same time attack, and, if he can, carry

Lookout Mountain. The enemy now seems to be looking for an attack on his left flank. This favors us. To further confirm this, Sherman's advance division will march direct from Whiteside to Trenton. The remainder of his force will pass over a new road just made from Whiteside to Kelly's Ferry, thus being concealed from the enemy, and leave him to suppose the whole force is going up Lookout Valley. Sherman's advance has only just reached Bridgeport. The rear will only reach there on the 16th. This will bring it to the 19th as the earliest day for making the combined movement as desired. Inform me if you think you can sustain yourself until this time. I can hardly conceive of the enemy breaking through at Kingston and pushing for Kentucky. If they should, however, a new problem would be left for solution. Thomas has ordered a division of cavalry to the vicinity of Sparta. I will ascertain if they have started, and inform you. It will be entirely out of the question to send you ten thousand men, not because they cannot be spared, but how would they be fed after they got even one day east from here? "

Longstreet, for some reason or other, stopped at Loudon until the 13th. That being the terminus of his railroad communications, it is probable he was directed to remain there awaiting orders. He was in a position threatening Knoxville and at the same time where he could be brought back speedily to Chattanooga. The day after Longstreet left Loudon, Sherman reached Bridgeport in person and proceeded on to see me that evening, the 14th, and reached Chattanooga the next day.

My orders for battle were all prepared in advance of Sherman's arrival,* except the dates, which could to not be fixed while troops to be engaged were so far away. The possession of Lookout Mountain was of no special advantage to us now. Hooker was instructed to send Howard's corps to the north side of the Tennessee, thence up behind the hills on the north side, and to go into camp opposite Chattanooga; with the remainder of the command, Hooker was, at a time to be afterwards appointed, to ascend the western slope between the upper and lower palisades, and so get into Chattanooga valley.

*CHATTANOOGA , November 18, 1863.

MAJOR-GENERAL W. T. SHERMAN:

Enclosed herewith I send you copy of instructions to Major General Thomas. You having been over the ground in person, and having heard the whole matter discussed, further instructions will not be necessary for you. It is particularly desirable that a force should be got through to the railroad between Cleveland and Dalton, and Longstreet thus cut off from communication with the South; but being confronted by a large force here, strongly located, it is not easy to tell how this is to be effected until the result of our first effort is known.

I will add, however, what is not shown in my instructions Thomas, that a brigade of cavalry has been ordered here which, if it arrives in time, will be thrown across the Tennessee above Chickamauga, and may be able to make the trip to Cleveland or thereabouts.

U. S. GRANT,
Maj. -Gen' l.
CHATTANOOGA , November 18, 1863.

MAJOR-GENERAL GEO. H. THOMAS,
Chattanooga:

All preparations should be made for attacking the enemy's position on Missionary Ridge by Saturday at daylight. Not being provided with a map giving names of roads, spurs of the mountains, and other places, such definite instructions cannot be given as might be desirable. However, the general plan, you understand, is for Sherman, with the force brought with him strengthened by a division from your command, to effect a crossing of the Tennessee River just below the mouth of Chickamauga; his crossing to be protected by artillery from the heights on the north bank of the river (to be located by your chief of artillery), and to secure the heights on the northern extremity to about the railroad tunnel before the enemy can concentrate against him. You will co-operate with Sherman. The troops in Chattanooga Valley should be well concentrated on your left flank, leaving only the necessary force to defend fortifications on the right and centre, and a movable column of one division in readiness to move wherever ordered. This division should show itself as threateningly as possible on the most practicable line for making an attack up the valley. Your effort then will be to form a junction with Sherman, making your advance well towards the northern end of Missionary Ridge, and moving as near simultaneously with him as possible. The junction once formed and the ridge carried, communications will be at once established between the two armies by roads on the south bank of the river. Further movements will then depend on those of the enemy. Lookout Valley, I think, will be easily held by Geary's division and what troops you may still have there belonging to the old Army of the Cumberland. Howard's corps can then be held in readiness to act either with you at Chattanooga or with Sherman. It should be marched on Friday night to a position on the north side of the river, not lower down than the first pontoon-bridge, and there held in readiness for such orders as may become necessary. All these troops will be provided with two days cooked rations in haversacks, and one hundred rounds of ammunition on the person of each infantry soldier. Special care should be taken by all officers to see that ammunition is not wasted or unnecessarily fired away. You will call on the engineer department for such preparations as you may deem necessary for carrying your infantry and artillery over the creek.

U.S. GRANT,
Major-General.

The plan of battle was for Sherman to attack the enemy's right flank, form a line across it, extend our left over South Chickamauga River so as to threaten or hold the railroad in Bragg's rear, and thus force him either to weaken his lines elsewhere or lose his connection with his base at Chickamauga Station. Hooker was to perform like service on our right. His problem was to get from Lookout Valley to Chattanooga Valley in the most expeditious way possible; cross the latter valley rapidly to Rossville, south of Bragg's line on Missionary Ridge, form line there across the ridge facing north, with his right flank extended to Chickamauga Valley east of the ridge, thus threatening the enemy's rear on that flank and compelling him to reinforce this also. Thomas, with the Army of the Cumberland, occupied the centre, and was to assault while the enemy was engaged with most of his forces on his two flanks.

To carry out this plan, Sherman was to cross the Tennessee at Brown' Ferry and move east of Chattanooga to a point opposite the north end of Mission Ridge, and to place his command back of the foothills out of sight of the enemy on the ridge. There are two streams called Chickamauga emptying into the Tennessee River east of Chattanooga, North Chickamauga, taking its rise in Tennessee, flowing south, and emptying into the river some seven or eight miles east; while the South Chickamauga, which takes its rise in Georgia, flows northward, and empties into the Tennessee some three or four miles above the town. There were now one hundred and sixteen pontoons in the North Chickamauga River, their presence there being unknown to the enemy.

At night a division was to be marched up to that point, and at two o'clock in the morning moved down with the current, thirty men in each boat. A few were to land east of the mouth of the South Chickamauga, capture the pickets there, and then lay a bridge connecting the two banks of the river. The rest were to land on the south side of the Tennessee, where Missionary Ridge would strike it if prolonged, and a sufficient number of men to man the boats were to push to the north side to ferry over the main body of Sherman's command while those left on the south side intrenched themselves. Thomas was to move out from his lines facing the ridge, leaving enough of Palmer's corps to guard against an attack down the valley. Lookout Valley being of no present value to us, and being untenable by the enemy if we should secure Missionary Ridge, Hooker's orders were changed, His revised orders brought him to Chattanooga by the established route north of the Tennessee. He was then to move out to the right to Rossville.

Hooker's position in Lookout Valley was absolutely essential to us so long as Chattanooga was besieged. It was the key to our line for supplying the army. But it was not essential after the enemy was dispersed from our front, or even after the battle for this purpose was begun. Hooker's orders, therefore, were designed to get his force past Lookout Mountain and Chattanooga Valley, and up to Missionary Ridge. By crossing the north face of Lookout the troops would come into

Chattanooga Valley in rear of the line held by the enemy across the valley, and would necessarily force its evacuation. Orders were accordingly given to march by this route. But days before the battle began the advantages as well as the disadvantages of this plan of action were all considered. The passage over the mountain was a difficult one to make in the face of an enemy. It might consume so much time as to lose us the use of the troops engaged in it at other points where they were more wanted. After reaching Chattanooga Valley, the creek of the same name, quite a formidable stream to get an army over, had to be crossed. I was perfectly willing that the enemy should keep Lookout Mountain until we got through with the troops on Missionary Ridge. By marching Hooker to the north side of the river, thence up the stream, and re-crossing at the town, he could be got in position at any named time; when in this new position, he would have Chattanooga Creek behind him, and the attack on Missionary Ridge would unquestionably cause the evacuation by the enemy of his line across the valley and on Lookout Mountain. Hooker's order was changed accordingly. As explained elsewhere, the original order had to be reverted to, because of a flood in the river rendering the bridge at Brown's Ferry unsafe for the passage of troops at the exact juncture when it was wanted to bring all the troops together against Missionary Ridge.

The next day after Sherman's arrival I took him, with Generals Thomas and Smith and other officers, to the north side of the river, and showed them the ground over which Sherman had to march, and pointed out generally what he was expected to do. I, as well as the authorities in Washington, was still in a great state of anxiety for Burnside's safety. Burnside himself, I believe, was the only one who did not share in this anxiety. Nothing could be done for him, however, until Sherman's troops were up. As soon, therefore, as the inspection was over, Sherman started for Bridgeport to hasten matters, rowing a boat himself, I believe, from Kelly's Ferry. Sherman had left Bridgeport the night of the 14th, reached Chattanooga the evening of the 15th, made the above described inspection on the morning of the 16th, and started back the same evening to hurry up his command, fully appreciating the importance of time.

His march was conducted with as much expedition as the roads and season would admit of. By the 20th he was himself at Brown's Ferry with the head of column, but many of his troops were far behind, and one division (Ewing's) was at Trenton, sent that way to create the impression that Lookout was to be taken from the south. Sherman received his orders at the ferry, and was asked if he could not be ready for the assault the following morning. News had been received that the battle had been commenced at Knoxville. Burnside had been cut off from telegraphic communications. The President, the Secretary of War, and General Halleck, were in an agony of suspense. My suspense was also great, but more endurable, because I was where I could soon do something to relieve the situation. It was impossible to get Sherman's troops up for the next day. I then asked him if they could not be got up to make the assault on the morning of the 22d, and ordered Thomas to move on that date. But the elements were against us. It rained all the 20th and 21st. The river rose so rapidly that it was difficult to keep the pontoons in place.

General Orlando B. Willcox, a division commander under Burnside, was at this time occupying a position farther up the valley than Knoxville -about Maynardville- and was still in telegraphic communication with the North. A dispatch was received from him saying that he was threatened from the east. The following was sent in reply:

"If you can communicate with General Burnside, say to him that our attack on Bragg will commence in the morning. If successful, such a move will be made as I think will relieve East Tennessee, if he can hold out. Longstreet passing through our lines to Kentucky need not cause alarm. He would find the country so bare that he would lose his transportation and artillery before reaching Kentucky, and would meet such a force before he got through, that he could not return."

Meantime, Sherman continued his crossing without intermission as fast as his troops could be got up. The crossing had to be effected in full view of the enemy on the top of Lookout Mountain. Once over, however, the troops soon disappeared behind the detached hills on the north side, and would not come to view again, either to watchmen on Lookout Mountain or Missionary Ridge, until they emerged between the hills to strike the bank of the river. But when Sherman's advance reached a point opposite the town of Chattanooga, Howard, who, it will be remembered, had been concealed behind the hills on the north side, took up his line of march to join the troops on the south side. His crossing was in full view both from Missionary Ridge and the top of Lookout, and the enemy of course supposed these troops to be Sherman's. This enabled Sherman to get to his assigned position without discovery.

CHAPTER XLIII

PREPARATIONS FOR BATTLE - THOMAS CARRIES THE FIRST LINE OF THE ENEMY - SHERMAN CARRIES MISSIONARY RIDGE - BATTLE OF LOOKOUT MOUNTAIN - GENERAL HOOKER'S FIGHT

ON the 20th, when so much was occurring to discourage -rains falling so heavily as to delay the passage of troops over the river at Brown's Ferry and threatening the entire breaking of the bridge; news coming of a battle raging at Knoxville; of Willcox being threatened by a force from the east, a letter was received from Bragg which contained these words: "As there may still be some noncombatants in Chattanooga, I deem it proper to notify you that prudence would dictate their early withdrawal." Of course, I understood that this was a device intended to deceive; but I did not know what the intended deception was. On the 22d, however, a deserter came in who informed me that Bragg was leaving our front, and on that day Buckner's division was sent to reinforce Longstreet at Knoxville, and another division started to follow but was recalled. The object of Bragg's letter, no doubt, was in some way to detain me until Knoxville could be captured, and his troops there be returned to Chattanooga.

During the night of the 21st the rest of the pontoon boats, completed, one hundred and sixteen in all, were carried up to and placed in North Chickamauga. The material for the roadway over these was deposited out of view of the enemy within a few hundred yards of the bank of the Tennessee, where the north end of the bridge was to rest.

Hearing nothing from Burnside, and hearing much of the distress in Washington on his account, I could no longer defer operations for his relief. I determined, therefore, to do on the 23d, with the Army of the Cumberland, what had been intended to be done on the 24th.

The position occupied by the Army of the Cumberland had been made very strong for defence during the months it had been besieged.

The line was about a mile from the town, and extended from Citico Creek, a small stream running near the base of Missionary Ridge and emptying into the Tennessee about two miles below the mouth of the South Chickamauga, on the left, to Chattanooga Creek on the right. All commanding points on the line were well fortified and well equipped with artillery. The important elevations within the line had all been carefully fortified and supplied with a proper armament. Among the elevations so fortified was one to the east of the town, named Fort Wood. It owed its importance chiefly to the fact that it lay between the town and Missionary Ridge, where most of the strength of the enemy was. Fort Wood had in it twenty-two pieces of artillery, most of which would reach the nearer points of the enemy's line. On the morning of the 23d Thomas, according to instructions, moved Granger's corps of two divisions, Sheridan and T.J. Wood commanding, to the foot of Fort Wood, and formed them into line as if going on parade, Sheridan on the right, Wood to the left, extending to or near Citico Creek. Palmer, commanding the 14th corps, held that part of our line facing south and southwest. He supported Sheridan with one division (Baird's), while his other division under Johnson remained in the trenches, under arms, ready to be moved to any point. Howard's corps was moved in rear of the centre. The picket lines were within a few hundred yards of each other. At two o'clock in the afternoon all were ready to advance. By this time the clouds had lifted so that the enemy could see from his elevated position all that was going on. The signal for advance was given by a booming of cannon from Fort Wood and other points on the line. The rebel pickets were soon driven back upon the main guards, which occupied minor and detached heights between the main ridge and our lines. These too were carried before halting, and before the enemy had time to reinforce their advance guards. But it was not without loss on both sides. This movement secured to us a line fully a mile in advance of the one we occupied in the morning, and the one which the enemy had occupied up to this time. The fortifications were rapidly turned to face the other way. During the following night they were made strong. We

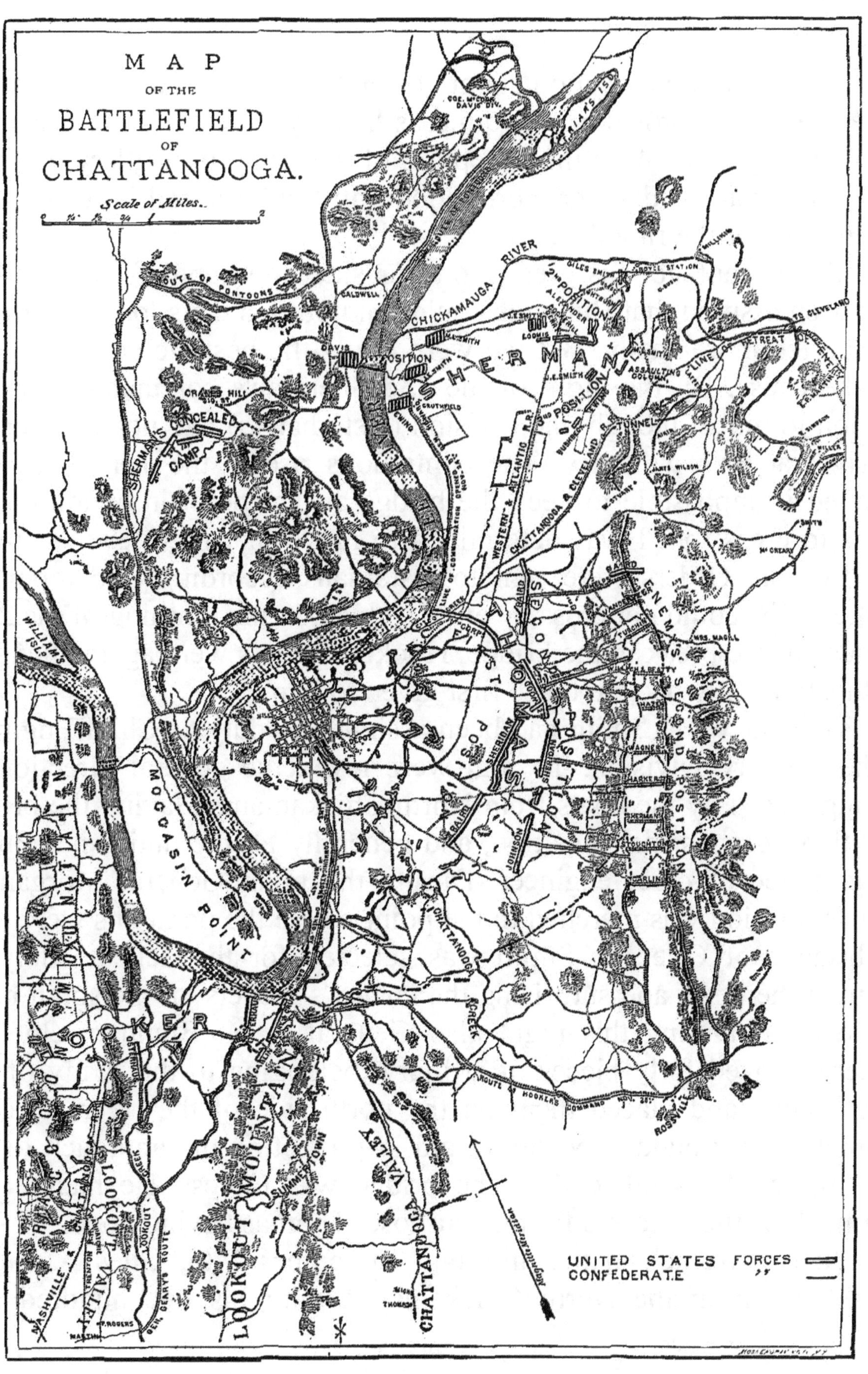

MAP
OF THE
BATTLEFIELD
OF
CHATTANOOGA.
Scale of Miles.
UNITED STATES FORCES
CONFEDERATE
CHICKAMAUGA RIVER
SHERMAN
TENNESSEE RIVER
MOCCASIN POINT
WILLIAM'S ISL.
LOOKOUT MOUNTAIN
LOOKOUT VALLEY
CHATTANOOGA VALLEY
CHATTANOOGA CREEK
HOOKER
ROUTE OF PONTOONS
SHERMAN'S CONCEALED CAMP
CRAVEN'S HILL
CALDWELL
DAVIS
ENEMY'S SECOND POSITION
ROUTE OF HOOKER'S COMMAND NOV. 25
ROSSVILLE
TUNNEL
WESTERN & ATLANTIC R.R.
CHATTANOOGA & CLEVELAND R.R.
TO CLEVELAND
SUMMERTOWN
SHERIDAN
WOOD
JOHNSON
WAGNER
HARKER
SHERMAN
STOUGHTON
MRS. MAGILL
NASHVILLE R.R.
GEN. GEARY'S ROUTE
MARTIN
W. ROGERS
COE. W. DAVIS DIV.
GILES SMITH
2nd POSITION
3rd POSITION
1st POSITION
ASSAULTING COLUMN
LINE OF BATTLE
RETREAT OF ENEMY

lost in this preliminary action about eleven hundred killed and wounded, while the enemy probably lost quite as heavily, including the prisoners that were captured. With the exception of the firing of artillery, kept up from Missionary Ridge and Fort Wood until night closed in, this ended the fighting for the first day.

The advantage was greatly on our side now, and if I could only have been assured that Burnside could hold out ten days longer I should have rested more easily. But we were doing the best we could for him and the cause. By the night of the 23d Sherman's command was in a position to move, though one division (Osterhaus's) had not yet crossed the river at Brown's Ferry. The continuous rise in the Tennessee had rendered it impossible to keep the bridge at that point in condition for troops to cross; but I was determined to move that night even without this division. Orders were sent to Osterhaus accordingly to report to Hooker, if he could not cross by eight o'clock on the morning of the 24th. Because of the break in the bridge, Hooker's orders were again changed, but this time only back to those first given to him.

General W. F. Smith had been assigned to duty as Chief Engineer of the Military Division. To him were given the general direction of moving troops by the boats from North Chickamauga, laying the bridge after they reached their position, and generally all the duties pertaining to his office of chief engineer. During the night General Morgan L. Smith's division was marched to the point where the pontoons were, and the brigade of Giles A. Smith was selected for the delicate duty of manning the boats and surprising the enemy's pickets on the south bank of the river. During this night also General J. M. Brannan, chief of artillery, moved forty pieces of artillery, belonging to the Army of the Cumberland, and placed them on the north side of the river so as to command the ground opposite, to aid in protecting the approach to the point where the south end of the bridge was to rest. He had to use Sherman's artillery horses for this purpose, Thomas having none.

At two o'clock in the morning, November 24th, Giles A. Smith pushed out from the North Chickamauga with his one hundred and sixteen boats, each loaded with thirty brave and well armed men. The boats with their precious freight dropped down quietly with the current to avoid attracting the attention of any one who could convey information to the enemy, until arriving near the mouth of South Chickamauga. Here a few boats were landed, the troops debarked, and a rush was made upon the picket guard known to be at that point. The guard were surprised, and twenty of their number captured. The remainder of the troops effected a landing at the point where the bridge was to start, with equally good results. The work of ferrying over Sherman's command from the north side of the Tennessee was at once commenced, using the pontoons for the purpose. A steamer was also brought up from the town to assist. The rest of M.L. Smith's division came first, then the division of John E. Smith. The troops as they landed were put to work intrenching their position. By daylight the two entire divisions were over and well covered by the works they had built.

The work of laying the bridge, on which to cross the artillery and cavalry, was now begun. The ferrying over the infantry was continued with the steamer and the pontoons, taking the pontoons, however, as fast as they were wanted to put in their place in the bridge. By a little past noon the bridge was completed, as well as one over the South Chickamauga connecting the troops left on that side with their comrades below, and all the infantry and artillery were on the south bank of the Tennessee.

Sherman at once formed his troops for assault on Missionary Ridge. By one o'clock he started with M.L. Smith on his left, keeping nearly the course of Chickamauga River; J. E. Smith next to the right and a little to the rear; and Ewing still. farther to the right and also a little to the rear of J. E. Smith's command, in column, ready to deploy to the right if an enemy should come from that direction. A good skirmish line preceded each of these columns. Soon the foot of the hill was reached; the skirmishers pushed directly up, followed closely by their supports. By half-past three Sherman was in possession of the height without having sustained much loss. A brigade from each division was now brought up, and artillery was dragged to the top of the hill by hand. The enemy did not seem to be aware of this movement until the top of the hill was gained. There had been a drizzling rain during the day, and the clouds were so low that Lookout Mountain and the top of Missionary Ridge were obscured from the view of persons in the valley. But now the enemy opened fire upon their assailants, and made several attempts with their skirmishers to drive them away, but without avail. Later in the day a more determined attack was made, but this, too, failed, and Sherman was left to fortify what he had gained.

Sherman's cavalry took up its line of march soon after the bridge was completed, and by half-past three the whole of it was over both bridges and on its way to strike the enemy's communications at Chickamauga Station. All of Sherman's command was now south of the Tennessee. During the afternoon General Giles A. Smith was severely wounded and carried from the field.

Thomas having done on the 23d what was expected of him on the 9th, there was nothing for him to do this day except to strengthen his position. Howard, however, effected a crossing of Citico Creek and a junction with Sherman, and was directed to report to him. With two or three regiments of his command he moved in the morning along the banks of the Tennessee, and reached the point where the bridge was being laid. He went out on the bridge as far as it was completed from the south end, and saw Sherman superintending the work from the north side and moving himself south as fast as an additional boat was put in and the roadway put upon it. Howard reported to his new chief across the chasm between them, which was now narrow and in a few minutes closed.

While these operations were going on to the east of Chattanooga, Hooker was engaged on the west. He had three divisions: Osterhaus's, of the 15th corps, Army of the Tennessee; Geary's, 12th corps, Army of the Potomac; and Cruft's, 14th corps, Army of the Cumberland. Geary was on the right at Wauhatchie, Cruft at the centre, and Osterhaus near Brown's Ferry. These troops were all west of Lookout Creek. The enemy had the east bank of the creek strongly picketed and intrenched, and three brigades of troops in the rear to reinforce them if attacked. These brigades occupied the summit of the mountain. General Carter L. Stevenson was in command of the whole. Why any troops, except artillery with a small infantry guard, were kept on the mountaintop, I do not see. A hundred men could have held the summit -which is a palisade for more than thirty feet down- against the assault of any number of men from the position Hooker occupied.

The side of Lookout Mountain confronting Hooker's command was rugged, heavily timbered, and full of chasms, making it difficult to advance with troops, even in the absence of an opposing force. Farther up, the ground becomes more even and level, and was in cultivation. On the east side the slope is much more gradual, and a good wagon road, zigzagging up it, connects the town of Chattanooga with the summit.

Early on the morning of the 24th Hooker Geary's division, supported by a brigade of Cruft's, up Lookout Creek, to effect a crossing. The remainder of Cruft's division was to seize the bridge over the creek, near the crossing of the railroad. Osterhaus was to move up to the bridge and cross it. The bridge was seized by Gross's brigade after a slight skirmish with the pickets guarding it. This attracted the enemy so that Geary's movement farther up was not observed. A heavy mist obscured him from the view of the troops on the top of the mountain. He crossed the creek almost unobserved, and captured the picket of over forty men on guard near by. He then commenced ascending the mountain directly in his front. By this time the enemy was seen coming down from their camps on the mountain slope, and filing into their rifle-pits to contest the crossing of the bridge. By eleven o'clock the bridge was complete. Osterhaus was up, and after some sharp skirmishing the enemy was driven away with considerable loss in killed and captured.

While the operations at the bridge were progressing, Geary was pushing up the hill over great obstacles, resisted by the enemy directly in his front, and in face of the guns on top of the mountain. The enemy, seeing their left flank and rear menaced, gave way, and were followed by Cruft and Osterhaus. Soon these were up abreast of Geary, and the whole command pushed up the hill, driving the enemy in advance. By noon Geary had gained the open ground on the north slope of the mountain, with his right close up to the base of the upper palisade, but there were strong fortifications in his front. The rest of the command coming up, a line was formed from the base of the upper palisade to the mouth of Chattanooga Creek.

Thomas and I were on the top of Orchard Knob. Hooker's advance now made our line a continuous one. It was in full view, extending from the Tennessee River, where Sherman had crossed, up Chickamauga River to the base of Mission Ridge, over the top of the north end of the ridge to Chattanooga Valley, then along parallel to the ridge a mile or more, across the valley to the mouth of Chattanooga Creek, thence up the slope of Lookout Mountain to the foot of the upper palisade. The day was hazy, so that Hooker's operations were not visible to us except at moments when the clouds would rise. But the sound of his artillery and musketry was heard incessantly. The enemy on his front was partially fortified, but was soon driven out of his works. During the afternoon the clouds, which had so obscured the top of Lookout all day as to hide whatever was going on from the view of those below, settled down and made it so dark where Hooker was as to stop operations for the time. At four o'clock Hooker reported his position as impregnable. By a little after five direct communication was established, and a brigade of troops was sent from Chattanooga to reinforce him. These troops had to cross Chattanooga Creek and met with some opposition, but soon overcame it, and by night the commander, General Carlin, reported to Hooker and was assigned to his left. I now telegraphed to Washington: "The fight today progressed favorably. Sherman carried the end of Missionary Ridge, and his right is now at the tunnel, and his left at Chickamauga Creek. Troops from Lookout Valley carried the point of the mountain, and now hold the eastern slope and a point high up. Hooker reports two thousand prisoners taken, besides which a small number have fallen into our hands from Missionary Ridge." The next day the President replied:

"Your dispatches as to fighting on Monday and Tuesday are here. Well done. Many thanks to all. Remember Burnside." And Halleck also telegraphed: "I congratulate you on the success thus far of your plans. I fear that Burnside is hard pushed, and that any further delay may prove fatal. I know you will do all in your power to relieve him."

The division of Jefferson C. Davis, Army of the Cumberland, had been sent to the North Chickamauga to guard the pontoons as they were deposited in the river, and to prevent all ingress or egress of citizens. On the night of the 24th his division, having crossed with Sherman, occupied our extreme left from the upper bridge over the plain to the north base of Missionary Ridge. Firing continued to a late hour in the night, but it was not connected with an assault at any point.

CHAPTER XLIV

BATTLE OF CHATTANOOGA - A GALLANT CHARGE - COMPLETE ROUT OF THE ENEMY - PURSUIT OF THE CONFEDERATES - GENERAL BRAGG - REMARKS ON CHATTANOOGA

AT twelve o'clock at night, when all was quiet, I began to give orders for the next day, and sent a dispatch to Willcox to encourage Burnside. Sherman was directed to attack at daylight. Hooker was ordered to move at the same hour, and endeavor to intercept the enemy's retreat if he still remained; if he had gone, then to move directly to Rossville and operate against the left and rear of the force on Missionary Ridge. Thomas was not to move until Hooker had reached Missionary Ridge. As I was with him on Orchard Knob, he would not move without further orders from me.

The morning of the 25th opened clear and bright, and the whole field was in full view from the top of Orchard Knob. It remained so all day. Bragg's headquarters were in full view, and officers -presumably staff officers- could be seen coming and going constantly.

The point of ground which Sherman had carried on the 24th was almost disconnected from the main ridge occupied by the enemy. A low pass, over which there is a wagon road crossing the hill, and near which there is a railroad tunnel, intervenes between the two hills. The problem now was to get to the main ridge. The enemy was fortified on the point; and back farther, where the ground was still higher, was a second fortification commanding the first. Sherman was out as soon as it was light enough to see, and by sunrise his command was in motion. Three brigades held the hill already gained. Morgan L. Smith moved along the east base of Missionary Ridge; Loomis along the west base, supported by two brigades of John E. Smith's division; and Corse with his brigade was between the two, moving directly towards the hill to be captured.

The ridge is steep and heavily wooded on the east side, where M. L. Smith's troops were advancing, but cleared and with a more gentle slope on the west side. The troops advanced rapidly and carried the extreme end of the rebel works. Morgan L. Smith advanced to a point which cut the enemy off from the railroad bridge and the means of bringing up supplies by rail from Chickamauga Station, where the main depot was located. The enemy made brave and strenuous efforts to drive our troops from the position we had gained, but without success. The contest lasted for two hours. Corse, a brave and efficient commander, was badly wounded in this assault. Sherman now threatened both Braggs flank and his stores, and made it necessary for him to weaken other points of his line to strengthen his right. From the position I occupied I could see column after column of Bragg's forces moving against Sherman. Every Confederate gun that could be brought to bear upon the Union forces was concentrated upon him. J.E. Smith, with two brigades, charged up the west side of the ridge to the support of Corse's command, over open ground and in the face of a heavy fire of both artillery and musketry, and reached the very parapet of the enemy. He lay here for a time, but the enemy coming with a heavy force upon his right flank, he was compelled to fall back, followed by the foe. A few hundred yards brought Smith's troops into a wood, where they were speedily reformed, when they charged and drove the attacking party back to his intrenchments.

Seeing the advance, repulse, and second advance of J.E. Smith from the position I occupied, I directed Thomas to send a division to reinforce him. Baird's division was accordingly sent from the right of Orchard Knob. It had to march a considerable distance directly under the eyes of the enemy to reach its position. Bragg at once commenced massing in the same direction. This was what I wanted. But it had now got to be late in the afternoon, and I had expected before this to see Hooker crossing the ridge in the neighborhood of Rossville and compelling Bragg to mass in that direction also.

The enemy had evacuated Lookout Mountain during the night, as I expected he would. In crossing the valley he burned the bridge over Chattanooga Creek, and did all he could to obstruct the roads behind him. Hooker was off bright and early, with no obstructions in his front but distance and the destruction above named. He was detained four hours crossing Chattanooga Creek, and thus was lost the immediate advantage I expected from his forces. His reaching Bragg's flank and extending across it was to be the signal for Thomas's assault of the ridge. But Sherman's condition was getting so critical that the assault for his relief could not be delayed any longer.

Sheridan's and Wood's divisions had been lying under arms from early morning, ready to move the instant the signal was given. I now directed Thomas to order the charge at once.* I watched eagerly to see the effect, and became impatient at last that there was no indication of any charge being made. The centre of the line which was to make the charge was near where Thomas and I stood, but concealed from view by an intervening forest. Turning to Thomas to inquire what caused the delay, I was surprised to see Thomas J. Wood, one of the division commanders who was to make the charge, standing talking to him. I spoke to General Wood, asking him why he did not charge as ordered an hour before. He replied very promptly that this was the first he had heard of it, but that he had been ready all day to move at a moment's notice. I told him to make the charge at once He was off in a moment, and in an incredibly short time loud cheering was heard, and he and Sheridan were driving the enemy's advance before them towards Missionary Ridge. The Confederates were strongly intrenched on the crest of the ridge in front of us, and had a second line halfway down and another at the base. Our men drove the troops in front of the lower line of rifle-pits so rapidly, and followed them so closely, that rebel and Union troops went

---

* In this order authority was given for the troops to reform after taking the first line of rifle-pits preparatory to carrying the ridge.

over the first line of works almost at the same time. Many rebels were captured and sent to the rear under the fire of their own friends higher up the hill. Those that were not captured retreated, and were pursued. The retreating hordes being between friends and pursuers caused the enemy to fire high to avoid killing their own men. In fact, on that occasion the Union soldier nearest the enemy was in the safest position. Without awaiting further orders or stopping to reform, on our troops went to the second line of works; over that and on for the crest -thus effectually carrying out my orders of the 18th for the battle and of the 24th** for this charge.

I watched their progress with intense interest. The fire along the rebel line was terrific. Cannon and musket balls filled the air: but the damage done was in small proportion to the ammunition expended. The pursuit continued until the crest was reached, and soon our men were seen climbing over the Confederate barriers at different points in front

---

** CHATTANOOGA, November 24, 1863.

MAJOR-GENERAL GEO. H. THOMAS,
Chattanooga:
General Sherman carried Missionary Ridge as far as the tunnel with only slight skirmishing. His right now rests at the tunnel and on top of the hill, his left at Chickamauga Creek. I have instructed General Sherman to advance as soon as it is light in the morning, and your attack, which will be simultaneous, will be in co-operation. Your command will either carry the rifle-pits and ridge directly in front of them, or move to the left, as the presence of the enemy may require. If Hooker's position on the mountain [cannot be maintained] with a small force, and it is found impracticable to carry the top from where he is, it would be advisable for him to move up the valley with all the force he can spare, and ascend by the first practicable road.

U. S. GRANT,
Major-General.

---

of both Sheridan's and Wood's divisions. The retreat of the enemy along most of his line was precipitate and the panic so great that Bragg and his officers lost all control over their men. Many were captured, and thousands threw away their arms in their flight.

Sheridan pushed forward until he reached the Chickamauga River at a point above where the enemy crossed. He met some resistance from troops occupying a second hill in rear of Missionary Ridge, probably to cover the retreat of the main body and of the artillery and trains. It was now getting dark, but Sheridan, without halting on that account pushed his men forward up this second hill slowly and without attracting the attention of the men placed to defend it, while he detached to the right and left to surround the position. The enemy discovered the movement before these dispositions were complete, and beat a hasty retreat, leaving artillery, wagon trains, and many prisoners in our hands. To Sheridan's prompt movement the Army of the Cumberland, and the nation, are indebted for the bulk of the capture of prisoners, artillery, and small-arms that day. Except for his prompt pursuit, so much in this way would not have been accomplished.

While the advance up Mission Ridge was going forward, General Thomas with staff, General Gordon Granger, commander of the corps making the assault, and myself and staff occupied Orchard Knob, from which the entire field could be observed. The moment the troops were seen going over the last line of rebel defences, I ordered Granger to join his command, and mounting my horse I rode to the front. General Thomas left about the same time. Sheridan on the extreme right was already in pursuit of the enemy east of the ridge. Wood, who commanded the division to the left of Sheridan, accompanied his men on horseback in the charge, but did not join Sheridan in the pursuit. To the left, in Baird's front where Bragg's troops had massed against Sherman, the resistance was more stubborn and the contest lasted longer. I ordered Granger to follow the enemy with Wood's division, but he was so much excited, and kept up such a roar of musketry in the direction the enemy had taken, that by the time I could stop the firing the enemy had got well out of the way. The enemy confronting Sherman, now seeing everything to their left giving way, fled also. Sherman, however, was not aware of the extent of our success until after nightfall, when he received orders to pursue at daylight in the morning.

As soon as Sherman discovered that the enemy had left his front he directed his reserves, Davis's division of the Army of the Cumberland, to push over the pontoon-bridge at the mouth of the Chickamauga, and to move forward to Chickamauga Station. He ordered Howard to move up the stream some two miles to where there was an old bridge, repair it during the night, and follow Davis at four o'clock in the morning. Morgan L. Smith was ordered to reconnoitre the tunnel to see if that was still held. Nothing was found there but dead bodies of men of both armies. The rest of Sherman's command was directed to follow Howard at daylight in the morning to get on to the railroad towards Graysville.

Hooker, as stated, was detained at Chattanooga Creek by the destruction of the bridge at that point. He got his troops over, with the exception of the artillery, by fording the stream at a little after three o'clock. Leaving his artillery to follow when the bridge should be reconstructed, he pushed on with the remainder of his command. At Rossville he came upon the flank of a division of the enemy, which soon commenced a retreat along the ridge. This threw them on Palmer. They could make but little resistance in the position they were caught in, and as many of them as could do so escaped, Many, however, were captured. Hooker's position during the night of the 25th was near Rossville, extending east of the ridge. Palmer was on his left, on the road to Graysville.

During the night I telegraphed to Willcox that Bragg had been defeated, and that immediate relief would be sent to Burnside if he could hold out; to Halleck I sent an announcement of our victory, and informed him that forces would be sent up the valley to relieve Burnside.

Before the battle of Chattanooga opened I had taken measures for the relief of Burnside the moment the way should be clear. Thomas was directed to have the little steamer that had been built at Chattanooga loaded to its capacity with rations and ammunition. Granger's corps was to move by the south bank of the Tennessee River to the mouth of the

Holston, and up that to Knoxville, accompanied by the boat. In addition to the supplies transported by boat, the men were to carry forty rounds of ammunition in their cartridge-boxes, and four day's rations in haversacks.

In the battle of Chattanooga, troops from the Army of the Potomac, from the Army of the Tennessee, and from the Army of the Cumberland participated. In fact, the accidents growing out of the heavy rains and the sudden rise in the Tennessee River so mingled the troops that the organizations were not kept together, under their respective commanders, during the battle. Hooker, on the right, had Geary's division of the 12th corps, Army of the Potomac; Osterhaus's division of the 15th corps, Army of the Tennessee; and Cruft's division of the Army of the Cumberland. Sherman had three divisions of his own army, Howard's corps from the Army of the Potomac, and Jefferson C. Davis's division of the Army of the Cumberland. There was no jealousy -hardly rivalry. Indeed, I doubt whether officers or men took any note at the time of the fact of this intermingling of commands. All saw a defiant foe surrounding them, and took it for granted that every move was intended to dislodge him, and it made no difference where the troops came from so that the end was accomplished.

The victory at Chattanooga was won against great odds, considering the advantage the enemy had of position, and was accomplished more easily than was expected by reason of Bragg's making several grave mistakes, first, in sending away his ablest corps commander with over twenty thousand troops; second, in sending away a division of troops on the eve of battle; third, in placing so much of a force on the plain in front of his impregnable position.

It was known that Mr. Jefferson Davis had visited Bragg on Missionary Ridge a short time before my reaching Chattanooga. It was reported and believed that he had come out to reconcile a serious difference between Bragg and Longstreet, and finding this difficult to do, planned the campaign against Knoxville, to be conducted by the latter general. I had known both Bragg and Longstreet before the war, the latter very well. We had been three years at West Point together, and, after my graduation, for a time in the same regiment. Then we served together in the Mexican War. I had known Bragg in Mexico, and met him occasionally subsequently. I could well understand how there might be an irreconcilable difference between them.

Bragg was a remarkably intelligent and well -informed man, professionally and otherwise. He was also thoroughly upright. But he was possessed of an irascible temper, and was naturally disputatious. A man of the highest moral character and the most correct habits, yet in the old army he was in frequent trouble. As a subordinate he was always on the lookout to catch his commanding officer infringing his prerogatives; as a post commander he was equally vigilant to detect the slightest neglect, even of the most trivial order.

I have heard in the old army an anecdote very characteristic of Bragg. On one occasion, when stationed at a post of several companies commanded by a field officer, he was himself commanding one of the companies and at the same time acting as post quartermaster and commissary. He was first lieutenant at the time, but his captain was detached on other duty. As commander of the company he made a requisition upon the quartermaster-himself -for something he wanted. As quartermaster he declined to fill the requisition, and endorsed on the back of it his reasons for so doing. As company commander he responded to this, urging that his requisition called for nothing but what he was entitled to, and that it was the duty of the quartermaster to fill it. As quartermaster he still persisted that he was right. In this condition of affairs Bragg referred the whole matter to the commanding officer of the post. The latter, when he saw the nature of the matter referred, exclaimed: "My God, Mr. Bragg, you have quarreled with every officer in the army, and now you are quarrelling with yourself!"

Longstreet was an entirely different man. He was brave, honest, intelligent, a very capable soldier, subordinate to his superiors, just and kind to his subordinates, but jealous of his own rights, which he had the courage to maintain. He was never on the lookout to detect a slight, but saw one as soon as anybody when intentionally given,

It may be that Longstreet was not sent to Knoxville for the reason stated, but because Mr. Davis had an exalted opinion of his own military genius, and thought he saw a chance of "killing two birds with one stone." On several occasions during the war he came to the relief of the Union army by means of his *superior military genius.*

I speak advisedly when I say Mr. Davis prided himself on his military capacity. He says so himself, virtually, in his answer to the notice of his nomination to the Confederate presidency. Some of his generals have said so in their writings since the downfall of the Confederacy.

My recollection is that my first orders for the battle of Chattanooga were as fought. Sherman was to get on Missionary Ridge, as he did; Hooker to cross the north end of Lookout Mountain, as he did, sweep across Chattanooga Valley and get across the south end of the ridge near Rossville. When Hooker had secured that position the Army of the Cumberland was to assault in the centre. Before Sherman arrived, however, the order was so changed as that Hooker was directed to come to Chattanooga by the north bank of the Tennessee River. The waters in the river, owing to heavy rains, rose so fast that the bridge at Brown's Ferry could not be maintained in a condition to be used in crossing troops upon it. For this reason Hooker's orders were changed by telegraph back to what they were originally.

NOTE -From this point on this volume was written (with the exception of the campaign in the Wilderness, which had been previously written) by General Grant after his great illness in April, and the present arrangement of the subject matter was made by him between the 10th and 18th of July, 1885.

CHAPTER XLV

THE RELIEF OF KNOXVILLE
- HEADQUARTERS MOVEDTO NASHVILLE
- VISITING KNOXVILLE - CIPHER
DISPATCHES WITHHOLDING ORDERS

CHATTANOOGA now being secure to the National troops beyond any doubt, I immediately turned my attention to relieving Knoxville, about the situation of which the President, in particular, was very anxious. Prior to the battles, I had made preparations for sending troops to the relief of Burnside at the very earliest moment after securing Chattanooga. We had there two little steamers which had been built and fitted up from the remains of old boats and put in condition to run. General Thomas was directed to have one of these boats loaded with rations and ammunition and move up the Tennessee River to the mouth of the Holston, keeping the boat all the time abreast of the troops. General Granger, with the 4th corps reinforced to make twenty thousand men, was to start the moment Missionary Ridge was carried, and under no circumstances were the troops to return to their old camps. With the provisions carried, and the little that could be got in the country, it was supposed he could hold out until Longstreet was driven away, after which event East Tennessee would furnish abundance of food for Burnside's army and his own also.

While following the enemy on the 26th, and again on the morning of the 27th, part of the time by the road to Ringgold, I directed Thomas, verbally, not to start Granger until he received further orders from me ; advising him that I was going to the front to more fully see the situation. I was not right sure but that Bragg's troops might be over their stampede by the time they reached Dalton. In that case Bragg might think it well to take the road back to Cleveland, move thence towards Knoxville, and, uniting with Longstreet, make a sudden dash upon Burnside.

When I arrived at Ringgold, however, on the 27th, I saw that the retreat was most earnest. The enemy had been throwing away guns, caissons and small-arms, abandoning provisions, and, altogether, seemed to be moving like a disorganized mob, with the exception of Cleburne's division, which was acting as rear-guard to cover the retreat.

When Hooker moved from Rossville toward Ringgold Palmer's division took the road to Graysville, and Sherman moved by the way of Chickamauga Station toward the same point. As soon as I saw the situation at Ringgold I sent a staff officer back to Chattanooga to advise Thomas of the condition of affairs, and direct him by my orders to start Granger at once. Feeling now that the troops were already on the march for the relief of Burnside I was in no hurry to get back, but stayed at Ringgold through the day to prepare for the return of our troops.

Ringgold is in a valley in the mountains, situated between East Chickamauga Creek and Taylor's Ridge, and about twenty miles southeast from Chattanooga. I arrived just as the artillery that Hooker had left behind at Chattanooga Creek got up. His men were attacking Cleburne's division, which had taken a strong position in the adjacent hills so as to cover the retreat of the Confederate army through a narrow gorge which presents itself at that point. Just beyond the gorge the valley is narrow, and the creek so tortuous that it has to be crossed a great many times in the course of the first mile. This attack was unfortunate, and cost us some men unnecessarily. Hooker captured, however, 3 pieces of artillery and 230 prisoners, and 130 rebel dead were left upon the field.

I directed General Hooker to collect the flour and wheat in the neighboring mills for the use of the troops, and then to destroy the mills and all other property that could be of use to the enemy, but not to make any wanton destruction.

At this point Sherman came up; having reached Graysville with his troops, where he found Palmer had preceded him. Palmer had picked up many prisoners and much abandoned property on the route. I went back in the evening to Graysville with Sherman, remained there over night and did not return to Chattanooga until the following night, the 29th. I then found that Thomas had not yet started Granger, thus having lost a full day which I deemed of so much importance in determining the fate of Knoxville. Thomas and Granger were aware that on the 23d of the month Burnside had telegraphed that his supplies would last for ten or twelve days and during that time he could hold out against Longstreet, but if not relieved within the time indicated he would be obliged to surrender or attempt to retreat. To effect a retreat would have been an impossibility. He was already very low in ammunition, and with an army pursuing he would not have been able to gather supplies.

Finding that Granger had not only not started but was very reluctant to go, he having decided for himself that it was a very bad move to make, I sent word to General Sherman of the situation and directed him to march to the relief of Knoxville. I also gave him the problem that we had to solve that Burnside had now but four to six days supplies left, and that he must be relieved within that time.

Sherman, fortunately, had not started on his return from Graysville, having sent out detachments on the railroad which runs from Dalton to Cleveland and Knoxville to thoroughly destroy that road, and these troops had not yet returned to camp. I was very loath to send Sherman, because his men needed rest after their long march from Memphis and hard fighting at Chattanooga. But I had become satisfied that Burnside would not be rescued if his relief depended upon General Granger's movements.

Sherman had left his camp on the north side of the Tennessee River, near Chattanooga, on the night of the 23d, the men having two day's cooked rations in their haversacks. Expecting to be back in their tents by that time and to be engaged in battle while out, they took with them neither overcoats nor blankets. The weather was already cold, and at night they must have suffered more or less. The two day's rations had already lasted them five days; and they were now to go through a country which had been run over so much by Confederate troops that there was but little probability of finding much food. They did, however, succeed in capturing some flour. They also found a good deal of bran in some of the mills, which the men made up into bread ; and in this and other ways they eked out an existence until they could reach Knoxville.

I was so very anxious that Burnside should get news of the steps being taken for his relief, and thus induce him to hold out a little longer if it became necessary, that I determined to send a message to him. I therefore sent a member of my staff, Colonel J. H. Wilson, to get into Knoxville if he could, report to Burnside the situation fully, and give him all the encouragement possible. Mr. Charles A. Dana was at Chattanooga during the battle, and had been there even before I assumed command. Mr. Dana volunteered to accompany Colonel Wilson, and did accompany him. I put the information of what was being done for the relief of Knoxville into writing, and directed that in some way or other it must be secretly managed so as to have a copy of this fall into the hands of General Longstreet. They made the trip safely; General Longstreet did learn of Sherman's coming in advance of his reaching there, and Burnside was prepared to hold out even for a longer time if it had been necessary.

Burnside had stretched a boom across the Holston River to catch scows and flats as they floated down. On these, by previous arrangements with the loyal people of East Tennessee, were placed flour and corn, with forage and provisions generally, and were thus secured for the use of the Union troops. They also drove cattle into Knoxville by the east side, which was not covered by the enemy; so that when relief arrived Burnside had more provisions on hand than when he had last reported.

Our total loss (not including Burnside's) in all these engagements amounted to 757 killed, 4,529 wounded and 330 missing. We captured 6,142 prisoners about 50 per cent. more than the enemy reported for their total loss -40 pieces of artillery, 69 artillery carriages and caissons and over 7,000 stands of small-arms. The enemy's loss in arms was probably much greater than here reported, because we picked up a great many that were found abandoned.

I had at Chattanooga, in round numbers, about 60,000 men. Bragg had about half this number, but his position was supposed to be impregnable. It was his own fault that he did not have more men present. He had sent Longstreet away with his corps swelled by reinforcements up to over twenty thousand men, thus reducing his own force more than one third and depriving himself of the presence of the ablest general of his command. He did this, too, after our troops had opened a line of communication by way of Brown's and Kelly's ferries with Bridgeport, thus securing full rations and supplies of every kind; and also when he knew reinforcements were coming to me. Knoxville was of no earthly use to him while Chattanooga was in our hands. If he should capture Chattanooga, Knoxville with its garrison would have fallen into his hands without a struggle. I have never been able to see the wisdom of this move.

Then, too, after Sherman had arrived, and when Bragg knew that he was on the north side of the Tennessee River, he sent Buckner's division to reinforce Longstreet. He also started another division a day later, but our attack having commenced before it reached Knoxville Bragg ordered it back. It had got so far, however, that it could not return to Chattanooga in time to be of service there. It is possible this latter blunder may have been made by Bragg having become confused as to what was going on, on our side. Sherman had, as already stated, crossed to the north side of the Tennessee River at Brown's Ferry, in full view of Bragg's troops from Lookout Mountain, a few days before the attack. They then disappeared behind foot hills, and did not come to the view of the troops on Missionary Ridge until they met their assault. Bragg knew it was Sherman's troops that had crossed, and, they being so long out of view, may have supposed that they had gone up the north bank of the Tennessee River to the relief of Knoxville and that Longstreet was therefore in danger. But the first great blunder, detaching Longstreet, cannot be accounted for in any way I know of. If he had captured Chattanooga, East Tennessee would have fallen without a struggle. It would have been a, victory for us to have got our army away from

Chattanooga safely. It was a manifold greater victory to drive away the besieging army; a still greater one to defeat that army in his chosen ground and nearly annihilate it.

The probabilities are that our loss in killed was the heavier, as we were the attacking party. The enemy reported his loss in killed at 361: but as he reported his missing at 4,146, while we held over 6,000 of them as prisoners, and there must have been hundreds if not thousands who deserted, but little reliance can be placed on this report. There was certainly great dissatisfaction with Bragg on the part of the soldiers for his harsh treatment of them, and a disposition to get away if they could. Then, too, Chattanooga, following in the same half year with Gettysburg in the East and Vicksburg in the West, there was much the same feeling in the South at this time that there had been in the North the fall and winter before. If the same license had been allowed the people and press in the South that was allowed in the North, Chattanooga would probably have been the last battle fought for the preservation of the Union.

General William F. Smith's services in these battles had been such that I thought him eminently entitled to promotion. I was aware that he had previously been named by the President for promotion to the grade of major-general, but that the Senate had rejected the nomination. I was not aware of the reasons for this course, and therefore strongly recommended him for a major-generalcy. My recommendation was heeded and the appointment made.

Upon the raising of the siege of Knoxville I, of course, informed the authorities at Washington -the President and Secretary of War- of the fact, which caused great rejoicing there. The President especially was rejoiced that Knoxville had been relieved* without further bloodshed. The safety of Burnsides army and the loyal people of East Tennessee had been the subject of much anxiety to the President for several months, during which time

MAJ.-GENERAL U. S. GRANT:

Understanding that your lodgment at Knoxville and at Chattanooga is now secure, I wish to tender you, and all under your command, my more than thanks, my profoundest gratitude for the skill, courage, and perseverance with which you and they, over so great difficulties, have effected that important object. God bless you all.

A. LINCOLN,
President U. S.

---

he was doing all he could to relieve the situation; sending a new commander* with a few thousand troops by the way of Cumberland Gap, and telegraphing me daily, almost hourly, to "remember Burnside," "do something for Burnside," and other appeals of like tenor. He saw no escape for East Tennessee until after our victory at Chattanooga. Even then he was afraid that Burnside might be out of ammunition, in a starving condition, or overpowered: and his anxiety was still intense until he heard that Longstreet had been driven from the field.

Burnside followed Longstreet only to Strawberry Plains, some twenty miles or more east, and then stopped, believing that Longstreet would leave the State. The latter did not do so, however, but stopped only a short distance farther on and subsisted his army for the entire winter off East Tennessee. Foster now relieved Burnside. Sherman made disposition of his troops along the Tennessee River in accordance with instructions. I left Thomas in command at Chattanooga, and, about the 20th of December, moved my headquarters to Nashville, Tennessee.

Nashville was the most central point from which to communicate with my entire military division, and also with the authorities at

---

* General John G. Foster.

Washington. While remaining at Chattanooga I was liable to have my telegraphic communications cut so as to throw me out of communication with both my command and Washington.

Nothing occurred at Nashville worthy of mention during the winter,* so I set myself to the task of having troops in positions from which they could move to advantage, and in collecting all necessary supplies so as to be ready to claim a due. share of the enemy's attention upon the appearance of the first good weather in the spring. I expected to retain the command I then had, and prepared myself for the campaign against Atlanta. I also had great hopes of having a campaign made against Mobile from the Gulf. I expected after Atlanta fell to occupy that place permanently, and to cut off Lee's army from the West by way of the road running through Augusta to Atlanta and thence southwest. I was preparing to hold Atlanta with a small garrison, and it was my expectation to push through to Mobile if that city was in our possession: if not, to Savannah; and in this manner to get possession of the only east and west railroad that would then be left to the enemy. But the spring campaign against Mobile was not made.

The Army of the Ohio had been getting supplies over Cumberland Gap until their animals had nearly all starved. I now determined to go myself to see if there was any possible chance of using that route in the spring, and if not to abandon it. Accordingly I left Nashville in the latter part of December by rail for Chattanooga. From Chattanooga I took one of the little steamers previously spoken of as having been built there, and,

---

* During this winter the citizens of Jo Davies County, Ill., subscribed for and had a diamond hilted sword made for General Grant, which was always known as the Chattanooga sword. The scabbard was of gold, and was ornamented with a scroll running nearly its entire length, displaying in engraved letters the names of the battles in which General Grant had participated.

Congress also gave him a vote of thanks for the victories at Chattanooga, and voted him a gold medal for Vicksburg and Chattanooga. All such things are now in the possession of the government at Washington.

putting my horses aboard, went up to the junction of the Clinch with the Tennessee. From that point the railroad had been repaired up to Knoxville and out east to Strawberry Plains. I went by rail therefore to Knoxville, where I remained for several days. General John G. Foster was then commanding the Department of the Ohio. It was an intensely cold winter, the thermometer being down as low as zero every morning for more than a week while I was at Knoxville and on my way from there on horseback to Lexington, Kentucky, the first point where I could reach rail to carry me back to my headquarters at Nashville.

The road over Cumberland Gap, and back of it, was strewn with debris of broken wagons and dead animals, much as I had found it on my first trip to Chattanooga over Waldron's Ridge. The road had been cut up to as great a depth as clay could be by mules and wagons, and in that condition frozen; SO that the ride of six days from Strawberry Plains to Lexington over these holes and knobs in the road was a very cheerless one, and very disagreeable.

I found a great many people at home along that route, both in Tennessee and Kentucky, and, almost universally, intensely loyal. They would collect in little places where we would stop of evenings, to see me, generally hearing of my approach before we arrived. The people naturally expected to see the commanding general the oldest person in the party. I was then forty-one years of age, while my medical director was gray haired and probably twelve or more years my senior. The crowds would generally swarm around him, and thus give me an opportunity of quietly dismounting and getting into the house. It also gave me an opportunity of hearing passing remarks from one spectator to another about their general. Those remarks were apt to be more complimentary to the cause than to the appearance of the supposed general, owing to his being muffled up, and also owing to the travel worn condition we were all in after a hard day's ride. I was back in Nashville by the 13th of January, 1864.

When I started on this trip it was necessary for me to have some person along who could turn dispatches into cipher, and who could also read the cipher dispatches which I was liable to receive daily and almost hourly. Under the rules of the War Department at that time, Mr. Stanton had taken entire control of the matter of regulating the telegraph and determining how it should be used, and of saying who, and who alone, should have the ciphers. The operators possessed of the ciphers, as well as the ciphers used, were practically independent of the commanders whom they were serving immediately under, and had to report to the War Department through General Stager all the dispatches which they received or forwarded.

I was obliged to leave the telegraphic operator back at Nashville, because that was the point at which all dispatches to me would come, to be forwarded from there. As I have said, it was necessary for me also to have an operator during this inspection who had possession of this cipher to enable me to telegraph to my division and to the War Department without my dispatches being read by all the operators along the line of wires over which they were transmitted. Accordingly I ordered the cipher operator to turn over the key to Captain Cyrus B. Comstock, of the Corps of Engineers, whom I had selected as a wise and discreet man who certainly could be trusted with the cipher if the operator at my headquarters could.

The operator refused point blank to turn over the key to Captain Comstock as directed by me, stating that his orders from the War Department were not to give it to anybody, the commanding general or any one else. I told him I would see whether he would or not. He said that if he did he would be punished. I told him if he did not he most certainly would be punished. Finally, seeing that punishment was certain if he refused longer to obey my order, and being somewhat remote (even if he was not protected altogether from the consequences of his disobedience to his orders) from the War Department, he yielded. When I returned from Knoxville I found quite a commotion. The operator had been reprimanded very severely and ordered to be relieved. I informed the Secretary of War, or his assistant secretary in charge of the telegraph, Stager, that the man could not be relieved, for he had only obeyed my orders. It was absolutely necessary for me to have the cipher, and the man would most certainly have been punished if he had not delivered it; that they would have to punish me if they punished anybody or words to that effect.

This was about the only thing approaching a disagreeable difference between the Secretary of War and myself that occurred until the war was over, when we had another little spat. Owing to his natural disposition to assume all power and control in all matters that he had anything whatever to do with, he boldly took command of the armies, and, while issuing no orders on the subject, prohibited any order from me going out of the adjutant-general's office until he had approved it. This was done by directing the adjutant-general to hold any orders that came from me to be issued from the adjutant-general's office until he had examined them and given his approval. He never disturbed himself, either, in examining my orders until it was entirely convenient for him; so that orders which I had prepared would often lie there three or four days before he would sanction them. I remonstrated against this in writing, and the Secretary apologetically restored me to my rightful position of General-in-Chief of the Army. But he soon lapsed again and took control much as before.

After the relief of Knoxville Sherman had proposed to Burnside that he should go with him to drive Longstreet out of Tennessee; but Burnside assured him that with the troops which had been brought by Granger, and which were to be left, he would be amply prepared to dispose of Longstreet without availing himself of this offer. As before stated Sherman's command had left their camps north of the Tennessee, near Chattanooga, with two day's rations in their haversacks, without coats or blankets, and without many wagons, expecting to return to their camps by the end of that time. The weather was now cold and they were suffering, but still they were ready to make the further sacrifice, had it been required, for the good of the cause which had brought them into service. Sherman, having accomplished the object for which he was sent, marched back leisurely to his old camp on the Tennessee River.

CHAPTER XLVI

OPERATIONS IN MISSISSIPPI - LONGSTREET IN EAST TEN-NESSEE - COMMISSIONED LIEUTENANT - GENERAL - COMMANDING THE ARMIES OF THE UNITED STATES - FIRST INTERVIEW WITH PRESIDENT LINCOLN

SOON after his return from Knoxville I ordered Sherman to distribute his forces from Stevenson to Decatur and thence north to Nashville; Sherman suggested that he be permitted to go back to Mississippi, to the limits of his own department and where most of his army still remained, for the purpose of clearing out what Confederates might still be left on the east bank of the Mississippi River to impede its navigation by our boats. He expected also to have the cooperation of Banks to do the same thing on the west shore. Of course I approved heartily.

About the 10th of January Sherman was back in Memphis, where Hurlbut commanded, and got together his Memphis men, or ordered them collected and sent to Vicksburg. He then went to Vicksburg and out to where McPherson was in command, and had him organize his surplus troops so as to give him about 20,000 men in all.

Sherman knew that General (Bishop) Polk was occupying Meridian with his headquarters, and had two divisions of infantry with a considerable force of cavalry scattered west of him. He determined, therefore, to move directly upon Meridian.

I had sent some 2,500 cavalry under General Sooy Smith to Sherman's department, and they had mostly arrived before Sherman got to Memphis. Hurlbut had 7,000 cavalry, and Sherman ordered him to reinforce Smith so as to give the latter a force of about 7,000 with which to go against Forrest, who was then known to be southeast from Memphis. Smith was ordered to move about the 1st of February.

While Sherman was waiting at Vicksburg for the arrival of Hurlbut with his surplus men, he sent out scouts to ascertain the position and strength of the enemy and to bring back all the information they could gather. When these scouts returned it was through them that he got the information of General Polk's being at Meridian, and of the strength and disposition of his command.

Forrest had about 4,000 cavalry with him, composed of thoroughly well disciplined men, who under so able a leader were very effective. Smith's command was nearly double that of Forrest, but not equal, man to man, for the lack of a successful experience such as Forrest's men had had. The fact is, troops who have fought a few battles and won, and followed up their victories, improve upon what they were before to an extent that can hardly be counted by percentage. The difference in result is often decisive victory instead of inglorious defeat. This same difference, too, is often due to the way troops are officered and for the particular kind of warfare which Forrest had carried on neither army could present a more effective officer than he was.

Sherman got off on the 3d of February and moved out on his expedition, meeting with no opposition whatever until he crossed the Big Black, and with no great deal of opposition after that until he reached Jackson, Mississippi. This latter place he reached on the 6th or 7th, Brandon on the 8th, and Morton on the 9th. Up to this time he moved in two columns to enable him to get a good supply of forage, etc., and expedite the march. Here, however, there were indications of the concentration of Confederate infantry, and he was obliged to keep his army close together. He had no serious engagement; but he met some of the enemy who destroyed a few of his wagons about Decatur, Mississippi, where, by the way, Sherman himself came near being picked up.

He entered Meridian on the 14th of the month, the enemy having retreated toward Demopolis, Alabama. He spent several days in Meridian in thoroughly destroying the railroad to the north and south, and also for the purpose of hearing from Sooy Smith, who he supposed had met Forrest before this time and he hoped had gained a decisive victory because of a superiority of numbers. Hearing nothing of him, however, he started on his return trip to Vicksburg. There he learned that Smith, while waiting for a few of his men who had been ice bound in the Ohio River, instead of getting off on the 1st as expected, had not left until the 11th. Smith did meet Forrest, but the result was decidedly in Forrest's favor.

Sherman had written a letter to Banks, proposing a co-operative movement with him against Shreveport, subject to my approval. I disapproved of Sherman's going himself, because I had other important work for him to do, but consented that he might send a few troops to the aid of Banks, though their time to remain absent must be limited. We must have them for the spring campaign. The trans-Mississippi movement proved abortive.

My eldest son, who had accompanied me on the Vicksburg campaign and siege, had while there contracted disease, which grew worse, until he had grown so dangerously ill that on the 24th of January I obtained permission to go to St. Louis, where he was staying at the time, to see him, hardly expecting to find him alive on my arrival. While I was permitted to go, I was not permitted to turn over my command to any one else, but was directed to keep the headquarters with me and to communicate regularly with all parts of my division and with Washington, just as though I had remained at Nashville.

When I obtained this leave I was at Chattanooga, having gone there again to make preparations to have the troops of Thomas in the southern part of Tennessee co-operate with Sherman's movement in Mississippi. I directed Thomas, and Logan who was at Scottsboro, Alabama, to keep up a threatening movement to the south against J. E. Johnston, who had again relieved Bragg, for the purpose of making him keep as many troops as possible there.

I learned through Confederate sources that Johnston had already sent two divisions in the direction of Mobile, presumably to operate against Sherman, and two more divisions to Longstreet in East

Tennessee. Seeing that Johnston had depleted in this way, I directed Thomas to send at least ten thousand men, besides Stanley's division which was already to the east, into East Tennessee, and notified Schofield, who was now in command in East Tennessee, of this movement of troops into his department and also of the reinforcements Longstreet had received. My object was to drive Longstreet out of East Tennessee as a part of the preparations for my spring campaign.

About this time General Foster, who had been in command of the Department of the Ohio after Burnside until Schofield relieved him,* advised me that he thought it would be a good thing to keep Longstreet just where he was; that he was perfectly quiet in East Tennessee, and if he was forced to leave there, his whole well -equipped army would be free to go to any place where it could effect the most for their cause. I thought the advice was good, and, adopting that view, countermanded the orders for pursuit of Longstreet.

On the 12th of February I ordered Thomas to take Dalton and hold it, if possible; and I directed him to move without delay. Finding that he had not moved, on the 17th I urged him again to start, telling him how important it was, that the object of the movement was to co-operate with Sherman, who was moving eastward and might be in danger.

---

* WASHINGTON, D. C.,
December 29, 1863.

MAJ.-GENERAL U. S. GRANT:
General Foster has asked to be relieved from his command on account of disability from old wounds. Should his request be granted, who would you like as his successor? It is possible that Schofield will be sent to your command.

H. W. HALLECK, (Offical.)
General-in-Chief.

Then again on the 21st, he not yet having started, I asked him if he could not start the next day. He finally got off on the 22d or 23d. The enemy fell back from his front without a battle, but took a new position quite as strong and farther to the rear. Thomas reported that he could not go any farther, because it was impossible with his poor teams, nearly starved, to keep up supplies until the railroads were repaired. He soon fell back.

Schofield also had to return for the same reason. He could not carry supplies with him, and Longstreet was between him and the supplies still left in the country. Longstreet, in his retreat, would be moving towards his supplies, while our forces, following, would be receding from theirs. On the ad of March, however, I learned of Sherman's success, which eased my mind very much. The next day, the 3d, I was ordered to Washington.

The bill restoring the grade of lieutenant-general of the army had passed through Congress and became a law on the 26th of February. My nomination had been sent to the Senate on the 1st of March and confirmed the next day (the 2d). I was ordered to Washington on the 3d to receive my commission, and started the day following that. The commission was handed to me on the 9th. It was delivered to me at the Executive Mansion by President Lincoln in the presence of his Cabinet, my eldest son, those of my staff who were with me and a few other visitors.

The President in presenting my commission read from a paper -stating, however, as a preliminary, and prior to the delivery of it, that he had drawn that up on paper, knowing my disinclination to speak in public, and handed me a copy in advance so that I might prepare a few lines of reply. The President said:

"General Grant, the nation's appreciation of what you have done, and its reliance upon you for what remains to be done in the existing great struggle, are now presented, with this commission constituting you lieutenant-general in the Army of the United States. With this high honor, devolves upon you, also, a corresponding responsibility. As the country herein trusts you, so, under God, it will sustain you. I scarcely need to add, that, with what I here speak for the nation, goes my own hearty personal concurrence."

To this I replied: "Mr. President, I accept the commission, with gratitude for the high honor conferred. With the aid of the noble armies that have fought in so many fields for our common country, it will be my earnest endeavor not to disappoint your expectations. I feel the full weight of the responsibilities now devolving on me; and I know that if they are met, it will be due to those armies, and above all, to the favor of that Providence which leads both nations and men."

On the 10th I visited the headquarters of the Army of the Potomac at Brandy Station; then returned to Washington, and pushed west at once to make my arrangements for turning over the commands there and giving general directions for the preparations to be made for the spring campaign.

It had been my intention before this to remain in the West, even if I was made lieutenant-general; but when I got to Washington and saw the situation it was plain that here was the point for the commanding general to be. No one else could, probably, resist the pressure that would be brought to bear upon him to desist from his own plans and pursue others. I determined, therefore, before I started back to have Sherman advanced to my late position, McPherson to Sherman's in command of the department, and Logan to the command of McPherson's corps. These changes were all made on my recommendation and without hesitation. My commission as lieutenant general was given to me on the 9th of March, 1864. On the following day, as already stated, I visited General Meade, commanding the Army of the Potomac, at his headquarters at Brandy Station, north of the Rapidan. I had known General Meade slightly in the Mexican war, but had not met him since until this visit. I was a stranger to most of the Army of the Potomac, I might say to all except the officers of the regular army who had served in the Mexican war. There had been some changes ordered in the organization of that army before my promotion. One was the consolidation of five corps into three, thus throwing some officers of rank out of important commands. Meade evidently thought that I might want to make still one more change not yet ordered. He said to me that I might want an officer who had served with me in the West, mentioning Sherman specially, to take his place. If so, he begged me not to hesitate about making the change. He urged that the work before us was of such vast importance to the whole nation that the feeling or wishes of no one person should stand in the way of selecting the right men for all positions. For himself, he would serve to the best of his ability wherever placed. I assured him that I had no thought of substituting any one for him. As to Sherman, he could not be spared from the West.

This incident gave me even a more favorable opinion of Meade than did his great victory at Gettysburg the July before. It is men who wait to be selected, and not those who seek, from whom we may always expect the most efficient service.

Meade's position afterwards proved embarrassing to me if not to him. He was commanding an army and, for nearly a year previous to my taking command of all the armies, was in supreme command of the Army of the Potomac except from the authorities at Washington. All other general officers occupying similar positions were independent in their commands so far as any one present with them was concerned. I tried to make General Meade's position as nearly as possible what it would have been if I had been in Washington or any other place away from his command. I therefore gave all orders for the movements of the Army of the Potomac to Meade to have them executed. To avoid the necessity of having to give orders direct, I established my headquarters near his, unless there were reasons for locating them elsewhere. This sometimes happened, and I had on occasions to give orders direct to the troops affected. On the 11th I returned to Washington and, on the day after, orders were published by the War Department placing me in command of all the armies. I had left Washington the night before to return to my old command in the West and to meet Sherman whom I had telegraphed to join me in Nashville.

Sherman assumed command of the military division of the Mississippi on the 18th of March, and we left Nashville together for Cincinnati. I had Sherman accompany me that far on my way back to

Washington so that we could talk over the matters about which I wanted to see him, without losing any more time from my new command than was necessary. The first point which I wished to discuss was particularly about the co-operation of his command with mine when the spring campaign should commence. There were also other and minor points, minor as compared with the great importance of the question to be decided by sanguinary war -the restoration to duty of officers who had been relieved from important commands, namely McClellan, Burnside and Fremont in the East, and Buell, McCook, Negley and Crittenden in the West.

Sometime in the winter of 1863-64 I had been invited by the general-in-chief to give my views of the campaign I thought advisable for the command under me now Sherman's. General J.E. Johnston was defending Atlanta and the interior of Georgia with an army, the largest part of which was stationed at Dalton, about 38 miles south of Chattanooga. Dalton is at the junction of the railroad from Cleveland with the one from Chattanooga to Atlanta.

There could have been no difference of opinion as to the first duty of the armies of the military division of the Mississippi. Johnston's army was the first objective, and that important railroad centre, Atlanta, the second. At the time I wrote General Halleck giving my views of the approaching campaign, and at the time I met General Sherman, it was expected that General Banks would be through with the campaign which he had been ordered upon before my appointment to the command of all the armies, and would be ready to co-operate with the armies east of the Mississippi, his part in the programme being to move upon Mobile by land while the navy would close the harbor and assist to the best of its ability.* The plan therefore was for Sherman to attack Johnston and destroy his army if possible, to capture Atlanta and hold it, and with his troops and those of Banks to hold a line through to Mobile, or at least to hold Atlanta and command the railroad running east and west, and the troops from one or other of the armies to hold important points on the southern road, the only east and west road that would be left in the possession of the enemy. This would cut the Confederacy in two again, as our gaining possession of the Mississippi River had done before. Banks was not ready in time for the part assigned to him, and circumstances that could not be foreseen determined the campaign which was afterwards made, the success and grandeur of which has resounded throughout all lands.

---

* Letter to Banks, from General Grant's report,

"MAJOR-GENERAL N. P. BANKS."

Major-General Meade was instructed that Lee's army would be his objective point; that wherever Lee went he would go also. For his movement two plans presented themselves: One to cross the Rapidan below Lee, moving by his right flank; the other above, moving by his left. Each presented advantages over the other, with corresponding objections. By crossing above, Lee would be cut off from all chance of ignoring Richmond or going north on a raid. But if we took this route, all we did would have to be done whilst the rations we started with held out ; besides, it separated us from Butler, so that he could not be directed how to co-operate. If we took the other route, Brandy Station could be used as a base of supplies until another was secured on the York or James rivers. Of these, however, it was decided to take the lower route.

In regard to restoring officers who had been relieved from important commands to duty again, I left Sherman to look after those who had been removed in the West while I looked out for the rest. I directed, however, that he should make no assignment until I could speak to the Secretary of War about the matter. I shortly after recommended to the Secretary the assignment of General Buell to duty. I received the assurance that duty would be offered to him; and afterwards the Secretary told me that he had offered Buell an assignment and that the latter had declined it, saying that it would be degradation to accept the assignment offered. I understood afterwards that he refused to serve under either Sherman or Canby because he had ranked them both. Both graduated before him and ranked him in the old army. Sherman ranked him as a brigadier-general. All of them ranked me in the old army, and Sherman and Buell did as brigadiers. The worst excuse a soldier can make for declining service is that he once ranked the commander he is ordered to report to.

On the 23d of March I was back in Washington, and on the 26th took up my headquarters at Culpeper Court House, a few miles south of the headquarters of the Army of the Potomac.

Although hailing from Illinois myself, the State of the President, I never met Mr. Lincoln until called to the capital to receive my commission as lieutenant-general. I knew him, however, very well and favorably from the accounts given by officers under me at the West who had known him all their lives had also read the remarkable series of debates between Lincoln and Douglas a few years before, when they were rival candidates for the United States Senate. I was then a resident of Missouri, and by no means a "Lincoln Man" in that contest; but I recognized then his great ability.

In my first interview with Mr. Lincoln alone he stated to me that he had never professed to be a military man or to know how campaigns should be conducted, and never wanted to interfere in them: but that procrastination on the part of commanders, and the pressure from the people at the North and Congress, *which was always with him*, forced him into issuing his series of "Military Orders" one, two, three, etc. He did not know but they were all wrong, and did know that some of them were. All he wanted or had ever wanted was some one who would take the responsibility and act, and call on him for all the assistance needed, pledging himself to use all the power of the government in' rendering such assistance. Assuring him that I would do the best I could with the means at hand, and avoid as far as possible annoying him or the War Department, our first interview ended.

The Secretary of War I had met once before only, but felt that I knew him better.

While commanding in West Tennessee we had occasionally held conversations over the wires, at night, when they were not being otherwise used. He and General Halleck both cautioned me against giving the President my plans of campaign, saying that he was so kind hearted, so averse to refusing anything asked of him, that some friend would be sure to get from him all he knew. I should have said that in our interview the President told me he did not want to know what I proposed to do. But he submitted a plan of campaign of his own which he wanted me to hear and then do as I pleased about. He brought out a map of Virginia on which he had evidently marked every position occupied by the Federal and Confederate armies up to that time. He pointed out on the map two streams which empty into the Potomac, and suggested that the army might be moved on boats and landed between the mouths of these streams. We would then have the Potomac to bring our supplies, and the tributaries would protect our flanks while we moved out. I listened respectfully, but did not suggest that the same streams would protect Lee's flanks while he was shutting us up.

I did not communicate my plans to the President, nor did I to the Secretary of War or to General Halleck.

March the 26th my headquarters were, as stated, at Culpeper, and the work of preparing for an early campaign commenced.

CHAPTER XLVII

THE MILITARY SITUATION - PLANS FOR THE CAMPAIGN - SHERIDAN ASSIGNED TO COMMAND OF THE CAVALRY - FLANK MOVEMENTS - FORREST AT FORT PILLOW - GENERAL BANKS'S EXPEDITION - COLONEL MOSBY - AN INCIDENT OF THE WILDERNESS CAMPAIGN

WHEN I assumed command of all the armies the situation was about this: the Mississippi River was guarded from St. Louis to its mouth ; the line of the Arkansas was held, thus giving us all the Northwest north of that river. A few points in Louisiana not remote from the river were held by the Federal troops, as was also the mouth of the Rio Grande. East of the Mississippi we held substantially all north of the Memphis and Charleston Railroad as far east as Chattanooga, thence along the line of the Tennessee and Holston rivers, taking in nearly all of the State of Tennessee. West Virginia was in our hands; and that part of old Virginia north of the Rapidan and east of the Blue Ridge we also held, On the sea coast we had Fortress Monroe and Norfolk in Virginia; Plymouth, Washington and New Berne in North Carolina; Beaufort, Folly and Morris islands, Hilton Head, Port Royal and Fort Pulaski in South Carolina and Georgia; Fernandina, St. Augustine, Key West and Pensacola in Florida. The balance of the Southern territory, an empire in extent, was still in the hands of the enemy.

Sherman, who had succeeded me in the command of the military division of the Mississippi, commanded all the troops in the territory west of the Alleghenies and north of Natchez, with a large movable force about Chattanooga. His command was subdivided into four departments, but the commanders all reported to Sherman and were subject to his orders. This arrangement, however, insured the better protection of all lines of communication through the acquired territory, for the reason that these different department commanders could act promptly in case of a sudden or unexpected raid within their respective jurisdictions without awaiting the orders of the division commander.

In the East the opposing forces stood in substantially the same relations towards each other as three years before, or when the war began; they were both between the Federal and Confederate capitals. It is true, footholds had been secured by us on the sea coast, in Virginia and North Carolina, but, beyond that, no substantial advantage had been gained by either side. Battles had been fought of as great severity as had ever been known in war, over ground from the James River and Chickahominy, near Richmond, to Gettysburg and Chambersburg, in Pennsylvania, with indecisive results, sometimes favorable to the National army, sometimes to the Confederate army; but in every instance, I believe, claimed as victories for the South by the Southern press if not by the Southern generals. The Northern press, as a whole, did not discourage these claims; a portion of it always magnified rebel success and belittled ours, while another portion, most sincerely earnest in their desire for the preservation of the Union and the overwhelming success of the Federal armies, would nevertheless generally express dissatisfaction with whatever victories were gained because they were not more complete.

That portion of the Army of the Potomac not engaged in guarding lines of communication was on the northern bank of the Rapidan. The Army of Northern Virginia confronting it on the opposite bank of the same river was strongly intrenched and commanded by the acknowledged ablest general in the Confederate army. The country back to the James River is cut up with many streams, generally narrow, deep, and difficult to cross except where bridged. The region is heavily timbered, and the roads narrow, and very bad after the least rain. Such an enemy was not, of course, unprepared with adequate fortifications at convenient intervals all the way back to Richmond, so that when driven from one fortified position they would always have another farther to the rear to fall back into.

To provision an army, campaigning against so formidable a foe through such a country, from wagons alone seemed almost impossible. System and discipline were both essential to its accomplishment.

The Union armies were now divided into nineteen departments, though four of them in the West had been concentrated into a single military division. The Army of the Potomac was a separate command and had no territorial limits. There were thus seventeen distinct commanders. Before this time these various armies had acted separately and independently of each other, giving the enemy an opportunity often of depleting one command, not pressed, to reinforce another more actively engaged. I determined to stop this. To this end I regarded the Army of the Potomac as the centre, and all west to Memphis along the line described as our position at the time, and north of it, the right wing ; the Army of the James, under General Butler, as the left wing, and all the troops south, as a force in rear of the enemy. Some of these latter were occupying positions from which they could not render service proportionate to their numerical strength. All such were depleted to the minimum necessary to hold their positions as a guard against blockade runners; where they could not do this their positions were abandoned altogether. In this way ten thousand men were added to the Army of the James from South Carolina alone, with General Gillmore in command. It was not contemplated that General Gillmore should leave his department; but as most of his troops were taken, presumably for active service, he asked to accompany them and was permitted to do so. Officers and soldiers on furlough, of whom there were many thousands, were ordered to their proper commands; concentration was the order of the day, and to have it accomplished in time to advance at the earliest moment the roads would permit was the problem.

As reinforcement to the Army of the Potomac, or to act in support of it, the 9th army corps, over twenty thousand strong, under General Burnside, had been rendezvoused at Annapolis, Maryland. This was an admirable position for such a reinforcement, The corps could be brought at the last moment as a reinforcement to the Army of the Potomac, or it could be thrown on the sea coast, south of Norfolk, in Virginia or North Carolina, to operate against Richmond from that direction. In fact Burnside and the War Department both thought the 9th corps was intended for such an expedition up to the last moment.

My general plan now was to concentrate all the force possible against the Confederate armies in the field. There were but two such, as we have seen, east of the Mississippi River and facing north. The Army of Northern Virginia, General Robert E. Lee commanding, was on the south bank of the Rapidan, confronting the Army of the Potomac; the second, under General Joseph E. Johnston, was at Dalton, Georgia, opposed to Sherman who was still at Chattanooga. Beside these main armies the Confederates had to guard the Shenandoah Valley, a great storehouse to feed their armies from, and their line of communications from Richmond to Tennessee. Forrest, a brave and intrepid cavalry general, was in the West with a large force ; making a larger command necessary to hold what we had gained in Middle and West Tennessee. We could not abandon any territory north of the line held by the enemy because it would lay the Northern States open to invasion. But as the Army of the Potomac was the principal garrison for the protection of Washington even while it was moving on Lee, so all the forces to the west, and the Army of the James, guarded their special trusts when advancing from them as well as when remaining at them. Better indeed, for they forced the enemy to guard his own lines and resources at a greater distance from ours, and with a greater force. Little expeditions could not so well be sent out to destroy a bridge or tear up a few miles of railroad track, burn a storehouse, or inflict other little annoyances. Accordingly I arranged for a simultaneous movement all along the line. Sherman was to move from Chattanooga, Johnston's army and Atlanta being his objective points.* Crook, commanding in West Virginia, was to move from the mouth of the Gauley River with a cavalry force and some artillery, the Virginia and Tennessee Railroad to be his objective.

HEADQUARTERS ARMIES OF THE UNITED STATES,
WASHINGTON , D. C., April 4, 1864.

MAJOR-GENERAL W. T. SHERMAN,

Commanding Military Division of the Mississippi.

General: -It is my design, if the enemy keep quiet and allow me to take the initiative in the spring campaign, to work all parts of the army together, and somewhat towards a common centre. For your information I now write you my programme, as at present determined upon.

I have sent orders to Banks, by private messenger, to finish up his present expedition against Shreveport with all dispatch ; to turn over the defence of Red River to General Steele and the navy, and to return your troops to you and his own to New Orleans; to abandon all of Texas, except the Rio Grande, and to hold that with not to exceed four thousand men; to reduce the number of troops on the Mississippi to the lowest number necessary to hold it, and to collect from his command not less than twenty-five thousand men. To this I will add five thousand men from Missouri. With this force he is to commence operations against Mobile as soon as he can. It will be impossible for him to commence too early.

Gillmore joins Butler -with ten thousand men, and the two operate against Richmond from the south side of the James River. This will give Butler thirty-three thousand men to operate with, W. F. Smith commanding the right wing of his forces and Gillmore the left wing. I will stay with the Army of the Potomac, increased by Burnside's corps of not less than twenty-five thousand effective men, and operate directly against Lee's army, wherever it may be found.

Sigel collects all his available force in two columns, one, under Ord and Averell, to start from Beverly, Virginia, and the other, under Crook, to start from Charleston on the Kanawha, to move against the Virginia and Tennessee Railroad. Crook will have all cavalry, and will endeavor to get .in about Saltville, and move east from there to join Ord. His force will be all cavalry, while Ord will have from ten to twelve thousand men of all arms.

You I propose to move against Johnston's army, to break it up and to get into the interior of the enemy's country as far as you can, inflicting all the damage you can against their war resources.

I do not propose to lay down for you a plan of campaign, but simply lay down the work it is desirable to have done and leave you free to execute it in your own way. Submit to me, however, as early as you can, your plan of operations.

As stated, Banks is ordered to commence operations as soon as he can. Gillmore is ordered to report at Fortress Monroe by the 18th inst., or as soon thereafter as practicable. Sigel is concentrating now. None will move from their places of rendezvous until I direct, except Banks. I want to be ready to move by the 25th inst., if possible. But all I can now direct is that you get ready as soon as possible. I know you will have difficulties to encounter in getting through the mountains to where supplies are abundant, but I believe you will accomplish it.

From the expedition from the Department of West Virginia I do not calculate on very great results; but it is the only way I can take troops from there. With the long line of railroad Sigel has to protect, he can spare no troops except to move directly to his front. In this way he must get through to inflict great damage on the enemy, or the enemy must detach from one of his armies a large force to prevent it. In other words, if Sigel can't skin himself he can hold a leg while some one else skins.

I am, general, very respectfully, your obedient servant,

U.S. GRANT,
Lieutenant-General.

Either the enemy would have to keep a large force to protect their communications, or see them destroyed and a large amount of forage and provision, which they so much needed, fall into our hands. Sigel was in command in the Valley of Virginia. He was to advance up the valley, covering the North from an invasion through that channel as well while advancing as by remaining near Harper's Ferry. Every mile he advanced also gave us possession of stores on which Lee relied. Butler was to advance by the James River, having Richmond and Petersburg as his objective.

Before the advance commenced I visited Butler at Fort Monroe. This was the first time I had ever met him. Before giving him any order as to the part he was to play in the approaching campaign I invited his views. They were very much such as I intended to direct, and as I did direct, in writing, before leaving.*

---

* See instructions to Butler, in General Grant's report, Appendix Page

General W. F. Smith, who had been promoted to the rank of major-general shortly after the battle of Chattanooga on my recommendation, had not yet been confirmed. I found a decided prejudice against his confirmation by a majority of the Senate, but I insisted that his services had been such that he should be rewarded. My wishes were now reluctantly complied with, and I assigned him to the command of one of the corps under General Butler. I was not long in finding out that the objections to Smith's promotion were well founded.

In one of my early interviews with the President I expressed my dissatisfaction with the little that had been accomplished by the cavalry so far in the war, and the belief that it was capable of accomplishing much more than it had done if under a thorough leader. I said I wanted the very best man in the army for that command. Halleck was present and spoke up, saying: "How would Sheridan do?" I replied: "The very man I want." The President said I could have anybody I wanted. Sheridan was telegraphed for that day, and on his arrival was assigned to the command of the cavalry corps with the Army of the Potomac. This relieved General Alfred Pleasonton. It was not a reflection on that officer, however, for I did not know but that he had been as efficient as any other cavalry commander.

Banks in the Department of the Gulf was ordered to assemble all the troops he had at New Orleans in time to join in the general move, Mobile to be his objective.

At this time I was not entirely decided as to whether I should move the Army of the Potomac by the right flank of the enemy, or by his left. Each plan presented advantages.*

---

* IN FIELD, CULPEPER C.H., VA.,
April 9, 1864.

MAJ.-GENERAL GEO. G. MEADE.
    Com'd'g Army of the Potomac.

For information and as instruction to govern your preparations for the coming campaign, the following is communicated confidentially for your own perusal alone. So far as practicable all the armies are to move together, and towards one common centre. Banks has been instructed to turn over the guarding of the Red River to General Steele and the navy, to abandon Texas with the exception of the Rio Grande, and to concentrate all the force he can, not less than 25,000 men, to move on Mobile. This he is to do without reference to other movements. From the scattered condition of his command, however, he cannot possibly get it together to leave New Orleans before the 1st of May, if so soon. Sherman will move at the same time you do, or two or three days in advance, Jo. Johnston's army being his objective point, and the heart of Georgia his ultimate aim. If successful he will secure the line from Chattanooga to Mobile with the aid of Banks.

Sigel cannot spare troops from his army to reinforce either of the great armies, but he can aid them by moving directly to his front. This he has been directed to do, and is now making preparations for it. Two columns of his command will make south at the same time with the general move; one from Beverly, from ten to twelve thousand strong, under Major-General Ord; the other from Charleston, Va., principally cavalry, under Brig.-General Crook. The former of these will endeavor to reach the Tennessee and Virginia Railroad, about south of Covington, and if found practicable will work eastward to Lynchburg and return to its base by way of the Shenandoah Valley, or join you. The other will strike at Saltville, Va., and come eastward to join Ord. The cavalry from Ord's command will try to force a passage southward, if they are successful in reaching the Virginia and Tennessee Railroad, to cut the main lines of the road connecting Richmond with all the South and Southwest,

Gillmore will join Butler with about 10,000 men from South Carolina. Butler can reduce his garrison so as to take 23,000 men into the field directly to his front. The force will be commanded by Maj.-General W. F. Smith. With Smith and Gillmore, Butler will seize City Point, and operate against Richmond from the south side of the river. His movement will be simultaneous with yours.

Lee's army will be your objective point. Wherever Lee goes, there you will go also. The only point upon which I am now in doubt is, whether it will be better to cross the Rapidan above or below him. Each plan presents great advantages over the with corresponding objections. By crossing above, Lee is cut off from all chance of ignoring Richmond and going north on a raid. But if we take this route, all we do must be done whilst the rations we start with hold out. We separate from Butler so that he cannot be directed how to co-operate. By the other route Brandy Station can be used as a base of supplies until another is secured on the York or James rivers.

These advantages and objections I will talk over with you more fully than I can write them.

Burnside with a force of probably 25,000 men will reinforce you. Immediately upon his arrival, which will be shortly after the 20th inst., I will give him the defence of the road from Bull Run as far south as we wish to hold it. This will enable you to collect all your strength about Brandy Station and to the front.

There will be naval co-operation on the James River, and transports and ferries will be provided so that should Lee fall back into his intrenchments at Richmond, Butler's force and yours will be a unit, or at least can be made to act as such. What I would direct then, is that you commence at once reducing baggage to the very lowest possible standard. Two wagons to a regiment of five hundred men is the greatest number that should be allowed, for all baggage, exclusive of subsistence stores and ordnance stores. One wagon to brigade and one to division headquarters is sufficient and about two to corps headquarters.

Should by Lee's right flank be our route, you will want to make arrangements for having supplies of all sorts promptly forwarded to White House on the Pamunkey. Your estimates for this contingency should be made at once. If not wanted there, there is every probability they will be wanted on the James River or elsewhere.

If Lee's left is turned, large provision will have to be made for ordnance stores. I would say not much short of five hundred rounds of infantry ammunition would do. By the other, half the amount would be sufficient.

U.S. GRANT,
Lieutenant-General.

If by his right -my left- the Potomac, Chesapeake Bay and tributaries would furnish us an easy line over which to bring all supplies to within easy hauling distance other of every position the army could occupy from the Rapidan to the James River. But Lee could, if he chose, detach or move his whole army north on a line rather interior to the one I would have to take in following. A movement by his left -our right- would obviate this; but all that was done would have to be done with the supplies and ammunition we started with. All idea of adopting this latter plan was abandoned when the limited quantity of supplies possible to take with us was considered. The country over which we would have to pass was so exhausted of all food or forage that we would, be obliged to carry everything with us.

While these preparations were going on the enemy was not entirely idle. In the West Forrest made a raid in West Tennessee up to the northern border, capturing the garrison of four or five hundred men at Union City, and followed it up by an attack on Paducah, Kentucky, on the banks of the Ohio. While he was able to enter the city he failed to capture the forts or any part of the garrison. On the first intelligence of Forrest's raid I telegraphed Sherman to send all his cavalry against him, and not to let him get out of the trap he had put himself into. Sherman had anticipated me by sending troops against him before he got my order.

Forrest, however, fell back rapidly, and attacked the troops at Fort Pillow, a station for the protection of the navigation of the Mississippi River. The garrison consisted of a regiment of colored troops, infantry, and a detachment of Tennessee cavalry. These troops fought bravely, but were overpowered. I will leave Forrest in his dispatches to tell what he did with them.

"The river was dyed," he says, with the blood of the slaughtered for two hundred yards. The approximate loss was upward of five hundred killed, but few of the officers escaping. My loss was about twenty killed. It is hoped that these facts will demonstrate to the Northern people that Negro soldiers cannot cope with Southerners." Subsequently Forrest made a report in which he left out the part which shocks humanity to read.

At the East, also, the rebels were busy. I had said to Halleck that Plymouth and Washington, North Carolina, were unnecessary to hold. It would be better to have the garrisons engaged there added to Butler's command. If success attended our arms both places, and others too, would fall into our hands naturally. These places had been occupied by Federal troops before I took command of the armies, and I knew that the Executive would be reluctant to abandon them, and therefore explained my views; but before my views were carried out the rebels captured the garrison at Plymouth. I then ordered the abandonment of Washington, but directed the holding of New Berne at all hazards. This was essential because New Berne was a port into which blockade runners could enter.

General Banks had gone on an expedition up the Red River long before my promotion to general command. I had opposed the movement strenuously, but acquiesced because it was the order of my superior at the time. By direction of Halleck I had reinforced Banks with a corps of about ten thousand men from Sherman's command. This reinforcement was wanted back badly before the forward movement commenced. But Banks had got so far that it seemed best that he should take Shreveport on the Red River, and turn over the line of that river to Steele, who commanded in Arkansas, to hold instead of the line of the Arkansas. Orders were given accordingly, and with the expectation that the campaign would be ended in time for Banks to return A. J. Smith's command to where it belonged and get back to New Orleans himself in time to execute his part in the general plan. But the expedition was a failure. Banks did not get back in time to take part in the programme as laid down. Nor was Smith returned until long after the movements of May, 1864, had been begun. The services of forty thousand veteran troops, over and above the number required to hold all that was necessary in the Department of the Gulf, were thus paralyzed. It is but just to Banks, however, to say that his expedition was ordered from Washington and he was in no way responsible except for the conduct of it. I make no criticism on this point. He opposed the expedition.

By the 27th of April spring had so far advanced as to justify me in fixing a day for the great move. On that day Burnside left Annapolis to occupy Meade's position between Bull Run and the Rappahannock. Meade was notified and directed to bring his troops forward to his advance. On the following day Butler was notified of my intended advance on the 4th of May, and he was directed to move the night of the same day and get as far up the James River as possible by daylight, and push on from there to accomplish the task given him. He was also notified that reinforcements were being collected in Washington City, which would be forwarded to him should the enemy fall back into the trenches at Richmond. The same day Sherman was directed to get his forces up ready to advance on the 5th. Sigel was in Winchester and was notified to move in conjunction with the others.

The criticism has been made by writers on the campaign from the Rapidan to the James River that all the loss of life could have been obviated by moving the army there on transports. Richmond was fortified and intrenched so perfectly that one man inside to defend was more than equal to five outside besieging or assaulting. To get possession of Lee's army was the first great object. With the capture of his army Richmond would necessarily follow. It was better to fight him outside of his stronghold than in it. If the Army of the Potomac had been moved bodily to the James River by water Lee could have moved a part of his forces back to Richmond, called Beauregard from the south to reinforce it, and with the balance moved on to Washington. Then, too, I ordered a move, simultaneous with that of the Army of the Potomac, up the James River by a formidable army already collected at the mouth of the river.

While my headquarters were at Culpeper, from the 26th of March to the 4th of May, I generally visited Washington once a week to confer with the Secretary of War and President. On the last occasion, a few days before moving, a circumstance occurred which came near postponing my part in the campaign altogether. Colonel John S. Mosby had for a long time been commanding a partisan corps, or regiment, which operated in the rear of the Army of the Potomac. On my return to the field on this occasion, as the train approached Warrenton Junction, a heavy cloud of dust was seen to the east of the road as if made by a body of cavalry on a charge. Arriving at the junction the train was stopped and inquiries made as to the cause of the dust. There was but one man at the station, and he informed us that Mosby had crossed a few minutes before at full speed in pursuit of Federal cavalry. Had he seen our train coming, no doubt he would have let his prisoners escape to capture the train. I was on a special train, if I remember correctly, without any guard.

Since the close of the war I have come to know Colonel Mosby personally, and somewhat intimately. He is a different man entirely from what I had supposed. He is slender, not tall, wiry, and looks as if he could endure any amount of physical exercise. He is able, and thoroughly honest and truthful. There were probably but few men in the South who could have commanded successfully a separate detachment in the rear of an opposing army, and so near the border of hostilities, as long as he did without losing his entire command.

On this same visit to Washington I had my last interview with the President before reaching the James River. He had of course become acquainted with the fact that a general movement had been ordered all along the line, and seemed to think it a new feature in war. I explained to him that it was necessary to have a great number of troops to guard and hold the territory we had captured, and to prevent incursions into the Northern States. These troops could perform this service just as well by advancing as by remaining still; and by advancing they would compel the enemy to keep detachments to hold them back, or else lay his own territory open to invasion, His answer was: "Oh, yes ! I see that. As we say out West, if a man can't skin he must hold a leg while somebody else does."

There was a certain incident connected with the Wilderness campaign of which it may not be out of place to speak; and to avoid a digression further on I will mention it here.

A few days before my departure from Culpeper the Honorable E. B. Washburne visited me there, and remained with my headquarters for some distance south, through the battle in the Wilderness and, I think, to Spottsylvania. He was accompanied by a Mr. Swinton, whom he presented as a literary gentleman who wished to accompany the army with a view of writing a history of the war when it was over. He assured me -and I have no doubt Swinton gave him the assurance- that he was not present as a correspondent of the press. I expressed an entire willingness to have him (Swinton) accompany the army, and would have allowed him to do so as a correspondent, restricted, however, in the character of the information he could give. We received Richmond papers with about as much regularity as if there had been no war, and knew that our papers were received with equal regularity by the Confederates. It was desirable, therefore, that correspondents should not be privileged spies of the enemy within our lines.

Probably Mr. Swinton expected to be an invited guest at my headquarters, and was disappointed that he was not asked to become so. At all events he was not invited, and soon I found that he was corresponding with some paper (I have now forgotten which one) thus violating his word either expressed or implied. He knew of the assurance Washburne had given as to the character of his mission. I never saw the man from the day of our introduction to the present that I recollect. He accompanied us, however, for a time at least.

The second night after crossing the Rapidan (the night of the 5th of May) Colonel W. R. Rowley, of my staff, was acting as night officer at my headquarters. A short time before midnight I gave him verbal instructions for the night. Three days later I read in a Richmond paper a verbatim report of these instructions.

A few nights still later (after the first, and possibly after the second, day's fighting in the Wilderness) General Meade came to my tent for consultation, bringing with him some of his staff officers. Both his staff and mine retired to the campfire some yards in front of the tent, thinking our conversation should be private. There was a stump a little to one side, and between the front of the tent and campfire. One of my staff, Colonel T. S. Bowers, saw what he took to be a man seated on the ground and leaning against the stump, listening to the conversation between Meade and myself. He called the attention of Colonel Rowley to it. The latter immediately took the man by the shoulder and asked him, in language more forcible than polite, what he was doing there. The man proved to be Swinton, the "historian," and his replies to the question were evasive and unsatisfactory, and he was warned against further eaves-dropping.

The next I heard of Mr. Swinton was at Cold Harbor. General Meade came to my headquarters saying that General Burnside had arrested Swinton, who at some previous time had given great offence, and had ordered him to be shot that afternoon. I promptly ordered the prisoner to be released, but that he must be expelled from the lines of the army not to return again on pain of punishment.

CHAPTER XLVIII

COMMENCEMENT OF THE GRAND CAMPAIGN - GENERAL BUTLER'S POSITION - SHERIDAN'S FIRST RAID

THE armies were now all ready to move for the accomplishment of a single object. They were acting as a unit so far as such a thing was possible over such a vast field. Lee, with the capital of the Confederacy, was the main end to which all were working. Johnston, with Atlanta, was an important obstacle in the way of our accomplishing the result aimed at, and was therefore almost an independent objective. It was of less importance only because the capture of Johnston and his army would not produce so immediate and decisive a result in closing the rebellion as would the possession of Richmond, Lee and his army. All other troops were employed exclusively in support of these two movements. This was the plan; and I will now endeavor to give, as concisely as I can, the method of its execution, outlining first the operations of minor detached but co-operative columns.

As stated before, Banks failed to accomplish what he had been sent to do on the Red River, and eliminated the use of forty thousand veterans whose co-operation in the grand campaign had been expected, ten thousand with Sherman and thirty thousand against Mobile.

Sigel's record is almost equally brief. He moved out, it is true, according to programme; but just when I was hoping to hear of good work being done in the valley I received instead the following announcement from Halleck: "Sigel is in full retreat on Strasburg. He will do nothing but run; never did anything else." The enemy had intercepted him about New Market and handled him roughly, leaving him short six guns, and some nine hundred men out of his six thousand.

The plan had been for an advance of Sigel's forces in two columns. Though the one under his immediate command failed ingloriously the other proved more fortunate. Under Crook and Averell his western column advanced from the Gauley in West Virginia at the appointed time, and with more happy results. They reached the Virginia and Tennessee Railroad at Dublin and destroyed a depot of supplies, besides tearing up several miles of road and burning the bridge over New River. Having accomplished this, they re-crossed the Alleghenies to Meadow Bluffs and there awaited further orders.

Butler embarked at Fort Monroe with all his command, except the cavalry and some artillery which moved up the south bank of the James River. His steamers moved first up Chesapeake Bay and York River as if threatening the rear of Lee's army. At midnight they turned back, and Butler by daylight was far up the James River. He seized City Point and Bermuda Hundred early in the day, without loss and, no doubt, very much to the surprise of the enemy.

This was the accomplishment of the first step contemplated in my instructions to Butler. He was to act from here, looking to Richmond as his objective point. I had given him to understand that I should aim to fight Lee between the Rapidan and Richmond if he would stand ; but should Lee fall back into Richmond I would follow up and make a junction of the armies of the Potomac and the James on the James River. He was directed to secure a footing as far up the south side of the river as he could at as early a date as possible.

Butler was in position by the 6th of May and had begun intrenching, and on the 7th he sent out his cavalry from Suffolk to cut the Weldon Railroad. He also sent out detachments to destroy the railroad between Petersburg and Richmond, but no great success attended these latter efforts. He made no great effort to establish himself on that road and neglected to attack Petersburg, which was almost defenseless. About the 11th he advanced slowly until he reached the works at Drury's Bluff, about half way between Bermuda Hundred and Richmond. In the mean time Beauregard had been gathering reinforcements. On the 16th he attacked Butler with great vigor, and with such success as to limit very materially the further usefulness of the Army of the James as a distinct factor in the campaign. I afterward ordered a portion of it to join the Army of the Potomac, leaving a sufficient force with Butler to man his works, hold securely the footing he had already gained and maintain a threatening front toward the rear of the Confederate capital.

The position which General Butler had chosen between the two rivers, the James and Appomattox, was one of great natural strength, one where a large area of ground might be thoroughly inclosed by means of a single intrenched line, and that a very short one in comparison with the extent of territory which it thoroughly protected. His right was protected by the James River, his left by the Appomattox, and his rear by their junction -the two streams uniting near by. The bends of the two streams shortened the line that had been chosen for intrenchments, while it increased the area which the line inclosed.

Previous to ordering any troops from Butler I sent my chief engineer, General Barnard, from the Army of the Potomac to that of the James to inspect Butler's position and ascertain whether I could again safely make an order for General Butler's movement in cooperation with mine, now that I was getting so near Richmond; or, if I could not, whether his position was strong enough to justify me in withdrawing some of his troops and having them brought round by water to White House to join me and reinforce the Army of the Potomac. General Barnard reported the position very strong for defensive purposes, and that I could do the latter with great security; but that General Butler could not move from where he was, in co-operation, to produce any effect. He said that the general occupied a place between the James and Appomattox rivers which was of great strength, and where with an inferior force he could hold it for an indefinite length of time against a superior; but that he could do nothing offensively. I then asked him why Butler could not move out from his lines and push across the Richmond and Petersburg Railroad to the rear and on the south side of Richmond. He replied that it was impracticable, because the enemy had substantially the same line across the neck of land that General Butler had. He then took out his pencil and drew a sketch of the locality, remarking that the position was like a bottle and that Butler's line of intrenchments across the neck represented the cork; that the enemy had built an equally strong line immediately in front of him across the neck ; and it was therefore as if Butler was in a bottle. He was perfectly safe against an attack; but, as Barnard expressed it, the enemy had corked the bottle and with a small force could hold the cork in its place. This struck me as being very expressive of his position, particularly when I saw the hasty sketch which General Barnard had drawn; and in making my subsequent report I used that expression without adding quotation marks, never thinking that anything had been said that would attract attention - as this did, very much to the annoyance, no doubt, of General Butler and, I know, very much to my own. I found afterwards that this was mentioned in the notes of General Badeau's book, which, when they were shown to me, I asked to have stricken out; yet it was retained there, though against my wishes.

I make this statement here because, although I have often made it before, it has never been in my power until now to place it where it will correct history; and I desire to rectify all injustice that I may have done to individuals, particularly to officers who were gallantly serving their country during the trying period of the war for the preservation of the Union. General Butler certainly gave his very earnest support to the war; and he gave his own best efforts personally to the suppression of the rebellion:

The further operations of the Army of the James can best be treated of in connection with those of the Army of the Potomac, the two being so intimately associated and connected as to be substantially one body in which the individuality of the supporting wing is merged.

Before giving the reader a summary of Sherman's great Atlanta campaign, which must conclude my description of the various co-operative movements preparatory to proceeding with that of the operations of the centre, I will briefly mention Sheridan's first raid upon Lee's communications which, though an incident of the operations on the main line and not specifically marked out in the original plan, attained in its brilliant execution and results all the proportions of an independent campaign. By thus anticipating, in point of time, I will be able to more perfectly observe the continuity of events occurring in my immediate front when I shall have undertaken to describe our advance from the Rapidan.

On the 8th of May, just after the battle of the Wilderness and when we were moving on Spottsylvania I directed Sheridan verbally to cut loose from the Army of the Potomac, pass around the left of Lee's army and attack his cavalry: to cut the two roads, one running west through Gordonsville, Chariottesville and Lynchburg, the other to Richmond, and, when compelled to do so for want of forage and rations, to move on to the James River and draw these from Butler's supplies. This move took him past the entire rear of Lee's army. These orders were also given in writing through Meade.

The object of this move was three-fold. First, if successfully executed, and it was, he would annoy the enemy by cutting his line of supplies and telegraphic communications, and destroy or get for his own use supplies in store in the rear and coming up. Second, he would draw the enemy's cavalry after him, and thus better protect our flanks, rear and trains than by remaining with the army. Third, his absence would save the trains drawing his forage and other supplies from Fredericksburg, which had now become our base. He started at daylight the next morning, and accomplished more than was expected. It was sixteen days before he got back to the Army of the Potomac.

The course Sheridan took was directly to Richmond. Before night Stuart, commanding the Confederate cavalry, came on to the rear of his command. But the advance kept on, crossed the North Anna, and at Beaver Dam, a station on the Virginia Central Railroad, recaptured four hundred Union prisoners on their way to Richmond, destroyed the road. and used and destroyed a large amount of subsistence and medical stores.

Stuart, seeing that our cavalry was pushing towards Richmond, abandoned the pursuit on the morning of the 10th and, by a detour and an exhausting march, interposed between Sheridan and Richmond at Yellow Tavern, only about six miles north of the city. Sheridan destroyed the railroad and more supplies at Ashland and on the 11th arrived in Stuart's front. A severe engagement ensued in which the losses were heavy on both sides, but the rebels were beaten, their leader mortally wounded, and some guns and many prisoners were captured.

Sheridan passed through the outer defences of Richmond, and could, no doubt, have passed through the inner ones. But having no supports near, he could not have remained. After caring for his wounded he struck for the James River below the city, to communicate with Butler and to rest his men and horses as well as to get food and forage for them.

He moved first between the Chickahominy and the James, but in the morning (the 12th) he was stopped by batteries at Mechanicsville. He then turned to cross to the north side of the Chickahominy by Meadow Bridge. He found this barred, and the defeated Confederate cavalry, reorganized, occupying the opposite side. The panic created by his first entrance within the outer works of Richmond having subsided troops were sent out to attack his rear.

He was now in a perilous position, one from which but few generals could have extricated themselves. The defences of Richmond, manned, were to the right, the Chickahominy was to the left with no bridge remaining and the opposite bank guarded, to the rear was a force from Richmond, This force was attacked and beaten by Wilson's and Gregg's divisions, while Sheridan turned to the left with the remaining division and hastily built a bridge over the Chickahominy under the fire of the enemy, forced a crossing and soon dispersed the Confederates he found there. The enemy was held back from the stream by the fire of the troops not engaged in bridge building.

On the 13th Sheridan was at Bottom's Bridge, over the Chickahominy. On the 14th he crossed this stream and on that day went into camp on the James River at Haxall's Landing. He at once put himself into communication with General Butler, who directed all the supplies he wanted to be furnished.

Sheridan had left the Army of the Potomac at Spottsylvania, but did not know where either this or Lee's army was now. Great caution therefore had to be exercised in getting back. On the 17th, after resting his command for three days, he started on his return. He moved by the way of White House.

The bridge over the Pamunkey had been burned by the enemy, but a new one was speedily improvised and the cavalry crossed over it. On the 22d he was at Aylett's on the Matapony, where he learned the position of the two armies. On the 24th he joined us on the march from North Anna to Cold Harbor, in the vicinity of Chesterfield.

Sheridan in this memorable raid passed entirely around Lee's army: encountered his cavalry in four engagements, and defeated them in all; recaptured four hundred Union prisoners and killed and captured many of the enemy; destroyed and used many supplies and munitions of war; destroyed miles of railroad and telegraph, and freed us from annoyance by the cavalry of the enemy for more than two weeks.

CHAPTER XLIX

SHERMAN'S CAMPAIGN IN GEORGIA - SEIGE OF ATLANTA - DEATH OF GENERAL MCPHERSON - ATTEMPT TO CAPTURE ANDERSONVILLE - CAPTURE OF ATLANTA

AFTER separating from Sherman in Cincinnati I went on to Washington, as already stated, while he returned to Nashville to assume the duties of his new command. His military division was now composed of four departments and embraced all the territory west of the Alleghany Mountains and east of the Mississippi River, together with the State of Arkansas in the trans-Mississippi. The most easterly of these was the Department of the Ohio, General Schofield commanding; the next was the Department of the Cumberland, General Thomas commanding; the third the Department of the Tennessee, General McPherson commanding ; and General Steele still commanded the trans-Mississippi, or Department of Arkansas. The last named department was so far away that Sherman could not communicate with it very readily after starting on his spring campaign, and it was therefore soon transferred from his military division to that of the Gulf, where General Canby, who had relieved General Banks, was in command.

The movements of the armies, as I have stated in a former chapter, were to be simultaneous, I fixing the day to start when the season should be far enough advanced, it was hoped, for the roads to be in a condition for the troops to march.

General Sherman at once set himself to work preparing for the task which was assigned him to accomplish in the spring campaign. McPherson lay at Huntsville with about twenty-four thousand men, guarding those points of Tennessee which were regarded as most worth holding; Thomas, with over sixty thousand men of the Army of the Cumberland, was at Chattanooga; and Schofield, with about fourteen thousand men, was at Knoxville. With these three armies, numbering about one hundred thousand men in all, Sherman was to move on the

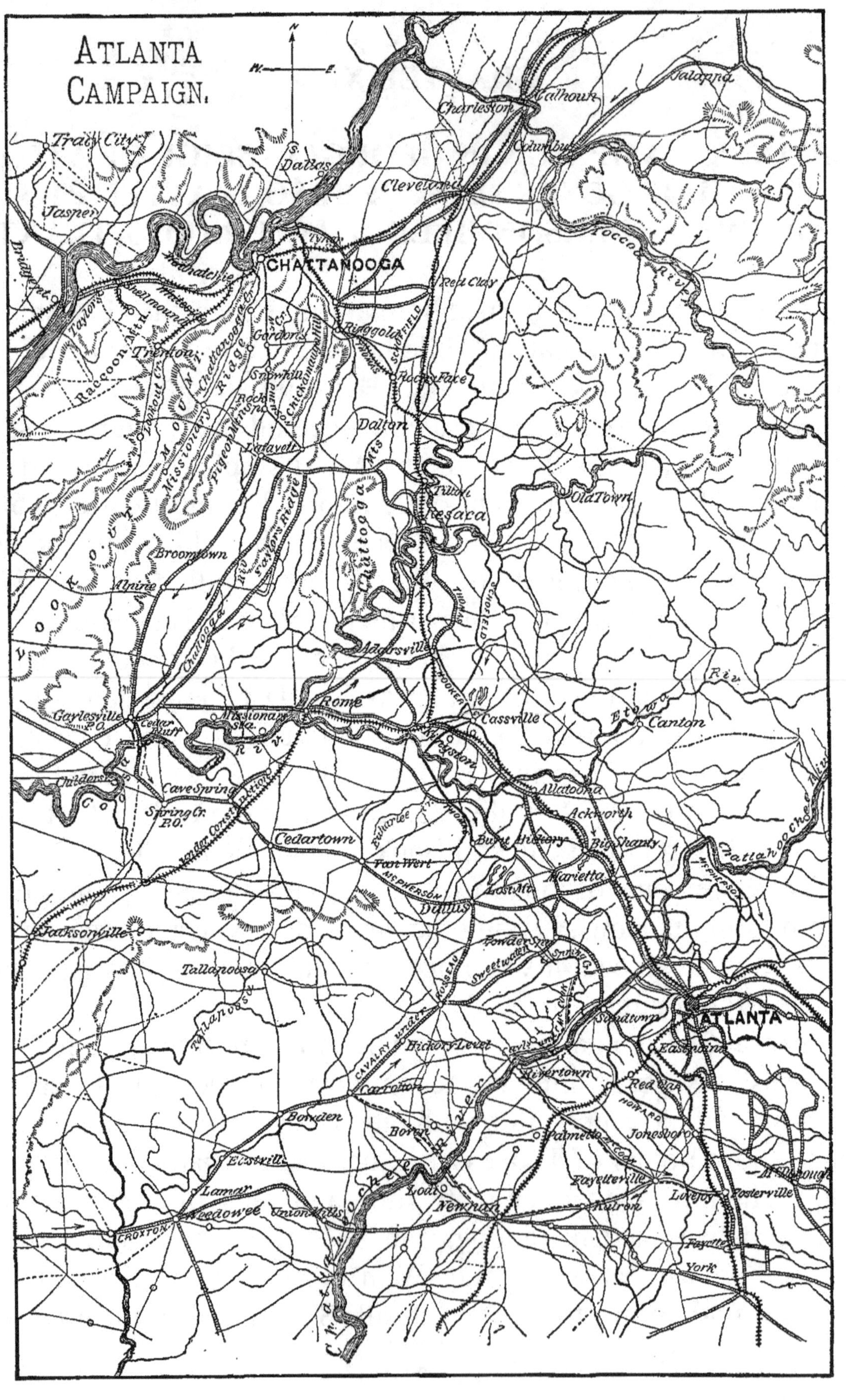

ATLANTA CAMPAIGN.
N
W — E
S
Train City?
Jasper
Bridgeport
Trenton
Raccoon
Taylor's
Whitmount
Chattanooga Cr.
CHATTANOOGA
Gordon's
Snowhill
Rock Spr.
Lafayette
Broomtown
Alpine
Chattooga River
Gaylesville P.O.
Cedar Bluff
Childersburg
Cave Spring
Spring Cr. P.O.
Cedartown
Jacksonville
Tallanoosa
Tallapoosa River
Needow'ee
Croxton
Lamar
Eckville
Bowden
Union Mills
Chattahoochee River
S. Dallas
Charleston
Cleveland
Tyner
Ringgold
Schofield
Ringgold
Rocky Face
Dalton
Chickamauga Cr.
Chattooga Mts.
Tilton
Resaca
Kingston
Missionary Sta.
Rome
Etowah
Cassville
Cartersville
Allatoona
Euharlee
Burnt Hickory
Big Shanty
Van Wert
McPherson
Dallas
Lost Mt.
Marietta
Powder Spr.
Sweetwater
Smyrna
Hickory Level
Carrolton
Rivertown
CAVALRY under STONEMAN
Goat
Newnan
Palmetto
Jonesboro
Fayetteville
Lovejoy
Fosterville
McDonough
York
Fayette
Calhoun
Columbus
Toccoa River
Red Clay
Old Town
Canton
Ackworth
Howard
Red Oak
East Point
ATLANTA
Soaptown
Talapoosa

day fixed for the general advance, with a view of destroying Johnston's army and capturing Atlanta. He visited each of these commands to inform himself as to their condition, and it was found to be, speaking generally, good.

One of the first matters to turn his attention to was that of getting, before the time arrived for starting, an accumulation of supplies forward to Chattanooga sufficiently large to warrant a movement. He found, when he got to that place, that the trains over the single-track railroad, which was frequently interrupted for a day or two at a time, were only sufficient to meet the daily wants of the troops without bringing forward any surplus of any kind. He found, however, that trains were being used to transport all the beef cattle, horses for the cavalry, and even teams that were being brought to the front. He at once changed all this, and required beef cattle, teams, cavalry horses, and everything that could travel, even the troops, to be marched, and used the road exclusively for transporting supplies. In this way he was able to accumulate an abundance before the time finally fixed upon for the move, the 4th of May.

As I have said already, Johnston was at Dalton, which was nearly one-fourth of the way between Chattanooga and Atlanta. The country is mountainous all the way to Atlanta, abounding in mountain streams, some of them of considerable volume. Dalton is on ground where water drains towards Atlanta and into one of the main streams rising northeast from there and flowing southwest, this being the general direction which all the main streams of that section taken with smaller tributaries entering into them. Johnston had been preparing himself for this campaign during the entire winter. The best positions for defence had been selected all the way from Dalton back to Atlanta, and very strongly intrenched; so that, as he might be forced to fall back from one position, he would have another to fall into in his rear. His position at Dalton was so very strongly intrenched that no doubt he expected, or at least hoped, to hold Sherman there and prevent him from getting any further. With a less skillful general, and one disposed to take no risks, I have no doubt that he would have succeeded.

Sherman's plan was to start Schofield, who was farthest back, a few days in advance from Knoxville, having him move on the direct road to Dalton. Thomas was to move out to Ringgold. It had been Sherman's intention to cross McPherson over the Tennessee River at Huntsville or Decatur, and move him south from there so as to have him come into the road running from Chattanooga to Atlanta a good distance to the rear of the point Johnston was occupying; but when that was contemplated it was hoped that McPherson alone would have troops enough to cope with Johnston, if the latter should move against him while unsupported by the balance of the army. In this he was disappointed. Two of McPherson's veteran divisions had reenlisted on the express provision that they were to have a furlough. This furlough had not yet expired, and they were not back.

Then, again, Sherman had lent Banks two divisions under A.J. Smith, the winter before, to co-operate with the trans-Mississippi forces, and this with the express pledge that they should be back by a time specified, so as to be prepared for this very campaign. It is hardly necessary to say they were not returned. That department continued to absorb troops to no purpose to the end of the war. This left McPherson so weak that the part of the plan above indicated had to be changed. He was therefore brought up to Chattanooga and moved from there on a road to the right of Thomas -the two coming together about Dalton. The three armies were abreast, all ready to start promptly on time.

Sherman soon found that Dalton was so strongly fortified that it was useless to make any attempt to carry it by assault; and even to carry it by regular approaches was impracticable. There was a narrowing up in the mountain, between the National and Confederate armies, through which a stream, a wagon road and a railroad ran. Besides, the stream had been dammed so that the valley was a lake. Through this gorge the troops would have to pass. McPherson was therefore sent around by the right, to come out by the way of Snake Creek Gap into the rear of the enemy. This was a surprise to Johnston, and about the 13th he decided to abandon his position at Dalton.

On the 15th there was very hard fighting about Resaca; but our cavalry having been sent around to the right got near the road in the enemy's rear. Again Johnston fell back, our army pursuing. The pursuit was continued to Kingston, which was reached on the 19th with very little fighting, except that Newton's division overtook the rear of Johnston's army and engaged it. Sherman was now obliged to halt for the purpose of bringing up his railroad trains. He was depending upon the railroad for all of his supplies, and as of course the railroad was wholly destroyed as Johnston fell back, it had to be rebuilt. This work was pushed forward night and day, and caused much less delay than most persons would naturally expect in a mountainous country where there were so many bridges to be rebuilt.

The campaign to Atlanta was managed with the most consummate skill, the enemy being flanked out of one position after another all the way there. It is true this was not accomplished without a good deal of fighting, some of it very hard fighting, rising to the dignity of very important battles -neither were single positions gained in a day. On the contrary, weeks were spent at some; and about Atlanta more than a month was consumed.

It was the 23d of May before the road was finished up to the rear of Sherman's army and the pursuit renewed. This pursuit brought him up to the vicinity of Allatoona. This place was very strongly intrenched, and naturally a very defensible position. An assault upon it was not thought of, but preparations were made to flank the enemy out of it. This was done by sending a large force around our right, by the way of Dallas, to reach the rear of the enemy. Before reaching there, however, they found the enemy fortified in their way, and there resulted hard fighting for about a week at a place called New Hope Church. On the left our troops also were fortified, and as close up to the enemy as they could get. They kept working still farther around to the left toward the railroad. This was the case more particularly with the cavalry. By the 4th of June Johnston found that he was being hemmed in so rapidly that he drew off and Allatoona was left in our possession.

Allatoona, being an important place, was strongly intrenched for occupation by our troops before advancing farther, and made a secondary base of supplies. The railroad was finished up to that point, the intrenchments completed, storehouses provided for food, and the army got in readiness for a further advance. The rains, however, were falling in such torrents that it was impossible to move the army by the side roads which they would have to move upon in order to turn Johnston out of his new position.

While Sherman's army lay here, General F.P. Blair returned to it, bringing with him the two divisions of veterans who had been on furlough.

Johnston had fallen back to Marietta and Kennesaw Mountain, where strong intrenchments awaited him. At this latter place our troops made an assault upon the enemy's lines after having got their own lines up close to him, and failed, sustaining considerable loss. But during the progress of the battle Schofield was gaining ground to the left; and the cavalry on his left were gaining still more toward the enemy's rear. These operations were completed by the 3d of July, when it was found that Johnston had evacuated the place. He was pursued at once. Sherman had made every preparation to abandon the railroad, leaving a strong guard in his intrenchments. He had intended, moving out with twenty days' rations and plenty of ammunition, to come in on the railroad again at the Chattahoochee River. Johnston frustrated this plan by himself starting back as above stated. This time he fell back to the Chattahoochee.

About the 5th of July he was besieged again, Sherman getting easy possession of the Chattahoochee River both above and below him. The enemy was again flanked out of his position, or so frightened by flanking movements that on the night of the 9th he fell back across the river.

Here Johnston made a stand until the 17th, when Sherman's old tactics prevailed again and the final movement toward Atlanta began. Johnston was now relieved of the command, and Hood superseded him.

Johnston's tactics in this campaign do not seem to have met with much favor, either in the eyes of the administration at Richmond, or of the people of that section of the South in which he was commanding. The very fact of a change of commanders being ordered under such circumstances was an indication of a change of policy, and that now they would become the aggressors -the very thing our troops wanted.

For my own part, I think that Johnston's tactics were right. Anything that could have prolonged the war a year beyond the time that it did finally close, would probably have exhausted the North to such an extent that they might then have abandoned the contest and agreed to a separation.

Atlanta was very strongly intrenched all the way around in a circle about a mile and a half outside of the city. In addition to this, there were advanced intrenchments which had to be taken before a close siege could be commenced.

Sure enough, as indicated by the change of commanders, the enemy was about to assume the offensive. On the 20th he came out and attacked the Army of the Cumberland most furiously. Hooker's corps, and Newton's and Johnson's divisions were the principal ones engaged in this contest, which lasted more than an hour; but the Confederates were then forced to fall back inside their main lines. The losses were quite heavy on both sides. On this day General Gresham, since our Postmaster-General, was very badly wounded. During the night Hood abandoned his outer lines, and our troops were advanced. The investment had not been relinquished for a moment during the day.

During the night of the 21st Hood moved out again, passing by our left flank, which was then in motion to get a position farther in rear of him, and a desperate battle ensued, which lasted most of the day of the 22d. At first the battle went very much in favor of the Confederates, our troops being somewhat surprised. While our troops were advancing they

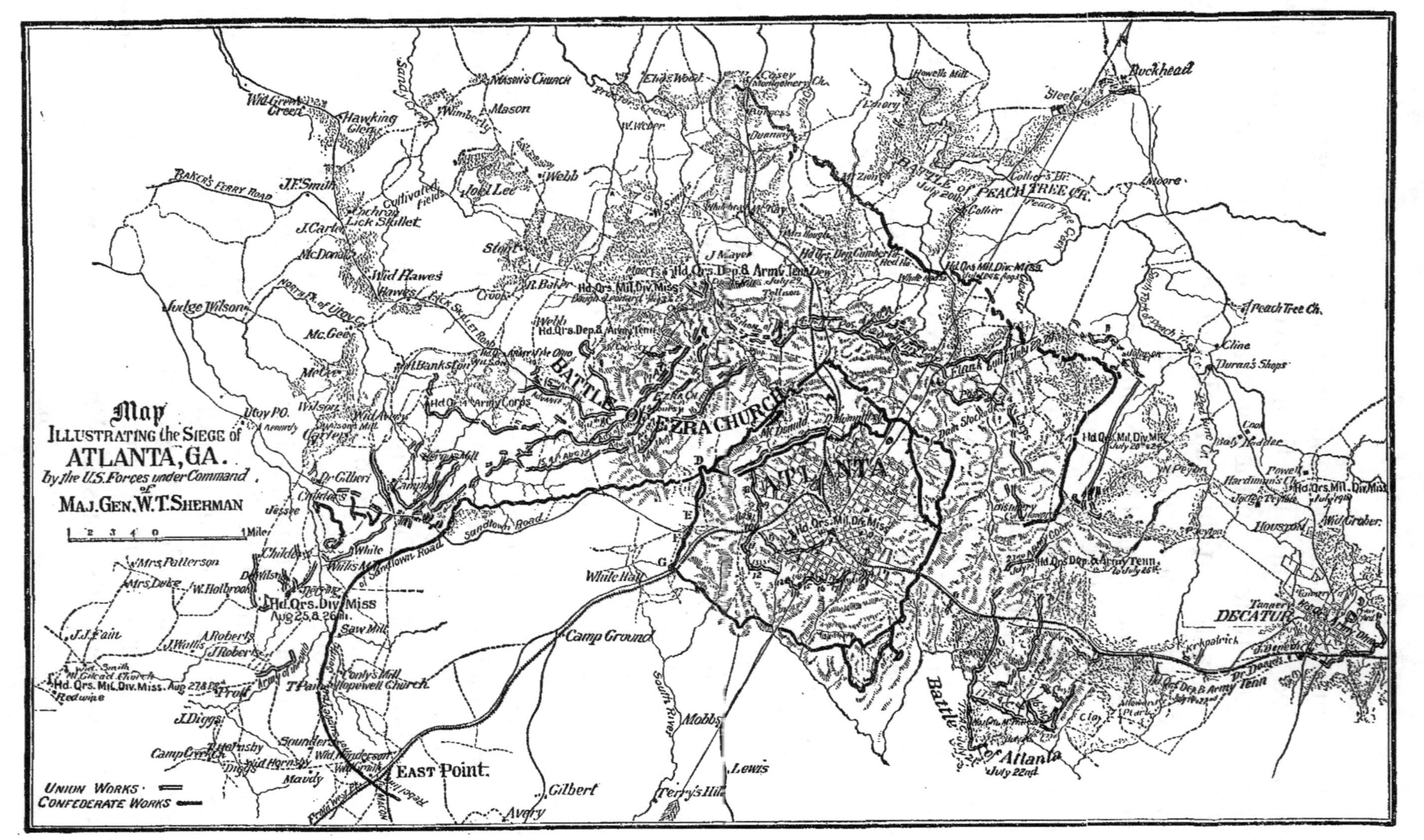

Map
ILLUSTRATING the SIEGE of
ATLANTA, GA.
by the U.S. Forces under Command of
MAJ. GEN. W.T. SHERMAN
1 Mile
UNION WORKS
CONFEDERATE WORKS
BATTLE of EZRA CHURCH
BATTLE of PEACH TREE CR.
July 20th
Battle of Atlanta
July 22nd
ATLANTA
DECATUR
East Point.
Buckhead
Camp Ground
South River
Sandtown Road
Baker's Ferry Road
Hawking Glen
Mason's Church
Wild Green Creek
Sandy Creek
Wimberly
Mason
J.F. Smith
Cochran
Lick Skillet
Cultivated fields
Joel Lee
Webb
J. Carter
McDonald
Wild Hawes
Hawes
Judge Wilson
North Pk. of Utoy Cr.
Mc.Gee
McLee
Wild Bankston
Lick Skillet Road
Utoy P.O.
Wilson
Wild Avery
Dr. Gilbert
Campbell
Childers
Jessee
Mrs. Patterson
Mrs. Duke
W. Holbrook
Childers
White
Willis Mill
Hd. Qrs. Div. Miss
Aug 25 & 26th.
Saw Mill
J.J. Fain
J. Wallis
J. Roberts
Mt. Gilead Church
Hd. Qrs. Mil. Div. Miss. Aug 27 & 28
Redwine
J. Diggs
Camp Creek
Hornsby
Wild Hornsby
Wild Henderson
Wild Grant
Maudy
Gilbert
Avery
White Hall
Mobbs
Lewis
Terry's Hill
Hopewell Church
Conly's Mill
T. Paul
Howell's Mill
Steele
Moore
Collier
Collier's Br.
July 20th
Peach Tree Cr.
Cline
Duran's Shops
Red Tune Cr.
Buck Head
Kirkpatrick
Houston
Wild Graber
W. Peyton
Powell
Hardiman's Ch.
Hd. Qrs. Mil. Div. Miss
Hd. Qrs. Mil. Div. Miss
July 28 & 24
Mason's Church
Elias Wood
Casey
Montgomery Ch.
Emory
W. Smith
W. Weber
J. Mayer
Hd. Qrs. Dep. & Army Tenn Dep.
Hd. Qrs. Mil. Div. Miss
Webb
Hd. Qrs. Dep. & Army Tenn
Hd. Qrs. Army Corps
Crook
Mt. Baker
Tolleson
Hd. Qrs. Dep. & Army Tenn
South Fork of Peach
South Fork of Peach Tree Cr.

were struck in flank, and their flank was enveloped. But they had become too thorough veterans to be thrown into irreparable confusion by an unexpected attack when off their guard, and soon they were in order and engaging the enemy, with the advantage now of knowing where their antagonist was. The field of battle continued to expand until it embraced about seven miles of ground. Finally, however, and before night, the enemy was driven back into the city.*

It was during this battle that McPherson, while passing from one column to another, was instantly killed. In his death the army lost one of its ablest, purest and best generals.

Garrard had been sent out with his cavalry to get upon the railroad east of Atlanta and to cut it in the direction of Augusta. He was successful in this, and returned about the time of the battle. Rousseau had also come up from Tennessee with a small division of cavalry, having crossed the Tennessee River about Decatur and made a raid into Alabama. Finally, when hard pressed, he had come in, striking the railroad in rear of Sherman, and reported to him about this time.

The battle of the 22d is usually known as the Battle of Atlanta, although the city did not fall into our hands until the 2d of September. Preparations went on, as before, to flank the enemy out of his position. The work was tedious, and the lines that had to be maintained were very long. Our troops were gradually worked around to the east until they struck the road between Decatur and Atlanta. These lines were strongly fortified, as were those to the north and west of the city -all as close up

---

* General John A. Logan, upon whom devolved the command of the Army of the Tennessee during this battle, in his report gave our total loss in killed, wounded and missing at 3,521; and estimated that of the enemy to be not less than 10,000: and General G. M. Dodge, graphically describing to General Sherman the enemy' attack, the full weight of which fell first upon and was broken by his depleted command, remarks:. The disparity of forces can be seen from the fact that in the charge made by my two brigades under Fuller and Mersy they took 351 prisoners, representing forty-nine different regiments, eight brigades and three divisions; and brought back eight battle flags from the enemy.

to the enemy's lines as practicable in order to hold them with the smallest possible number of men, the design being to detach an army to move by our right and try to get upon the railroad down south of Atlanta.

On the 27th the movement by the right flank commenced. On the 28th the enemy struck our right flank, General Logan commanding, with great vigor. Logan intrenched himself hastily, and by that means was enabled to resist all assaults and inflict a great deal of damage upon the enemy. These assaults were continued to the middle of the afternoon, and resumed once or twice still later in the day. The enemy's losses in these unsuccessful assaults were fearful.

During that evening the enemy in Logan's front withdrew into the town. This now left Sherman's army -close up to the Confederate lines, extending from a point directly east of the city around by the north and west of it for a distance of fully ten miles; the whole of this line being intrenched, and made stronger every day they remained there.

In the latter part of July Sherman sent Stoneman to destroy the railroads to the south, about Macon. He was then to go east and, if possible, release our prisoners about Andersonville. There were painful stories current at the time about the great hardships these prisoners had to endure in the way of general bad treatment, in the way in which they were housed, and in the way in which they were fed. Great sympathy was felt for them; and it was thought that even if they could be turned loose upon the country it would be a great relief to them. But the attempt proved a failure. McCook, who commanded a small brigade, was first reported to have been captured; but he got back, having inflicted a good deal of damage upon the enemy. He had also taken some prisoners; but encountering afterwards a largely superior force of the enemy he was obliged to drop his prisoners and get back as best he, could with what men he had left. He had lost several hundred men out of his small command. On the 4th of August Colonel Adams, commanding a little brigade of about a thousand men, returned reporting Stoneman and all but himself as lost. I myself had heard around Richmond of the capture of Stoneman, and had sent Sherman word, which he received. The rumor was confirmed there, also, from other sources. A few days after Colonel Adams's return Colonel Capron also got in with a small detachment and confirmed the report of the capture of Stoneman with something less than a thousand men.

It seems that Stoneman, finding the escape of all his force was impossible, had made arrangements for the escape of two divisions. He covered the, movement of these divisions to the rear with a force of about seven hundred men, and at length surrendered himself and this detachment to the commanding Confederate. In this raid, however, much damage was inflicted upon the enemy by the destruction of cars, locomotives, army wagons, manufactories of military supplies, etc.

On the 4th and 5th Sherman endeavored to get upon the railroad to our right, where Schofield was in command, but these attempts failed utterly. General Palmer was charged with being the cause of this failure, to a great extent, by both General Sherman and General Schofield; but I am not prepared to say this, although a question seems to have arisen with Palmer as to whether Schofield had any right to command him. If he did raise this question while an action was going on, that act alone was exceedingly reprehensible.

About the same time Wheeler got upon our railroad north of Resaca and destroyed it nearly up to Dalton. This cut Sherman off from communication with the North for several days. Sherman responded to this attack on his lines of communication by directing one upon theirs.

Kilpatrick started on the night of the 18th of August to reach the Macon road about Jonesboro. He succeeded in doing so, passed entirely around the Confederate lines of Atlanta, and was back again in his former position on our left by the 22d. These little affairs, however, contributed but very little to the grand result. They annoyed, it is true, but any damage thus done to a railroad by any cavalry expedition is soon repaired.

Sherman made preparations for a repetition of his tactics; that is, for a flank movement with as large a force as could be got together to some point in the enemy's rear. Sherman commenced this last movement on the 25th of August, and on the 1st of September was well up towards the railroad twenty miles south of Atlanta. Here he found Hardee intrenched, ready to meet him. A battle ensued, but he was unable to drive Hardee away before night set in. Under cover of the night, however, Hardee left of his own accord. That night Hood blew up his military works, such as he thought would be valuable in our hands, and decamped.

The next morning at daylight General H. W. Slocum, who was commanding north of the city, moved in and took possession of Atlanta, and notified Sherman. Sherman then moved deliberately back, taking three days to reach the city, and occupied a line extending from Decatur on the left to Atlanta in the centre, with his troops extending out of the city for some distance to the right.

The campaign had lasted about four months, and was one of the most memorable in history. There was but little if anything in the whole campaign, now that it is over, to criticize at all, and nothing to criticize severely. It was creditable alike to the general who commanded and the army which had executed it. Sherman had on this campaign some bright, wide awake division and brigade commanders whose alertness added a host to the efficiency of his command.

The troops now went to work to make themselves comfortable, and to enjoy a little rest after their arduous campaign. The city of Atlanta was turned into a military base. The citizens were all compelled to leave. Sherman also very wisely prohibited the assembling of the army of sutlers and traders who always follow in the wake of an army in the field, if permitted to do so, from trading with the citizens and getting the money of the soldiers for articles of but little use to them, and for which they are made to pay most exorbitant prices. He limited the number of these traders to one for each of his three armies.

The news of Sherman's success reached the North instantaneously, and set the country all aglow. This was the first great political campaign for the Republicans in their canvass of 1864. It was followed later by Sheridan's campaign in the Shenandoah Valley; and these two campaigns probably had more effect in settling the election of the following November than all the speeches, all the bonfires, and all the parading with banners and bands of music in the North.

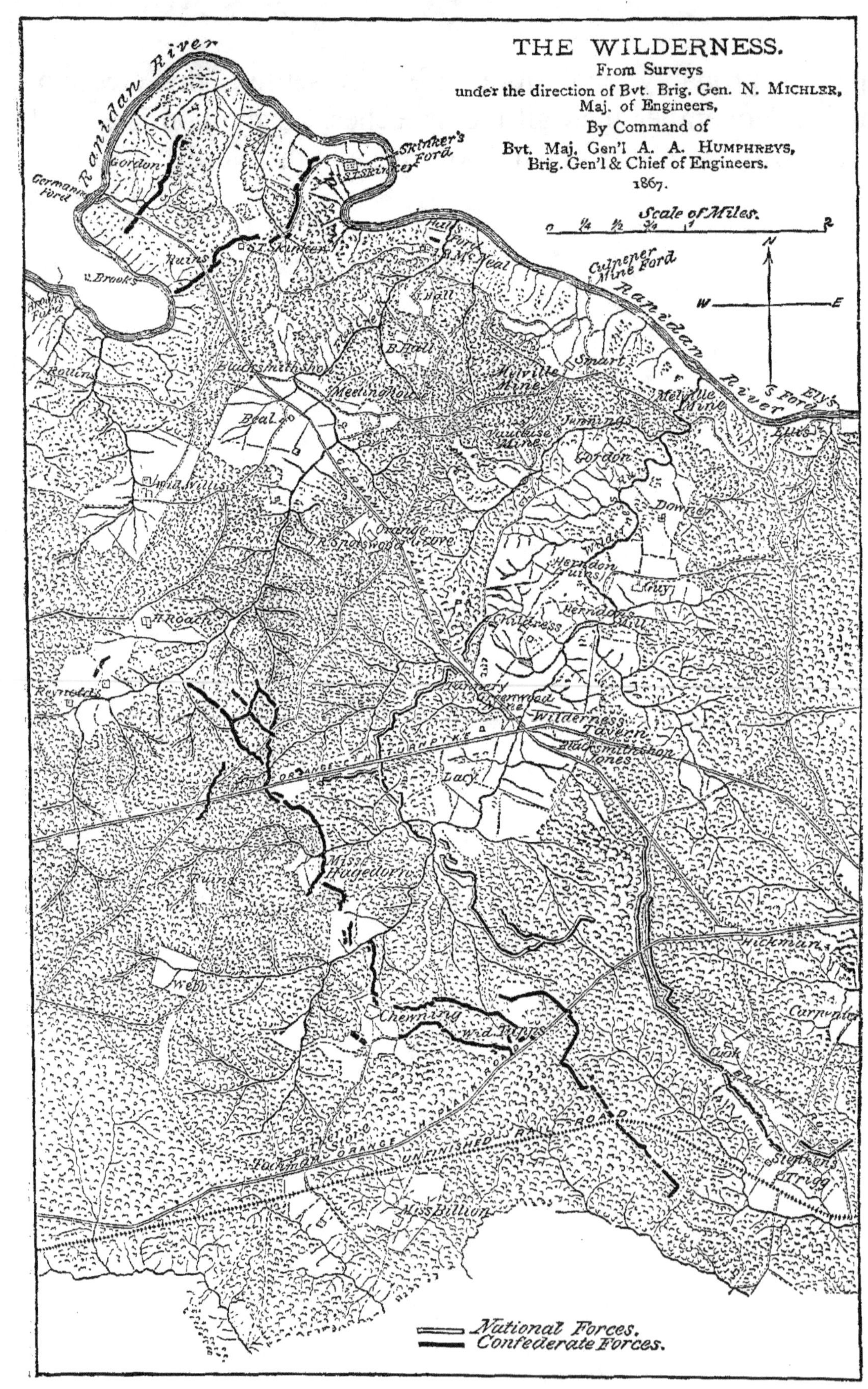

THE WILDERNESS.
From Surveys
under the direction of Bvt. Brig. Gen. N. MICHLER,
Maj. of Engineers,
By Command of
Bvt. Maj. Gen'l A. A. HUMPHREYS,
Brig. Gen'l & Chief of Engineers.
1867.
Scale of Miles.
0   1/4   1/2   3/4   1   2
N
W   E
S
Rapidan River
Germanna Ford
Gordon
Skinker's Ford
Skinker Ford
Culpeper Mine Ford
Ely's Ford
Rapidan River
U. Brooks
Brooks Ford
J. T. Skinker
Ruins
McNeal
Hall Ford
Hall
B. Hall
Rollins
Blacksmith shop
Meeting House
Jack Hill
Ayrville Mine
Smart
Melville Mine
Ellis
Beal
Jackson Mine
Jennings
Gordon
Wid. Willis
Downer
Orange Grove
Up. Spotswood
Herndon Jacks
Guy
Reynolds Hill
Childress
Reynolds
Cemetery
Greenwood
Wilderness Tavern
Blacksmith shop
Jones
Lacy
Mrs. Hagedorn
Ruins
Webb
Chewning
wd. Ripe
Hickman
Carpenter
Cook
Lochman Orange
UNFINISHED Rail
PLANK ROAD
Stephens Trigg
Miss Billion
National Forces.
Confederate Forces.

CHAPTER L

GRAND MOVEMENT OF THE ARMY OF THE POTOMAC CROSSING THE RAPIDAN - ENTERING THE WILDERNESS - BATTLE OF THE WILDERNESS - UNION ARMY ON THE RAPIDAN May 5 1864 - CONFEDERATE ARMY AUGUST 31 1864

Soon after midnight, May 3rd-4th the Army of the Potomac moved out from its position north of the Rapidan, to start upon that memorable campaign, destined to result in the capture of the Confederate capital and the army defending it. This was not to be accomplished, however, without as desperate fighting as the world has ever witnessed; not to be consummated in a day, a week, a month, or a single season. The losses inflicted, and endured, were destined to be severe ; but the armies now confronting each other had already been in deadly conflict for a period of three years, with immense losses in killed, by death from sickness, captured and wounded ; and neither had made any real progress toward accomplishing the final end. It is true the Confederates had, so far, held their capital, and they claimed this to be their sole object. But previously they had boldly proclaimed their intention to capture Philadelphia, New York, and the National Capital, and had made several attempts to do so, and once or twice had come fearfully near making their boast good too near for complacent contemplation by the loyal North. They had also come near losing their own capital on at least one occasion. So, here was a standoff. The campaign now begun was destined to result in heavier losses, to both armies, in a given time, than any previously suffered ; but the carnage was to be limited to a single year, and to accomplish all that had been anticipated or desired at the beginning in that time. We had to have hard fighting to achieve this. The two armies had been confronting each other so long, without any decisive result, that they hardly knew which could whip.

Ten days' rations, with a supply of forage and ammunition were taken in wagons. Beef cattle were driven with the trains, and butchered as wanted. Three days' rations in addition, in haversacks, and fifty rounds of cartridges, were carried on the person of each soldier.

The country over which the army had to operate, from the Rapidan to the crossing of the James River, is rather flat, and is cut by numerous streams which make their way to the Chesapeake Bay. The crossings of these streams by the army were generally made not far above tidewater, and where they formed a considerable obstacle to the rapid advance of troops even when the enemy did not appear in opposition. The country roads were narrow and poor. Most of the country is covered with a dense forest, in places, like the Wilderness and along the Chickahominy, almost impenetrable even for infantry except along the roads. All bridges were naturally destroyed before the National troops came to them.

The Army of the Potomac was composed of three infantry and one cavalry corps, commanded respectively by Generals W. S. Hancock, G. K. Warren, John Sedgwick and P. H. Sheridan. The artillery was commanded by General Henry J. Hunt. This arm was in such abundance that the fourth of it could not be used to advantage in such a country as we were destined to pass through. The surplus was much in the way, taking up as it did so much of the narrow and bad roads, and consuming so much of the forage and other stores brought up by the trains.

The 5th corps, General Warren commanding, was in advance on the right, and marched directly for Germania Ford, preceded by one division of cavalry, under General J. H. Wilson. General Sedgwick followed Warren with the 6th corps. Germania Ford was nine or ten miles below the right of Lee's line. Hancock, with the 2d corps, moved by another road, farther east, directly upon Ely's Ford, six miles below Germania, preceded by Gregg's division of cavalry, and followed by the artillery. Torbert's division of cavalry was left north of the Rapidan, for the time, to picket the river and prevent the enemy from crossing and getting into our rear. The cavalry seized the two crossings before daylight, drove the enemy's pickets guarding them away, and by six o'clock A.M. had the pontoons laid ready for the crossing of the infantry and artillery. This was undoubtedly a surprise to Lee. The fact that the movement was unopposed proves this.

Burnside, with the 9th corps, was left back at Warrenton, guarding the railroad from Bull Run forward to preserve control of it in case our crossing the Rapidan should be long delayed. He was instructed, however, to advance at once on receiving notice that the army had crossed; and a dispatch was sent to him a little after one P.M. giving the information that our crossing. had been successful.

The country was heavily wooded at all the points of crossing, particularly on the south side of the river. The battlefield from the crossing of the Rapidan until the final movement from the Wilderness toward Spottsylvania was of the same character. There were some clearings and small farms within what might be termed the battlefield; but generally the country was covered with a dense forest. The roads were narrow and bad. All the conditions were favorable for defensive operations.

There are two roads, good for that part of Virginia, running from Orange Court House to the battlefield. The most southerly of these roads is known as the Orange Court House Plank Road, the northern one as the Orange Turnpike. There are also roads from east of the battlefield running to Spottsylvania Court House, one from Chancellorsville, branching at Aldrich's ; the western branch going by Piney Branch Church, Alsop's, thence by the Brock Road to Spottsylvania; the east branch goes by Gates's, thence to Spottsylvania. The Brock Road runs from Germania Ford through the battlefield and on to the Court House. As Spottsylvania is approached the country is cut up with numerous roads, some going to the town direct, and others crossing so as to connect the farms with roads going there.

Lee's headquarters were at Orange Court House. From there to Fredericksburg he had the use of the two roads above described running nearly parallel to the Wilderness. This gave him unusual facilities, for that country, for concentrating his forces to his right. These roads strike the road from Germania Ford in the Wilderness.

As soon as the crossing of the infantry was assured, the cavalry pushed forward, Wilson's division by Wilderness Tavern to Parker's store, on the Orange Plank Road; Gregg to the left towards, Chancellorsville. Warren followed Wilson and reached the Wilderness Tavern by noon, took position there and intrenched. Sedgwick followed Warren. He was across the river and in camp on the south bank, on the right of Warren, by sundown. Hancock, with the 2d corps, moved parallel with Warren and camped about six miles east of him. Before night all the troops, and by the evening of the 5th the trains of more than four thousand wagons, were safely on the south side of the river.

There never was a corps better organized than was the quartermaster's corps with the Army of the Potomac in 1864. With a wagon train that would have extended from the Rapidan to Richmond, stretched along in single file and separated as the teams necessarily would be when moving, we could still carry only three days' forage and about ten to twelve days' rations, besides a supply of ammunition. To overcome all difficulties, the chief quartermaster, General Rufus Ingalls, had marked on each wagon the corps badge with the division color and the number of the brigade. At a glance, the particular brigade to which any wagon belonged could be told. The wagons were also marked to note the contents : if ammunition, whether for artillery or infantry ; if forage, whether grain or hay ; if rations, whether bread, pork, beans, rice, sugar, coffee or whatever it might be. Empty wagons were never allowed to follow the army or stay in camp. As soon as a wagon was empty it would return to the base of supply for a load of precisely the same article that had been taken from it. Empty trains were obliged to leave the road free for loaded ones. Arriving near the army they would be parked in fields nearest to the brigades they belonged to. Issues, except of ammunition, were made at night in all cases. By this system the hauling of forage for the supply train was almost wholly dispensed with. They consumed theirs at the depots.

I left Culpeper Court House after all the troops had been put in motion, and passing rapidly to the front, crossed the Rapidan in advance of Sedgwick's corps; and established headquarters for the afternoon and night in a deserted house near the river.

Orders had been given, long before this movement began, to cut down the baggage of officers and. men to the lowest point possible. Notwithstanding this I saw scattered along the road from Culpeper to Germania Ford wagon-loads of new blankets and overcoats, thrown away by the troops to lighten their knapsacks; an improvidence I had never witnessed before.

Lee, while his pickets and signal corps must have discovered at a very early hour on the morning of the 4th of May, that the Army of the Potomac was moving, evidently did not learn until about one o'clock in the afternoon by what route we would confront his army. This I judge from the fact that at 1:15 P.M., an hour and a quarter after Warren had reached Old Wilderness Tavern, our officers took off rebel signals which, when translated, were seen to be an order to his troops to occupy their intrenchments at Mine Run.

Here at night dispatches were received announcing that Sherman, Butler and Crook had moved according to programme.

On discovering the advance of the Army of the Potomac, Lee ordered Hill, Ewell and Longstreet, each commanding corps, to move to the right to attack us, Hill on the Orange Plank Road, Longstreet to follow on the same road. Longstreet was at this time -middle of the afternoon -at Gordonsville, twenty or more miles away. Ewell was ordered by the Orange Pike. He was near by and arrived some four miles east of Mine Run before bivouacking for the night.

My orders were given through General Meade for an early advance on the morning of the 5th. Warren was to move to Parker's store, and Wilson's cavalry -then at Parker's store -to move on to Craig's meeting house. Sedgwick followed Warren, closing in on his right. The Army of the Potomac was facing to the west, though our advance was made to the south, except when facing the enemy. Hancock was to move south westward to join on the left of Warren, his left to reach to Shady Grove Church.

At six o'clock, before reaching Parker's store, Warren discovered the enemy. He sent word back to this effect, and was ordered to halt and prepare to meet and attack him. Wright, with his division of Sedgwick's corps, was ordered, by any road he could find, to join on to Warren's right, and Getty with his division, also of Sedgwick's corps, was ordered to move rapidly by Warren's rear and get on his left. This was the speediest way to reinforce Warren who was confronting the enemy on both the Orange plank and turnpike roads.

Burnside had moved promptly on the 4th, on receiving word that the Army of the Potomac had safely crossed the Rapidan. By making a night march, although some of his troops had to march forty miles to reach the river, he was crossing with the head of his column early on the morning of the 5th.

Meade moved his headquarters on to Old Wilderness Tavern, four miles south of the river, as soon as it was light enough to see the road. I remained to hasten Burnside's crossing and to put him in position. Burnside at this time was not under Meade's command, and was his senior in rank. Getting information of the proximity of the enemy, I informed Meade, and without waiting to see Burnside, at once moved forward my headquarters to where Meade was.

It was my plan then, as it was on all other occasions, to take the initiative whenever the enemy could be drawn from his intrenchments if we were not intrenched ourselves. Warren had not yet reached the point where he was to halt, when he discovered the enemy near by. Neither party had any advantage of position. Warren was, therefore, ordered to attack as soon as he could prepare for it. At nine o'clock Hancock was ordered to come up to the support of Getty. He himself arrived at Getty's front about noon, but his troops were yet far in the rear. Getty was directed to hold his position at all hazards until relieved. About this hour Warren was ready, and attacked with favorable though not decisive results. Getty was somewhat isolated from Warren and was in a precarious condition for a time. Wilson, with his division of cavalry, was farther south, and was cut off from the rest of the army. At two o'clock Hancock's troops began to arrive, and immediately he was ordered to join Getty and attack the enemy. But the heavy timber and narrow roads prevented him from getting into position for attack as promptly as he generally did when receiving such orders. At four o'clock he again received his orders to attack, and General Getty received orders from Meade a few minutes later to attack whether Hancock was ready or not. He met the enemy under Heth within a few hundred yards.

Hancock immediately sent two divisions, commanded by Birney and Mott, and later two brigades, Carroll's and Owen's, to the support of Getty. This was timely and saved Getty. During the battle Getty and Carroll were wounded, but remained on the field. One of Birney's most gallant brigade commanders, Alexander Hays was killed.

I had been at West Point with Hays for three years, and had served with him through the Mexican war, a portion of the time in the same regiment. He was a most gallant officer, ready to lead his command wherever ordered. With him it was "Come, boys," not "Go."

Wadsworth's division and Baxter's brigade of the 2d division were sent to reinforce Hancock and Getty ; but the density of the intervening forest was such that, there being no road to march upon, they did not get up with the head of column until night, and bivouacked where they were without getting into position.

During the afternoon Sheridan sent Gregg's division of cavalry to Todd's Tavern in search of Wilson. This was fortunate. He found Wilson engaged with a superior force under General Rosser, supported by infantry, and falling back before it. Together they were strong enough to turn the tables upon the enemy and themselves become aggressive. They soon drove the rebel cavalry back beyond Corbin's Bridge.

Fighting between Hancock and Hill continued until night put a close to it. Neither side made any special progress.

After the close of the battle of the 5th of May my orders were given for the following morning. We knew Longstreet with 12,000 men was on his way to join Hill's right, near the Brock Road, and might arrive during the night. I was anxious that the rebels should not take the initiative in the morning, and therefore ordered Hancock to make an assault at 4.30 o'clock. Meade asked to have the hour changed to six. Deferring to his wishes as far as I was willing, the order was modified and five was fixed as the hour to move.

Hancock had now fully one-half of the Army of the Potomac. Wadsworth with his division, which had arrived the night before, lay in a line perpendicular to that held by Hill, and to the right of Hancock. He was directed to move at the same time, and to attack Hill's left.

Burnside, who was coming up with two divisions, was directed to get in between Warren and Wadsworth, and attack as soon as he could get in position to do so. Sedgwick and Warren were to make attacks in their front, to detain as many of the enemy as they could and to take advantage of any attempt to reinforce Hill from that quarter. Burnside was ordered if he should succeed in breaking the enemy's centre, to swing around to the left and envelop the right of Lee's army. Hancock was informed of all the movements ordered.

Burnside had three divisions, but one of them, a colored division was sent to guard the wagon train, and he did not see it again until July.

Lee was evidently very anxious that there should be no battle on his right until Longstreet got up. This is evident from the fact that notwithstanding the early hour at which I had ordered the assault, both for the purpose of being the attacking party and to strike before Longstreet got up, Lee was ahead in his assault on our right. His purpose was evident, but he failed.

Hancock was ready to advance by the hour named, but learning in time that Longstreet was moving a part of his corps by the Catharpin Road, thus threatening his left flank, sent a division of infantry, commanded by General Barlow, with all his artillery, to cover the approaches by which Longstreet was expected. This disposition was made in time to attack as ordered. Hancock moved by the left of the Orange Plank Road, and Wadsworth by the right of it. The fighting was desperate for about an hour, when the enemy began to break up in great confusion.

I believed then, and see no reason to change that opinion now, that if the country had been such that Hancock and his command could have seen the confusion and panic in the lines of the enemy, it would have been taken advantage of so effectually that Lee would not have made another stand outside of his Richmond defences.

Gibbon commanded Hancock's left, and was ordered to attack, but was not able to accomplish much.

On the morning of the 6th Sheridan was sent to connect with Hancock's left and attack the enemy's cavalry who were trying to get on our left and rear. He met them at the intersection of the Furnace and Brock roads and at Todd's Tavern, and defeated them at both places. Later he was attacked, and again the enemy was repulsed.

Hancock heard the firing between Sheridan and Stuart, and thinking the enemy coming by that road, still further reinforced his position guarding the entrance to the Brock Road. Another incident happened during the day to further induce Hancock to weaken his attacking column. Word reached him that troops were seen moving towards him from the direction of Todd's Tavern, and Brooke's brigade was detached to meet this new enemy; but the troops approaching proved to be several hundred convalescents coming from Chancellorsville, by the road Hancock had advanced upon, to join their respective commands. At 6:50 o'clock A.M., Burnside, who had passed Wilderness Tavern at six o'clock, was ordered to send a division to the support of Hancock, but to continue with the remainder of his command in the execution of his previous order. The difficulty of making a way through the dense forests prevented Burnside from getting up in time to be of any service on the forenoon of the sixth.

Hancock followed Hill's retreating forces, in the morning, a mile or more. He maintained this position until, along in the afternoon, Longstreet came upon him. The retreating column of Hill meeting reinforcements that had not yet been engaged became encouraged and returned with them. They were enabled, from the density of the forest, to approach within a few hundred yards of our advance before being discovered. Falling upon a brigade of Hancock's corps thrown to the advance, they swept it away almost instantly. The enemy followed up his advantage and soon came upon Mott's division, which fell back in great confusion. Hancock made dispositions to hold his advanced position, but after holding it for a time, fell back into the position that he had held in the morning, which was strongly intrenched. In this engagement the intrepid Wadsworth while trying to rally his men was mortally wounded and fell into the hands of the enemy. The enemy followed up, but made no immediate attack.

The Confederate General Jenkins was killed and Longstreet seriously wounded in this engagement. Longstreet had to leave the field, not to resume command for many weeks. His loss was a severe one to Lee, and compensated in a great measure for the mishap, or mis-apprehensions, which had fallen to our lot during the day.

After Longstreet's removal from the field Lee took command of his right in person. He was not able, however, to rally his men to attack Hancock's position, and withdrew from our front for the purpose of reforming. Hancock sent a brigade to clear his front of all remnants that might be left of Longstreet's or Hill's commands. This brigade having been formed at right angles to the intrenchments held by Hancock's command, swept down the whole length of them from left to right. A brigade of the enemy was encountered in this move; but it broke and disappeared without a contest.

Firing was continued after this, but with less fury. Burnside had not yet been able to get up to render any assistance. But it was now only about nine in the morning, and he was getting into position on Hancock's right.

At 4:15 in the afternoon Lee attacked our left. His line moved up to within a hundred yards of ours and opened a heavy fire. This status was maintained for about half an hour. Then a part of Mott's division and Ward's brigade of Birney's division gave way and retired in disorder.

The enemy under R. H. Anderson took advantage of this and pushed through our line, planting their flags on a part of the intrenchments not on fire. But owing to the efforts of Hancock, their success was but temporary. Carroll, of Gibbon's division, moved at a double quick with his brigade and drove back the enemy, inflicting great loss. Fighting had continued from five in the morning sometimes along the whole line, at other times only in places. The ground fought over had varied in width, but averaged three-quarters of a mile. The killed, and many of the severely wounded, of both armies, lay within this belt where it was impossible to reach them, woods were set on fire by the bursting shells, and the conflagration raged. The wounded who had not strength to move themselves were either suffocated or burned to death. Finally the fire communicated with our breastworks, in places. Being constructed of wood, they burned with great fury. But the battle still raged, our men firing through the flames until it became too hot to remain longer.

Lee was now in distress. His men were in confusion, and his personal efforts failed to restore order. These facts, however, were learned subsequently, or we would have taken advantage of his condition and no doubt gained a decisive success. His troops were withdrawn now, but I revoked the order, which I had given previously to this assault, for Hancock to attack, because his troops had exhausted their ammunition and did not have time to replenish from the train, which was at some distance.

Burnside, Sedgwick, and Warren had all kept up an assault during all this time; but their efforts had no other effect than to prevent the enemy from reinforcing his right from the troops in their front.

I had, on the 5th, ordered all the bridges over the Rapidan to be taken up except one at Germania Ford.

The troops on Sedgwick's right had been sent to reinforce our left. This left our right in danger of being turned, and us of being cut off from all present base of supplies. Sedgwick had refused his right and intrenched it for protection against attack. But late in the afternoon of the 6th Early came out from his lines in considerable force and got in upon

Sedgwick's right, notwithstanding the precautions taken, and created considerable confusion. Early captured several hundred prisoners, among them two general officers. The defence, however, was vigorous; and night coming on, the enemy was thrown into as much confusion as our troops, engaged, were. Early says in his Memoirs that if we had discovered the confusion in his lines we might have brought fresh troops to his great discomfort. Many officers, who had not been attacked by Early, continued coming to my headquarters even after Sedgwick had rectified his lines a little farther to the rear, with news of the disaster, fully impressed with the idea that the enemy was pushing on and would soon be upon me.

During the night. all of Lee's army withdrew within their intrenchments. On the morning of the 7th General Custer drove the enemy's cavalry from Catharpin Furnace to Todd's Tavern. Pickets and skirmishers were sent along our entire front to find the position of the enemy. Some went as far as a mile and a half before finding him. But Lee showed no disposition to come out of his works. There was no battle during the day, and but little firing except in Warren's front; he being directed about noon to make a reconnaissance in force. This drew some sharp firing, but there was no attempt on the part of Lee to drive him back. This ended the Battle of the Wilderness.

Union Army on the Rapidan, May 5, 1864
[Compiled]

Lieutenant- General U.S. Grant, Commander in Chief
Major-General George G. Meade, Commanding Army of the Potomac

Major-General W.S. Hancock, Commanding Second Army Corps.			
1st Division, Brig-Gen. Francis C. Barlow.	2nd Division, Brig.-Gen. John Gibbon.	3rd Division, Maj.-Gen. David B. Birney.	4th Division, Brig.-Gen. Gershom Mott
1st Brigade, Col. Nelson A. Miles	1st Brigade, Brig.-Gen. Alex A. Webb	1st Brigade, Brig.-Gen. J.H.H. Ward	1st Brigade, Col. Robert McAllister
2nd Brigade, Col. Thomas Smyth	2nd Brigade, Brig.-Gen. Joshua T. Owen	2nd Brigade, Brig.-Gen. Alexander Hayes	2nd Brigade, Col. Wm. R. Brewster
3rd Brigade, Col. Paul Frank	3rd Brigade, Col. Samuel S. Carroll		Artillary Brigade, Col. John C. Tidball
4th Brigade, Col. John R. Brooke			

Major-General G.K. Warren Commanding 5th Army Corps.			
1st Division, Brig.-Gen. Charles Griffen	2nd Division, Brig.-Gen. John C. Robinson	3rd Division, Brig-Gen. Samuel W. Crawford	4th Division, Brig.-Gen. James S. Wadsworth
1st Brigade, Brig.-Gen. Romeyen B. Ayers	1st. Brigade, Col. Samuel H. Leonard	1st. Brigade, Col. William McCandless	1st Brigade, Brig-Gen. Lysander Cutler

2nd Brigade, Col. Jacob B. Sweitzer	2nd Brigade, Brig.-Gen. Harry Baxter		2nd Brigade, Brig.-Gen. James C. Rice
3rd Brigade, Brig. Gen. J.J. Bartlett	3rd Brigade, Col. Andrew W. Denison	3rd Brigade, Col. Joseph W. Fisher	3rd Brigade, Col. Roy Stone
			Artillery Brigade, Col. C.S. Wainwright

Major-General John Sedgwick, Commanding Sixth Army Corps.		
1st Division, Brig.-Gen. H.G. Wright	2nd Division, Brig.-Gen. George W. Getty	3rd Division, Brig.-Gen. James B. Ricketts
1st Brigade, Col. Henry W. Brown	1st Brigade, Brig.-Gen. Frank Wheaton	1st Brigade, Brig.-Gen William H. Morris
2nd Brigade, Col. Emory Upton	2nd Brigade, Col. Lewis A. Grant	2nd Brigade, Brig.-Gen. T. Seymour
3rd Brigade, Brig.-Gen. D.A. Russell	3rd Brigade, Brig.-Gen. Thos. H. Neill	
4th Brigade, Brig.-Gen. Alexander Shaler	4th Brigade, Brig.-Gen. Henry L. Eustis	Artillery Brigade, Col. C.H. Tompkins

Major-General A.E. Burnside, Commanding Ninth Army Corps.			
1st Division, Brig.-Gen. T.G. Stevenson	2nd Division, Brig.-Gen Robert B. Potter	3rd Division, Brig.-Gen O. B. Wilcox	4th Division, Brig.-Gen Edward Ferrero
1st Brigade, Col. Sumner Carruth	1st Brigade, Col. Zenas R. Bliss	1st Brigade, Col. John F. Hartranft	1st Brigade, Col. Joshua K. Sigfried

2nd Brigade, Col. Daniel Leasure	2nd Brigade, Col. Simon G. Griffin	2nd Brigade, Col. Beni C. Christ	2nd Brigade, Col. Henry G. Thomas
			Provisional Brigade, ol. Elisha G. Marshal

Major-General P.H. Sheridan, Commanding Cavalry Corps.		
1st Division, Brig-Gen. A.T.A.	2nd Division, Brig.-Gen. D. McM. Gregg	3rd Division, Brig.-Gen. J.H. Wilson
1st Brigade, Brig.-Gen. G.A. Custer	1st Brigade, Brig.-Gen. Henry E. Davis, Jr.	1st Brigade, Col. T.M. Bryan, Jr.
2nd Brigade, Col. Thos. C. Devin	2nd Brigade, Col. J. Irwin Gregg	2nd Brigade, Col. George H. Chapman
Reserve Brigade, Brig.-Gen. Wesley Merritt		

Brigadier-General Henry J. Hunt, Commanding Artillery	
Reserve Col. H.S. Hunt	
1st Brigade, Col. J.H. Kitching	1st Brigade Horse Artillery Capt. J.M Robertson
2nd Brigade, Major J.A. Thompkins	2nd Brigade, Horse Artillery Capt. D.R. Ransom
3rd Brigade, Major R.H. Fitzhugh	
General Headquarters	
Provost Guard, Brig.-Gen. M.R. Patrick	Volunteer Engineers, Brig.-Gen H.W. Benham

Confederate Army

Organization of the Army of Northern Virginia, Commanded by General Robert E. Lee, August 31st 1864.

First Army Corps: Lieut.-Gen. R.H. Andersen Commanding		
Maj.-Gen. Geo. E. Pickett's Division	Maj.-Gen. C.W. Field's Division (b)	Maj.-Gen. J.B. Kershaw's Division (d)
Brigades	Brigades	Brigades
Brig.-Gen.'s	Brig.-Gen.'s	Brig.-Gen.'s
Seth M. Barton (a)	G.T. Anderson	W.T. Wofford
M.D. Corse	E.M. Law (c)	B.G. Humphrey
Eppa Hunton	John Bratton	Goode Bryan
Wm. R. Terry		Kershaw's (old)

Second Army Corps: Major-Gen. Jubal A. Early. Commanding		
Maj.-Gen. John B. Gordon's Division	Maj.-Gen. Edward Johnson's Division	Maj.-Gen. R.E. Rode's Division
Brigades	Brigades	Brigades
Brig.-Gen.'s	Stonewall Brigade	Brig.-Gen.'s
H.T. Hays (e)	Brig.-Gen.'s	J. Daniel (i)
John Pegram (f)	J.A. Walker (h)	Geo. Dole (k)
Gordon's (g)	J.M. Jones (h)	S.D. Ramseur
R.F Hoke's	Geo. H. Stewart (h)	C.A. Battle
	L.A. Stafford (e)	R.D. Johnston (f)

Note:

(a) Col. W.R. Aylett was in command Aug. 29th, and probably at above date.

(b) Inspection report of this division shoes that it also contained Benning's and Gregg's Brigades.

(c) Commanded by Colonel P.D. Bowles.

(d) Only two brigadier generals reported for duty: names not indicated.

Organization of the Army of the Valley District.

(e) Constituting York's Brigade.
(f) In Ramseur's Division.
(g) Evan's Brigade, Colonel E.N. Atkinson commanding, and containing 12th Georgia Battalion.
(h) The Virginia Regiments constituted Terry's Brigade, Gordon's Division
(i) Grimes Brigade
(k) Cook's

Third Army Corp: Lieut.-Gen A.P. Hill Commanding		
Maj.-Gen. Wm. Mahone's Division (l)	Maj.-Gen. C.M. Wilcox's Division	Maj.-Gen. H. Heth's Division
Brigades	Brigades	Brigades
Brig.-Gen.'s	Brig.-Gen.'s	Brig.-Gen.'s
J.C.C. Sanders	E.L. Thomas (n)	J.R. Davis
Mahone	James H. Lane	John R. Cooke
H.N. Harris (m)	Sam'l McGowen	D. McRae
A.R. Wright	Alfred M. Scale	J.J, Archer
Joseph Finegan's		H.H. Walker
Unattached: 5th Alabama Battalion		

Notes
(l) Returns report but one general officer present for duty; name not indicated
(m) Colonel Joseph M. Jayne, commanding
(n) Colonel Thomas J. Simmons, commanding
(o) Four brigadier-generals reported present for duty; names not indicated

Cavalry Corps: Lieut.-General Wade Hampton, Commanding (p)		
Maj.-Gen. Fitzhugh Lee's Division	Maj.-Gen. M.C. Butler's Division	Maj.-Gen. W.H.F. Lee's Division
Brigades	Brigades	Brigades
Brig.-Gen's W.C. Wickham L.L. Lomax	Brig.-Gen's John Dunovant P.M.B Young Thomas Rosser	Brig.-Gen's Rufus Barringer J.R. Chambliss

Note: (p) On face of returns appears to have consisted of Hampton's, Fitz-Lee's and W.H.F. Lee's Division and Dearing's Brigade.

Artillery Reserve: Brig.-Gen. W.N. Pendleton, Commanding			
Brig.-Gen E.P. Alexanders Division.*			
Cabell's Battalion	Haskell's Battalion	Huger's Battalion	Gibb's Battalion
Battery	Battery	Battery	Battery
Manly's1st Co. Richmond Howitzers Carelton Calloway	Branch Nelson Garden Rowan	Smith Moodoy Woolfolk Parker Taylor Fickling Martin	Davidson Dickens Otley

Brig.-Gen A.L. Long's Division Artillery and Howitzers				
Braxton's Battalion	Cutshaw's Battalion	Carter's Battalion	Nelson's Battalion	Brown's Battalion
Lee Battery 1st Md. Stafford Allegany	Charlottesville Staunton Courtney	Morris Orange King William Jeff Davis	Amherst Milledge Fluvauna	Powhatten 2nd & 3rd Richmond Howitzers Rockbridge Salem Flying

Colonel R.L. Walker's Division Artillery and Batteries				
Cutt's Battalion	Richardson's Battalion	McIntosh's Battalion	Pegram's Battalion	Poague's Battalion
Ross	Lewis	Johnson	Peedee	Madison
Patterson	Donaldsonville	Hardaway	Fredericksburg	Albermarle
Irwin	Norfolk	Danville	Letcher	Brooke
	Huger	2nd Rockbridge	Purcell	Charlotte
			Crenshaw	

* But one general officer reported present for duty in the artillery, and Alexander's name not on original.

CHAPTER LI

AFTER THE BATTLE - TELEGRAPH AND SIGNAL SERVICE - MOVEMENT BY THE LEFT FLANK

MORE desperate fighting has not been witnessed on this continent than that of the 5th and 6th of May. Our victory consisted in having successfully crossed a formidable stream, almost in the face of an enemy, and in getting the army together as a unit. We gained an advantage on the morning of the 6th, which, if it had been followed up, must have proven very decisive. In the evening the enemy gained an advantage; but was speedily repulsed. As we stood at the close, the two armies were relatively in about the same condition to meet each other as when the river divided them. But the fact of having safely crossed was a victory.

Our losses in the Wilderness were very severe. Those of the Confederates must have been even more so; but I have no means of speaking with accuracy upon this point. The Germania Ford Bridge was transferred to Ely's Ford to facilitate the transportation of the wounded to Washington.

It may be as well here as elsewhere to state two things connected with all movements of the Army of the Potomac: first, in every change of position or halt for the night, whether confronting the enemy or not, the moment arms were stacked the men intrenched themselves. For this purpose they would build up piles of logs or rails if they could be found in their front, and dig a ditch, throwing the dirt forward on the timber. Thus the digging they did counted in making a depression to stand in, and increased the elevation in front of them. It was wonderful how quickly they could in this way construct defences of considerable strength. When a halt was made with the view of assaulting the enemy, or in his presence, these would be strengthened or their positions changed under the direction of engineer officers. The second was, the use made of the telegraph and signal corps. Nothing could be more complete than the organization and discipline of this body of brave and

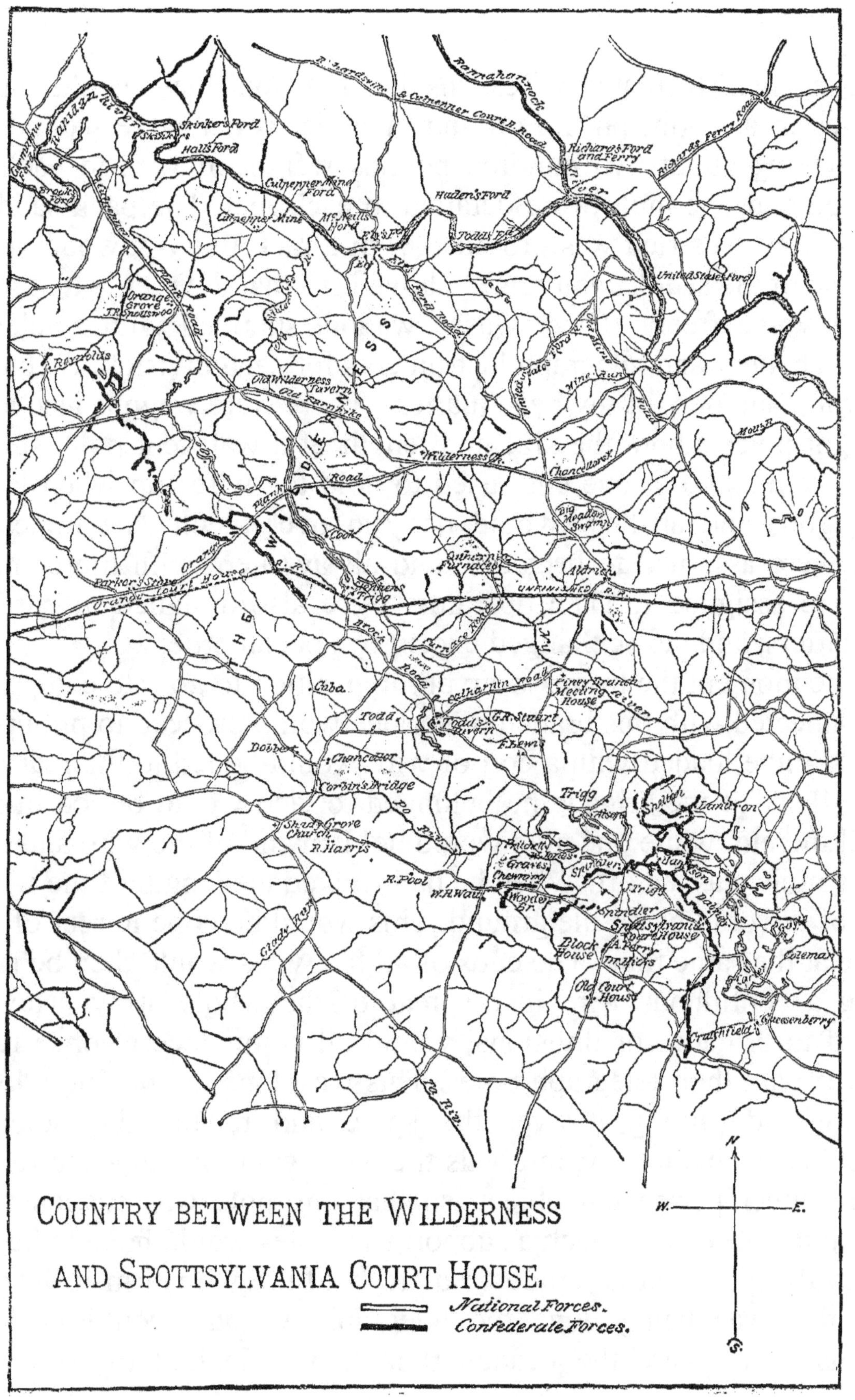

COUNTRY BETWEEN THE WILDERNESS

AND SPOTTSYLVANIA COURT HOUSE.

intelligent men. Insulated wires, insulated so that they would transmit messages in a storm, on the ground or under water were wound upon reels, making about two hundred pounds weight of wire to each reel. Two men and one mule were detailed to each reel. The pack-saddle on which this was carried was provided with a rack like a sawbuck placed crosswise of the saddle, and raised above it so that the reel, with its wire, would revolve freely. There was a wagon, supplied with a telegraph operator, battery and telegraph instruments for each division, each corps, each army, and one for my headquarters. There were wagons also loaded with light poles, about the size and length of a wall tent pole, supplied with an iron spike in one end, used to hold the wires up when laid, so that wagons and artillery would not run over them. The mules thus loaded were assigned to brigades, and always kept with the command they were assigned to. The operators were also assigned to particular headquarters, and never changed except by special orders.

The moment the troops were put in position to go into camp all the men connected with this branch of service would proceed to put up their wires. A mule loaded with a coil of wire would be led to the rear of the nearest flank of the brigade he belonged to, and would be led in a line parallel thereto, while one man would hold an end of the wire and uncoil it as the mule was led off. When he had walked the length of the wire the whole of it would be on the ground. This would be done in rear of every brigade at the same time. The ends of all the wires would then be joined, making a continuous wire in the rear of the whole army. The men, attached to brigades or divisions, would all commence at once raising the wires with their telegraph poles. This was done by making a loop in the wire and putting it over the spike and raising the pole to a perpendicular position. At intervals the wire would be attached to trees, or some other permanent object, so that one pole was sufficient at a place. In the absence of such a support two poles would have to be used, at intervals, placed at an angle so as to hold the wire firm in its place. While this was being done the telegraph wagons would take their positions near where the headquarters they belonged to were to be established, and would connect with the wire. Thus, in a few minutes longer time than it took a mule to walk the length of its coil, telegraphic communication would be effected between all the headquarters of the army. No orders ever had to be given to establish the telegraph.

The signal service was used on the march. The men composing this corps were assigned to specified commands. When movements were made, they would go in advance, or on the flanks, and seize upon high points of ground giving a commanding view of the country, if cleared, or would climb tall trees on the highest points if not cleared, and would denote, by signals, the positions of different parts of our own army, and often the movements of the enemy. They would also take off the signals of the enemy and transmit them. It would sometimes take too long a time to make translations of intercepted dispatches for us to receive any benefit from them. But sometimes they gave useful information.

On the afternoon of the 7th I received news from Washington announcing that Sherman had probably attacked Johnston that day, and that Butler had reached City Point safely and taken it by surprise on the 5th. I had given orders for a movement by the left flank, fearing that Lee might move rapidly to Richmond to crush Butler before I could get there.

My order for this movement was as follows:

HEADQUARTERS ARMIES OF T HE U. S.,
May 7, 1864, 6:30 A.M.

MAJOR-GENERAL MEADE,
Commanding A. P.

Make all preparations during the day for a night march to take position at Spottsylvania C. H. with one army corps, at Todd's Tavern with one, and another near the intersection of the Piney Branch and Spottsylvania road with the road from Alsop's to Old Court House. If this move is made the trains should be thrown forward early in the morning to the Ny River.

I think it would be advisable in making the change to leave Hancock where he is until Warren passes him. He could then follow and become the right of the new line. Burnside will move to Piney Branch Church. Sedgwick can move along the pike to Chancellorsville and on to his destination. Burnside will move on the plank road to the intersection of it with the Orange and Fredericksburg plank road, then follow Sedgwick to his place of destination.

All vehicles should be got out of hearing of the enemy before the troops move, and then move off quietly.

It is more than probable that the enemy concentrate for a heavy attack on Hancock this afternoon. In case they do we must be prepared to resist them, and follow up any success we may gain, with our whole force. Such a result would necessarily modify these instructions.

All the hospitals should be moved today to Chancellorsville.

U.S. GRANT,
Lieut.-General.

During the 7th Sheridan had a fight with the rebel cavalry at Todd's Tavern, but routed them, thus opening the way for the troops that were to go by that route at night. Soon after dark Warren withdrew from the front of the enemy, and was soon followed by Sedgwick. Warren's march carried him immediately behind the works where Hancock's command lay on the Brock Road. With my staff and a small escort of cavalry I preceded the troops. Meade with his staff accompanied me. The greatest enthusiasm was manifested by Hancock's men as we passed by. No doubt it was inspired by the fact that the movement was south. It indicated to them that they had passed through the "beginning of the end" in the battle just fought. The cheering was so lusty that the enemy must have taken it for a night attack. At all events it drew from him a furious fusillade of artillery and musketry, plainly heard but not felt by us.

Meade and I rode in advance. We had passed but a little way beyond our left when the road forked. We looked to see, if we could, which road Sheridan had taken with his cavalry during the day. It seemed to be the right-hand one, and accordingly we took it. We had not gone far, however, when Colonel C.B. Comstock, of my staff, with the instinct of the engineer, suspecting that we were on a road that would lead us into the lines of the enemy, if he, too, should be moving, dashed by at a rapid gallop and all alone. In a few minutes he returned and reported that Lee was moving, and that the road we were on would bring us into his lines in a short distance. We returned to the forks of the road, left a man to indicate the right road to the head of Warren's column when it should come up, and continued our journey to Todd's Tavern, where we arrived after midnight.

My object in moving to Spottsylvania was two-fold: first, I did not want Lee to get back to Richmond in time to attempt to crush Butler before I could get there; second, I wanted to get between his army and Richmond if possible; and, if not, to draw him into the open field. But Lee, by accident, beat us to Spottsylvania. Our wagon trains had been ordered easterly of the roads the troops were to march upon before the movement commenced. Lee interpreted this as a semi-retreat of the Army of the Potomac to Fredericksburg, and so informed his government. Accordingly he ordered Longstreet's corps, now commanded by Anderson, to move in the morning (the 8th) to Spottsylvania. But the woods being still on fire, Anderson could not go into bivouac, and marched directly on to his destination that night. By this accident Lee got possession of Spottsylvania. It is impossible to say now what would have been the result if Lee's orders had been obeyed as given; but it is certain that we would have been in Spottsylvania, and between him and his capital, My belief is that there would have been a race between the two armies to see which could reach Richmond first, and the Army of the Potomac would have had the shorter line. Thus, twice since crossing the Rapidan we came near closing the campaign, so far as battles were concerned, from the Rapidan to the James River or Richmond. The first failure was caused by our not following up the success gained over Hill's corps on the morning of the 6th, as before described: the second, when fires caused by that battle drove Anderson to make a march during the night of the 7th-8th which he was ordered to commence on the morning of the 8th. But accident often decides the fate of battle.

Sheridan's cavalry had had considerable fighting during the afternoon of the 7th, lasting at Todd's Tavern until after night, with the field his at the close. He issued the necessary orders for seizing Spottsylvania and holding the bridge over the PO River, which Lee's troops would have to cross to get to Spottsylvania. But Meade changed Sheridan's orders to Merritt, who was holding the bridge on his arrival at Todd's Tavern, and thereby left the road free for Anderson when he came up. Wilson, who was ordered to seize the town, did so, with his division of cavalry; but he could not hold it against the Confederate corps which had not been detained at the crossing of the Po, as it would have been but for the unfortunate change in Merritt's orders. Had he been permitted to execute the orders Sheridan gave him, he would have been guarding with two brigades of cavalry the bridge over the PO River which Anderson had to cross, and must have detained him long enough to enable Warren to reinforce Wilson and hold the town.

Anderson soon intrenched himself; if indeed the intrenchments were not already made, immediately across Warren's front. Warren was not aware of his presence, but probably supposed it was the cavalry which Merritt had engaged earlier in the day. He assaulted at once, but was repulsed. He soon organized his men, as they were not pursued by the enemy, and made a second attack, this time with his whole corps. This time he succeeded in gaining a position immediately in the enemy's front, where he intrenched. His right and left divisions; the former Crawford's, the latter Wadsworth's, now commanded by Cutler, drove the enemy back some distance.

At this time my headquarters had been advanced to Piney Branch Church. I was anxious to crush Anderson before Lee could get a force to his support. To this end Sedgwick, who was at Piney Branch Church, was ordered to Warren's support. Hancock, who was at Todd's Tavern, was notified of Warren's engagement, and was directed to be in readiness to come up. Burnside, who was with the wagon trains at Aldrich's on our extreme left, received the same instructions. Sedgwick was slow in getting up for some reason; probably unavoidable, because he was never at fault when serious work was to be done, so that it was near night before the combined forces were ready to attack. Even then all of Sedgwick's command did not get into the engagement. Warren led the last assault, one division at a time, and of course it failed.

Warren's difficulty was twofold: when he received an order to do anything, it would at once occur to his mind how all the balance of the army should be engaged so as properly to co-operate with him. His ideas were generally good, but he would forget that the person giving him orders had thought of others at the time he had of him. In like manner, when he did get ready to execute an order, after giving most intelligent instructions to division commanders, he would go in with one division, holding the others in reserve until he could superintend their movements in person also, forgetting that division commanders could execute an order without his presence. His difficulty was constitutional and beyond his control. He was an officer of superior ability, quick perceptions, and personal courage to accomplish anything that could be done with a small command.

Lee had ordered Hill's corps; now commanded by Early, to move by the very road we had marched upon. This shows that even early in the morning of the 8th Lee had not yet become acquainted with my move, but still thought that the Army of the Potomac had gone to Fredericksburg. Indeed, he informed the authorities at Richmond that he had possession of Spottsylvania and was thus on my flank. Anderson was in possession of Spottsylvania, through, no foresight of Lee, however. Early only found that he had been following us when he ran against Hancock at Todd's Tavern. His coming detained Hancock from the battlefield of Spottsylvania for that day; but he, in like manner, kept Early back and forced him to move by another route.

Had I ordered the movement for the night of the 7th by my left flank, it would have put Hancock in the lead. It would also have given us an hour or more earlier start. It took all that time for Warren to get the head of his column to the left of Hancock after he had got his troops out of their line confronting the enemy. This hour, and Hancock's capacity to use his whole force when necessary, would, no doubt, have enabled him to crush Anderson before he could be reinforced. But the movement made was tactical. It kept the troops in mass against a possible assault by the enemy. Our left occupied its intrenchments while the two corps to the right passed. If an attack had been made by the enemy he would have found the 2d corps in position, fortified, and, practically, the 5th and 6th corps in position as reserves, until his entire front was passed. By a left flank movement the army would have been scattered while still passing the front of the enemy, and before the extreme right had got by it would have been very much exposed. Then, too, I had not yet learned the special qualifications of the different corps commanders. At that time my judgment was that Warren was the man I would suggest to succeed Meade should anything happen to that gallant soldier to take him from the field. As I have before said, Warren was a gallant soldier, an able man; and he was beside thoroughly imbued with the solemnity and importance of the duty he had to perform.

CHAPTER LII

BATTLE OF SPOTTSYLVANIA - HANCOCK'S POSITION - ASSAULT OF WARREN'S AND WRIGHT'S CORPS - UPTON PROMOTED ON THE FIELD - GOOD NEWS FROM BUTLER AND SHERIDAN

THE Mattapony River is formed by the junction of the Mat, the Ta, the Po and the Ny rivers, the last being the northernmost of the four. It takes its rise about a mile south and a little east of the Wilderness Tavern. The Po rises southwest of the same place, but farther away. Spottsylvania is on the ridge dividing these two streams, and where they are but a few miles apart. The Brock Road reaches Spottsylvania without crossing either of these streams. Lee's army coming up by the Catharpin Road had to cross the Po at Wooden Bridge. Warren and Hancock came by the Brock Road. Sedgwick crossed the Ny at Catharpin Furnace. Burnside coming by Aldrich's to Gates's house had to cross the Ny near the enemy. He found pickets at the bridge, but they were soon driven off by a brigade of Willcox's division, and the stream was crossed. This brigade was furiously attacked; but the remainder of the division coming up, they were enabled to hold their position, and soon fortified it.

About the time I received the news of this attack, word came from Hancock that Early had left his front. He had been forced over to the Catharpin Road, crossing the Po at Corbin's and again at Wooden Bridge. These are the bridges Sheridan had given orders to his cavalry to occupy on the 8th, while one division should occupy Spottsylvania. These movements of the enemy gave me the idea that Lee was about to make the attempt to get to, or towards, Fredericksburg to cut off my supplies. I made arrangements to attack his right and get between him and Richmond if he should try to execute this design. If he had any such intention it was abandoned as soon as Burnside was established south of the Ny.

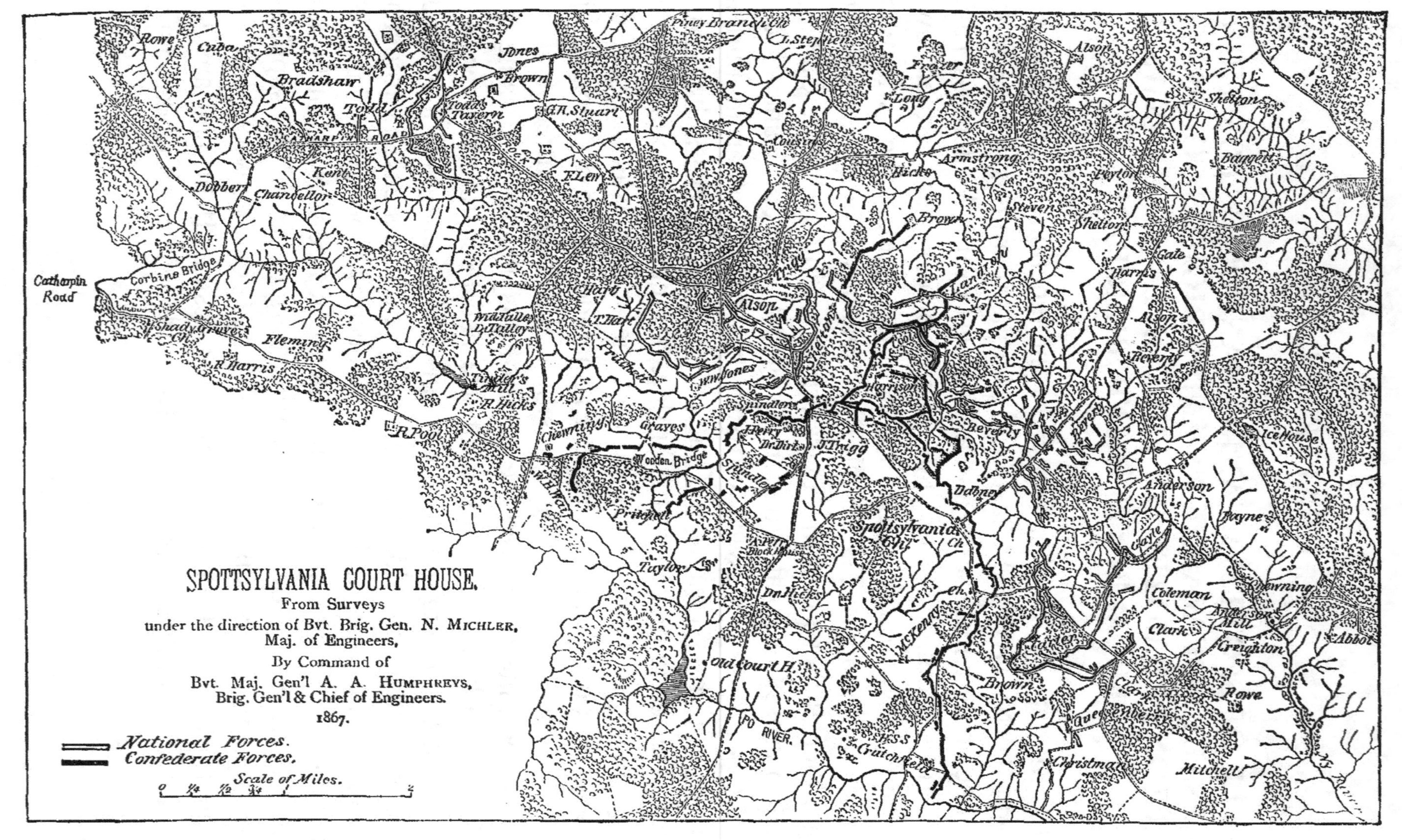

SPOTTSYLVANIA COURT HOUSE.
From Surveys
under the direction of Bvt. Brig. Gen. N. Michler,
Maj. of Engineers,
By Command of
Bvt. Maj. Gen'l A. A. Humphreys,
Brig. Gen'l & Chief of Engineers.
1867.
National Forces.
Confederate Forces.
Scale of Miles.
Catharpin Road
Corbins Bridge
Shady Grove
Fleming
R. Harris
Rowe
Cuba
Bradshaw
Todd
Todd's Tavern
Kent
Dobber
Chancellor
BROCK ROAD
Jones
Brown
G.R. Stuart
Flen
Piney Branch Ch.
L. Stephen
Long
Cousins
Hicks
Armstrong
Peyton
Alson
Shelton
Baggett
Steven
Shelton
Brown
Landrum
Alson
Beverly
Gate
Harris
Alson
Revere
Ice House
Tinder's Hill
R. Hicks
R. Pool
Chewning
Graves
Wooden Bridge
W.H. Wall
Pritchett
Taylor
Block House
Jones
Spindle
Heth
Dr. Birks
J. Trigg
Shudo
Spottsylvania C.H.
Ddones
Anderson
Payne
Gayle
Coleman
Downing
Anderson Mill
Clark
Creighton
Abbot
Dr. Hicks
McKenney
Old Court H.
PO RIVER.
Crutchfield
Brown
Que
Rowe
Christman
Mitchell
0   1/4   1/2   3/4   1   2

The Po and the Ny are narrow little streams, but deep, with abrupt banks, and bordered by heavily wooded and marshy bottoms -at the time we were there and difficult to cross except where bridged. The country about was generally heavily timbered, but with occasional clearings. It was a much better country to conduct a defensive campaign in than an offensive one.

By noon of the 9th the position of the two armies was as follows: Lee occupied a semicircle facing north, northwest and northeast, enclosing the town. Anderson was on his left extending to the Po, Ewell came next, then Early. Warren occupied our right, covering the Brock and other roads converging at Spottsylvania; Sedgwick was to his left and Burnside on our extreme left. Hancock was yet back at Todd's Tavern, but as soon as it was known that Early had left Hancock's front the latter was ordered up to Warren's right. He formed a line with three divisions on the hill overlooking the Po early in the afternoon, and was ordered to cross the Po and get on the enemy's flank. The fourth division of Hancock's corps, Mott commanding, was left at Todd's when the corps first came up; but in the afternoon it was brought up and placed to the left of Sedgwick's, now Wright's 6th corps. In the morning General Sedgwick had been killed near the right of his intrenchments by rebel sharpshooters. His loss was a severe one to the Army of the Potomac and to the Nation. General H.G. Wright succeeded him in the command of his corps.

Hancock was now, nine P.M. of the 9th of May, across the left flank of Lee's army, but separated from it, and also from the remainder of Meade's army, by the Po River. But for the lateness of the hour and the darkness of the night he would have attempted to cross the river again at Wooden Bridge, thus bringing himself on the same side with both friend and foe.

The Po at the points where Hancock's corps crossed runs nearly due east. Just below his lower crossing -the troops crossed at three points- it turns due south, and after passing under Wooden Bridge soon resumes a more easterly direction. During the night this corps built three bridges over the Po; but these were in rear.

The position assumed by Hancock's corps forced Lee to reinforce his left during the night. Accordingly on the morning of the 10th, when Hancock renewed his effort to get over the Po to his front, he found himself confronted by some of Early's command, which had been brought from the extreme right of the enemy during the night. He succeeded in effecting a crossing with one brigade, however, but finding the enemy intrenched in his front, no more were crossed.

Hancock reconnoitred his front on the morning of the 10th, with the view of forcing a crossing, if it was found that an advantage could be gained. The enemy -was found strongly intrenched on the high ground overlooking the river, and commanding the Wooden Bridge with artillery. Anderson's left rested on the Po, where it turns south ; therefore, for Hancock to cross over -although it would bring him to the same side of the stream with the rest the army- would still farther isolate him from it. The stream would have to be crossed twice in the face of the enemy to unite with the main body. The idea of crossing was therefore abandoned.

Lee had weakened the other parts of his line to meet this movement of Hancock's, and I determined to take advantage of it. Accordingly in the morning, orders were issued for an attack in the afternoon on the centre by Warren's and Wright's corps, Hancock to command all the attacking force. Two of his divisions were brought to the north side of the Po. Gibbon was placed to the right of Warren, and Birney in his rear as a reserve. Barlow's division was left south of the stream, and Mott of the same corps was still to the left of Wright's corps. Burnside was ordered to reconnoitre his front in force, and, if an opportunity presented, to attack with vigor. The enemy seeing Barlow's division isolated from the rest of the army, came out and attacked with fury. Barlow repulsed the assault with great slaughter, and with considerable loss to himself. But the enemy reorganized and renewed the assault. Birney was now moved to the high ground overlooking the river crossings built by our troops, and covered the crossings. The second assault was repulsed, again with severe loss to the enemy, and Barlow was withdrawn without further molestation. General T. G. Stevenson was killed in this move.

Between the lines, where Warren's assault was to take place, there was a ravine grown up with large trees and underbrush, making it almost impenetrable by man. The slopes on both sides were also covered with a heavy growth of timber. Warren, before noon, reconnoitred his front twice, the first time with one and the second with two divisions. He was repulsed on both occasions, but gained such information of the ground as to induce him to report recommending the assault.

Wright also reconnoitred his front and gained a considerably advanced position from the one he started from. He then organized a storming party, consisting of twelve regiments, and assigned Colonel Emory Upton, of the 121st New York Volunteers, to the command of it. About four o'clock in the afternoon the assault was ordered, Warren's and Wright's corps, with Mott's division of Hancock's corps, to move simultaneously. The movement was prompt, and in a few minutes the fiercest of struggles began. The battlefield was so densely covered with forest that but little could be seen, by any one person, as to the progress made. Meade and I occupied the best position we could get, in rear of Warren.

Warren was repulsed with heavy loss, General J.C. Rice being among the killed. He was not followed, however, by the enemy, and was thereby enabled to reorganize his command as soon as covered from the guns of the enemy. To the left our success was decided, but the advantage was lost by the feeble action of Mott. Upton with his assaulting party pushed forward and crossed the enemy's intrenchments. Turning to the right and left he captured several guns and some hundreds of prisoners. Mott was ordered to his assistance but failed utterly. So much time was lost in trying to get up the troops which were in the right position to reinforce, that I ordered Upton to withdraw; but the officers and men of his command were so averse to giving up the advantage they had gained that I withdrew the order. To relieve them, I ordered a renewal of the assault. By this time Hancock, who had gone with Birney's division to relieve Barlow, had returned, bringing the division with him. His corps was now joined with Warren's and Wright's in this last assault. It was gallantly made, many men getting up to, and over, the works of the enemy; but they were not able to hold them. At night they were withdrawn. Upton brought his prisoners with him, but the guns he had captured he was obliged to abandon. Upton had gained an important advantage, but a lack in others of the spirit and dash possessed by him lost it to us. Before leaving Washington I had been authorized to promote officers on the field for special acts of gallantry. By this authority I conferred the rank of brigadier-general upon Upton on the spot, and this act was confirmed by the President. Upton had been badly wounded in this fight.

Burnside on the left had got up to within a few hundred yards of Spottsylvania Court House, completely turning Lee's right. He was not aware of the importance of the advantage he had gained, and I, being with the troops where the heavy fighting was, did not know of it at the time. He had gained his position with but little fighting, and almost without loss. Burnside's position now separated him widely from Wright's corps, the corps nearest to him. At night he was ordered to join on to this, this brought him back about a mile, and lost to us an important advantage. I attach no blame to Burnside for this, but I do to myself for not having had a staff officer with him to report to me his position.

The enemy had not dared to come out of his line at any point to follow up his advantage, except in the single instance of his attack on Barlow. Then he was twice repulsed with heavy loss, though he had an entire corps against two brigades. Barlow took up his bridges in the presence of this force.

On the 11th there was no battle and but little firing; none except by Mott who made a reconnaissance to ascertain if there was a weak point in the enemy's line.

I wrote the following letter to General Halleck:

NEAR SPOTTSYLVANIA C.H.,
May 11, 1864-8:30 A.M.

MAJOR-GENERAL HALLECK. Chief of Staff of the Army,
Washington, D. C.

We have now ended the 6th day of very hard fighting. The result up to this time is much in our favor. But our losses have been heavy as well as those of the enemy. We have lost to this time eleven general officers killed, wounded and missing, and probably twenty thousand men. I think the loss of the enemy must be greater -we having taken over four thousand prisoners in battle, whilst he has taken from us but few except a few stragglers. I am now sending back to Belle Plain all my wagons for a fresh supply of provisions and ammunition, and purpose to fight it out on this line if it takes all summer.

The arrival of reinforcements here will be very encouraging to the men, and I hope they will be sent as fast as possible, and in as great numbers. My object in having them sent to Belle Plain was to use them as an escort to our supply trains. If it is more convenient to send them out by train to march from the railroad to Belle Plain or Fredericksburg, send them so.

I am satisfied the enemy are very shaky, and are only kept up to the mark by the greatest exertions on the part of their officers, and by keeping them intrenched in every position they take.

Up to this time there is no indication of any portion of Lee's army being detached for the defence of Richmond.

U.S. GRANT,
Lieut.-General.

And also, I received information, through the War Department, from General Butler that his cavalry under Kautz had cut the railroad south of Petersburg, separating Beauregard from Richmond, and had whipped Hill, killing, wounding and capturing many. Also that he was intrenched, and could maintain himself. On this same day came news from Sheridan to the effect that he had destroyed ten miles of the railroad and telegraph between Lee and Richmond, one and a half million rations, and most of the medical stores for his army.

On the 8th I had directed Sheridan verbally to cut loose from the Army of the Potomac and pass around the left of Lee's army and attack his cavalry and communications, which was successfully executed in the manner I have already described.

CHAPTER LIII

HANCOCK'S ASSAULT - LOSSES OF THE CONFEDERATES - PROMOTIONS RECOMMENDED - DISCOMFITURE OF THE ENEMY - WELL'S ATTACK - REDUCING THE ARTILLERY

IN the reconnaissance made by Mott on the 11th, a salient was discovered at the right centre. I determined that an assault should be made at that point.* Accordingly in the afternoon Hancock was ordered to move his command by the rear of Warren and Wright, under cover of night, to Wright's left, and there form it for an assault at four o'clock the next morning. The night was dark, it rained heavily, and the road was difficult, so that it was midnight when he reached the point where he was to halt. It took most of the night to get the men in position for their advance in the morning. The men got but little rest. Burnside was ordered to attack* on the left of the salient at the same hour. I sent two of my staff officers to impress upon him the importance of pushing forward vigorously

---

*HEADQUARTERS ARMIES U. S.,
May 11, 1864.-3 P.M.

MAJOR-GENERAL MEADE,
Commanding Army of the Potomac.

Move three divisions of the 2nd corps by the rear of the 5th and 6th corps, under cover of night, so as to join the 9th corps in a vigorous assault on the enemy at four o'clock A.M. tomorrow. I will send one or two staff officers over tonight to stay with Burnside, and impress him with the importance of a prompt and vigorous attack. Warren and Wright should hold their corps as close to the enemy as possible, to take advantage of any diversion caused by this attack, and to push in if any opportunity presents itself. There is but little doubt in my mind that the assault last evening would have proved entirely successful if it had commenced one hour earlier and had been heartily entered into by Mott's division and the 9th corps.

U.S. GRANT, Lieut.-General.

Hancock was notified of this. Warren and Wright were ordered to hold themselves in readiness to join in the assault if circumstances made it advisable. I occupied a central position most convenient for receiving information from all points. Hancock put Barlow on his left, in double column, and Birney to his right. Mott followed Birney, and Gibbon was held in reserve.

*HEADQUARTERS, ARMIES U. S.,
May 11, 1864 - 4 P.M

MAJOR-GENERAL A.E. BURNSIDE,
Commanding 9th Army Corps.

Major-General Hancock has been ordered to move his corps under cover of night to join you in a vigorous attack against the enemy at 4 o'clock A.M. tomorrow. You will move against the enemy with your entire force promptly and with all possible vigor at precisely 4 o'clock A.M. tomorrow the 12th inst. Let your preparations for this attack be conducted with the utmost secrecy and veiled entirely from the enemy.

I send two of my staff officers; Colonels Comstock and Babcock, in whom I have great confidence and who are acquainted with the direction the attack is to be made from here, to remain with you and General Hancock with instructions to render you every assistance in their power. Generals Warren and Wright will hold their corps as close to the enemy as possible, to take advantage of any diversion caused by yours and Hancock's attack, and will push in their whole force if any opportunity presents itself.

U.S. GRANT,
Lieut.-General.

The morning of the 12th opened foggy, delaying the start more than half an hour.

The ground over which Hancock had to pass to reach the enemy, was ascending and heavily wooded to within two or three hundred yards of the enemy's intrenchments. In front of Birney there was also a marsh to cross. But, notwithstanding all these difficulties, the troops pushed on in quick time without firing a gun, and when within four or five hundred yards of the enemy's line broke out in loud cheers, and with a rush went up to and over the breastworks. Barlow and Birney entered almost simultaneously. Here a desperate hand-to-hand conflict took place. The men of the two sides were too close together to fire, but used their guns as clubs. The hand conflict was soon over. Hancock's corps captured some four thousand prisoners -among them a division and a brigade commander-twenty or more guns with their horses, caissons, and ammunition, several thousand stand of arms, and many colors. Hancock, as soon as the hand-to-hand conflict was over, turned the guns of the enemy against him and advanced inside the rebel lines. About six o'clock I ordered Warren's corps to the support of Hancock's. Burnside, on the left, had advanced up east of the salient to the very parapet of the enemy. Potter, commanding one of his divisions, got over but was not able to remain there. However, he inflicted a heavy loss upon the enemy; but not without loss in return.

This victory was important, and one that Lee could not afford to leave us in full possession of. He made the most strenuous efforts to regain the position he had lost. Troops were brought up from his left and attacked Hancock furiously. Hancock was forced to fall back: but he did so slowly, with his face to the enemy, inflicting on him heavy loss, until behind the breastworks he had captured. These he turned, facing them the other way, and continued to hold. Wright was ordered up to reinforce Hancock, and arrived by six o'clock. He was wounded soon after coming up but did not relinquish the command of his corps, although the fighting lasted until one o'clock the next morning. At eight o'clock Warren was ordered up again, but was so slow in making his dispositions that his orders were frequently repeated, and with emphasis. At eleven o'clock I gave Meade written orders to relieve Warren from his command if he failed to move promptly. Hancock placed batteries on high ground in his rear, which he used against the enemy, firing over the heads of his own troops.

Burnside accomplished but little on our left of a positive nature, but negatively a great deal. He kept Lee from reinforcing his centre from that quarter. If the 5th corps, or rather if Warren had been as prompt as Wright was with the 6th corps, better results might have been obtained.

Lee massed heavily from his left flank on the broken point of his line. Five times during the day he assaulted furiously, but without dislodging our troops from their new position. His losses must have been fearful. Sometimes the belligerents would be separated by but a few feet. In one place a tree, eighteen inches in diameter, was cut entirely down by musket balls. All the trees between the lines were very much cut to pieces by artillery and musketry. It was three o'clock next morning before the fighting ceased. Some of our troops had then been twenty hours under fire. In this engagement we did not lose a single organization, not even a company. The enemy lost one division with its commander, one brigade and one regiment, with heavy losses elsewhere.* Our losses were heavy, but, as stated, no whole company was captured. At night Lee took a position in rear of his former one, and by the following morning he was strongly intrenched in it.

---

*HEADQUARTERS ARMIES U. S.,
May 12, 1864, 6:30 P.M.

MAJOR-GENERAL HALLECK,
Washington, D. C.

The eighth day of the battle closes, leaving between three and four thousand prisoners in our hands for the day's work, including two general officers, and over thirty pieces of artillery. The enemy are obstinate, and seem to have found the last ditch. We have lost no organizations, not even that of a company, whilst we have destroyed and captured one division (Johnson's), one brigade (Doles'), and one regiment entire from the enemy.

U.S. GRANT,
Lieut.-General.

Warren's corps was now temporarily broken up, Cutler's division sent to Wright, and Griffin's to Hancock. Meade ordered his chief of staff, General Humphreys, to remain with Warren and the remaining division, and authorized him to give it orders in his name.

During the day I was passing along the line from wing to wing continuously. About the centre stood a house which proved to be occupied by an old lady and her daughter. She showed such unmistakable signs of being strongly Union that I stopped. She said she had not seen a Union flag for so long a time that it did her heart good to look upon it again. She said her husband and son, being Union men, had had to leave early in the war, and were now somewhere in the Union army, if alive. She was without food or nearly so, so I ordered rations issued to her, and promised to find out if I could where the husband and son were.

There was no fighting on the 13th, further than a little skirmishing between Mott's division and the enemy. I was afraid that Lee might be moving out, and I did not want him to go without my knowing it. The indications were that he was moving, but it was found that he was only taking his new position back from the salient that had been captured. Our dead were buried this day. Mott's division was reduced to a brigade, and assigned to Birney's division.

During this day I wrote to Washington recommending Sherman and Meade * for promotion to the grade of Major-General in the regular army; Hancock for Brigadier-General; Wright, Gibbon and Humphreys to be Major-Generals of Volunteers; and Upton and Carroll to be Brigadiers. Upton had already been named as such, but the appointment had to be confirmed by the Senate on the nomination of the President.

---

* SPOTTSYLVANIA C.H.
May 13, 1864.

HON. E.M. STANTON, SECRETARY OF WAR,
Washington, D. C.

I beg leave to recommend the following promotions be made for gallant and distinguished services in the last eight days' battles, to wit: Brigadier-General H. G. Wright and Brigadier-General John Gibbon to be Major-Generals; Colonel S. S. Carroll, 8th Ohio Volunteers; Colonel E. Upton, 121st New York Volunteers; Colonel William McCandless, 2d Pennsylvania Reserves, to be Brigadier-Generals. I would also recommend Major-General W.S. Hancock for Brigadier-General in the regular army. His services and qualifications are eminently deserving of this recognition. In making these recommendations I do not wish the claims of General G. M. Dodge for promotion forgotten, but recommend his name to be sent in at the same time. I would also ask to have General Wright assigned to the command of the Sixth Army Corps. I would further ask the confirmation of General Humphreys to the rank of Major-General.

General Meade has more than met my most sanguine expectations. He and Sherman are the fittest officers for large commands I have come in contact with. If their services can be rewarded by promotion to the rank of Major-Generals in the regular army the honor would be worthily bestowed, and I would feel personally gratified. I would not like to see one of these promotions at this time without seeing both.

U.S. GRANT,
Lieut. -General.

The night of the 13th Warren and Wright were moved by the rear to the left of Burnside. The night was very dark and it rained heavily, the roads were so bad that the troops had to cut trees and corduroy the road a part of the way, to get through. It was midnight before they got to the point where they were to halt, and daylight before the troops could be organized to advance to their position in line, They gained their position in line, however, without any fighting, except a little in Wright's front. Here Upton had to contend for an elevation which we wanted and which the enemy was not disposed to yield. Upton first drove the enemy, and was then repulsed in turn. Ayres coming to his support with his brigade (of Griffin's division, Warren's corps), the position was secured and fortified. There was no more battle during the 14th. This brought our line east of the Court House and running north and south and facing west.

During the night of the 14th-15th Lee moved to cover this new front. This left Hancock without an enemy confronting him. He was brought to the rear of our new centre, ready to be moved in any direction he might be wanted.

On the 15th news came from Butler and Averill. The former reported the capture of the outer works at Drury's Bluff, on the James River, and that his cavalry had cut the railroad and telegraph south of Richmond on the Danville road : and the latter, the destruction of a depot of supplies at Dublin, West Virginia, and the breaking of New River Bridge on the Virginia and Tennessee Railroad. The next day news came from Sherman and Sheridan. Sherman had forced Johnston out of Dalton, Georgia, and was following him south. The report from Sheridan embraced his operations up to his passing the outer defences of Richmond. The prospect must now have been dismal in Richmond. The road and telegraph were cut between the capital and Lee. The roads and wires were cut in every direction from the rebel capital. Temporarily that city was cut off from all communication with the outside except by courier. This condition of affairs, however, was of but short duration. I wrote Halleck:

NEAR SPOTTSYLVANIA C.H.,
May 16, 1864, 8 A.M.

MAJOR -GENERAL HALLECK,
Washington, D. C.:

We have had five days almost constant rain without any prospect yet of it clearing up. The roads have now become so impassable that ambulances with wounded men can no longer run between here and Fredericksburg. All offensive operations necessarily cease until We can have twenty-four hours of dry weather. The army is in the best of spirits, and feel the greatest confidence of ultimate success.

You can assure the President and Secretary of War that the elements alone have suspended hostilities and that it is in no manner due to weakness or exhaustion on our part.

U. S. GRANT, Lieut.-General.

The condition of the roads was such that nothing was done on the 17th. But that night Hancock and Wright were to make a night march back to their old positions, and to make an assault at four o'clock in the morning. Lee got troops back in time to protect his old line, so the assault was unsuccessful. On this day (18th) the news was almost as discouraging to us as it had been two days before in the rebel capital. As stated above, Hancock's and Wright's corps had made an unsuccessful assault. News came that Sigel had been defeated at New Market, badly, and was retreating down the valley. Not two hours before, I had sent the inquiry to Halleck whether Sigel could not get to Staunton to stop supplies coming from there to Lee. I asked at once that Sigel might be relieved, and some one else put in his place. Hunter's name was suggested, and I heartily approved. Further news from Butler reported him driven from Drury's Bluff, but still in possession of the Petersburg road. Banks had been defeated in Louisiana, relieved, and Canby put in his place. This change of commander was not on my suggestion. All this news was very discouraging. All of it must have been known by the enemy before it was by me. In fact, the good news (for the enemy) must have been known to him at the moment I thought he was in despair, and his anguish had been already relieved when we were enjoying his supposed discomfiture. But this was no time for repining. I immediately gave orders for a movement by the left flank, on towards Richmond, to commence on the night of the 19th. I also asked Halleck to secure the co-operation of the navy in changing our base of supplies from Fredericksburg to Port Royal, on the Rappahannock.

Up to this time had received no reinforcements, except six' thousand raw troops under Brigadier-General Robert O. Tyler, just arrived. They had not yet joined their command, Hancock's corps, but were on our right. This corps had been brought to the rear of the centre, ready to move in any direction. Lee, probably suspecting some move on my part, and seeing our right entirely abandoned, moved Ewell's corps about five o'clock in the afternoon, with Early's as a reserve, to attack us in that quarter. Tyler had come up from Fredericksburg, and had been halted on the road to the right of our line, near Kitching's brigade of Warren's corps. Tyler received the attack with his raw troops, and they maintained their position, until reinforced, in a manner worthy of veterans.

Hancock was in a position to reinforce speedily, and was the soldier to do it without waiting to make dispositions. Birney was thrown to Tyler's right and Crawford to his left, with Gibbon as a reserve; and Ewell was whirled back speedily and with heavy loss.

Warren had been ordered to get on Ewell's flank and in his rear, to cut him off from his intrenchments. But his efforts were so feeble that under the cover of night Ewell got back with only the loss of a few hundred prisoners, besides his killed and wounded. The army being engaged until after dark, I rescinded the order for the march by our left flank that night.

As soon as it was discovered that the enemy were coming out to attack, I naturally supposed they would detach a force to destroy our trains. The withdrawal of Hancock from the right uncovered one road from Spottsylvania to Fredericksburg over which trains drew our supplies. This was guarded by a division of colored troops, commanded by General Ferrero, belonging to Burnside's corps. Ferrero was therefore promptly notified, and ordered to throw his cavalry pickets out to the south and be prepared to meet the enemy if he should come; if he had to retreat to do so towards Fredericksburg. The enemy did detach as expected, and captured twenty-five or thirty wagons which, however, were soon retaken.

In consequence of the disasters that had befallen us in the past few days, Lee could be reinforced largely, and I had no doubt he would be. Beauregard had come up from the south with troops to guard the Confederate capital when it was in danger. Butler being driven back, most of the troops could be sent to Lee. Hoke was no longer needed in North Carolina ; and Sigel's troops having gone back to Cedar Creek, whipped, many troops could be spared from the valley.

The Wilderness and Spottsylvania battles convinced me that we had more artillery than could ever be brought into action at any one time. It occupied much of the road in marching, and taxed the trains in bringing up forage. Artillery is very useful when it can be brought into action, but it is a very burdensome luxury where it cannot be used. Before leaving Spottsylvania, therefore, I sent back to the defences of Washington over one hundred pieces of artillery, with the horses and caissons. This relieved the roads over which we were to march of more than two hundred six-horse teams, and still left us more artillery than could be advantageously used. In fact, before reaching the James River I again reduced the artillery with the army largely.

I believed that, if one corps of the army was exposed on the road to Richmond, and at a distance from the main army, Lee would endeavor to attack the exposed corps before reinforcements could come up; in which case the main army could follow Lee up and attack him before he had time to intrench.

So I issued the following orders:

NEAR SPOTTSYLVANIA C. H., VA.,
May 18, 1864

MAJOR-GENERAL MEADE,
Commanding Army of the Potomac.

Before daylight tomorrow morning I propose to draw Hancock and Burnside from the position they now hold, and put Burnside to the left of Wright. Wright and Burnside should then force their way up as close to the enemy as they can get without a general engagement, or with a general engagement if the enemy will come out of their works to fight, and intrench. Hancock should march and take up a position as if in support of the two left corps. Tomorrow night, at twelve or one o'clock, he will be moved southeast with all his force and as much cavalry as can be given to him, to get as far towards Richmond on the line of the Fredericksburg Railroad as he can make, fighting the enemy in whatever force he can find him. If the enemy make a general move to meet this, they will be followed by the other three corps of the army, and attacked, if possible, before time is given to intrench.

Suitable directions will at once be given for all trains and surplus artillery to conform to this movement.

U. S. GRANT

On the 20th, Lee showing no signs of coming out of his lines, orders were renewed for a left-flank movement, to commence after night.

CHAPTER LIV

MOVEMENT BY THE LEFT FLANK - BATTLE OF NORTH ANNA - AN INCIDENT OF THE MARCH - MOVING ON RICHMOND - SOUTH OF THE PAMUNKEY - POSITION OF THE NATIONAL ARMY

WE were now to operate in a different country from any we had before seen in Virginia. The roads were wide and good, and the country well cultivated. No men were seen except those bearing arms, even the black man having been sent away. The country, however, was new to us, and we had neither guides nor maps to tell us where the roads were, or where they led to. Engineer and staff officers were put to the dangerous duty of supplying the place of both maps and guides. By reconnoitring they were enabled to locate the roads in the vicinity of each army corps. Our course was south, and we took all roads leading in that direction which would not separate the army too widely.

Hancock who had the lead had marched easterly to Guiney's Station, on the Fredericksburg Railroad, thence southerly to Bowling Green and Milford. He was at Milford by the night of the 21st. Here he met a detachment of Pickett's division coming from Richmond to reinforce Lee. They were speedily driven away, and several hundred captured. Warren followed on the morning of the 21st, and reached Guiney's Station that night without molestation. Burnside and Wright were retained at Spottsylvania to keep up the appearance of an intended assault, and to hold Lee, if possible, while Hancock and Warren should get start enough to interpose between him and Richmond.

Lee had now a superb opportunity to take the initiative either by attacking Wright and Burnside alone, or by following by the Telegraph Road and striking Hancock's and Warren's corps, or even Hancock's alone, before reinforcements could come up. But he did not avail himself of either opportunity. He seemed really to be misled as to my designs; but moved by his interior line -the Telegraph Road- to make sure of

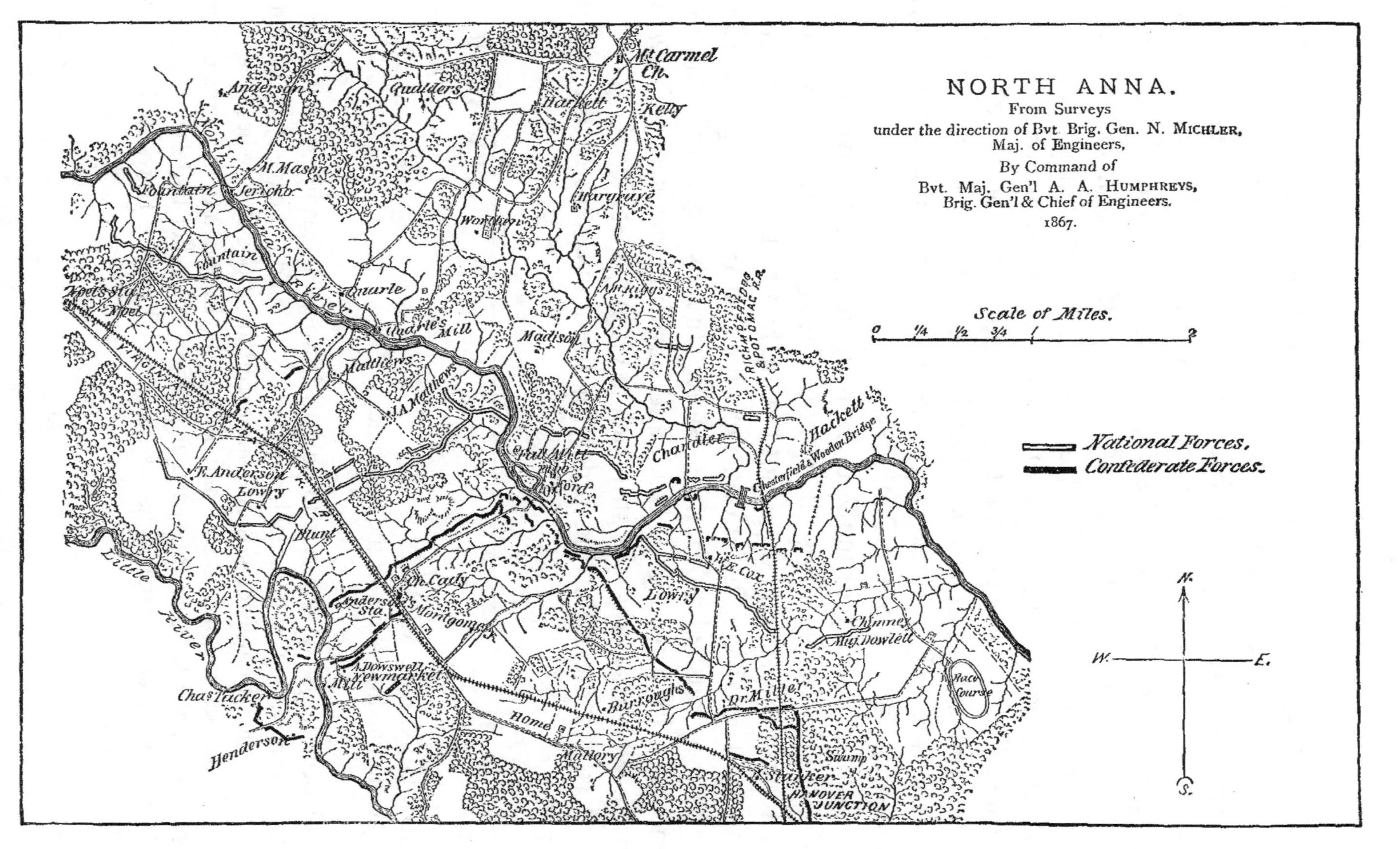

NORTH ANNA.
From Surveys
under the direction of Bvt. Brig. Gen. N. MICHLER,
Maj. of Engineers,
By Command of
Bvt. Maj. Gen'l A. A. HUMPHREYS,
Brig. Gen'l & Chief of Engineers.
1867.
Scale of Miles.
0   1/4   1/2   3/4   1   2
National Forces.
Confederate Forces.
N.
W.   E.
S.
Mt Carmel Ch.
Anderson
Gudders
Hackett
Kelly
M. Mason
Mountain
Jericho
Worsham
Hargrave
Fountain
North Anna River
Quarle
Noel's Sta.
Aper
VIRGINIA
Quarle's Mill
Madison
J. Riggs
Matthews
J. A. Matthews
RICHM'D FRED'BG & POTOMAC R.R.
Hackett
Chandler
Gun Mill
Ox Ford
Chesterfield & Wooden Bridge
J. E. Anderson
Lowry
Hunt
Little River
Dr. Cody
Anderson's Sta.
Montgomy
W. E. Cox
Lowry
Chimney
Maj. Dowlell
Race Course
A. Dowswell
Newmarket Mill
Burroughs
Dr. Miller
Cha's Tucker
Henderson
Home
Mallory
Swamp
Stamper
HANOVER JUNCTION

keeping between his capital and the Army of the Potomac. He never again had such an opportunity of dealing a heavy blow.

The evening of the 21st Burnside, 9th corps, moved out followed by Wright, 6th corps. Burnside was to take the Telegraph Road; but finding Stanard's Ford, over the Po, fortified and guarded, he turned east to the road taken by Hancock and Warren without an attempt to dislodge the enemy. The night of the 21st I had my headquarters near the 6th corps, at Guiney's Station, and the enemy's cavalry was between us and Hancock. There was a slight attack on Burnside's and Wright's corps as they moved out of their lines; but it was easily repulsed. The object probably was only to make sure that we were not leaving a force to follow upon the rear of the Confederates.

By the morning of the 22d Burnside and Wright were at Guiney's Station. Hancock's corps had now been marching and fighting continuously for several days, not having had rest even at night much of the time. They were, therefore, permitted to rest during the 22d. But Warren was pushed to Harris's Store, directly west of Milford, and connected with it by a good road, and Burnside was sent to New Bethel Church. Wright's corps was still back at Guiney's Station.

I issued the following order for the movement of the troops the next day:

NEW BETHEL, VA.,
May 22, 1864.

MAJOR-GENERAL MEADE,
    Commanding Army of the Potomac.

Direct corps commanders to hold their troops in readiness to march at five A.M. tomorrow. At that hour each command will send out cavalry and infantry on all roads to their front leading south, and ascertain, if possible, where the enemy is. If beyond the South Anna, the 5th and 6th corps will march to the forks of the road, where one branch leads to Beaver Dam Station, the other to Jericho Bridge, then south by roads reaching the Anna, as near to and east of Hawkins Creek as they can be found.

The ad corps will move to Chesterfield Ford. The 9th corps will be directed to move at the same time to Jericho Bridge. The map only shows two roads for the four corps to march upon, but, no doubt, by the use of plantation roads, and pressing in guides, others can be found, to give one for each corps.

The troops will follow their respective reconnoitring parties. The trains will be moved at the same time to Milford Station.

Headquarters will follow the 9th corps.

U.S. GRANT,
Lieut.-General.

Warren's corps was moved from Harris's Store to Jericho Ford, Wright's following. Warren arrived at the ford early in the afternoon, and by five o'clock effected a crossing under the protection of sharpshooters. The men had to wade in water up to their waists. As soon as enough troops were over to guard the ford, pontoons were laid and the artillery and the rest of the troops crossed. The line formed was almost perpendicular to the course of the river, Crawford on the left, next to the river, Griffin in the centre, and Cutler on the right. Lee was found intrenched along the front of their line. The whole of Hill's corps was sent against Warren's right before it had got in position. A brigade of Cutler's division was driven back, the enemy following, but assistance coming up the enemy was in turn driven back into his trenches with heavy loss in killed and wounded, with about five hundred prisoners left in our hands. By night Wright's corps was up ready to reinforce Warren.

On the 23rd Hancock's corps was moved to the wooden bridge which spans the North Anna River just west of where the Fredericksburg Railroad crosses. It was near night when the troops arrived. They found the bridge guarded, with troops intrenched, on the north side. Hancock sent two brigades, Egans's and Pierce's, to the right and left, and when properly disposed they charged simultaneously. The bridge was carried quickly, the enemy retreating over it so hastily that many were shoved into the river, and some of them were drowned. Several hundred prisoners were captured. The hour was so late that Hancock did not cross until next morning.

Burnside's corps was moved by a middle road running between those described above, and which strikes the North Anna at Ox Ford, midway between Telegraph Road and Jericho Ford. The hour of its arrival was too late to cross that night.

On the 24th Hancock's corps crossed to the south side of the river without opposition, and formed line facing nearly west. The railroad in rear was taken possession of and destroyed as far as possible. Wright's corps crossed at Jericho early the same day, and took position to the right of Warren's corps, extending south of the Virginia Central Railroad. This road was torn up for a considerable distance to the rear (west), the ties burned, and the rails bent and twisted by heating them over the burning ties. It was found, however, that Burnside's corps could not cross at Ox Ford. Lee had taken a position with his centre on the river at this point, with the two wings thrown back, his line making an acute angle where it overlooked the river.

Before the exact position of the whole of Lee's line was accurately known, I directed Hancock and Warren each to send a brigade to Ox Ford by the south side of the river. They found the enemy too strong to justify a serious attack. A third ford was found between Ox Ford and Jericho. Burnside was directed to cross a division over this ford, and to send one division to Hancock. Crittenden was crossed by this newly discovered ford, and formed up the river to connect with Crawford's left. Potter joined Hancock by way of the wooden bridge. Crittenden had a severe engagement with some of Hill's corps on his crossing the river, and lost heavily. When joined to Warren's corps he was no further molested. Burnside still guarded Ox Ford from the north side.

Lee now had his entire army south of the North Anna. Our lines covered his front, with the six miles separating the two wings guarded by but a single division. To get from one wing to the other the river would have to be crossed twice. Lee could reinforce any part of his line from all points of it in a very short march; or could concentrate the whole of it wherever he might choose to assault. We were, for the time, practically two armies besieging.

Lee had been reinforced, and was being reinforced, largely. About this time the very troops whose coming I had predicted, had arrived or were coming in. Pickett with a full division from Richmond was up; Hoke from North Carolina had come with a brigade; and Breckinridge was there: in all probably not less than fifteen thousand men. But he did not attempt to drive us from the field.

On the 22d or 23d I received dispatches from Washington saying that Sherman had taken Kingston, crossed the Etowah River and was advancing. into Georgia.

I was seated at the time on the porch of a fine plantation house waiting for Burnside's corps to pass. Meade and his staff, besides my own staff, were with me. The lady of the house, a Mrs. Tyler, and an elderly lady, were present. Burnside seeing us, came up on the porch, his big spurs and saber rattling as he walked. He touched his hat politely to the ladies, and remarked that he supposed they had never seen so many "live Yankees" before in their lives. The elderly lady spoke up promptly saying, "Oh yes, I have; many more" "Where? "said Burnside." In Richmond." Prisoners, of course, was understood.

I read my dispatch aloud, when it was received. This threw the younger lady into tears. I found the information she had received (and I suppose it was the information generally in circulation through the South) was that Lee was driving us from the State in the most demoralized condition, and that in the Southwest our troops were but little better than prisoners of war. Seeing our troops moving south was ocular proof that a part of her information was incorrect, and she asked me if my news from Sherman was true. I assured her that there was no doubt about it. I left a guard to protect the house from intrusion until the troops should have all passed, and assured her that if her husband was in hiding she could bring him in and he should be protected also. But I presume he was in the Confederate army.

On the 25th I gave orders, through Halleck, to Hunter, who had relieved Sigel, to move up the Valley of Virginia, cross over the Blue Ridge to Charlottesville and go as far as Lynchburg if possible, living upon the country and cutting the railroads and canal as he went. After doing this he could find his way back to his base, or join me.

On the same day news was received that Lee was falling back on Richmond. This proved not to be true. But we could do nothing where we were unless Lee would assume the offensive. I determined, therefore, to draw out of our present position and make one more effort to get between him and Richmond. I had no expectation now, however, of succeeding in this; but I did expect to hold him far enough west to enable me to reach the James River high up. Sheridan was now again with the Army of the Potomac.

On the 26th I informed the government at Washington of the position of the two armies; of the reinforcements the enemy had received; of the move I proposed to make; * and directed that our base of supplies should be shifted to White House, on the Pamunkey.

---

*QUARLES' MILLS, VA.,
May 26, 1864.

MAJOR-GENERAL HALLECK,
    Washington, D. C.

The relative position of the two armies is now as follows: Lee's right rests on a swamp east of the Richmond and Fredericksburg road and south of the North Anna, his centre on the river at Ox Ford, and his left at Little River with the crossings of Little River guarded as far up as we have gone. Hancock with his corps and one division of the 9th corps crossed at Chesterfield Ford and covers the right wing of Lee's army. One division of the 9th corps is on the north bank of the Anna at Ox Ford, with bridges above and below at points nearest to it where both banks are held by us, so that it could reinforce either wing of our army with equal facility. The 5th and 6th corps with one division of the 9th corps run from the south bank of the Anna from a short distance above Ox Ford to Little River, and parallel with and near to the enemy.

To make a direct attack from either wing would cause a slaughter of our men that even success would not justify. To turn the enemy by his right, between the two Annas, is impossible on account of the swamp upon which his right rests. To turn him by the left leaves Little River, New Found River and South Anna River, all of them streams presenting considerable obstacles to the movement of our army, to be crossed. I have determined therefore to turn the enemy's right by crossing at or near Hanover Town. This crosses all three streams at once, and leaves us still where we can draw supplies.

During the last night the teams and artillery not in position, belonging to the right wing of our army, and one division of that wing were quietly withdrawn to the north bank of the river and moved down to the rear of the left. As soon as it is dark this division with most of the cavalry will commence a forced march for Hanover Town to seize and hold the crossings. The balance of the right wing will withdraw at the same hour, and follow as rapidly as possible. The left wing will also withdraw from the south bank of the river tonight and follow in rear of the right wing.

Lee's army is really whipped. The prisoners we now take show it, and the action of his army shows it unmistakably. A battle with them outside of intrenchments cannot be had. Our men feel that they have gained the morale over the enemy, and attack him with confidence. I may be mistaken, but I feel that our success over Lee's army is already assured. The promptness and rapidity with which you have forwarded reinforcements has contributed largely to the feeling of confidence inspired in our men, and to break down that of the enemy.

We are destroying all the rails we can on the Central and Fredericksburg roads. I want to leave a gap on the roads north of Richmond so big that to get a single track they will have to import rail from elsewhere.

Even if a crossing is not effected at Hanover Town it will probably be necessary for us to move on down the Pamunkey until a crossing is effected. I think it advisable therefore to change our base of supplies from Port Royal to the White House. I wish you would direct this change at once, and also direct Smith to put the railroad bridge there in condition for crossing troops and artillery and leave men to hold it.

U.S. GRANT,
Lieut.-General.

The wagon train and guards moved directly from Port Royal to White House. Supplies moved around by water, guarded by the navy. Orders had previously been sent, through Halleck, for Butler to send Smith's corps to White House. This order was repeated on the 25th, with directions that they should be landed on the north side of the Pamunkey, and marched until they joined the Army of the Potomac.

It was a delicate move to get the right wing of the Army of the Potomac from its position south of the North Anna in the presence of the enemy. To accomplish it I issued the following order:

QUARLES' MILLS, VA.,
May 25, 1864.

MAJOR GENERAL MEADE,
    Commanding A. P.

Direct Generals Warren and Wright to withdraw all their teams and artillery, not in position, to the north side of the river tomorrow. Send that belonging to General Wright's corps as far on the road to Hanover Town as it can go, without attracting attention to the fact. Send with it Wright's best division or division under his ablest commander. Have their places filled up in the line so if possible the enemy will not notice their withdrawal. Send the cavalry tomorrow afternoon, or as much of it as you may deem necessary, to watch and seize, if they can, Littlepage's Bridge and Taylor's Ford, and to remain on one or other side of the river at these points until the infantry and artillery all pass. As soon as it is dark tomorrow night start the division which you withdraw first from Wright's corps to make a forced march to Hanover Town, taking with them no teams to impede their march. At the same time this division starts commence withdrawing all of the 5th and 6th corps from the south side of the river, and march them for the same place. The two divisions of the 9th corps not now with Hancock, may be moved down the north bank of the river where they will be handy to support Hancock if necessary, or will be that much on their road to follow the 5th and 6th corps. Hancock should hold his command in readiness to follow as soon as the way is clear for him. Tomorrow it will leave nothing for him to do, but as soon as he can he should get all his teams and spare artillery on the road or roads which he will have to take. As soon as the troops reach Hanover Town they should get possession of all the crossings they can in that neighborhood. I think it would be well to make a heavy cavalry demonstration on the enemy's left, tomorrow afternoon, also.

U.S. GRANT,
Lieut.-General.

Wilson's division of cavalry was brought up from the left and moved by our right south to Little River. Here he manuvred to give the impression that we were going to attack the left flank of Lee's army.

Under cover of night our right wing was withdrawn to the north side of the river, Lee being completely deceived by Wilson's feint. On the afternoon of the 26th Sheridan -moved, sending Gregg's and Torbert's cavalry to Taylor's and Littlepage's fords towards Hanover. As soon as it was dark both divisions moved quietly to Hanover Ferry, leaving small guards behind to keep up the impression that crossings were to be attempted in the morning. Sheridan was followed by a division of infantry under General Russell. On the morning of the 2.th the crossing was effected with but little loss, the enemy losing thirty or forty, taken prisoners. Thus a position was secured south of the Pamunkey.

Russell stopped at the crossing while the cavalry pushed on to Hanover Town. Here Barringer's, formerly Gordon's, brigade of rebel cavalry was encountered, but it was speedily driven away.

Warren's and Wright's corps were moved by the rear of Burnside's and Hancock's corps. When out of the way these latter corps followed, leaving pickets confronting the enemy. Wilson's cavalry followed last, watching all the fords until everything had re-crossed; then taking up the pontoons and destroying other bridges, became the rear guard.

Two roads were traversed by the troops in this move. The one nearest to and north of the North Anna and Pamunkey was taken by Wright, followed by Hancock. Warren, followed by Burnside, moved by a road farther north, and longer. The trains moved by a road still farther north, and had to travel a still greater distance. All the troops that had crossed the Pamunkey on the morning of the 27th remained quiet during the rest of the day, while the troops north of that stream marched to reach the crossing that had been secured for them.

Lee had evidently been deceived by our movement from North Anna; for on the morning of the 27th he telegraphed to Richmond: "Enemy crossed to north side, and cavalry and infantry crossed at Hanover Town." The troops that had then crossed left his front the night of the 25th.

The country we were now in was a difficult one to move troops over. The streams were numerous, deep and sluggish, sometimes spreading out into swamps grown up with impenetrable growths of trees and underbrush. The banks were generally low and marshy, making the streams difficult to approach except where there were roads and bridges.

Hanover Town is about twenty miles from Richmond. There are two roads leading there; the most direct and shortest one crossing the Chickahominy at Meadow Bridge, near the Virginia Central Railroad, the second going by New and Old Cold Harbor. A few miles out from Hanover Town there is a third road by way of Mechanicsville to Richmond. New Cold Harbor was important to us because while there we both covered the roads back to White House (where our supplies came from), and the roads southeast over which we would have to pass to get to the James River below the Richmond defences.

On the morning of the 28th the army made an early start, and by noon all had crossed except Burnside's corps. This was left on the north side temporarily to guard the large wagon train. A line was at once formed extending south from the river, Wright's corps on the right, Hancock's in the centre, and Warren's on the left, ready to meet the enemy if he should come.

At the same time Sheridan was directed to reconnoitre towards Mechanicsville to find Lee's position. At Hawe's Shop, just where the middle road leaves the direct road to Richmond, he encountered the Confederate cavalry dismounted and partially intrenched. Gregg attacked with his division, but was unable to move the enemy. In the evening Custer came up with a brigade. The attack was now renewed, the cavalry dismounting and charging as infantry. This time the assault was successful, both sides losing a considerable number of men. But our troops had to bury the dead, and found that more Confederate than Union soldiers had been killed. The position was easily held, because our infantry was near.

On the 29th a reconnaissance was made in force, to find the position of Lee. Wright's corps pushed to Hanover Court House. Hancock's corps pushed toward Totopotomoy Creek; Warren's corps to the left on the Shady Grove Church Road, while Burnside was held in reserve. Our advance was pushed forward three miles on the left with but little fighting. There was now an appearance of a movement past our left flank, and Sheridan was sent to meet it.

On the 30th Hancock moved to the Totopotomoy, where he found the enemy strongly fortified. Wright was moved to the right of Hancock's corps, and Burnside was brought forward and crossed, taking position to the left of Hancock. Warren moved up near Huntley Corners on the Shady Grove Church Road. There was some skirmishing along the centre, and in the evening Early attacked Warren with some vigor, driving him back at first, and threatening to turn our left flank. As the best means of reinforcing the left, Hancock was ordered to attack in his front. He carried and held the rifle-pits. While this was going on Warren got his men up, repulsed Early, and drove him more than a mile.

On this day I wrote to Halleck ordering all the pontoons in Washington to be sent to City Point. In the evening news was received of the arrival of Smith with his corps at White House. I notified Meade, in writing, as follows:

NEAR HAWES' SHOP, VA.,
6.40 P.M., May 30, 1664.

MAJOR - GENERAL MEADE,
Commanding A.P.

General Smith will debark his force at the White House tonight and start up the south bank of the Pamunkey at an early hour, probably at 3 A.M. in the morning. It is not improbable that the enemy, being aware of Smith's movement, will be feeling to get on our left flank for the purpose of cutting him off, or by a dash to crush him and get back before we are aware of it. Sheridan ought to be notified to watch the enemy's movements well out towards Cold Harbor, and also on the Mechanicsville road. Wright should be got well massed on Hancock's right, so that, if it becomes necessary, he can take the place of the latter readily whilst troops are being thrown east of the Totopotomoy if necessary.

I want Sheridan to send a cavalry force of at least half a brigade, if not a whole brigade, at 5 A.M. in the morning, to communicate with Smith and to return with him. I will send orders for Smith by the messenger you send to Sheridan with his orders.

U.S. GRANT.

I also notified Smith of his danger, and the precautions that would be taken to protect him.

The night of the 30th Lee's position was substantially from Atlee's Station on the Virginia Central Railroad south and east to the vicinity of Cold Harbor. Ours was: The left of Warren's corps was on the Shady Grove Road, extending to the Mechanicsville Road and about three miles south of the Totopotomoy. Burnside to his right, then Hancock, and Wright on the extreme right, extending towards Hanover Court House, six miles southeast of it. Sheridan with two divisions of cavalry was watching our left front towards Cold Harbor. Wilson with his division on our right was sent to get on the Virginia Central Railroad and destroy it as far back as possible. He got possession of Hanover Court House the next day after a skirmish with Young's cavalry brigade. The enemy attacked Sheridan's pickets, but reinforcements were sent up and the attack was speedily repulsed and the enemy followed some distance towards Cold Harbor.

CHAPTER LV

ADVANCE ON COLD HARBOR - AN ANECDOTE OF THE WAR - BATTLE OF COLD HARBOR - CORRESPONDENCE WITH LEE - RETROSPECTIVE

ON the 31st Sheridan advanced to near Old Cold Harbor. He found it intrenched and occupied by cavalry and infantry. A hard fight ensued but the place was carried. The enemy well knew the importance of Cold Harbor to us, and seemed determined that we should not hold it. He returned with such a large force that Sheridan was about withdrawing without making any effort to hold it against such odds; but about the time he commenced the evacuation he received orders to hold the place at all hazards, until reinforcements could be sent to him. He speedily turned the rebel works to face against them and placed his men in position for defence. Night came on before the enemy was ready for assault.

Wright's corps was ordered early in the evening to march directly to Cold Harbor passing by the rear of the army. It was expected to arrive by daylight or before; but the night was dark and the distance great, so that it was nine o'clock the 1st of June before it reached its destination. Before the arrival of Wright the enemy had made two assaults on Sheridan, both of which were repulsed with heavy loss to the enemy. Wright's corps coming up, there was no further assault on Cold Harbor.

Smith, who was coming up from White House, was also directed to march directly to Cold Harbor, and was expected early on the morning of the 1st of June; but by some blunder the order which reached Smith directed him to Newcastle instead of Cold Harbor. Through this blunder Smith did not reach his destination until three o'clock in the afternoon, and then with tired and worn out men from their long and dusty march. He landed twelve thousand five hundred men from Butler's command, but a division was left at White House temporarily and many men had fallen out of ranks in their long march.

Before the removal of Wright's corps from our right, after dark on the 31st, the two lines, Federal and Confederate, were so close together at that point that either side could detect directly any movement made by the other. Finding at daylight that Wright had left his front, Lee evidently divined that he had gone to our left. At all events, soon after light on the 1st of June Anderson, who commanded the corps on Lee's left, was seen moving along Warren's front. Warren was ordered to attack him vigorously in flank, while Wright was directed to move out and get on his front. Warren fired his artillery at the enemy; but lost so much time in making ready that the enemy got by, and at three o'clock he reported the enemy was strongly intrenched in his front, and besides his lines were so long that he had no mass of troops to move with. He seemed to have forgotten that lines in rear of an army hold themselves while their defenders are fighting in their front. Wright reconnoitred some distance to his front: but the enemy finding Old Cold Harbor already taken had halted and fortified some distance west.

By six o'clock in the afternoon Wright and Smith were ready to make an assault. In front of both the ground was clear for several hundred yards, and then became wooded. Both charged across this open space and into the wood, capturing and holding the first line of rifle-pits of the enemy, and also capturing seven or eight hundred prisoners.

While this was going on, the enemy charged Warren three separate times with vigor, but were repulsed each time with loss. There was no officer more capable, nor one more prompt in acting, than Warren when the enemy forced him to it. There was also an attack upon Hancock's and Burnside's corps at the same time; but it was feeble and probably only intended to relieve Anderson who was being pressed by Wright and Smith.

During the night the enemy made frequent attacks with the view of dispossessing us of the important position we had gained, but without effecting their object.

Hancock was moved from his place in line during the night and ordered to the left of Wright. I expected to take the offensive on the

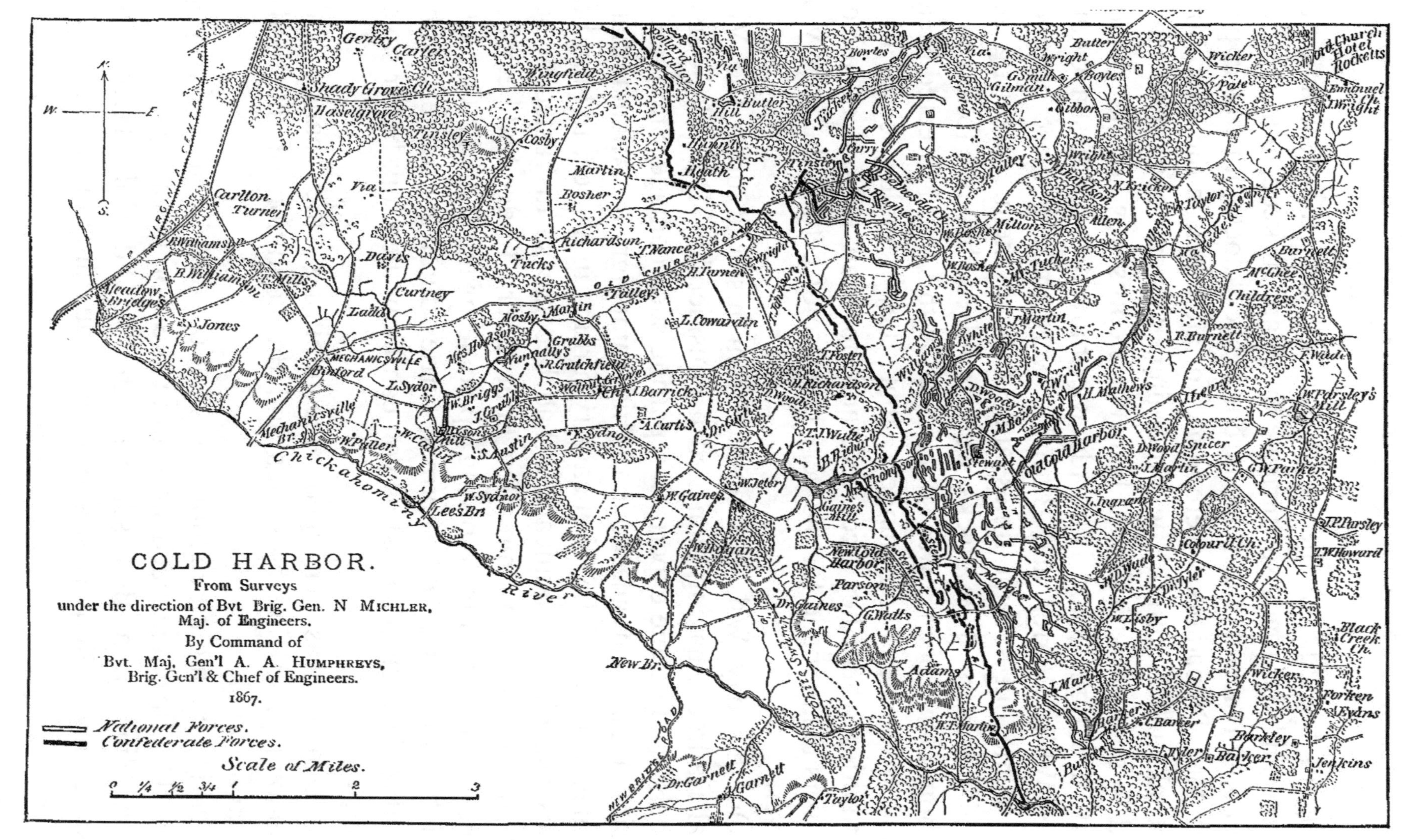

COLD HARBOR.
From Surveys
under the direction of Bvt. Brig. Gen. N. MICHLER,
Maj. of Engineers.
By Command of
Bvt. Maj. Gen'l A. A. HUMPHREYS,
Brig. Gen'l & Chief of Engineers.
1867.
National Forces.
Confederate Forces.
Scale of Miles.
0 ¼ ½ ¾ 1   2   3

morning of the 2d, but the night was so dark, the heat and dust so excessive and the roads so intricate and hard to keep, that the head of column only reached Old Cold Harbor at six o'clock, but was in position at 7.30 A.M. Preparations were made for an attack in the afternoon, but did not take place until the next morning. Warren's corps was moved to the left to connect with Smith: Hancock's corps was got into position to the left of Wright's, and Burnside was moved to Bethesda Church in reserve. While Warren and Burnside were making these changes the enemy came out several times and attacked them, capturing several hundred prisoners. The attacks were repulsed, but not followed up as they should have been. I was so annoyed at this that I directed Meade to instruct his corps commanders that they should seize all such opportunities when they occurred, and not wait for orders, all of our maneuvers being made for the very purpose of getting the enemy out of his cover.

On this day Wilson returned from his raid upon the Virginia Central Railroad, having damaged it considerably. But, like ourselves, the rebels had become experts in repairing such damage. Sherman, in his memoirs, relates an anecdote of his campaign to Atlanta that well illustrates this point. The rebel cavalry lurking in his rear to burn bridges and obstruct his communications had become so disgusted at hearing trains go whistling by within a few hours after a bridge had been burned, that they proposed to try blowing up some of the tunnels. One of them said, I No use, boys, Old Sherman carries duplicate tunnels with him, and will replace them as fast as you can blow them up; better save your powder."

Sheridan was engaged reconnoitring the banks of the Chickahominy, to find crossings and the condition of the roads. He reported favorably.

During the night Lee moved his left up to make his line correspond to ours. His lines extended now from the Totopotomoy to New Cold Harbor. Mine from Bethesda Church by Old Cold Harbor to the Chickahominy, with a division of cavalry guarding our right. An assault was ordered for the 3d, to be made mainly by the corps of Hancock, Wright and Smith; but Warren and Burnside were to support it by threatening Lee's left, and to attack with great earnestness if he should either reinforce more threatened points by drawing from that quarter or if a favorable opportunity should present itself.

The corps commanders were to select the points in their respective fronts where they would make their assaults. The move was to commence at half-past four in the morning. Hancock sent Barlow and Gibbon forward at the appointed hour, with Birney as a reserve. Barlow pushed forward with great vigor, under a heavy fire of both artillery and musketry, through thickets and swamps. Not withstanding all the resistance of the enemy and the natural obstructions to overcome, he carried a position occupied by the enemy outside their main line where the road makes a deep cut through a bank affording as good a shelter for troops as if it had been made for that purpose. Three pieces of artillery had been captured here, and several hundred prisoners. The guns were immediately turned against the men who had just been using them. No

---

NEAR COLD HARBOR, JUNE 3, 1864, 7 A.M.

MAJOR-GENERAL MEADE,
    Commanding A. P.

The moment it becomes certain that an assault cannot succeed, suspend the offensive; but when one does succeed, push it vigorously and if necessary pile in troops at the successful point from wherever they can be taken. I shall go to where you are in the course of an hour.

U.S. GRANT,
Lieut.-General.

---

assistance coming to him, he (Barlow) intrenched under fire and continued to hold his place. Gibbon was not so fortunate in his front. He found the ground over which he had to pass cut up with deep ravines and a morass difficult to cross. But his men struggled on until some of them got up to the very parapet covering the enemy. Gibbon gained ground much nearer the enemy than that which he left, and here he intrenched and held fast.

Wright's corps moving in two lines captured the outer rifle-pits in their front, but accomplished nothing more. Smith's corps also gained the outer rifle-pits in its front. The ground over which this corps (18th) had to move was the most exposed of any over which charges were made. An open plain intervened between the contending forces at this point, which was exposed both to a direct and a cross fire. Smith, however, finding a ravine running towards his front, sufficiently deep to protect men in it from cross fire, and somewhat from a direct fire, put Martindale's division in it, and with Brooks supporting him on the left and Devens on the right succeeded in gaining the outer probably picket rifle-pits. Warren and Burnside also advanced and gained ground which brought the whole army on one line.

This assault cost us heavily and probably without benefit to compensate: but the enemy was not cheered by the occurrence sufficiently to induce him to take the offensive. In fact, nowhere after the battle of the Wilderness did Lee show any disposition to leave his defences far behind him.

Fighting was substantially over by half past seven in the morning. At eleven o'clock I started to visit all the corps commanders to see for myself the different positions gained and to get their opinion of the practicability of doing anything more in their respective fronts.

Hancock gave the opinion that in his front the enemy was too strong to make any further assault promise success. Wright thought he could gain the lines of the enemy, but it would require the co-operation of Hancock's and Smith's corps. Smith thought a lodgment possible, but was not sanguine: Burnside thought something could be done in his front, but Warren differed. I concluded, therefore, to make no more assaults, and a little after twelve directed in the following letter that all offensive action should cease.

COLD HARBOR, June 3, 1864.-12:30 P.M.

MAJOR -GENERAL MEADE,
    Commanding A. P.

The opinion of corps commanders not being sanguine of success in case an assault is ordered, you may direct a suspension of farther advance for the present. Hold our most advanced positions and strengthen them. Whilst on the defensive our line may be contracted from the right if practicable. Reconnaissances should be made in front of every corps and advances made to advantageous positions by regular approaches. To aid the expedition under General Hunter it is necessary that we should detain all the army now with Lee until the former gets well on his way to Lynchburg. To do this effectually it will be better to keep the enemy out of the intrenchments of Richmond than to have them go back there.

Wright and Hancock should be ready to assault in case the enemy should break through General Smith's lines, and all should be ready to resist an assault.

U.S. GRANT,
Lieutenant-General.

The remainder of the day was spent in strengthening the line we now held. By night we were as strong against Lee as he was against us.

During the night the enemy quitted our right front, abandoning some of their wounded, and without burying their dead. These we were able to care for. But there were many dead and wounded men between the lines of the contending forces, which were now close together, who could not be cared for without a cessation of hostilities.

So I wrote the following:

COLD HARBOR, VA., June 5, 1864.

GENERAL R.E. LEE,

Commanding Confederate Army.

It is reported to me that there are wounded men, probably of both armies, now lying exposed and suffering between the lines occupied respectively by the two armies. Humanity would dictate that some provision should be made to provide against such hardships. I would propose, therefore, that hereafter, when no battle is raging, either party be authorized to send to any point between the pickets or skirmish lines, unarmed men bearing litters to pick up their dead or wounded, without being fired upon by the other party. Any other method, equally fair to both parties, you may propose for meeting the end desired will be accepted by me.

U.S. GRANT,
Lieut.-General.

Lee replied that he feared such an arrangement would lead to misunderstanding, and proposed that in future, when either party wished to remove their dead and wounded, a flag of truce be sent. I answered this immediately by saying:

COLD HARBOR, VA., June 6, 1864.

GENERAL R. E. LEE,
        Commanding Army of N. Va.

"Your communication of yesterday's date is received. I will send immediately, as you propose, to collect the dead and wounded between the lines of the two armies, and will also instruct that you be allowed to do the same. I propose that the time for doing this be between the hours of 12 M. and 3 P.M. today. I will direct all parties going out to bear a white flag, and not to attempt to go beyond where we have dead or wounded, and not beyond or on ground occupied by your troops.

U.S. GRANT,
Lieut-General.

Lee's response was that he could not consent to the burial of the dead and removal of the wounded in the way I proposed, but when either party desired such permission it should be asked for by flag of truce; and he had directed that any parties I may have sent out, as mentioned in my letter, to be turned back. I answered:

163

COLD HARBOR. VA, June 6, 1864.

GENERAL R.E. LEE,
      Commanding Army, N. Va.

The knowledge that wounded men are now suffering from want of attention, between the two armies, compels me to ask a suspension of hostilities for sufficient time to collect them in, say two hours. Permit me to say that the hours you may fix upon for this will be agreeable to me, and the same privilege will be extended to such parties as you may wish to send out on the same duty without further application.

U.S. GRANT,
Lieut.-General.

Lee acceded to this; but delays in transmitting the correspondence brought it to the 7th of June, forty-eight hours after it commenced, before parties were got out to collect the men left upon the field. In the meantime all but two of the wounded had died. And I wrote to Lee:

COLD HARBOR, VA., June 7, 1864.
10.10 A.M.

GENERAL. R.E. LEE,
      Commanding Army of N. Va.

I regret that your note of seven P.M. yesterday should have been received at the nearest corps headquarters, to where it was delivered, after the hour which had been given for the removal of the dead and wounded had expired; 10.45 P.M. was the hour at which it was received at corps headquarters, and between eleven and twelve it reached my headquarters. As a consequence, it was not understood by the troops of this army that there was a cessation of hostilities for the purpose of collecting the dead and wounded, and none were collected. Two officers and six men of the 8th and 25th North Carolina Regts., who were out in search of the bodies of officers of their respective regiments, were captured and brought into our lines, owing to this want of understanding. I regret this, but will state that as soon as I learned the fact, I directed that they should not be held as prisoners, but must be returned to their commands. These officers and men having been carelessly brought through our lines to the rear, I have not determined whether they will be sent back the way they came, or whether they will be sent by some other route.

Regretting that all my efforts for alleviating the sufferings of wounded men left upon the battlefield have been rendered nugatory, I remain, &c.,

U.S. GRANT,
Lieutenant-General.

I have always regretted that the last assault at Cold Harbor was ever made. I might say the same thing of the assault of the 22d of May, 1863, at Vicksburg. At Cold Harbor no advantage whatever was gained to compensate for the heavy loss we sustained. Indeed, the advantages other than those of relative losses were on the Confederate side. Before that, the Army of Northern Virginia seemed to have acquired a wholesome regard for the courage, endurance, and soldierly qualities generally of the Army of the Potomac. They no longer wanted to fight them "one Confederate to five Yanks." Indeed, they seemed to have given up any idea of gaining any advantage of their antagonist in the open field. They had come to much prefer breastworks in their front to the Army of the Potomac. This charge seemed to revive their hopes temporarily; but it was of short duration. The effect upon the Army of the Potomac was the reverse. When we reached the James River, however, all effects of the battle of Cold Harbor seemed to have disappeared.

There was more justification for the assault at Vicksburg. We were in a Southern climate, at the beginning of the hot season. The Army of the Tennessee had won five successive victories over the garrison of Vicksburg in the three preceding weeks. They had driven a portion of that army from Port Gibson with considerable loss, after having flanked them out of their stronghold at Grand Gulf. They had attacked another portion of the same army at Raymond, more than fifty miles farther in the interior of the State, and driven them back into Jackson with great loss in killed, wounded, captured and missing, besides loss of large and small arms: they had captured the capital of the State of Mississippi, with a large amount of materials of war and manufactures. Only a few days before, they had beaten the enemy then penned up in the town first at Champion's Hill, next at Big Black River Bridge, inflicting upon him a loss of fifteen thousand or more men (including those cut off from returning) besides large losses in arms and ammunition. The Army of the Tennessee had come to believe that they could beat their antagonist under any circumstances. There was no telling how long a regular siege might last. As I have stated, it was the beginning of the hot season in a Southern climate. There was no telling what the casualties might be among Northern troops working and living in trenches, drinking surface water filtered through rich vegetation, under a tropical sun. If Vicksburg could have been carried in May, it would not only have saved the army the risk it ran of a greater danger than from the bullets of the enemy, but it would have given us a splendid army, well equipped and officered, to operate else where with. These are reasons justifying the assault. The only benefit we gained -and it was a slight one for so great a sacrifice- was that the men worked cheerfully in the trenches after that, being satisfied with digging the enemy out. Had the assault not been made, I have no doubt that the majority of those engaged in the siege of Vicksburg would have believed that had we assaulted it would have proven successful, and would have saved life, health and comfort.

CHAPTER LVI

LEFT FLANK MOVEMENT ACROSS THE CHICKAHOMINY AND JAMES - GENERAL LEE-VISIT TO BUTLER - THE MOVEMENT ON PETERSBURG - THE INVESTMENT OF PETERSBURG

LEE'S position was now so near Richmond, and the intervening swamps of the Chickahominy so great an obstacle to the movement of troops in the face of an enemy, that I determined to make my next left flank move carry the Army of the Potomac south of the James River.* Preparations for this were promptly commenced. The move was a hazardous one to make: the Chickahominy River, with its marshy and heavily timbered approaches, had to be crossed; all the bridges over it east of Lee were destroyed; the enemy had a shorter line and better roads to travel on to confront me in crossing; more than fifty miles intervened

---

*COLD HARBOR, June 5, 1864.

MAJOR-GENERAL HALLECK,
Chief of Staff of the Army, Washington, D. C.

A full survey of all the ground satisfies me that it would be impracticable to hold a line northeast of Richmond that would protect the Fredericksburg Railroad to enable us to use that road for supplying the army. To do so would give us a long vulnerable line of road to protect, exhausting much of our strength to guard it, and would leave open to the enemy all of his lines of communication on the south side of the James. My idea from the start has been to beat Lee's army if possible north of Richmond; then after destroying his lines of communication on the north side of the James River to transfer the army to the south side and besiege Lee in Richmond, or follow him south if he should retreat.

I now find, after over thirty days of trial, the enemy deems it of the first importance to run no risks with the armies they now have. They act purely on the defensive behind breastworks, or feebly on the offensive immediately in front of them, and where in case of repulse they can instantly retire behind them. Without a greater sacrifice of human life than I am willing to make all cannot be accomplished that I had designed outside of the city. I have therefore resolved upon the following plan:

I will continue to hold substantially the ground now occupied by the Army of the Potomac, taking advantage of any favorable circumstance that may present itself until the cavalry can be sent west to destroy the Virginia Central Railroad from about Beaver Dam for some twenty-five or thirty miles west. When this is effected I will move the army to the south side of the James River, either by crossing the Chickahominy and marching near to City Point, or by going to the mouth of the Chickahominy on north side and crossing there. To provide for this last and most possible contingency, several ferryboats of the largest class ought to be immediately provided.

Once on the south side of the James River, I can cut off all sources of supply to the enemy except what is furnished by the canal. If Hunter succeeds in reaching Lynchburg, that will be lost to him also. Should Hunter not succeed, I will still make the effort to destroy the canal by sending cavalry up the south side of the river with a pontoon train to cross wherever they can.

The feeling of the two armies now seems to be that the rebels can protect themselves only by strong intrenchments, whilst our army is not only confident of protecting itself without intrenchments, but that it can beat and drive the enemy wherever and whenever he can be found without this protection.

U.S. GRANT,
Lieutenant-General.

---

between me and Butler, by the roads I should have to travel, with both the James and the Chickahominy unbridged to cross; and last, the Army of the Potomac had to be got out of a position but a few hundred yards from the enemy at the widest place. Lee, if he did not choose to follow me, might, with his shorter distance to travel and his bridges over the Chickahominy and the James, move rapidly on Butler and crush him before the army with me could come to his relief. Then too he might spare troops enough to send against Hunter who was approaching Lynchburg, living upon the country he passed through, and without ammunition further than what he carried with him.

But the move had to be made, and I relied upon Lee's not seeing my danger as I saw it. Besides we had armies on both sides of the James

River and not far from the Confederate capital. I knew that its safety would be a matter of the first consideration with the executive, legislative and judicial branches of the so called Confederate government, if it was not with the military commanders. But I took all the precaution I knew of to guard against all dangers.

Sheridan was sent with two divisions, to communicate with Hunter and to break up the Virginia Central Railroad and the James River Canal, on the 7th of June, taking instructions to Hunter to come back with him.* Hunter was also informed by way of Washington and the Valley that Sheridan was on the way to meet him. The canal and Central Road, and the regions penetrated by them, were of vast importance to the

---

*COLD HARBOR, VA., June 6, 1864.

MAJOR GENERAL D. HUNTER,
     Commanding Dept. W. Va.

General Sheridan leaves here tomorrow morning, with instructions to proceed to Charlottesville, Va., and to commence there the destruction of the Va. Cen. R. R., destroying this way as much as possible. The complete destruction of this road and of the canal on James River is of great importance to us. According to the instructions I sent to General Halleck for your guidance, you were to proceed to Lynchburg and commence there. It would be of great value to us to get possession of Lynchburg for a single day. But that point is of so much importance to the enemy, that in attempting to get it such resistance may be met as to defeat your getting onto the road or canal at all. I see, in looking over the letter to General Halleck on the subject of your instructions that it rather indicates that your route should be from Staunton via Charlottesville. If you have so understood it, you will be doing just what I want. The direction I would now give is, that if this letter reaches you in the valley between Staunton and Lynchburg, you immediately turn east by the most practicable road until you strike the Lynchburg branch of the Va. Central road. From thence move eastward along the line of the road, destroying it completely and thoroughly, until you join General Sheridan. After the work laid out for General Sheridan and yourself is thoroughly done, proceed to join the Army of the Potomac by the route laid out in General Sheridan's instructions.

If any portion of your force, especially your cavalry, is needed back in your Department, you are authorized to send it back.

If on receipt of this you should be near to Lynchburg and deem it practicable to reach that point, you will exercise your judgment about going there.

If you should be on the railroad between Charlottesville and Lynchburg, it may be practicable to detach a cavalry force to destroy the canal. Lose no opportunity to destroy the canal.

U.S. GRANT,
Lieut. - General.

---

enemy, furnishing and carrying a large per cent, of all the supplies for the Army of Northern Virginia and the people of Richmond. Before Sheridan got off on the 7th news was received from Hunter reporting his advance to Staunton and successful engagement with the enemy near that place on the 5th, in which the Confederate commander, W. S. Jones, was killed. On the 4th of June the enemy having withdrawn his left corps, Burnside on our right was moved up between Warren and Smith. On the 5th Birney returned to Hancock, which extended his left now to the Chickahominy, and Warren was withdrawn to Cold Harbor. Wright was directed to send two divisions to the left to extend down the banks of that stream to Bottom's Bridge. The cavalry extended still farther east to Jones's Bridge.

On the 7th Abercrombie, who was in command at White House, and who had been in command at our base of supplies in all the changes made from the start -was ordered to take up the iron from the York River Railroad and put it on boats, and to be in readiness to move by water to City Point.

On the 8th Meade was directed to fortify a line down the bank overlooking the Chickahominy, under cover of which the army could move.

On the 9th Abercrombie was directed to send all organized troops arriving at White House, without debarking from their transports, to report to Butler. Halleck was at this time instructed to send all reinforcements to City Point.

On the 11th I wrote:

COLD HARBOR, VA., June 11, 1864.

MAJOR - GEN. B. F. BUTLER,
    Commanding Department of Va. and S. C.

The movement to transfer this army to the south side of the James River mill commence after dark tomorrow night. Cal. Cornstock, of my staff, was sent specially to ascertain what was necessary to make your position secure in the interval during which the enemy might use most of his force against you, and also, to ascertain what point on the river we should reach to effect a crossing if it should not be practicable to reach this side of the river at Bermuda Hundred. Colonel Comstock has not yet returned, so that I cannot make instructions as definite as I would wish, but the time between this and Sunday night being so short in which to get word to you, I must do the best I can. Colonel Dent goes to make arrangements for gunboats and transportation to send up the Chickahominy to take to you the 18th corps. The corps will leave its position in the trenches as early in the evening, tomorrow, as possible, and make a forced march to Cole's Landing or Ferry, where it should reach by 10 A.M. the following morning. This corps numbers now 15,300 men. They take with them neither wagons nor artillery; these latter marching with the balance of the army to the James River. The remainder of the army will cross the Chickahominy at Long Bridge and at Jones's, and strike the river at the most practicable crossing below City Point.

I directed several days ago that all reinforcements for the army should be sent to you. I am not advised of the number that may have gone, but suppose you have received from six to ten thousand. General Smith will also reach you as soon as the enemy could, going by the way of Richmond. The balance of the force will not be more than one day behind, unless detained by the whole of Lee's army, in which case you will be strong enough. I wish you would direct the proper staff officers, your chief-engineer and your chief-quartermaster, to commence at once the collection of all the means in their reach for crossing the army on its arrival. If there is a point below City Point where a pontoon bridge can be thrown, have it laid. Expecting the arrival of the 18th corps by Monday night, if you deem it practicable from the force you have to seize and hold Petersburg, you may prepare to start, on the arrival of troops to hold your present lines. I do not want Petersburg visited, however, unless it is held, nor an attempt to take it, unless you feel a reasonable degree of confidence of success. If you should go there, I think troops should take nothing with them except what they can carry, depending upon supplies being sent after the place is secured. If Colonel Dent should not succeed in securing the requisite amount of transportation for the 18th corps before reaching you, please have the balance supplied.

U.S. GRANT,
Lieut.-General.

P.S. -On reflection I will send the 18th corps by way of White House. The distance which they will have to march will be enough shorter to enable them to reach you about the same time, and the uncertainty of navigation on the Chickahominy will be avoided. U.S. GRANT.

COLD HARBOR, VA., June 11, 1864.

MAJOR-GENERAL G.G. MEADE,
    Commanding Army of the Potomac.

Colonel Comstock, who visited the James River for the purpose of ascertaining the best point below Bermuda Hundred to which to march the army has not yet returned. It is now getting so late, however, that all preparations may be made for the move tomorrow night without waiting longer. The movement will be made as heretofore agreed upon, that is, the 18th corps make a rapid march with the infantry alone, their wagons and artillery accompanying the balance of the army to Cole's Landing or Ferry, and there embark for City Point, losing no time for rest until they reach the latter point. The 5th corps will seize Long Bridge and move out on the Long Bridge Road to its junction with Quaker Road, or until stopped by the enemy. The other three corps will follow in such order as you may direct, one of them crossing at Long Bridge, and two at Jones's Bridge. After the crossing is effected, the most practicable roads will be taken to reach about Fort Powhattan. Of course, this is supposing the enemy makes no opposition to our advance. The 5th corps, after securing the passage of the balance of the army, will join or follow in rear of the corps which crosses the same bridge with themselves.

The wagon trains should be kept well east of the troops, and if a crossing can be found, or made lower down than Jones's they should take it.

U.S. GRANT,
Lieut.-General.

P.S.-In view of the long march to reach Cole's Landing, and the uncertainty of being able to embark a large number of men there, the direction of the 18th corps may be changed to White House. They should be directed to load up transports, and start them as fast as loaded without waiting for the whole corps or even whole divisions to go together. U.S. GRANT.

About this time word was received (through the Richmond papers of the 11th) that Crook and Averell had united and were moving east. This, with the news of Hunter's successful engagement near Staunton, was no doubt known to Lee before it was to me. Then Sheridan leaving with two divisions of cavalry, looked indeed threatening, both to Lee's communications and supplies. Much of his cavalry was sent after Sheridan, and Early with Ewell's entire corps was sent to the Valley. Supplies were growing scarce in Richmond, and the sources from which to draw them were in our hands. People from outside began to pour into Richmond to help eat up the little on hand. Consternation reigned there.

On the 12th Smith was ordered to move at night to White House, not to stop until he reached there, and to take boats at once for City Point, leaving his trains and artillery to move by land.

Soon after dark some of the cavalry at Long Bridge effected a crossing by wading and floundering through the water and mud, leaving their horses behind, and drove away the cavalry pickets. A pontoon bridge was speedily thrown across, over which the remainder of the army soon passed and pushed out for a mile or two to watch and detain any advance that might be made from the other side. Warren followed the cavalry, and by the morning of the 13th had his whole corps over, Hancock followed Warren. Burnside took the road to Jones's Bridge, followed by Wright. Ferrero's division, with the wagon train, moved farther east, by Window Shades and Cole's Ferry, our rear being covered by cavalry.

It was known that the enemy had some gunboats at Richmond. These might run down at night and inflict great damage upon us before they could be sunk or captured by our navy. General Butler had, in advance, loaded some vessels with stone ready to be sunk so as to obstruct the channel in an emergency. On the 13th I sent orders to have these sunk as high up the river as we could guard them, and prevent their removal by the enemy.

As soon as Warren's corps was over the Chickahominy it marched out and joined the cavalry in holding the roads from Richmond while the army passed. No attempt was made by the enemy to impede our march, however, but Warren and Wilson reported the enemy strongly fortified in their front. By the evening of the 13th Hancock's corps was at Charles City Court House on the James River. Burnside's and Wright's corps were on the Chickahominy, and crossed during the night, Warren's corps and the cavalry still covering the army. The material for a pontoon bridge was already at hand and the work of laying it was commenced immediately, under the superintendence of Brigadier-General Benham, commanding the engineer brigade. On the evening of the 14th the crossing commenced, Hancock in advance, using both the bridge and boats.

When the Wilderness campaign commenced the Army of the Potomac, including Burnside's corps -which was a separate command until the 24th of May when it was incorporated with the main army numbered about 116,000 men. During the progress of the campaign about 40,000 reinforcements were received. At the crossing of the James River June 14th-15th the army numbered about 115,000. Besides the ordinary losses incident to a campaign of six weeks' nearly constant fighting or skirmishing, about one-half of the artillery was sent back to Washington, and many men were discharged by reason of the expiration of their term of service.* In estimating our strength every enlisted man and every commissioned officer present is included, no matter how employed; in bands, sick in field hospitals, hospital attendants, company cooks and all. Operating in an enemy's country, and being supplied always from a distant base, large detachments had at all times to be sent from the front, not only to guard the base of supplies and the roads to it, but all the roads leading to our flanks and rear. We were also operating in a country unknown to us, and without competent guides or maps showing the roads accurately.

The manner of estimating numbers in the two armies differs materially. In the Confederate army often only bayonets are taken into account, never, I believe, do they estimate more than are handling the guns of the artillery and armed with muskets or carbines.

<u>*FROM A STATEMENT OF LOSSES COMPILED IN THE ADJUTANT-GENERAL'S OFFICE.</u>

Field of Action and Date	Killed	Wounded	Missing	Aggregate
Wilderness, May 5th to 7th	2,261	8,785	2,902	13,259
Spottsylvania, May 8th to21st	2,271	9,360	1,970	13,601
North Anna, May 23d to 27th	186	792	165	1143
Totopotomoy, May 27th to 31st	99	358	52	509
Cold Harbor, May 31st to June 12th	1,769	6752	1537	10058
Total	6,586	26,047	6,626	39,259

Generally the latter are far enough away to be excluded from the count in any one field. Officers and details of enlisted men are not included. In the Northern armies the estimate is most liberal, taking in all connected with the army and drawing pay.

Estimated in the same manner as ours, Lee had not less than 80,000 men at the start. His reinforcements were about equal to ours during the campaign, deducting the discharged men and those sent back. He was on the defensive, and in a country in which every stream, every road, every obstacle to the movement of troops and every natural defence was familiar to him and his army. The citizens were all friendly to him and his cause, and could and did furnish him with accurate reports of our every move. Rear guards were not necessary for him, and having always a railroad at his back, large wagon trains were not required. All circumstances considered we did not have any advantage in numbers.

General Lee, who had led the Army of Northern Virginia in all these contests, was a very highly estimated man in the Confederate army and States, and filled also a very high place in the estimation of the people and press of the Northern States. His praise was sounded throughout the entire North after every action he was engaged in: the number of his forces was always lowered and that of the National forces exaggerated. He was a large, austere man, and I judge difficult of approach to his subordinates. To be extolled by the entire press of the South after every engagement, and by a portion of the press North with equal vehemence, was calculated to give him the entire confidence of his troops and to make him feared by his antagonists. It was not an uncommon thing for my staff-officers to hear from Eastern officers, "Well, Grant has never met Bobby Lee yet." There were good and true officers who believe now that the Army of Northern Virginia was superior to the Army of the Potomac man to man. I do not believe so, except as the advantages spoken of above made them so. Before the end I believe the difference was the other way. The Army of Northern Virginia became despondent and saw the end. It did not please them. The National army saw the same thing, and were encouraged by it.

The advance of the Army of the Potomac reached the James on the 14th of June. Preparations were at once commenced for laying the pontoon bridges and crossing the river. As already stated, I had previously ordered General Butler to have two vessels loaded with stone and carried up the river to a point above that occupied by our gunboats, where the channel was narrow, and sunk there so as to obstruct the passage and prevent Confederate gunboats from coming down the river. Butler had had these boats filled and put in position, but had not had them sunk before my arrival. I ordered this done, and also directed that he should turn over all material and boats not then in use in the river to be used in ferrying the troops across.

I then, on the 14th, took a steamer and ran up to Bermuda Hundred to see General Butler for the purpose of directing a movement against Petersburg, while our troops of the Army of the Potomac were crossing.

I had sent General W. F. Smith back from Cold Harbor by the way of White House, thence on steamers to City Point for the purpose of giving General Butler more troops with which to accomplish this result. General Butler was ordered to send Smith with his troops reinforced, as far as that could be conveniently done, from other parts of the Army of the James. He gave Smith about six thousand reinforcements, including some twenty-five hundred cavalry under Kautz, and about thirty-five hundred colored infantry under Hinks.

The distance which Smith had to move to reach the enemy's lines was about six miles, and the Confederate advance line of works was but two miles outside of Petersburg. Smith was to move under cover of night, up close to the enemy's works, and assault as soon as he could after daylight. I believed then, and still believe, that Petersburg could have been easily captured at that time. It only had about 2,500 men in the defences besides some irregular troops, consisting of citizens and employees in the city who took up arms in case of emergency. Smith started as proposed, but his advance encountered a rebel force intrenched between City Point and their lines outside of Petersburg. This position he carried, with some loss to the enemy; but there was so much delay that it was daylight before his troops really got off from there. While there I informed General Butler that Hancock's corps would cross the river and move to Petersburg to support Smith in case the latter was successful, and that I could reinforce there more rapidly than Lee could reinforce from his position.

I returned down the river to where the troops of the Army of the Potomac now were, communicated to General Meade, in writing, the directions I had given to General Butler and directed him (Meade) to cross Hancock's corps over under cover of night, and push them forward in the morning to Petersburg; halting them, however, at a designated point until they could hear from Smith. I also informed General Meade that I had ordered rations from Bermuda Hundred for Hancock's corps, and desired him to issue them speedily, and to lose no more time than was absolutely necessary. The rations did not reach him, however, and Hancock, while he got all his corps over during the night, remained until half past ten in the hope of receiving them. He then moved without them, and on the road received a note from General W. F. Smith, asking him to come on. This seems to be the first information that General Hancock had received of the fact that he was to go to Petersburg, or that anything particular was expected of him. Otherwise he would have been there by four o'clock in the afternoon.

Smith arrived in front of the enemy's lines early in the forenoon of the 15th, and spent the day until after seven o'clock in the evening in reconnoitering what appeared to be empty works. The enemy's line consisted of redans occupying commanding positions, with rifle-pits connecting them. To the east side of Petersburg, from the Appomattox back, there were thirteen of these redans extending a distance of several miles, probably three. If they had been properly manned they could have held out against any force that could have attacked them, at least until reinforcements could have got up from the north of Richmond.

Smith assaulted with the colored troops, and with success. By nine o'clock at night he was in possession of five of these redans and, of course, of the connecting lines of rifle-pits. All of them contained artillery, which fell into our hands. Hancock came up and proposed to take any part assigned to him; and Smith asked him to relieve his men who were in the trenches.

Next morning, the 16th, Hancock himself was in command, and captured another redan. Meade came up in the afternoon and succeeded Hancock, who had to be relieved, temporarily, from the command of his corps on account of the breaking out afresh of the wound he had received at Gettysburg. During the day Meade assaulted and carried one more redan to his right and two to his left. In all this we lost very heavily.

The works were not strongly manned, but they all had guns in them which fell into our hands, together with the men who were handling them in the effort to repel these assaults.

Up to this time Beauregard, who had commanded south of Richmond, had received no reinforcements, except Hoke's division from Drury's Bluff,* which had arrived on the morning of the 16th; though he had urged the authorities very strongly to send them, believing, as he did, that Petersburg would be a valuable prize which we might seek.

---

* CITY POINT, VA., June 17, 1864- 11 A.M.

MAJOR-GEN. HALLECK,
    Washington, D. C.

The enemy in their endeavor to reinforce Petersburg abandoned their intrenchments in front of Bermuda Hundred. They no doubt expected troops from north of the James River to take their place before we discovered it. General Butler took advantage of this and moved a force at once upon the railroad and plank road between Richmond and Petersburg, which I hope to retain possession of. Too much credit cannot be given to the troops and their commanders for the energy and fortitude displayed during the last five days. Day and night has been all the same, no delays being allowed on any account.

U.S. GRANT,
Lieut.-General.

During the 17th the fighting was very severe and the losses heavy; and at night our troops occupied about the same position they had occupied in the morning, except that they held a redan which had been captured by Potter during the day. During the night, however, Beauregard fell back to the line which had been already selected, and commenced fortifying it. Our troops advanced on the 19th to the line which he had abandoned, and found that the Confederate loss had been very severe, many of the enemy's dead still remaining in the ditches and in front of them.

Colonel J.L Chamberlain, of the 20th Maine, was wounded on the 18th. He was gallantly leading his brigade at the time, as he had been in the habit of doing in all the engagements in which he had previously been engaged. He had several times been recommended for a brigadier-generalcy for gallant and meritorious conduct. On this occasion, however, I promoted him on the spot, and forwarded a copy of my order to the War Department, asking that my act might be confirmed and Chamberlain's name sent to the Senate for confirmation without any delay. This was done, and at last a gallant and meritorious officer received partial justice at the hands of his government, which he had served so faithfully and so well.

If General Hancock's orders of the 15th had been communicated to him, that officer, with his usual promptness, would undoubtedly have been upon the ground around Petersburg as early as four o'clock in the afternoon of the 15th. The days were long and it would have given him considerable time before night. I do not think there is any doubt that Petersburg itself could have been carried without much loss; or, at least, if protected by inner detached works, that a line could have been established very much in rear of the one then occupied by the enemy. This would have given us control of both the Weldon and South Side railroads. This would also have saved an immense amount of hard fighting which had to be done from the 15th to the 18th, and would have given us greatly the advantage in the long siege which ensued.

I now ordered the troops to be put under cover and allowed some of the rest which they had so long needed. They remained quiet, except that there was more or less firing every day, until the 22d, when General Meade ordered an advance towards the Weldon Railroad. We were very anxious to get to that road, and even round to the South Side Railroad if possible.

Meade moved Hancock's corps, now commanded by Birney, to the left, with a view to at least force the enemy to stay within the limits of his own line. General Wright, with the 6th corps, was ordered by a road farther south, to march directly for the Weldon road. The enemy passed in between these two corps and attacked vigorously, and with very serious results to the National troops, who were then withdrawn from their advanced position.

The Army of the Potomac was given the investment of Petersburg, while the Army of the James held Bermuda Hundred and all the ground we possessed north of the James River. The 9th corps, Burnside's, was placed upon the right at Petersburg; the 5th, Warren's, next; the 2d, Birney's, next; then the 6th, Wright's, broken off to the left and south. Thus began the siege of Petersburg.

CHAPTER LVII

RAID ON THE VIRGINIA CENTRAL RAILROAD - RAID ON THE WELDON RAILROAD - EARLY'S MOVEMENT UPON WASHINGTON - MINING THE WORKS BEFORE PETERS- BURG - EXPLOSION OF THE MINE BEFORE PETERS- BURG - CAMPAIGN IN THE SHENANDOAH VALLEY - CAPTURE OF THE WELDON RAILROAD

ON the 7th of June, while at Cold Harbor, I had as already indicated sent Sheridan with two divisions of cavalry to destroy as much as he could of the Virginia Central Railroad. General Hunter had been operating up the Shenandoah Valley with some success, having fought a battle near Staunton where he captured a great many prisoners, besides killing and wounding a good many men. After the battle he formed a junction at Staunton with Averell and Crook, who had come up from the Kanawha, or Gauley River. It was supposed, therefore, that General Hunter would be about Charlottesville, Virginia, by the time Sheridan could get there, doing on the way the damage that he was sent to do.

I gave Sheridan instructions to have Hunter, in case he should meet him about Charlottesville, join and return with him to the Army of the Potomac. Lee, hearing of Hunter's success in the valley, started Breckinridge out for its defence at once. Learning later of Sheridan's going with two divisions; he also sent Hampton with two divisions of cavalry, his own and Fitz-Hugh Lee's.

Sheridan moved to the north side of the North Anna to get out west, and learned of the movement of these troops to the south side of the same stream almost as soon as they had started. He pushed on to get to Trevilian Station to commence his destruction at that point. On the night of the 10th he bivouacked some six or seven miles east of Trevilian, while Fitz-Hugh Lee was the same night at Trevilian Station and Hampton but a few miles away.

During the night Hampton ordered an advance on Sheridan, hoping, no doubt, to surprise and very badly cripple him. Sheridan, however, by a counter move sent Custer on a rapid march to get between the two divisions of the enemy and into their rear. This he did successfully, so that at daylight, when the assault was made, the enemy found himself at the same time resisted in front and attacked in rear, and broke in some confusion. The losses were probably very light on both sides in killed and wounded, but Sheridan got away with some five hundred prisoners and sent them to City Point.

During that day, the 11th, Sheridan moved into Trevilian Station, and the following day proceeded to tear up the road east and west. There was considerable fighting during the whole of the day, but the work of destruction went on. In the meantime, at night, the enemy had taken possession of the crossing which Sheridan had proposed to take to go north when he left Trevilian. Sheridan learned, however, from some of the prisoners he had captured here, that General Hunter was about Lynchburg, and therefore that there was no use of his going on to Charlottesville with a view to meet him.

Sheridan started back during the night of the 12th, and made his way north and farther east, coming around by the north side of White House, and arriving there on the 21st. Here he found an abundance of forage for his animals, food for his men, and security while resting. He had been obliged to leave about ninety of his own men in the field hospital which he had established near Trevilian, and these necessarily fell into the hands of the enemy.

White House up to this time had been a depot; but now that our troops were all on the James River, it was no longer wanted as a store of supplies. Sheridan was, therefore, directed to break it up; which he did on the 22d of June, bringing the garrison and an immense wagon train with him. All these were over the James River by the 26th of the month, and Sheridan ready to follow.

In the meantime Meade had sent Wilson's division on a raid to destroy the Weldon and South Side roads. Now that Sheridan was safe and Hampton free to return to Richmond with his cavalry, Wilson's position became precarious. Meade therefore, on the 27th, ordered Sheridan over the river to make a demonstration in favor of Wilson. Wilson got back, though not without severe loss, having struck both roads, but the damage done was soon repaired.

After these events comparative quiet reigned about Petersburg until late in July. The time, however, was spent in strengthening the intrenchments and making our position generally more secure against a sudden attack. In the meantime I had to look after other portions of my command, where things had not been going on so favorably, always, as I could have wished.

General Hunter who had been appointed to succeed Sigel in the Shenandoah Valley immediately took up the offensive. He met the enemy on the 5th of June at Piedmont, and defeated him. On the 8th he formed a junction with Crook and Averell at Staunton, from which place he moved direct on Lynchburg, via Lexington, which he reached and invested on the 16th. Up to this time he was very successful ; and but for the difficulty of taking with him sufficient ordnance stores over so long a march, through a hostile country, he would, no doubt, have captured Lynchburg. The destruction of the enemy's supplies and manufactories had been very great. To meet this movement under General Hunter, General Lee sent Early with his corps, a part of which reached Lynchburg before Hunter. After some skirmishing on the 17th and 18th, General Hunter, owing to a want of ammunition to give battle, retired from before the place. Unfortunately, this want of ammunition left him no choice of route for his return but by the way of the Gauley and Kanawha rivers, thence up the Ohio River, returning to Harper's Ferry by way of the Baltimore and Ohio Railroad. A long time was consumed in making this movement. Meantime the valley was left open to Early's troops, and others in that quarter; and Washington also was uncovered. Early took advantage of this condition of affairs and moved on Washington.

In the absence of Hunter, General Lew Wallace, with headquarters at Baltimore, commanded the department in which the Shenandoah lay. His surplus of troops with which to move against the enemy was small in number. Most of these were raw and, consequently, very much inferior to our veterans and to the veterans which Early had with him; but the situation of Washington was precarious, and Wallace moved with commendable promptitude to meet the enemy at the Monocacy. He could hardly have expected to defeat him badly, but he hoped to cripple and delay him until Washington could be put into a state of preparation for his reception. I had previously ordered General Meade to send a division to Baltimore for the purpose of adding to the defences of Washington, and he had sent Ricketts's division of the 6th corps (Wright's), which arrived in Baltimore on the 8th of July. Finding that Wallace had gone to the front with his command, Ricketts immediately took the cars and followed him to the Monocacy with his entire division. They met the enemy and, as might have been expected, were defeated; but they succeeded in stopping him for the day on which the battle took place. The next morning Early started on his march to the capital of the Nation, arriving before it on the 11th.

Learning of the gravity of the situation I had directed General Meade to also order Wright with the rest of his corps directly to Washington for the relief of that place, and the latter reached there the very day that Early arrived before it. The 19th corps, which had been stationed in Louisiana, having been ordered up to reinforce the armies about Richmond, had about this time arrived at Fortress Monroe, on their way to join us. I diverted them from that point to Washington, which place they reached, almost simultaneously with Wright, on the 11th. The 19th corps was commanded by Major-General Emory.

Early made his reconnaissance with a view of attacking on the following morning, the 12th; but the next morning he found our intrenchments, which were very strong, fully manned. He at once commenced to retreat, Wright following. There is no telling how much this result was contributed to by General Lew Wallace's leading what might well be considered almost a forlorn hope. If Early had been but one day earlier he might have entered the capital before the arrival of the reinforcements I had sent. Whether the delay caused by the battle amounted to a day or not, General Wallace contributed on this occasion, by the defeat of the troops under him a greater benefit to the cause than often falls to the lot of a commander of an equal force to render by means of a victory.

Farther west also the troubles were threatening. Some time before, Forrest had met Sturgis in command of some of our cavalry in Mississippi and handled him very roughly, gaining a very great victory over him. This left Forrest free to go almost where he pleased, and to cut the roads in rear of Sherman who was then advancing. Sherman was abundantly able to look after the army that he was immediately with, and all of his military division so long as he could communicate with it ; but it was my place to see that he had the means with which to hold his rear. Two divisions under A. J. Smith had been sent to Banks in Louisiana some months before. Sherman ordered these back, with directions to attack Forrest. Smith met and defeated him very badly. I then directed that Smith should hang to Forrest and not let him go; and to prevent by all means his getting upon the Memphis and Nashville Railroad. Sherman had anticipated me in this matter, and given the same orders in substance; but receiving my directions for this order to Smith, he repeated it.

On the 25th of June General Burnside had commenced running a mine from about the centre of his front under the Confederate works confronting him. He was induced to do this by Colonel Pleasants, of the Pennsylvania Volunteers, whose regiment was mostly composed of miners, and who was himself a practical miner. Burnside had submitted the scheme to Meade and myself, and we both approved of it, as a means of keeping the men occupied. His position was very favorable for carrying on this work, but not so favorable for the operations to follow its completion. The position of the two lines at that point were only about a hundred yards apart with a comparatively deep ravine intervening. In the bottom of this ravine the work commenced. The position was unfavorable in this particular: that the enemy's line at that point was reentering, so that its front was commanded by their own lines both to the right and left. Then, too, the ground was sloping upward back of the Confederate line for a considerable distance, and it was presumable that the enemy had, at least, a detached work on this highest point. The work progressed, and on the 23d of July the mine was finished ready for charging; but I had this work of charging deferred until we were ready for it.

On the 17th of July several deserters came in and said that there was great consternation in Richmond, and that Lee was coming out to make an attack upon us; the object being to put us on the defensive so that he might detach troops to go to Georgia where the army Sherman was operating against was said to be in great trouble. I put the army commanders, Meade and Butler, on the lookout, but the attack was not made.

I concluded, then, a few days later, to do something in the way of offensive movement myself, having in view something of the same object that Lee had had. Wright's and Emorys's corps were in Washington, and with this reduction of my force Lee might very readily have spared some troops from the defences to send West. I had other objects in view, however, besides keeping Lee where he was. The mine was constructed and ready to be exploded, and I wanted to take that occasion to carry Petersburg if I could. It was the object, therefore, to get as many of Lee's troops away from the south side of the James River as possible. Accordingly, on the 26th, we commenced a movement with Hancock's corps and Sheridan's cavalry to the north side by the way of, Deep Bottom, where Butler had a pontoon bridge laid. The plan, in the main, was to let the cavalry cut loose and, joining with Kautz's cavalry of the Army of the James, get by Lee's lines and destroy as much as they could of the Virginia Central Railroad, while, in the mean time, the infantry was to move out so as to protect their rear and cover their retreat back when they should have got through with their work. We were successful in drawing the enemy's troops to the north side of the James as I expected. The mine was ordered to be charged, and the morning of the 30th of July was the time fixed for its explosion. I gave Meade minute orders* on the 24th directing how I wanted the assault conducted,

---

*CITY POINT, VA., July 24, 1864.
MAJOR-GENERAL MEADE, Commanding, etc.

The engineer officers who made a survey of the front from Bermuda Hundred report against the probability of success from an attack there. The chances they think will be better on Burnside's front. If this is attempted it will be necessary to concentrate all the force possible at the point in the enemy's line we expect to penetrate. All officers should be fully impressed with the absolute necessity of pushing entirely beyond the enemy's present line, if they should succeed in penetrating it, and of getting back to their present line promptly if they should not succeed in breaking through.

To the right and left of the point of assault all the artillery possible should be brought to play upon the enemy in front during the assault. Their lines would be sufficient for the support of the artillery, and all the reserves could be brought on the flanks of their commands nearest to the point of assault, ready to follow in if successful. The field artillery and infantry held in the lines during the first assault should be in readiness to move at a moment's notice either to their front or to follow the main assault, as they should receive orders. One thing, however, should be impressed on corps commanders. If they see the enemy giving away on their front or moving from it to reinforce a heavily assaulted portion of their line, they should take advantage of such knowledge and act promptly without waiting for orders from army commanders. General Ord can cooperate with his corps in this movement, and about five thousand troops from Bermuda Hundred can be sent to reinforce you or can be used to threaten an assault between the Appomattox and James rivers, as may be deemed best.

This should be done by Tuesday morning, if done at all. If not attempted, we will then start at the date indicated to destroy the railroad as far as Hicksford at least, and to Weldon if possible.

Whether we send an expedition on the road or assault at Petersburg, Burnside's mine will be blown up.

U.S. GRANT, Lieutenant-General.

---

which orders he amplified into general instructions for the guidance of the troops that were to be engaged.

Meade's instructions, which I, of course, approved most heartily, were all that I can see now was necessary. The only further precaution which he could have taken, and which he could not foresee, would have been to have different men to execute them.

The gallery to the mine was over five hundred feet long from where it entered the ground to the point where it was under the enemy's works, and with a cross gallery of something over eighty feet running under their lines. Eight chambers had been left, requiring a ton of powder each to charge them. All was ready by the time I had prescribed; and on the 29th Hancock and Sheridan were brought back near the James River with their troops. Under cover of night they started to recross the bridge at Deep Bottom, and to march directly for that part of our lines in front of the mine.

Warren was to hold his line of intrenchments with a sufficient number of men and concentrate the balance on the right next to Burnside's corps, while Ord, now commanding the 18th corps, temporarily under Meade, was to form in the rear of Burnside to support him when he went in. All were to clear off the parapets and the abatis in their front so as to leave the space as open as possible, and be able to charge the moment the mine had been sprung and Burnside had taken possession. Burnside's corps was not to stop in the crater at all but push on to the top of the hill, supported on the right and left by Ord's and Warren's corps.

Warren and Ord fulfilled their instructions perfectly so far as making ready was concerned. Burnside seemed to have paid no attention whatever to the instructions, and left all the obstruction in his own front for his troops to get over in the best way they could. The four divisions of his corps were commanded by Generals Potter, Willcox, Ledlie and Ferrero. The last was a colored division; and Burnside selected it to make the assault. Meade interfered with this. Burnside then took Ledlie's division -a worse selection than the first could have been. In fact, Potter and Willcox were the only division commanders Burnside had who were equal to the occasion. Ledlie besides being otherwise inefficient proved also to possess disqualification less common among soldiers.

There was some delay about the explosion of the mine so that it did not go off until about five o'clock in the morning. When it did explode it was very successful, making a crater twenty feet deep and something like a hundred feet in length. Instantly one hundred and ten cannon and fifty mortars, which had been placed in the most commanding positions covering the ground to the right   and left of where the troops were to enter the enemy's lines, commenced playing. Ledlie's division marched into the crater immediately on the explosion, but most of the men stopped there in the absence of any one to give directions; their commander having found some safe retreat to get into before they started. There was some delay on the left and right in advancing, but some of the troops did get in and turn to the right and left, carrying the rifle-pits as I expected they would do.

There had been great consternation in Petersburg, as we were well aware, about a rumored mine that we were going to explode. They knew we were mining, and they had failed to cut our mine off by countermining, though Beauregard had taken the precaution to run up a line of intrenchments to the rear of that part of their line fronting where they could see that our men were at work. We had learned through deserters who had come in that the people had very wild rumors about what was going on on our side. They said that we had undermined the whole of Petersburg; that they were resting upon a slumbering volcano and did not know at what moment they might expect an eruption. I somewhat based my calculations upon this state of feeling, and expected that when the mine was exploded the troops to the right and left would flee in all directions, and that our troops, if they moved promptly, could get in and strengthen themselves before the enemy had come to a realization of the true situation. It was just as I expected it would be. We could see the men running without any apparent object except to get away. It was half an hour before musketry firing, to amount to anything, was opened upon our men in the crater. It was an hour before the enemy got artillery up to play upon them ; and it was nine o'clock before Lee got up reinforcements from his right to join in expelling our troops.

The effort was a stupendous failure. It cost us about four thousand men, mostly, however, captured; and all due to inefficiency on the part of the corps commander and the incompetency of the division commander who was sent to lead the assault.

After being fully assured of the failure of the mine, and finding that most of that part of Lee's army which had been drawn north of the James River were still there, I gave Meade directions to send a corps of infantry and the cavalry next morning, before Lee could get his forces back, to destroy fifteen or twenty miles of the Weldon Railroad. But misfortunes never come singly. I learned during that same afternoon that Wright's pursuit of Early was feeble because of the constant and contrary orders he had been receiving from Washington, while I was cut off from immediate communication by reason of our cable across Chesapeake Bay being broken. Early, however, was not aware of the fact that Wright was not pursuing until he had reached Strasburg. Finding that he was not pursued he turned back to Winchester, where Crook was stationed with a small force, and drove him out. He then pushed north until he had reached the Potomac, then he sent McCausland across to Chambersburg, Pa., to destroy that town. Chambersburg was a purely defenseless town with no garrison whatever, and no fortifications; yet McCausland, under Early's orders, burned the place and left about three hundred families houseless. This occurred on the 30th of July. I rescinded my orders for the troops to go out to destroy the Weldon Railroad, and directed them to embark for Washington City. After burning Chambersburg McCausland retreated, pursued by our cavalry, towards Cumberland. They were met and defeated by General Kelley and driven into Virginia.

The Shenandoah Valley was very important to the Confederates, because it was the principal storehouse they now had for feeding their armies about Richmond. It was well known that they would make a desperate struggle to maintain it. It had been the source of a great deal of trouble to us heretofore to guard that outlet to the north, partly because of the incompetency of some of the commanders, but chiefly because of interference from Washington. It seemed to be the policy of General Halleck and Secretary Stanton to keep any force sent there, in pursuit of the invading army, moving right and left so as to keep between the enemy and our capital; and, generally speaking, they pursued this policy until all knowledge of the whereabouts of the enemy was lost. They were left, therefore, free to supply themselves with horses, beef cattle, and such provisions as they could carry away from Western Maryland and Pennsylvania. I determined to put a stop to this. I started Sheridan at once for that field of operation, and on the following day sent another division of his cavalry.

I had previously asked to have Sheridan assigned to that command, but Mr. Stanton objected, on the ground that he was too young for so important a command. On the 1st of August when I sent reinforcements for the protection of Washington, I sent the following orders:

CITY POINT, VA.,
August 1, 1864, 11.30 A.M.

MAJOR -GENERAL HALLECK,
    Washington, D. C.

I am sending General Sheridan for temporary duty whilst the enemy is being expelled from the border. Unless General Hunter is in the field in person, I want Sheridan put in command of all
the troops in the field, with instructions to put himself south of the enemy and follow him to the death. Wherever the enemy goes let our troops go also. Once started up the valley they ought to be followed until we get possession of the Virginia Central Railroad. If General Hunter is in the field, give Sheridan direct command of the 6th corps and cavalry division. All the cavalry, I presume, will reach Washington in the course of tomorrow.

U.S. GRANT,
Lieutenant-General.

The President in some way or other got to see this dispatch of mine directing certain instructions to be given to the commanders in the field, operating against Early, and sent me the following very characteristic dispatch:

OFFICE U. S. MILITARY TELEGRAPH,
WAR DEPARTMENT,
WASHINGTON, D. C., August 3, 1864.

Cypher. 6 P.M.,
    LT.GENERAL GRANT,
        City Point, Va.

I have seen your despatch in which you say, "I want Sheridan put in command of all the troops in the field, with instructions to put himself south of the enemy, and follow him to the death. Wherever the enemy goes, let our troops go also." This, I think, is exactly right, as to how our forces should move. But please look over the despatches you may have received from here, even since you made that order, and discover, if you can, that there is any idea in the head of any one here, of "putting our army south of the enemy," or of "following him to the death " in any direction. I repeat to you it will neither be done nor attempted unless you watch it every day, and hour, and force it.

A. LINCOLN.

I replied to this that "I would start in two hours for Washington," and soon got off, going directly to the Monocacy without stopping at Washington on my way. I found General Hunter's army encamped there, scattered over the fields along the banks of the Monocacy, with many hundreds of cars and locomotives, belonging to the Baltimore and Ohio Railroad, which he had taken the precaution to bring back and collect at that point. I asked the general where the enemy was. He replied that he did not know. He said the fact was, that he was so embarrassed with orders from Washington moving him first to the right and then to the left that he had lost all trace of the enemy.

I then told the general that I would find out where the enemy was, and at once ordered steam got up and trains made up, giving directions to push for Halltown, some four miles above Harper's Ferry, in the Shenandoah Valley. The cavalry and the wagon trains were to march, but all the troops that could be transported by the cars were to go in that way. I knew that the valley was of such importance to the enemy that, no matter how much he was scattered at that time, he would in a very short time be found in front of our troops moving south.

I then wrote out General Hunter's instructions.* I told him that Sheridan was in Washington, and still another division was on its way; and suggested that he establish the headquarters of the department at any point that would suit him best, Cumberland, Baltimore, or elsewhere, and give Sheridan command of the troops in the field. The general replied to this, that he thought he had better be relieved entirely. He said that General Halleck seemed so much to distrust his fitness for the position he was in that he thought somebody else ought to be there. He did not want, in any way, to embarrass the cause; thus showing a patriotism that was none too common in the army. There were not many major-generals who would voluntarily have asked to have the command of a department taken from them on the supposition that for some particular reason, or for any reason, the service would be better performed. I told him, "very well then," and telegraphed at once for Sheridan to come to the Monocacy, and suggested that I would wait and meet him there.

Sheridan came at once by special train, but reached there after the troops were all off. I went to the station and remained there until he arrived. Myself and one or two of my staff were about all the Union people, except General Hunter and his staff, who were left at the Monocacy when Sheridan arrived. I hastily told Sheridan what had been done and what I wanted him to do, giving him, at the same time, the written instructions which had been prepared for General Hunter and

---

*See letter, August 5th, Appendix page 581.

directed to that officer.

Sheridan now had about 30,000 men to move with, 8,000 of them being cavalry. Early had about the same number, but the superior ability of the National commander over the Confederate commander was so great that all the latter's advantage of being on the defensive was more than counterbalanced by this circumstance. As I had predicted, Early was soon found in front of Sheridan in the valley, and Pennsylvania and Maryland were speedily freed from the invaders. The importance of the valley was so great to the Confederates that Lee reinforced Early, but not to the extent that we thought and feared he would.

To prevent as much as possible these reinforcements from being sent out from Richmond, I had to do something to compel Lee to retain his forces about his capital. I therefore gave orders for another move to the north side of the James River, to threaten Richmond. Hancock's corps, part of the 10th corps under Birney, and Gregg's division of cavalry were crossed to the north side of the James during the night of the 13th-14th of August. A threatening position was maintained for a number of days, with more or less skirmishing, and some tolerably hard fighting; although it was my object and my instructions that anything like a battle should be avoided, unless opportunities should present themselves which would insure great success, General Meade was left in command of the few troops around Petersburg, strongly intrenched; and was instructed to keep a close watch upon the enemy in that quarter, and himself to take advantage of any weakening that might occur through an effort on the part of the enemy to reinforce the north side. There was no particular victory gained on either side; but during that time no more reinforcements were sent to the valley.

I informed Sheridan of what had been done to prevent reinforcements being sent from Richmond against him, and also that the efforts we had made had proven that one of the divisions which we supposed had gone to the valley was still at Richmond, because we had captured six or seven hundred prisoners from that division, each of its four brigades having contributed to our list of captures. I also informed him that but one division had gone, and it was possible that I should be able to prevent the going of any more.

To add to my embarrassment at this time Sherman, who was now near Atlanta, wanted reinforcements. He was perfectly willing to take the raw troops then being raised in the North-west, saying that he could teach them more soldiering in one day among his troops than they would learn in a week in a camp of instruction. I therefore asked that all troops in camps of instruction in the North-west be sent to him. Sherman also wanted to be assured that no Eastern troops were moving out against him. I informed him of what I had done and assured him that I would hold all the troops there that it was possible for me to hold, and that up to that time none had gone. I also informed him that his real danger was from Kirby Smith, who commanded the trans-Mississippi Department. If Smith should escape Steele, and get across the Mississippi River, he might move against him. I had, therefore, asked to have an expedition ready to move from New Orleans against Mobile in case Kirby Smith should get across. This would have a tendency to draw him to the defence of that place, instead of going against Sherman.

Right in the midst of all these embarrassments Halleck informed me that there was an organized scheme on foot in the North to resist the draft, and suggested that it might become necessary to draw troops from the field to put it down. He also advised taking in sail, and not going too fast.

The troops were withdrawn from the north side of the James River on the night of the 20th. Before they were withdrawn, however, and while most of Lee's force was on that side of the river, Warren had been sent with most of the 5th corps to capture the Weldon Railroad. He took up his line of march well back to the rear, south of the enemy, while the troops remaining in the trenches extended so as to cover that part of the line which he had vacated by moving out. From our left, near the old line, it was about three miles to the Weldon Railroad. A division was ordered from the right of the Petersburg line to reinforce Warren, while a division was brought back from the north side of the James River to take its place.

This road was very important to the enemy. The limits from which his supplies had been drawn were already very much contracted, and I knew that he must fight desperately to protect it. Warren carried the road, though with heavy loss on both sides. He fortified his new position, and our trenches were then extended from the left of our main line to connect with his new one. Lee made repeated attempts to dislodge Warren's corps, but without success, and with heavy loss.

As soon as Warren was fortified and reinforcements reached him, troops were sent south to destroy the bridges on the Weldon Railroad; and with such success that the enemy had to draw in wagons, for a distance of about thirty miles, all the supplies they got thereafter from that source. It was on the 21st that Lee seemed to have given up the Weldon Railroad as having been lost to him; but along about the 24th or 25th he made renewed attempts to recapture it ; again he failed and with very heavy losses to him as compared with ours.

On the night of the 20th our troops on the north side of the James were withdrawn, and Hancock and Gregg were sent south to destroy the Weldon Railroad. They were attacked on the 25th at Ream's Station, and after desperate fighting a part of our line gave way, losing five pieces of artillery. But the Weldon Railroad never went out of our possession from the 18th of August to the close of the war.

CHAPTER LVIII

SHERIDAN'S ADVANCE - VISIT TO SHERIDAN - SHERIDAN'S VICTORY IN THE SHENANDOAH - SHERIDAN'S RIDE TO WINCHESTER - CLOSE OF THE CAMPAIGN FOR THE WINTER

WE had our troops on the Weldon Railroad contending against a large force that regarded this road of so much importance that they could afford to expend many lives in retaking it; Sherman just getting through to Atlanta with great losses of men from casualties, discharges and detachments left along as guards to occupy and hold the road in rear of him; Washington threatened, but a short time before, and now Early being strengthened in the valley so as, probably, to renew that attempt. It kept me pretty active in looking after all these points.

On the 10th of August Sheridan had advanced on Early up the Shenandoah Valley, Early falling back to Strasburg. On the 12th I learned that Lee had sent twenty pieces of artillery, two divisions of infantry and a considerable cavalry force to strengthen Early. It was important that Sheridan should be informed of this, so I sent the information to Washington by telegraph, and directed a courier to be sent from there to get the message to Sheridan at all hazards, giving him the information. The messenger, an officer of the army, pushed through with great energy and reached Sheridan just in time. The officer went through by way of Snicker's Gap, escorted by some cavalry. He found Sheridan just making his preparations to attack Early in his chosen position. Now, however, he was thrown back on the defensive.

On the 15th of September I started to visit General Sheridan in the Shenandoah Valley. My purpose was to have him attack Early, or drive him out of the valley and destroy that source of supplies for Lee's army. I knew it was impossible for me to get orders through Washington to Sheridan to make a move, because they would be stopped there and such orders as Halleck's caution (and that of the Secretary of War) would suggest would be given instead, and would, no doubt, be contradictory to mine. I therefore, without stopping at Washington, went directly through to Charlestown, some ten miles above Harper's Ferry, and waited there to see General Sheridan, having sent a courier in advance to inform him where to meet me.

When Sheridan arrived I asked him if he had a map showing the positions of his army and that of the enemy. He at once drew one out of his side pocket, showing all roads and streams, and the camps of the two armies. He said that if he had permission he would move so and so (pointing out how) against the Confederates, and that he could "whip them." Before starting I had drawn up a plan of campaign for Sheridan, which I had brought with me ; but, seeing that he was so clear and so positive in his views and so confident of success, I said nothing about this and did not take it out of my pocket.

Sheridan's wagon trains were kept at Harper's Ferry, where all of his stores were. By keeping the teams at that place, their forage did not have to be hauled to them. As supplies of ammunition, provisions and rations for the men were wanted, trains would be made up to deliver the stores to the commissaries and quartermasters encamped at Winchester. Knowing that he, in making preparations to move at a given day, would have to bring up wagon trains from Harper's Ferry, I asked him if he could be ready to get off by the following Tuesday. This was on Friday. "O yes," he said, he "could be off before daylight on Monday." I told him then to make the attack at that time and according to his own plan; and I immediately started to return to the army about Richmond. After visiting Baltimore and Burlington, New Jersey, I arrived at City Point on the 19th.

On the way out to Harper's Ferry I had met Mr. Robert Garrett, President of the Baltimore and Ohio Railroad. He seemed very anxious to know when workmen might be put upon the road again so as to make repairs and put it in shape for running. It was a large piece of property to have standing idle. I told him I could not answer then positively but would try and inform him before a great while. On my return Mr. Garrett met me again with the same question and I told him I thought that by the following Wednesday he might send his workmen out on his road. I gave him no further information however, and he had no suspicion of how I expected to have the road cleared for his workmen.

Sheridan moved at the time he had fixed upon. He met Early at the crossing of Opequon Creek, and won a most decisive victory -one which electrified the country. Early had invited this attack himself by his bad generalship and made the victory easy. He had sent G.T. Anderson's division east of the Blue Ridge before I went to Harper's Ferry ; and about the time I arrived there he started with two other divisions (leaving but two in their camps) to march to Martinsburg for the purpose of destroying the Baltimore and Ohio Railroad at that point. Early here learned that I had been with Sheridan and, supposing there was some movement on foot, started back as soon as he got the information. But his forces were separated and, as I have said, he was very badly defeated. He fell back to Fisher's Hill, Sheridan following.

The valley is narrow at that point, and Early made another stand there, behind works which extended across. But Sheridan turned both his flanks and again sent him speeding up the valley, following in hot pursuit. The pursuit was continued up the valley to Mount Jackson and New Market. Sheridan captured about eleven hundred prisoners and sixteen guns. The houses which he passed all along the route were found to be filled with Early's wounded, and the country swarmed with his deserters. Finally, on the 25th, Early turned from the valley eastward, leaving Sheridan at Harrisonburg in undisputed possession.

Now one of the main objects of the expedition began to be accomplished. Sheridan went to work with his command, gathering in the crops, cattle, and everything in the upper part of the valley required by our troops; and especially taking what might be of use to the enemy. What he could not take away he destroyed, so that the enemy would not be invited to come back there. I congratulated Sheridan upon his recent great victory and had a salute of a hundred guns fired in honor of it, the guns being aimed at the enemy around Petersburg. I also notified the other commanders throughout the country, who also fired salutes in honor of his victory.

I had reason to believe that the administration was a little afraid to have a decisive battle fought at that time, for fear it might go against us and have a bad effect on the November elections. The convention which had met and made its nomination of the Democratic candidate for the presidency had declared the war a failure. Treason was talked as boldly in Chicago at that convention as ever it had been in Charleston. It was a question whether the government would then have had the power to make arrests and punish those who thus talked treason. But this decisive victory was the most effective campaign argument made in the canvass.

Sheridan, in his pursuit, got beyond where they could hear from him in Washington, and the President became very much frightened about him. He was afraid that the hot pursuit had been a little like that of General Cass was said to have been, in one of our Indian wars, when he was an officer of the army. Cass was pursuing the Indians so closely that the first thing he knew he found himself in their front, and the Indians pursuing him. The President was afraid that Sheridan had got on the other side of Early and that Early was in behind him. He was afraid that Sheridan was getting so far away that reinforcements would be sent out from Richmond to enable Early to beat him. I replied to the President that I had taken steps to prevent Lee from sending reinforcements to Early, by attacking the former where he was.

On the 28th of September, to retain Lee in his position, I sent Ord with the 18th corps and Birney with the 10th corps to make an advance on Richmond, to threaten it. Ord moved with the left wing up to Chaffin's Bluff; Birney with the 10th corps took a road farther north; while Kautz with the cavalry took the Darby road, still farther to the north. They got across the river by the next morning, and made an effort to surprise the enemy. In that, however, they were unsuccessful

The enemy's lines were very strong and very intricate. Stannard's division of the 18th corps with General Burnham's brigade leading, tried an assault against Fort Harrison and captured it with sixteen guns and a good many prisoners. Burnham was killed in the assault. Colonel Stevens who succeeded him was badly wounded; and his successor also fell in the same way. Some works to the right and left were also carried with the guns in them -six in number -and a few more prisoners. Birney's troops to the right captured the enemy's intrenched picketlines, but were unsuccessful in their efforts upon the main line.

Our troops fortified their new position, bringing Fort Harrison into the new line and extending it to the river. This brought us pretty close to the enemy on the north side of the James, and the two opposing lines maintained their relative positions to the close of the siege.

In the afternoon a further attempt was made to advance, but it failed. Ord fell badly wounded, and had to be relieved; the command devolved upon General Heckman, and later General Weitzel was assigned to the command of the 18th corps. During the night Lee reinforced his troops about Fort Gilmer, which was at the right of Fort Harrison, by transferring eight additional brigades from Petersburg, and attempted to retake the works which we had captured by concentrating ten brigades against them. All their efforts failed, their attacks being all repulsed with very heavy loss. In one of these assaults upon us General Stannard, a gallant officer, who was defending Fort Harrison, lost an arm. Our casualties during these operations amounted to 394 killed, 1,554 wounded and 324 missing.

Whilst this was going on General Meade was instructed to keep up an appearance of moving troops to our extreme left. Parke and Warren were kept with two divisions, each under arms, ready to move, leaving their enclosed batteries manned, with a scattering line on the other intrenchments. The object of this was to prevent reinforcements from going to the north side of the river. Meade was instructed to watch, the enemy closely and, if Lee weakened his lines, to make an attack.

On the 30th these troops moved out, under Warren, and captured an advanced intrenched camp at Peeble's farm, driving the enemy back to the main line, Our troops followed and made an attack in the hope of carrying the enemy's main line; but in this they were unsuccessful and lost a large number of men, mostly captured. The number of killed and wounded was not large. The next day our troops advanced again and established themselves, intrenching a new line about a mile in front of the enemy. This advanced Warren's position on the Weldon Railroad very considerably.

Sheridan having driven the enemy out of the valley, and taken the productions of the valley so that instead of going there for supplies the enemy would have to bring his provisions with him if he again entered it, recommended a reduction of his own force, the surplus to be sent where it could be of more use. I approved of his suggestion, and ordered him to send Wright's corps back to the James River. I further directed him to repair the railroad up the Shenandoah Valley towards the advanced position which we would hold with a small force. The troops were to be sent to Washington by the way of Culpeper, in order to watch the east side of the Blue Ridge, and prevent the enemy from getting into the rear of Sheridan while he was still doing his work of destruction.

The valley was so very important, however, to the Confederate army that, contrary to our expectations, they determined to make one more strike, and save it if possible before the supplies should be all destroyed. Reinforcements were sent therefore to Early, and this before any of our troops had been withdrawn. Early prepared to strike Sheridan at Harrisonburg; but the latter had not remained there.

On the 6th of October Sheridan commenced retiring down the valley, taking or destroying all the food and forage and driving the cattle before him, Early following. At Fisher's Hill Sheridan turned his cavalry back on that of Early, which, under the lead of Rosser, was pursuing closely, and routed it most completely, capturing eleven guns and a large number of prisoners. Sheridan lost only about sixty men. His cavalry pursued the enemy back some twenty-five miles. On the 10th of October the march down the valley was again resumed, Early again following.

I now ordered Sheridan to halt, and to improve the opportunity if afforded by the enemy's having been sufficiently weakened, to move back again and cut the James River Canal and Virginia Central Railroad.

But this order had to go through Washington where it was intercepted; and when Sheridan received what purported to be a statement of what I wanted him to do it was something entirely different. Halleck informed Sheridan that it was my wish for him to hold a forward position as a base from which to act against Charlottesville and Gordonsville; that he should fortify this position and provision it.

Sheridan objected to this most decidedly; and I was impelled to telegraph him, on the 14th, as follows

---

CITY POINT, VA.,
October 14, 1864. -12.30 P.M.

MAJOR-GENERAL SHERIDAN,
> Cedar Creek, Va.

What I want is for you to threaten the Virginia Central Railroad and canal in the manner your judgment tells you is best, holding yourself ready to advance, if the enemy draw off their forces. If you make the enemy hold a force equal to your own for the protection of those thoroughfares, it will accomplish nearly as much as their destruction. If you cannot do this, then the next best thing to do is to send here all the force you can. I deem a good cavalry force necessary for your offensive, as well as defensive operations. You need not therefore send here more than one division of cavalry.

U.S. GRANT,
Lieutenant-General.

Sheridan having been summoned to Washington City, started on the 15th leaving Wright in command. His army was then at Cedar Creek, some twenty miles south -of Winchester. The next morning while at Front Royal, Sheridan received a dispatch from Wright, saying that a dispatch from Longstreet to Early had been intercepted. It directed the latter to be ready to move and to crush Sheridan as soon as he, Longstreet, arrived. On the receipt of this news Sheridan ordered the cavalry up the valley to join Wright.

On the 18th of October Early was ready to move, and during the night succeeded in getting his troops in the rear of our left flank, which fled precipitately and in great confusion down the valley, losing eighteen pieces of artillery and a thousand or more prisoners. The right under General Getty maintained a firm and steady front, falling back to Middletown where it took a position and made a stand. The cavalry went to the rear, seized the roads leading to Winchester and held them for the use of our troops in falling back, General Wright having ordered a retreat back to that place.

Sheridan having left Washington on the 18th, reached Winchester that night. The following morning he started to join his command. He had scarcely got out of town, when he met his men returning in panic from the front and also heard heavy firing to the south. He immediately ordered the cavalry at Winchester to be deployed across the valley to stop the stragglers. Leaving members of his staff to take care of Winchester and the public property there, he set out with a small escort directly for the scene of battle. As he met the fugitives he ordered them to turn back, reminding them that they were going the wrong way. His presence soon restored confidence. Finding themselves worse frightened than hurt the men did halt and turn back. Many of those who had run ten miles got back in time to redeem their reputation as gallant soldiers before night.

When Sheridan got to the front he found Getty and Custer still holding their ground firmly between the Confederates and our retreating troops. Every thing in the rear was now ordered up. Sheridan at once proceeded to intrench his position; and he awaited an assault from the enemy. This was made with vigor, and was directed principally against Emory's corps, which had sustained the principal loss in the first attack. By one o'clock the attack was repulsed. Early was so badly damaged that he seemed disinclined to make another attack, but went to work to intrench himself with a view to holding the position he had already gained. He thought, no doubt, that Sheridan would be glad enough to leave him unmolested; but in this he was mistaken.

About the middle of the afternoon Sheridan advanced. He sent his cavalry by both flanks, and they penetrated to the enemy's rear. The contest was close for a time, but at length the left of the enemy broke, and disintegration along the whole line soon followed. Early tried to rally his men, but they were followed so closely that they had to give way very quickly every time they attempted to make a stand. Our cavalry, having pushed on and got in the rear of the Confederates, captured twenty-four pieces of artillery, besides retaking what had been lost in the morning. This victory pretty much closed the campaigning in the Valley of Virginia. All the Confederate troops were sent back to Richmond with the exception of one division of infantry and a little cavalry. Wright's corps was ordered back to the Army of the Potomac, and two other divisions were withdrawn from the valley. Early had lost more men in killed, wounded and captured in the valley than Sheridan had commanded from first to last.

On more than one occasion in these engagements General R. B. Hayes, who succeeded me as President of the United States, bore a very honorable part. His conduct on the field was marked by conspicuous gallantry as well as the display of qualities of a higher order than that of mere personal daring. This might well have been expected of one who could write at the time he is said to have done so. "Any officer fit for duty who at this crisis would abandon his post to electioneer for a seat in Congress, ought to be scalped." Having entered the army as a Major of Volunteers at the beginning of the war, General Hayes attained by meritorious service the rank of Brevet Major-General before its close.

On the north side of the James River the enemy attacked Kautz's cavalry on the 7th of October, and drove it back with heavy loss in killed, wounded and prisoners, and the loss of all the artillery. This was followed up by an attack on our intrenched infantry line, but was repulsed with severe slaughter. On the 13th a reconnaissance was sent out by General Butler, with a view to drive the enemy from some new works he was constructing, which resulted in heavy loss to us.

On the 24th I ordered General Meade to attempt to get possession of the South Side Railroad, and for that purpose to advance on the 27th. The attempt proved a failure, however, the most advanced of our troops not getting nearer than within six miles of the point aimed for. Seeing the impossibility of its accomplishment I ordered the troops to withdraw, and they were all back in their former positions the next day.

Butler, by my directions, also made a demonstration on the north side of the James River in order to support this move, by detaining there the Confederate troops who were on that side. He succeeded in this, but failed of further results by not marching past the enemy's left before turning in on the Darby road and by reason of simply coming up against their lines in place.

This closed active operations around Richmond for the winter. Of course there was frequent skirmishing between pickets, but no serious battle was fought near either Petersburg or Richmond. It would prolong this work to give a detailed account of all that took place from day to day around Petersburg and at other parts of my command, and it would not interest the general reader if given. All these details can be found by the military student in a series of books published by the Scribners, Badeau's history of my campaigns, and also in the publications of the War Department, including both the National and Confederate reports.

In the latter part of November General Hancock was relieved from the command of the 2d corps by the Secretary of War and ordered to Washington, to organize and command a corps of veteran troops to be designated the 1st corps. It was expected that this would give him a large command to co-operate with in the spring. It was my expectation, at the time, that in the final operations Hancock should move either up the valley, or else east of the Blue Ridge to Lynchburg; the idea being to make the spring campaign the close of the war. I expected, with Sherman coming up from the South, Meade south of Petersburg and around Richmond, and Thomas's command in Tennessee with depots of supplies established in the eastern part of that State, to move from the direction of Washington or the valley towards Lynchburg. We would then have Lee so surrounded that his supplies would be cut off entirely, making it impossible for him to support his army.

General Humphreys, chief-of-staff of the Army of the Potomac, was assigned to the command of the 2d corps, to succeed Hancock.

CHAPTER LIX

THE CAMPAIGN IN GEORGIA -
SHERMAN'S MARCH TO THE SEA - WAR ANECDOTES - THE
MARCH ON SAVANNAH - INVESTMENT OF SAVANNAH -
CAPTURE OF SAVANNAH

LET us now return to the operations in the military division of the Mississippi, and accompany Sherman in his march to the sea.

The possession of Atlanta by us narrowed the territory of the enemy very materially and cut off one of his two remaining lines of roads from east to west.

A short time after the fall of Atlanta Mr. Davis visited Palmetto and Macon and made speeches at each place. He spoke at Palmetto on the 20th of September and at Macon on the 22d. Inasmuch as he had relieved Johnston and appointed Hood, and Hood had immediately taken the initiative, it is natural to suppose that Mr. Davis was disappointed with General Johnston's policy. My own judgment is that Johnston acted very wisely: he husbanded his men and saved as much of his territory as he could, without fighting decisive battles in which all might be lost. As Sherman advanced, as I have shown, his army became spread out, until, if this had been continued, it would have been easy to destroy it in detail. I know that both Sherman and I were rejoiced when we heard of the change. Hood was unquestionably a brave, gallant soldier and not destitute of ability; but unfortunately his policy was to fight the enemy wherever he saw him, without thinking much of the consequences of defeat.

In his speeches Mr. Davis denounced Governor Brown, of Georgia, and General Johnston in unmeasured terms, even insinuating that their loyalty to the Southern cause was doubtful. So far as General Johnston is concerned, I think Davis did him a great injustice in this particular. I had known the general before the war and strongly believed it would be impossible for him to accept a high commission for the purpose of betraying the cause he had espoused. Then, as I have said, I think that his policy was the best one that could have been pursued by the whole South -protract the war, which was all that was necessary to enable them to gain recognition in the end. The North was already growing weary, as the South evidently was also, but with this difference. In the North the people governed, and could stop hostilities whenever they chose to stop supplies. The South was a military camp, controlled absolutely by the govermment with soldiers to back it, and the war could have been protracted, no matter to what extent the discontent reached, up to the point of open mutiny of the soldiers themselves. Mr. Davis's speeches were frank appeals to the people of Georgia and that portion of the South to come to their relief. He tried to assure his frightened hearers that the Yankees were rapidly digging their own graves; that measures were already being taken to cut them off from supplies from the North; and that with a force in front, and cut off from the rear, they must soon starve in the midst of a hostile people. Papers containing reports of these speeches immediately reached the Northern States, and they were republished. Of course, that caused no alarm so long as telegraphic communication was kept up with Sherman.

When Hood was forced to retreat from Atlanta he moved to the southwest and was followed by a portion of Sherman's army. He soon appeared upon the railroad in Sherman's rear, and with his whole army began destroying the road. At the same time also the work was begun in Tennessee and Kentucky which Mr. Davis had assured his hearers at Palmetto and Macon would take place. He ordered Forrest (about the ablest cavalry general in the South) north for this purpose; and Forrest and Wheeler carried out their orders with more or less destruction, occasionally picking up a garrison. Forrest indeed performed the very remarkable feat of capturing, with cavalry, two gunboats and a number of transports, something the accomplishment of which is very hard to account for. Hood's army had been weakened by Governor Brown's withdrawing the Georgia State troops for the purpose of gathering in the season's crops for the use of the people and for the use of the army. This not only depleted Hood's forces but it served a most excellent purpose in gathering in supplies of food and forage for the use of our army in its subsequent march. Sherman was obliged to push on with his force and go himself with portions of it hither and thither, until it was clearly demonstrated to him that with the army he then had it would be impossible to hold the line from Atlanta back and leave him any force whatever with which to take the offensive. Had that plan been adhered to, very large reinforcements would have been necessary ; and Mr. Davis's prediction of the destruction of the army would have been realized, or else Sherman would have been obliged to make a successful retreat, which Mr. Davis said in his speeches would prove more disastrous than Napoleon's retreat from Moscow.

These speeches of Mr. Davis were not long in reaching Sherman. He took advantage of the information they gave, and made all the preparation possible for him to make to meet what now became expected, attempts to break his communications. Something else had to be done: and to Sherman's sensible and soldierly mind the idea was not long in dawning upon him, not only that something else had to be done, but what that something else should be.

On September 16th I telegraphed Sherman as follows:

CITY POINT, VA., Sept. 10, 1864.

MAJOR-GENERAL SHERMAN,

Atlanta, Georgia.

So soon as your men are sufficiently rested, and preparations can be made, it is desirable that another campaign should be commenced. We want to keep the enemy constantly pressed to the end of the war. If we give him no peace whilst the war lasts, the end cannot be distant. Now that we have all of Mobile Bay that is valuable, I do not know but it will be the best move to transfer Canby's troops to act upon Savannah, whilst you move on Augusta. I should like to hear from you, however, in this matter.

U.S. GRANT, Lieutenant-General.

Sherman replied promptly:

"If I could be sure of finding provisions and ammunition at Augusta, or Columbus, Georgia, I can march to Milledgeville, and compel Hood to give up Augusta or Macon, and then turn on the other. * * * If you can manage to take the Savannah River as high up as Augusta, or the Chattahoochee as far up as Columbus, I can sweep the whole State of Georgia."

On the 12th I sent a special messenger, one of my own staff, with a letter inviting Sherman's views about the next campaign.

CITY POINT, VA., Sept. 12, 1864.

MAJOR-GENERAL W. T. SHERMAN,
       Commanding Mil. Division of the Mississippi.

I send Lieutenant-Colonel Porter, of my staff, with this. Colonel Porter will explain to you the exact condition of affairs here better than I can do in the limits of a letter. Although I feel myself strong enough for offensive operations, I am holding on quietly to get advantage of recruits and convalescents, who are coming forward very rapidly. My lines are necessarily very long, extending from Deep Bottom north of the James across the peninsula formed by the Appomattox and the James, and south of the Appomattox to the Weldon Road. This line is very strongly fortified, and can be held with comparatively few men, but from its great length takes many in the aggregate. I propose, when I do move, to extend my left so as to control what is known as the South Side, or Lynchburg and Petersburg Road, then if possible to keep the Danville Road cut. At the same time this move is made, I want to send a force of from six to ten thousand men against Wilmington.

The way I propose to do this is to land the men north of Fort Fisher, and hold that point. At the same time a large naval fleet will be assembled there, and the ironclads will run the batteries as they did at Mobile. This will give us the same control of the harbor of Wilmington that we now have of the harbor of Mobile. What you are to do with the forces at your command, I do not see. The difficulties of supplying your army, except when you are constantly moving, beyond where you are, I plainly see. If it had not been for Price's movements Canby would have sent twelve thousand more men to Mobile. From your command on the Mississippi an equal number could have been taken. With these forces my idea would have been to divide them, sending one half to Mobile and the other half to Savannah. You could then move as proposed in your telegram, so as to threaten Macon and Augusta equally. Whichever was abandoned by the enemy you could take and open up a new base of supplies. My object now in sending a, staff officer is not so much to suggest operations for you, as to get your views and have plans matured by the time everything can be got ready. It will probably be the 5th of October before any of the plans herein indicated will be executed.

If you have any promotions to recommend, send the names forward and I will approve them. * * *

U.S. GRANT, Lieutenant-General.

This reached Sherman on September 20th.

On the 25th of September Sherman reported to Washington that Hood's troops were in his rear. He had provided against this by sending a division to Chattanooga and a division to Rome, Georgia, which was in the rear of Hood, supposing that Hood would fall back in the direction from which he had come to reach the railroad. At the same time Sherman and Hood kept up a correspondence relative to the exchange of prisoners, the treatment of citizens. and other matters suitable to be arranged between hostile commanders in the field. On the 27th of September I telegraphed Sherman as follows:

CITY POINT, VA.,
September 27, 1864.-10.30 A.M.

MAJOR-GENERAL SHERMAN:

I have directed all recruits and new troops from the Western States to be sent to Nashville, to receive their further orders from you. * * *

U.S. GRANT, Lieutenant-General.

On the 29th Sherman sent Thomas back to Chattanooga, and afterwards to Nashville, with another division (Morgan's) of the advanced army. Sherman then suggested that, when he was prepared, his movements should take place against Milledgeville and then to Savannah. His expectation at that time was, to make this movement as soon as he could get up his supplies. Hood was moving in his own country, and was moving light so that he could make two miles to Sherman's one. He depended upon the country to gather his supplies, and so was not affected by delays.

As I have said, until this unexpected state of affairs happened, Mobile had been looked upon as the objective point of Sherman's army, It had been a favorite move of mine from 1862, when I first suggested to the then commander-in-chief that the troops in Louisiana, instead of frittering away their time in the trans-Mississippi, should move against Mobile. I recommended this from time to time until I came into command of the army, the last of March 1864. Having the power in my own hands, I now ordered the concentration of supplies, stores and troops, in the department of the Gulf about New Orleans, with a view to a move against Mobile, in support of, and in conjunction with, the other armies operating in the field. Before I came into command, these troops had been scattered over the trans-Mississippi department in such a way that they could not be, or were not, gotten back in time to take any part in the original movement; hence the consideration, which had caused Mobile to be selected as the objective point for Sherman's army to find his next base of supplies after having cut loose from Atlanta, no longer existed.

General G.M. Dodge, an exceedingly efficient officer, having been badly wounded, had to leave the army about the first of October. He was in command of two divisions of the 16th corps, consolidated into one. Sherman then divided his army into the right and left wings--the right commanded by General O.O. Howard and the left by General Slocum. General Dodge's two divisions were assigned, one to each of these wings. Howard's command embraced the 15th and 17th corps, and Slocum's the 14th and 20th corps, commanded by Generals Jeff. C. Davis and A.S. Williams. Generals Logan and Blair commanded the two corps composing the right wing. About this time they left to take part in the presidential election, which took place that year, leaving their corps to Osterhaus and Ransom. I have no doubt that their leaving was at the earnest solicitation of the War Department. General Blair got back in time to resume his command and to proceed with it throughout the march to the sea and back to the grand review at Washington. General Logan did not return to his command until after it reached Savannah.

Logan felt very much aggrieved at the transfer of General Howard from that portion of the Army of the Potomac which was then with the Western Army, to the command of the Army of the Tennessee, with which army General Logan had served from the battle of Belmont to the fall of Atlanta -having passed successively through all grades from colonel commanding a regiment to general commanding a brigade, division and army corps, until upon the death of McPherson the command of the entire Army of the Tennessee devolved upon him in the midst of a hotly contested battle. He conceived that he had done his full duty as commander in that engagement; and I can bear testimony, from personal observation, that he had proved himself fully equal to all the lower positions which he had occupied as a soldier. I will not pretend to question the motive which actuated Sherman in taking an officer from another army to supersede General Logan. I have no doubt, whatever, that he did this for what he considered would be to the good of the service, which was more important than that the personal feelings of any individual should not be aggrieved; though I doubt whether he had an officer with him who could have filled the place as Logan would have done. Differences of opinion must exist between the best of friends as to policies in war, and of judgment as to men's fitness. The officer who has the command, however, should be allowed to judge of the fitness of the officers under him, unless he is very manifestly wrong.

Sherman's army, after all the depletions, numbered about sixty thousand effective men. All weak men had been left to hold the rear, and those remaining were not only well men, but strong and hardy, so that he had sixty thousand as good soldiers as ever trod the earth; better than any European soldiers, because they not only worked like a machine but the machine thought. European armies know very little what they are fighting for, and care less. Included in these sixty thousand troops, there were two small divisions of cavalry, numbering altogether about four thousand men. Hood had about thirty-five to forty thousand men, independent of Forrest, whose forces were operating in Tennessee and Kentucky, as Mr. Davis had promised they should. This part of Mr. Davis's military plan was admirable, and promised the best results of anything he could have done, according to my judgment. I say this because I have criticized his military judgment in the removal of Johnston, and also in the appointment of Hood. I am aware, however, that there was high feeling existing at that time between Davis and his subordinate, whom I regarded as one of his ablest lieutenants.

On the 5th of October the railroad back from Atlanta was again very badly broken, Hood having got on the track with his army. Sherman saw after night, from a high point, the road burning for miles. The defence of the railroad by our troops was very gallant, but they could not hold points between their intrenched positions against Hood's whole army; in fact they made no attempt to do so; but generally the intrenched positions were held, as well as important bridges, and stores located at them. Allatoona, for instance, was defended by a small force of men under the command of General Corse, one of the very able and efficient volunteer officers produced by the war. He, with a small force, was cut off from the remainder of the National army and was attacked with great vigor by many times his own number. Sherman from his high position could see the battle raging, with the Confederate troops between him and his subordinate. He sent men, of course, to raise the temporary siege, but the time that would be necessarily consumed in reaching Corse, would be so great that all occupying the intrenchments might be dead. Corse was a man who would never surrender. From a high position some of Sherman's signal corps discovered a signal flag waving from a hole in the block house at Allatoona. It was from Corse. He had been shot through the face, but he signaled to his chief a message which left no doubt of his determination to hold his post at all hazards. It was at this point probably, that Sherman first realized that with the forces at his disposal, the keeping open of his line of communications with the North would be impossible if he expected to retain any force with which to operate offensively beyond Atlanta. He proposed, therefore, to destroy the roads back to Chattanooga, when all ready to move, and leave the latter place garrisoned. Yet, before abandoning the railroad, it was necessary that he should repair damages already done, and hold the road until he could get forward such supplies, ordnance stores and small rations, as he wanted to carry with him on his proposed march, and to return to the north his surplus artillery; his object being to move light and to have no more artillery than could be used to advantage on the field.

Sherman thought Hood would follow him, though he proposed to prepare for the contingency of the latter moving the other way while he was moving south, by making Thomas strong enough to hold Tennessee and Kentucky. I, myself, was thoroughly satisfied that Hood would go north, as he did. On the 2d of November I telegraphed Sherman authorizing him definitely to move according to the plan he had proposed: that is, cutting loose from his base, giving up Atlanta and the railroad back to Chattanooga. To strengthen Thomas he sent Stanley (4th corps) back and also ordered Schofield, commanding the Army of the Ohio, twelve thousand strong, to report to him. In addition to this, A. J. Smith, who, with two divisions of Sherman's army, was in Missouri aiding Rosecrans in driving the enemy from that State, was under orders to return to Thomas and, under the most unfavorable circumstances, might be expected to arrive there long before Hood could reach Nashville.

In addition to this, the new levies of troops that were being raised in the Northwest went to Thomas as rapidly as enrolled and equipped. Thomas, without any of these additions spoken of, had a garrison at Chattanooga -which had been strengthened by one division- and garrisons at Bridgeport, Stevenson, Decatur, Murfreesboro, and Florence.

There were already with him in Nashville ten thousand soldiers in round numbers, and many thousands of employees in the quartermaster's and other departments who could be put in the intrenchments in front of Nashville, for its defence. Also, Wilson was there with ten thousand dismounted cavalrymen, who were being equipped for the field. Thomas had at this time about forty-five thousand men without any of the reinforcements here above enumerated. These reinforcements gave him altogether about seventy thousand men, without counting what might be added by the new levies already spoken of.

About this time Beauregard arrived upon the field, not to supersede Hood in command, but to take general charge over the entire district in which Hood and Sherman were, or might be, operating. He made the most frantic appeals to the citizens for assistance to be rendered in every way: by sending reinforcements, by destroying supplies on the line of march of the invaders, by destroying the bridges over which they would have to cross, and by, in every way, obstructing the roads to their front. But it was hard to convince the people of the propriety of destroying supplies which were so much needed by themselves, and each one hoped that his own possessions might escape.

Hood soon started north, and went into camp near Decatur, Alabama, where he remained until the 29th of October, but without making an attack on the garrison of that place.

The Tennessee River was patrolled by gunboats, from Muscle Shoals east; and, also, below the second shoals out to the Ohio River. These, with the troops that might be concentrated from the garrisons along the river at any point where Hood might choose to attempt to cross, made it impossible for him to cross the Tennessee at any place where it was navigable. But Muscle Shoals is not navigable, and below them again is another shoal which also obstructs navigation. Hood therefore moved down to a point nearly opposite Florence, Alabama, crossed over and remained there for some time, collecting supplies of food, forage and ammunition. All of these had to come from a considerable distance south, because the region in which he was then situated was mountainous, with small valleys which produced but little, and what they had produced had long since been exhausted. On the 1st of November I suggested to Sherman, and also asked his views thereon, the propriety of destroying Hood before he started on his campaign.

On the 2d of November, as stated, I approved definitely his making his proposed campaign through Georgia, leaving Hood behind to the tender mercy of Thomas and the troops in his command. Sherman fixed the 10th of November as the day of starting.

Sherman started on that day to get back to Atlanta, and on the 15th the real march to the sea commenced. The right wing, under Howard, and the cavalry went to Jonesboro, Milledgeville, then the capital of Georgia, being Sherman's objective or stopping place on the way to Savannah. The left wing moved to Stone Mountain, along roads much farther east than those taken by the right wing. Slocum was in command, and threatened Augusta as the point to which he was moving, but he was to turn off and meet the right wing at Milledgeville.

Atlanta was destroyed so far as to render it worthless for military purposes before starting, Sherman himself remaining over a day to superintend the work, and see that it was well done. Sherman's orders for this campaign were perfect. Before starting, he had sent back all sick, disabled and weak men, retaining nothing but the hardy, well inured soldiers to accompany him on his long march in prospect. His artillery was reduced to sixty-five guns. The ammunition carried with them was two hundred rounds for musket and gun. Small rations were taken in a small wagon train, which was loaded to its capacity for rapid movement. The army was expected to live on the country, and to always keep the wagons full of forage and provisions against a possible delay of a few days.

The troops, both of the right and left wings, made most of their advance along the line of railroads, which they destroyed. The method adopted to perform this work, was to burn and destroy all the bridges and culverts, and for a long distance, at places, to tear up the track and bend the rails. Soldiers to do this rapidly would form a line along one side of the road with crowbars and poles, place these under the rails and, hoisting all at once, turn over many rods of road at one time. The ties would then be placed in piles, and the rails, as they were loosened, would be carried and put across these log heaps. When a sufficient number of rails were placed upon a pile of ties it would be set on fire. This would heat the rails very much more in the middle, that being over the main part of the fire, than at the ends, so that they would naturally bend of their own weight; but the soldiers, to increase the damage, would take tongs and, one or two men at each end of the rail, carry it with force against the nearest tree and twist it around, thus leaving rails forming bands to ornament the forest trees of Georgia. All this work was going on at the same time, there being a sufficient number of men detailed for that purpose. Some piled the logs and built the fire; some put the rails upon the fire; while others would bend those that were sufficiently heated: so that, by the time the last bit of road was torn up, that it was designed to destroy at a certain place, the rails previously taken up were already destroyed.

The organization for supplying the army was very complete. Each brigade furnished a company to gather supplies of forage and provisions for the command to which they belonged. Strict injunctions were issued against pillaging, or otherwise unnecessarily annoying the people; but everything in shape of food for man and forage for beast was taken. The supplies were turned over to the brigade commissary and quartermaster, and were issued by them to their respective commands precisely the same as if they had been purchased. The captures consisted largely of cattle, sheep, poultry, some bacon, cornmeal, often molasses, and occasionally coffee or other small rations.

The skill of these men, called by themselves and the army "bummers," in collecting their loads and getting back to their respective commands, was marvelous. When they started out in the morning, they were always on foot; but scarcely one of them returned in the evening without being mounted on a horse or mule. These would be turned in for the general use of the army, and the next day these men would start out afoot and return again in the evening mounted. Many of the exploits of these men would fall under the head of romance; indeed, I am afraid that in telling some of their experiences, the romance got the better of the truth upon which the story was founded, and that, in the way many of these anecdotes are told, very little of the foundation is left. I suspect that most of them consist chiefly of the fiction added to make the stories better. In one instance it was reported that a few men of Sherman's army passed a house where they discovered some chickens under the dwelling. They immediately proceeded to capture them, to add to the army's supplies. The lady of the house, who happened to be at home, made piteous appeals to have these spared, saying they were a few she had put away to save by permission of other parties who had preceded and who had taken all the others that she had. The soldiers seemed moved at her appeal; but looking at the chickens again they were tempted and one of them replied: "The rebellion must be suppressed if it takes the last chicken in the Confederacy," and proceeded to appropriate the last one.

Another anecdote characteristic of these times has been told. The South, prior to the rebellion, kept bloodhounds to pursue runaway slaves who took refuge in the neighboring swamps, and also to hunt convicts. Orders were issued to kill all these animals as they were met with. On one occasion a soldier picked up a poodle, the favorite pet of its mistress, and was carrying it off to execution when the lady made a strong appeal to him to spare it. The soldier replied, "Madam, our orders are to kill every bloodhound." "But this is not a bloodhound," said the lady. "Well, madam, we cannot tell what it will grow into if we leave it behind," said the soldier as he went off with it.

Notwithstanding these anecdotes, and the necessary hardship they would seem to imply, I do not believe there was much unwarrantable pillaging considering that we were in the enemy's territory and without any supplies except such as the country afforded.

On the 23d Sherman, with the left wing, reached Milledgeville. The right wing was not far off: but proceeded on its way towards Savannah destroying the road as it went. The troops at Milledgeville remained over a day to destroy factories, buildings used for military purposes, etc., before resuming its march.

The governor, who had been almost defying Mr. Davis before this, now fled precipitately, as did the legislature of the State and all the State officers. The governor, Sherman says, was careful to carry away even his garden vegetables, while he left the archives of the State to fall into our hands. The only military force that was opposed to Sherman's forward march was the Georgia militia, a division under the command of General G.W. Smith, and a battalion under Harry Wayne. Neither the quality of the forces nor their numbers was sufficient to even retard the progress of Sherman's army.

The people at the South became so frantic at this time at the successful invasion of Georgia that they took the cadets from the military college and added them to the ranks of the militia. They even liberated the State convicts under promise from them that they would serve in the army. I have but little doubt that the worst acts that were attributed to Sherman's army were committed by these convicts, and by other Southern people who ought to have been under sentence -such people as could be found in every community, North and South -who took advantage of their country being invaded to commit crime. They were in but little danger of detection, or of arrest even if detected.

The Southern papers in commenting upon Sherman's movements pictured him as in the most deplorable condition: stating that his men were starving, that they were demoralized and wandering about almost without object, aiming only to reach the sea coast and get under the protection of our navy. These papers got to the North and had more or less effect upon the minds of the people, causing much distress to all loyal persons -particularly to those who had husbands, sons or brothers with Sherman. Mr. Lincoln seeing these accounts, had a letter written asking me if I could give him anything that he could say to the loyal people that would comfort them. I told him there was not the slightest occasion for alarm; that with 60,000 such men as Sherman had with him, such a commanding officer as he was could not be cut off in the open country. He might possibly be prevented from reaching the point he had started out to reach, but he would get through somewhere and would finally get to his chosen destination: and even if worst came to worst he could return North. I heard afterwards of Mr. Lincoln's saying, to those who would inquire of him as to what he thought about the safety of Sherman's army, that Sherman was all right: "Grant says they are safe with such a general, and that if they cannot get out where they want to, they can crawl back by the hole they went in at."

While at Milledgeville the soldiers met at the State House, organized a legislature, and proceeded to business precisely as if they were the legislative body belonging to the State of Georgia. The debates were exciting, and were upon the subject of the situation the South was in at that time, particularly the State of Georgia. They went so far as to repeal, after a spirited and acrimonious debate, the ordinance of secession. The next day (24th) Sherman continued his march, going by the way of Waynesboro and Louisville, Millen being the next objective and where the two columns (the right and left wings) were to meet. The left wing moved to the left of the direct road, and the cavalry still farther off so as to make it look as though Augusta was the point they were aiming for. They moved on all the roads they could find leading in that direction. The cavalry was sent to make a rapid march in hope of surprising Millen before the Union prisoners could be carried away; but they failed in this.

The distance from Milledgeville to Millen was about one hundred miles. At this point Wheeler, who had been ordered from Tennessee, arrived and swelled the numbers and efficiency of the troops confronting Sherman. Hardee, a native of Georgia, also came, but brought no troops with him. It was intended that he should raise as large an army as possible with which to intercept Sherman's march. He did succeed in raising some troops, and with these and those under the command of Wheeler and Wayne, had an army sufficient to cause some annoyance but no great detention. Our cavalry and Wheeler's had a pretty severe engagement, in which Wheeler was driven towards Augusta, thus giving the idea that Sherman was probably making for that point.

Millen was reached on the 3d of December, and the march was resumed the following day for Savannah, the final objective. Bragg had now been sent to Augusta with some troops. Wade Hampton was there also trying to raise cavalry sufficient to destroy Sherman's army. If he ever raised a force it was too late to do the work expected of it. Hardee's whole force probably numbered less than ten thousand men.

From Millen to Savannah the country is sandy and poor, and affords but very little forage other than rice straw, which was then growing. This answered a very good purpose as forage, and the rice grain was an addition to the soldier's rations. No further resistance worthy of note was met with, until within a few miles of Savannah. This place was found to be intrenched and garrisoned. Sherman proceeded at once on his arrival to invest the place, and found that the enemy had placed torpedoes in the ground, which were to explode when stepped on by man or beast. One of these exploded under an officer's horse, blowing the animal to pieces and tearing one of the legs of the officer so badly that it had to be amputated. Sherman at once ordered his prisoners to the front, moving them in a compact body in advance, to either explode the torpedoes or dig them up. No further explosion took place.

On the 10th of December the siege of Savannah commenced. Sherman then, before proceeding any further with operations for the capture of the place, started with some troops to open communication with our fleet, which he expected to find in the lower harbor or as near by as the forts of the enemy would permit. In marching to the coast he encountered Fort McAllister, which it was necessary to reduce before the supplies he might find on shipboard could be made available. Fort McAllister was soon captured by an assault made by General Hazen's division. Communication was then established with the fleet. The capture of Savannah then only occupied a few days, and involved no great loss of life. The garrison, however, as we shall see, was enabled to escape by crossing the river and moving eastward.

When Sherman had opened communication with the fleet he found there a steamer, which I had forwarded to him, carrying the accumulated mails for his army, also supplies which I supposed he would be in need of. General J. G. Foster, who commanded all the troops south of North Carolina on the Atlantic sea-board, visited General Sherman before he had opened communication with the fleet, with the view of ascertaining what assistance he could be to him. Foster returned immediately to his own headquarters at Hilton Head, for the purpose of sending Sherman siege guns, and also if he should find he had them to spare, supplies of clothing, hard bread, etc., thinking that these articles might not be found outside. The mail on the steamer which I sent down, had been collected by Colonel A. H. Markland of the Post Office Deparment, who went in charge of it. On this same vessel I sent an officer of my staff (Lieutenant Dunn) with the following letter to General Sherman:

CITY POINT, VA., Dec. 3, 1864.

MAJOR-GENERAL W. T. SHERMAN,
> Commanding Armies near Savannah, Ga.

The little information gleaned from the Southern press, indicat-ing no great obstacle to your progress, I have directed your mails (which had been previously collected at Baltimore by Colonel Markland, Special Agent of the Post Office Department) to be sent as far as the blockading squadron off Savannah, to be forwarded to you as soon as heard from on the coast.

Not liking to rejoice before the victory is assured, I abstain from congratulating you and those under your command, until bottom has been struck. I have never had a fear, however, for the result.

Since you left Atlanta, no very great progress has been made here. The enemy has been closely watched though, and prevented from detaching against you. I think not one man has gone "from here, except some twelve or fifteen hundred dismounted cavalry. Bragg has gone from Wilmington. I am trying to take advantage of his absence to get possession of that place. Owing to some preparations Admiral Porter and General Butler are making to blow up Fort Fisher (which, while hoping for the best, I do not believe a particle in), there is a delay in getting this expedition off. I hope they will be ready to start by the 7th, and that Bragg will not have started back by that time.

In this letter I do not intend to give you anything like directions for future action, but will state a general idea I have, and will get your views after you have established yourself on the sea-coast. With your veteran army I hope to get control of the only two through routes from east to west possessed by the enemy before the fall of Atlanta. The condition will be filled by holding Savannah and Augusta, or by holding any other port to the east of Savannah and Branchville. If Wilmington falls, a force from there can co-operate with you.

Thomas has got back into the defences of Nashville, with Hood close upon him. Decatur has been abandoned, and so have all the roads except the main one leading to Chattanooga. Part of this falling back was undoubtedly necessary, and all of it may have been. It did not look so, however, to me. In my opinion, Thomas far outnumbers Hood in infantry. In cavalry, Hood has the advantage in morale and numbers. I hope yet that Hood will be badly crippled if not destroyed. The general news you will learn from the papers better than I could give it.
After all becomes quiet, and roads become so bad up here that there is likely to be a week or two when nothing can be done, I will run down the coast to see you. If you desire it, I will ask Mrs. Sherman to go with me.

Yours truly,
U.S. GRANT,
Lieutenant-General.

I quote this letter because it gives the reader a full knowledge of the events of that period.

Sherman now (the 15th) returned to Savannah to complete its investment and insure the surrender of the garrison. The country about Savannah is low and marshy, and the city was well intrenched from the river above to the river below, and assaults could not be made except along a comparatively narrow causeway. For this reason assaults must have resulted in serious destruction of life to the Union troops, with the chance of failing altogether. Sherman therefore decided upon a complete investment of the place. When he believed this investment completed, he summoned the garrison to surrender. General Hardee, who was in command, replied in substance that the condition of affairs was not such as Sherman had described. He said he was in full communication with his department and was receiving supplies constantly.

Hardee, however, was cut off entirely from all communication with the west side of the river, and by the river itself to the north and south. On the South Carolina side the country was all rice fields, through which it would have been impossible to bring supplies -so that Hardee had no possible communication with the outside world except by a dilapidated plank road starting from the west bank of the river. Sherman, receiving this reply, proceeded in person to a point on the coast, where General Foster had troops stationed under General Hatch, for the purpose of making arrangements with the latter officer to go through by one of the numerous channels running inland along that part of the coast of South Carolina, to the plank road which General Hardee still possessed, and thus to cut him off from the last means he had of getting supplies, if not of communication.

While arranging for this movement and before the attempt to execute the plan had been commenced, Sherman received information through one of his staff officers that the enemy had evacuated Savannah the night before. This was the night of the 21st of December. Before evacuating the place Hardee had blown up the navy yard. Some iron-clads had been destroyed, as well as other property that might have been valuable to us ; but he left an immense amount of stores untouched, consisting of cotton, railroad cars, workshops, numerous pieces of artillery, and several thousand stands of small arms.

A little incident occurred, soon after the fall of Savannah, which Sherman relates in his Memoirs, and which is worthy of repetition. Savannah was one of the points where blockade runners entered. Shortly after the city fell into our possession, a blockade runner came sailing up serenely, not doubting but the Confederates were still in possession. It was not molested, and the captain did not find out his mistake until he had tied up and gone to the Custom House, where he found a new occupant of the building, and made a less profitable disposition of his vessel and cargo than he had expected.

As there was some discussion as to the authorship of Sherman's march to the sea, by critics of his book when it appeared before the public, I want to state here that no question upon that subject was ever raised between General Sherman and myself. Circumstances made the plan on which Sherman expected to act impracticable, and as commander of the forces he necessarily had to devise a new one which would give, more promise of success: consequently he recommended the destruction of the railroad back to Chattanooga, and that he should be authorized then to move, as he did, from Atlanta forward. His suggestions were finally approved, although they did not immediately find favor in Washington. Even when it came to the time of starting, the greatest apprehension, as to the propriety of the campaign he was about to commence, filled the mind of the President, induced no doubt by his advisers. This went so far as to move the President to ask me to suspend Sherman's march for a day or two until I could think the matter over. My recollection is, though I find no record to show it, that out of deference to the President's wish I did send a dispatch to Sherman asking him to wait a day or two, or else the connections between us were already cut so that I could not do so. However this may be, the question of who devised the plan of march from Atlanta to Savannah is easily answered: it was clearly Sherman, and to him also belongs the credit of its brilliant execution. It was hardly possible that any one else than those on the spot could have devised a new plan of campaign to supersede one that did not promise success.*

I was in favor of Sherman's plan from the time it was first submitted to me. My chief of staff, however, was very bitterly opposed to it and, as I learned subsequently, finding that he could not move me, he appealed to the authorities at Washington to stop it.

---

*See Appendix, letters of Oct. 11th.

CHAPTER LX

THE BATTLE OF FRANKLIN -
THE BATTLE OF NASHVILLE

AS we have seen, Hood succeeded in crossing the Tennessee River between Muscle Shoals and the lower shoals at the end of October, 1864. Thomas sent Schofield with the 4th and 23d corps, together with three brigades of Wilson's cavalry to Pulaski to watch him. On the 17th of November Hood started and moved in such a manner as to avoid Schofield, thereby turning his position. Hood had with him three infantry corps, commanded respectively by Stephen D. Lee, Stewart and Cheatham. These, with his cavalry, numbered about forty-five thousand men. Schofield had, of all arms, about thirty thousand. Thomas's orders were, therefore, for Schofield to watch the movements of the enemy, but not to fight a battle if he could avoid it; but to fall back in case of an advance on Nashville, and to fight the enemy, as he fell back, so as to retard the enemy's movements until he could be reinforced by Thomas himself. As soon as Schofield saw this movement of Hood's, he sent his trains to the rear, but did not fall back himself until the 21st, and then only to Columbia. At Columbia there was a slight skirmish but no battle. From this place Schofield then retreated to Franklin. He had sent his wagons in advance, and Stanley had gone with them with two divisions to protect them. Cheatham's corps of Hood's army pursued the wagon train and went into camp at Spring Hill, for the night of the 29th.

Schofield retreating from Columbia on the 29th passed Spring Hill, where Cheatham was bivouacked, during the night without molestation, though within half a mile of where the Confederates were encamped. On the morning of the 30th he had arrived at Franklin.

Hood followed closely and reached Franklin in time to make an attack the same day. The fight was very desperate and sanguinary. The Confederate generals led their men in the repeated charges, and the loss among them was of unusual proportions. This fighting continued with great severity until long after the night closed in, when the Confederates drew off. General Stanley, who commanded two divisions of the Union troops, and whose troops bore the brunt of the battle, was wounded in the fight, but maintained his position.

The enemy's loss at Franklin, according to Thomas's report, was 1,750 buried upon the field by our troops, 3,800 in the hospital, and 702 prisoners besides. Schofield's loss, as officially reported, was 189 killed, 1,033 wounded, and 1,104 captured and missing.

Thomas made no effort to reinforce Schofield at Franklin, as it seemed to me at the time he should have done, and fight out the battle there. He simply ordered Schofield to continue his retreat to Nashville, which the latter did during that night and the next day.

Thomas, in the meantime, was making his preparations to receive Hood. The road to Chattanooga was still well guarded with strong garrisons at Murfreesboro, Stevenson, Bridgeport and Chattanooga. Thomas had previously given up Decatur and had been reinforced by A.J. Smith's two divisions just returned from Missouri. He also had Steedman's division and R.S. Granger's, which he had drawn from the front. His quartermaster's men, about ten thousand in number, had been organized and armed under the command of the chief quartermaster, General J.L. Donaldson, and placed in the fortifications under the general supervision of General Z.B. Tower, of the United States Engineers.

Hood was allowed to move upon Nashville, and to invest that place almost without interference. Thomas was strongly fortified in his position, so that he would have been safe against the attack of Hood. He had troops enough even to annihilate him in the open field. To me his delay was unaccountable -sitting there and permitting himself to be invested, so that, in the end, to raise the siege he would have to fight the enemy strongly posted behind fortifications. It is true the weather was very bad. The rain was falling and freezing as it fell, so that the ground was covered with a sheet of ice that made it very difficult to move. But I was afraid that the enemy would find means of moving, elude Thomas

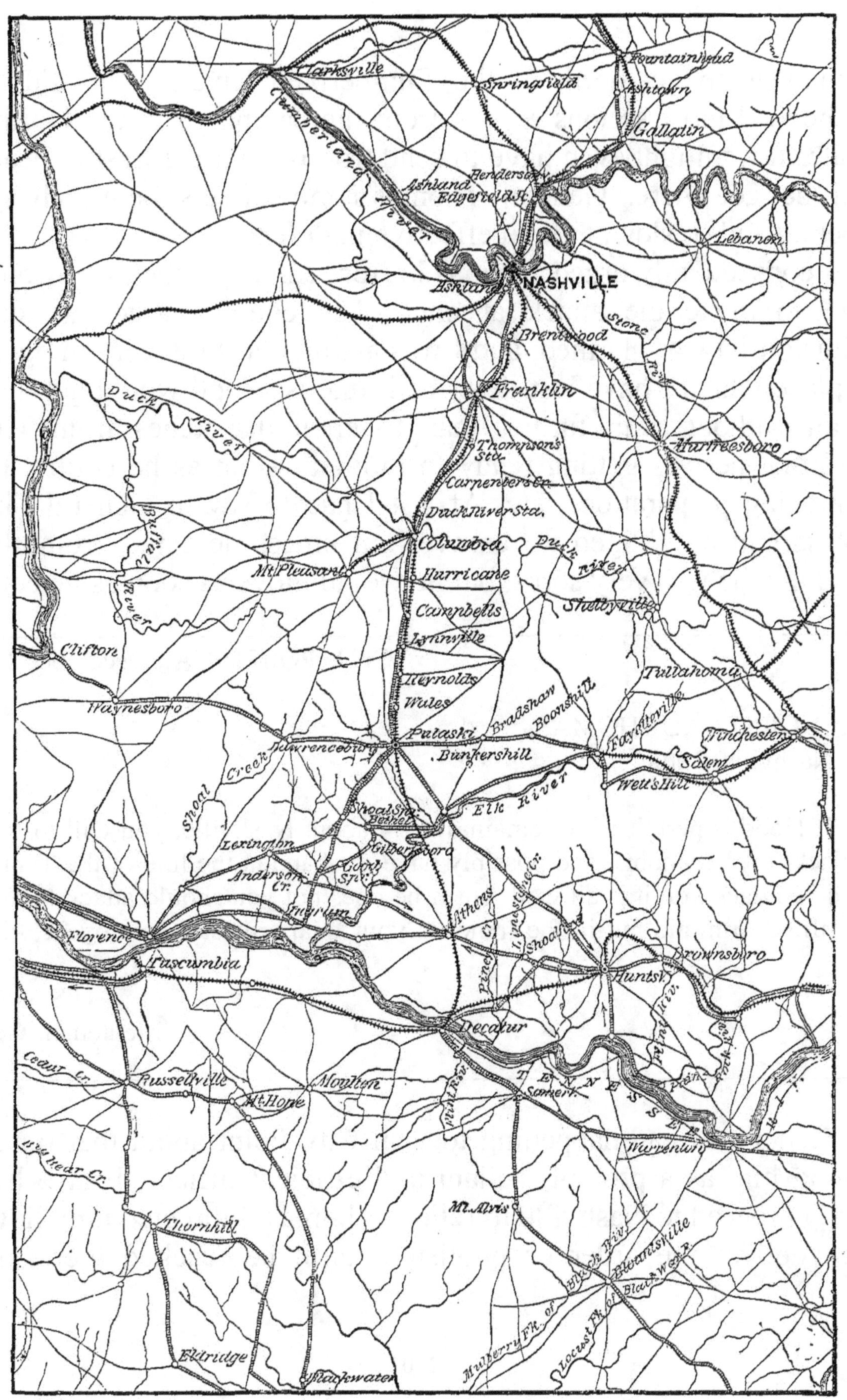

Clarksville
Springfield
Fountainhead
Ashtown
Gallatin
Cumberland River
Henderson
Ashland
Edgefield Jc.
Lebanon
Ashland NASHVILLE
Brentwood
Stone R.
Duck River
Franklin
Murfreesboro
Thompson's Sta.
Carpenters Sta.
Duck River Sta.
Columbia
Duck River
Mt Pleasant
Hurricane
Shelbyville
Campbells
Buffalo River
Lynnville
Clifton
Reynolds
Tullahoma
Waynesboro
Wales
Bradshaw
Boonshill
Fayetteville
Winchester
Pulaski
Lawrenceburg
Bunkershill
Salem
Shoal Creek
Elk River
Well's Hill
Shoal Sta.
Bethel
Gilbersboro
Lexington
Good Spr.
Anderson Cr.
Pine Cr.
Limestone Cr.
Shoalford
Merium
Athens
Florence
Brownsboro
Tuscumbia
Huntsv.
Paine Riv.
Decatur
Cedar Cr.
Russellville
Moulton
Somerv.
Paint Rock Riv.
Mt.Hope
T E N N E S S E E
Warrenton
Big Near Cr.
Mt.Alvis
Thornhill
Mulberry Fk. of Black Riv.
Locust Fk. of Black Riv.
Blountsville
Blackwer R.
Eldridge
Blackwater

and manage to get north of the Cumberland River. If he did this, I apprehended most serious results from the campaign in the North, and was afraid we might even have to send troops from the East to head him off if he got there, General Thomas's movements being always so deliberate and so slow, though effective in defence.

I consequently urged Thomas in frequent dispatches sent from City Point* to make the attack at once. The country was alarmed, the administration was alarmed, and I was alarmed lest the very thing would take place which I have just described -that is, Hood would get north. It was all without avail further than to elicit dispatches from Thomas saying that he was getting ready to move as soon as he could, that he was making preparations, etc. At last I had to say to General Thomas that I should be obliged to remove him unless he acted promptly. He replied that he was very sorry, but he would move as soon as he could.

---

*CITY POINT, VA., December 2, 1864.

MAJOR-GENERAL THOMAS,
    Nashville, Tenn.

If Hood is permitted to remain quietly about Nashville, you will lose all the road back to Chattanooga and possibly have to abandon the line of the Tennessee. Should he attack you it is all well, but if he does not you should attack him before he fortifies. Arm and put in the trenches your quartermaster employees, citizens, etc.

U.S. GRANT,
Lieutenant-General.

General Logan happening to visit City Point about that time, and knowing him as a prompt, gallant and efficient officer, I gave him an order to proceed to Nashville to relieve Thomas. I directed him, however, not to deliver the order or publish it until he reached there, and if

Thomas had moved, then not to deliver it at all, but communicate with me by telegraph. After Logan started, in thinking over the situation, I

CITY POINT, VA., December 2, 1864.--1:30 P.M.

MAJOR-GENERAL THOMAS,
  Nashville, Tenn.
  With your citizen employees armed, you can move out of Nashville with all your army and force the enemy to retire or fight upon ground of your own choosing. After the repulse of Hood at Franklin, it looks to me that instead of falling back to Nashville we should have taken the offensive against the enemy where he was. At this distance, however, I may err as to the best method of dealing with the enemy. You will now suffer incalculable injury upon your railroads if Hood is not speedily disposed of. Put forth therefore every possible exertion to attain this end. Should you get him to retreating give him no peace.

U.S. GRANT,
Lieutenant-General.

---

became restless, and concluded to go myself. I went as far as Washington City, when a dispatch was received from General Thomas announcing his readiness at last to move, and designating the time of his movement. I concluded to wait until that time. He did move, and was successful from the start. This was on the 15th of December. General Logan was at Louisville at the time this movement was made, and telegraphed the fact to Washington, and proceeded no farther himself.

CITY POINT, VA., December 5, 1864.

MAJOR -GENERAL THOMAS,
Nashville, Tenn.

  Is there not danger of Forrest moving down the Cumberland to where he can cross it? It seems to me whilst you should be getting up your cavalry as rapidly as possible to look after Forrest, Hood should be attacked where he is. Time strengthens him in all possibility as much as it does you.

U.S. GRANT,
Lieutenant-General.

CITY POINT, VA., December 6, 1864.-4 P.M.

MAJOR-GENERAL THOMAS,
>Nashville, Tenn.

Attack Hood at once and wait no longer for a remnant of your cavalry. There is great danger of delay resulting in a campaign back to the Ohio River.

U.S. GRANT,
Lieutenant-General:

The battle during the 15th was severe, but favorable to the Union troops, and continued until night closed in upon the combat. The next day the battle was renewed. After a successful assault upon Hood's men in their intrenchments the enemy fled in disorder, routed and broken, leaving their dead, their artillery and small arms in great numbers on the field, besides the wounded that were captured. Our cavalry had fought on foot as infantry, and had not their horses with them; so that they were not ready to join in the pursuit the moment the enemy retreated. They sent back, however, for their horses, and endeavored to get to Franklin ahead of Hood's broken army by the Granny White Road, but too much time was consumed in getting started.

CITY POINT, VA., December 8, 1864-8.30 P.M.

MAJOR -GENERAL THOMAS,
>Nashville, Tenn.

Your dispatch of yesterday received. It looks to me evident the enemy are trying to cross the Cumberland River, and are scattered. Why not attack at once? By all means avoid the contingency of a foot race to see which, you or Hood, can beat to the Ohio. If you think necessary call on the governors of States to send a force into Louisville to meet the enemy if he should cross the river. You clearly never should cross except in rear of the enemy. Now is one of the finest opportunities ever presented of destroying one of the three armies of the enemy. If destroyed he never can replace it. Use the means at your command, and you can do this and cause a rejoicing that will resound from one end of the land to the other.

U. S. GRANT,
Lieutenant-General.

CITY POINT, VA., December 11, 1864.-4 P.M.

MAJOR-GENERAL THOMAS,
Nashville, Tenn.

If you delay attack longer the mortifying spectacle will be witnessed of a rebel army moving for the Ohio River, and you will be forced to act, accepting such weather as you find. Let there be no further delay. Hood cannot even stand a drawn battle so far from his supplies of ordnance stores. If he retreats and you follow, he must lose his material and much of his army. I am in hopes of receiving a dispatch from you today announcing that you have moved. Delay no longer for weather or reinforcements.

U.S. GRANT,
Lieutenant-General.

WASHINGTON, D. C., December 15, 1864.

MAJOR - GENERAL THOMAS,
Nashville, Tenn.
I was just on my way to Nashville, but receiving a dispatch from Van Duzer detailing your splendid success of today, I shall go no further. Push the enemy now and give him no rest until he is entirely destroyed. Your army will cheerfully suffer many privations to break up Hood's army and render it useless for future operations. Do not stop for trains or supplies, but take them from the country as the enemy have done. Much is now expected.

U.S. GRANT.
Lieutenant-General.

They had got but a few miles beyond the scene of the battle when they found the enemy's cavalry dismounted and behind intrenchments covering the road on which they were advancing. Here another battle ensued, our men dismounting and fighting on foot, in which the Confederates were again routed and driven in great disorder. Our cavalry then went into bivouac, and renewed the pursuit on the following morning. They were too late. The enemy already had possession of Franklin, and was beyond them. It now became a chase in which the Confederates had the lead.

Our troops continued the pursuit to within a few miles of Columbia, where they found the rebels had destroyed the railroad bridge as well as all other bridges over Duck River. The heavy rains of a few days before had swelled the stream into a mad torrent, impassable except on bridges. Unfortunately, either through a mistake in the wording of the order or otherwise, the pontoon bridge which was to have been sent by rail out to Franklin, to be taken thence with the pursuing column, had gone toward Chattanooga. There was, consequently, a delay of some four days in building bridges out of the remains of the old railroad bridge. Of course Hood got such a start in this time that farther pursuit was useless, although it was continued for some distance, but without coming upon him again.

CHAPTER LXI

EXPEDITION AGAINST FORT FISHER - ATTACK ON THE FORT - FAILURE OF THE EXPEDITION - SECOND EXPEDITION AGAINST THE FORT - CAPTURE OF FORT FISHER

UP to January, 1865, the enemy occupied Fort Fisher, at the mouth of Cape Fear River and below the City of Wilmington. This port was of immense importance to the Confederates, because it formed their principal inlet for blockade runners by means of which they brought in from abroad such supplies and munitions of war as they could not produce at home. It was equally important to us to get possession of it, not only because it was desirable to cut off their supplies so as to insure a speedy termination of the war, but also because foreign governments, particularly the British Government, were constantly threatening that unless ours could maintain the blockade of that coast they should cease to recognize any blockade. For these reasons I determined, with the concurrence of the Navy Department, in December, to send an expedition against Fort Fisher for the purpose of capturing it.

To show the difficulty experienced in maintaining the blockade, I will mention a circumstance that took place at Fort Fisher after its fall. Two English blockade runners came in at night. Their commanders, not supposing the fort had fallen, worked their way through all our fleet and got into the river unobserved. They then signaled the fort, announcing their arrival. There was a colored man in the fort who had been there before and who understood these signals. He informed General Terry what reply he should make to have them come in, and Terry did as he advised. The vessels came in, their officers entirely unconscious that they were falling into the hands of the Union forces. Even after they were brought in to the fort they were entertained in conversation for some little time before suspecting that the Union troops were occupying

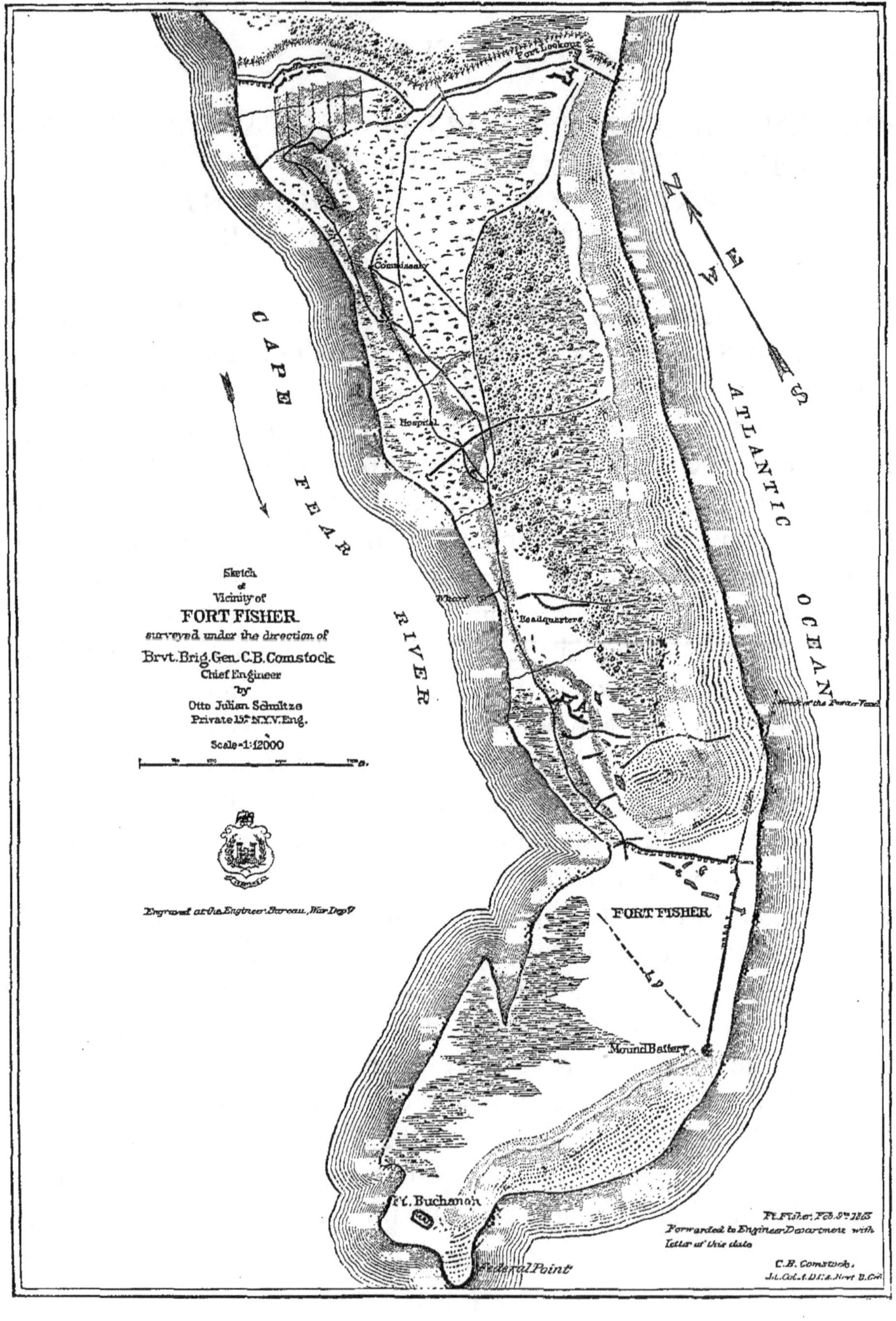

Fort Lookout
Commissary
Hospital
Wharf
Headquarters
CAPE FEAR RIVER
ATLANTIC OCEAN
N W E S
Sketch of Vicinity of FORT FISHER surveyed under the direction of Brvt. Brig. Gen. C. B. Comstock Chief Engineer by Otto Julian Schultze Private 15th N.Y.V. Eng.
Scale = 1:12000
Engraved at the Engineer Bureau, War Dep.t
Wreck of the Porter Yard
FORT FISHER
Mound Battery
Ft. Buchanan
Federal Point
Ft. Fisher, Feb. 9th 1865
Forwarded to Engineer Department with letter of this date
C. B. Comstock
Lt. Col. A.D.C. & Bvt. B. Gen.

the fort. They were finally informed that their vessels and cargoes were prizes.

I selected General Weitzel, of the Army of the James, to go with the expedition, but gave instructions through General Butler. He commanded the department within whose geographical limits Fort Fisher was situated, as well as Beaufort and other points on that coast held by our troops; he was, therefore, entitled to the right of fitting out the expedition against Fort Fisher.

General Butler conceived the idea that if a steamer loaded heavily with powder could be run up to near the shore under the fort and exploded, it would create great havoc and make the capture an easy matter. Admiral Porter, who was to command the naval squadron, seemed to fall in with the idea, and it was not disapproved of in Washington; the navy was therefore given the task of preparing the steamer for this purpose. I had no confidence in the success of the scheme, and so expressed myself; but as no serious harm could come of the experiment, and the authorities at Washington seemed desirous to have it tried, I permitted it. The steamer was sent to Beaufort, North Carolina, and was there loaded with powder and prepared for the part she was to play in the reduction of Fort Fisher.

General Butler chose to go in command of the expedition himself, and was all ready to sail by the 9th of December (1864). Very heavy storms prevailed, however, at that time along that part of the seacoast, and prevented him from getting off until the 13th or 14th. His advance arrived off Fort Fisher on the 15th. The naval force had been already assembled, or was assembling, but they were obliged to run into Beaufort for munitions, coal, etc.; then, too, the powder-boat was not yet fully prepared. The fleet was ready to proceed on the 18th; but Butler, who had remained outside from the 15th up to that time, now found himself out of coal, fresh water, etc., and had to put into Beaufort to replenish. Another storm overtook him, and several days more were lost before the army and navy were both ready at the same time to co-operate.

On the night of the 23d the powder-boat was towed in by a gunboat as near to the fort as it was safe to run. She was then propelled by her own machinery to within about five hundred yards of the shore. There the clockwork, which was to explode her within a certain length of time, was set and she was abandoned. Everybody left, and even the vessels put out to sea to prevent the effect of the explosion upon them. At two o'clock in the morning the explosion took place -and produced no more effect on the fort, or anything else on land, than the bursting of a boiler anywhere on the Atlantic Ocean would have done. Indeed when the troops in Fort Fisher heard the explosion they supposed it was the bursting of a boiler in one of the Yankee gunboats.

Fort Fisher was situated upon a low, flat peninsula north of Cape Fear River. The soil is sandy. Back a little the peninsula is very heavily wooded, and covered with freshwater swamps. The fort ran across this peninsula, about five hundred yards in width, and extended along the sea coast about thirteen hundred yards. The fort had an armament of 21 guns and 3 mortars on the land side, and 24 guns on the sea front. At that time it was only garrisoned by four companies of infantry, one light battery and the gunners at the heavy guns -less than seven hundred men- with a reserve of less than a thousand men five miles up the peninsula. General Whiting of the Confederate army was in command, and General Bragg was in command of the force at Wilmington, Both commenced calling for reinforcements the moment they saw our troops landing, The Governor of North Carolina called for everybody who could stand behind a parapet and shoot a gun, to join them. In this way they got two or three hundred additional men into Fort Fisher; and Hoke's division, five or six thousand strong, was sent down from Richmond. A few of these troops arrived the very day that Butler was ready to advance.

On the 24th the fleet formed for an attack in arcs of concentric circles, their heavy ironclads going in very close range, being nearest the shore, and leaving intervals or spaces so that the outer vessels could fire between them. Porter was thus enabled to throw one hundred and fifteen shells per minute. The damage done to the fort by these shells was very slight, only two or three cannon being disabled in the fort. But the firing silenced all the guns by making it too hot for the men to maintain their positions about them and compelling them to seek shelter in the bomb-proofs.

On the next day part of Butler's troops under General Adelbert Ames effected a landing out of range of the fort without difficulty. This was accomplished under the protection of gunboats sent for the purpose, and under cover of a renewed attack upon the fort by the fleet. They formed a line across the peninsula and advanced, part going north and part toward the fort, covering themselves as they did so. Curtis pushed forward and came near to Fort Fisher, capturing the small garrison at what was called the Flag Pond Battery. Weitzel accompanied him to within a half a mile of the works. Here he saw that the fort had not been injured, and so reported to Butler, advising against an assault. Ames, who had gone north in his advance, captured 228 of the reserves. These prisoners reported to Butler that sixteen hundred of Hoke's division of six thousand from Richmond had already arrived and the rest would soon be in his rear.

Upon these reports Butler determined to withdraw his troops from the peninsula and return to the fleet. At that time there had not been a man on our side injured except by one of the shells from the fleet. Curtis had got within a few yards of the works. Some of his men had snatched a flag from the parapet of the fort, and others had taken a horse from the inside of the stockade. At night Butler informed Porter of his withdrawal, giving the reasons above stated, and announced his purpose as soon as his men could embark to start for Hampton Roads. Porter represented to him that he had sent to Beaufort for more ammunition. He could fire much faster than he had been doing, and would keep the enemy from showing himself until our men were within twenty yards of the fort, and he begged that Butler would leave some brave fellows like those who had snatched the flag from the parapet and taken the horse from the fort.

Butler was unchangeable. He got all his troops aboard, except Curtis's brigade, and started back. In doing this, Butler made a fearful mistake. My instructions to him, or to the officer who went in command of the expedition, were explicit in the statement that to effect a landing would be of itself a great victory, and if one should be effected, the foothold must not be relinquished; on the contrary, a regular siege of the fort must be commenced and, to guard against interference by reason of storms, supplies of provisions must be laid in as soon as they could be got on shore. But General Butler seems to have lost sight of this part of his instructions, and was back at Fort Monroe on the 28th.

I telegraphed to the President as follows:

CITY POINT, VA.,
Dec. 28, 1864.-8:30 P.M.

The Wilmington expedition has proven a gross and culpable failure. Many of the troops are back here. Delays and free talk of the object of the expedition enabled the enemy to move troops to Wilmington to defeat it. After the expedition sailed from Fort Monroe, three days of fine weather were squandered, during which the enemy was without a force to protect himself. Who is to blame will, I hope, be known.

U.S. GRANT,
Lieutenant-General.

Porter sent dispatches to the Navy Department in which he complained bitterly of having been abandoned by the army just when the fort was nearly in our possession, and begged that our troops might be sent back again to cooperate, but with a different commander. As soon as I heard this I sent a messenger to Porter with a letter asking him to hold on. I assured him that I fully sympathized with him in his disappointment, and that I would send the same troops back with a different commander, with some reinforcements to offset those which the enemy had received. I told him it would take some little time to get transportation for the additional troops; but as soon as it could be had the men should be on their way to him, and there would be no delay on my part. I selected A.H. Terry to command.

It was the 6th of January before the transports could be got ready and the troops aboard. They sailed from Fortress Monroe on that day. The object and destination of the second expedition were at the time kept a secret to all except a few in the Navy Department and in the army to whom it was necessary to impart the information. General Terry had not the slightest idea of where he was going or what he was to do. He simply knew that he was going to sea and that he had his orders with him, which were to be opened when out at sea.

He was instructed to communicate freely with Porter and have entire harmony between army and navy, because the work before them would require the best efforts of both arms of the service. They arrived off Beaufort on the 8th. A heavy storm, however, prevented a landing at Fort Fisher until the 13th. The navy prepared itself for attack about as before, and at the same time assisted the army in landing, this time five miles away. Only ironclads fired at first; the object being to draw the fire of the enemy's guns so as to ascertain their positions. This object being accomplished, they then let in their shots thick and fast. Very soon the guns were all silenced, and the fort showed evident signs of being much injured.

Terry deployed his men across the peninsula as had been done before, and at two o'clock on the following morning was up within two miles of the fort with a respectable abatis in front of his line. His artillery was all landed on that day, the 14th. Again Curtis's brigade of Ames's division had the lead. By noon they had carried an unfinished work less than a half mile from the fort, and turned it so as to face the other way.

Terry now saw Porter and arranged for an assault on the following day. The two commanders arranged their signals so that they could communicate with each other from time to time as they might have occasion. At daylight the fleet commenced its firing. The time agreed upon for the assault was the middle of the afternoon, and Ames who commanded the assaulting column moved at 3:30. Porter landed a force of sailors and marines to move against the sea-front in cooperation with Ames's assault. They were under Commander Breese of the navy. These sailors and marines had worked their way up to within a couple of hundred yards of the fort before the assault. The signal was given and the assault was made; but the poor sailors and marines were repulsed and very badly handled by the enemy, losing 280 killed and wounded out of their number.

Curtis's brigade charged successfully though met by a heavy fire, some of the men having to wade through the swamp up to their waists to reach the fort. Many were wounded, of course, and some killed; but they soon reached the palisades. These they cut away, and pushed on through. The other troops then came up, Pennypacker's following Curtis, and Bell, who commanded the 3d brigade of Ames's division, following Pennypacker. But the fort was not yet captured though the parapet was gained.

The works were very extensive. The large parapet around the work would have been but very little protection to those inside except when they were close up under it. Traverses had, therefore, been run until really the work was a succession of small forts enclosed by a large one. The rebels made a desperate effort to hold the fort, and had to be driven from these traverses one by one. The fight continued till long after night. Our troops gained first one traverse and then another, and by 10 o'clock at night the place was carried. During this engagement the sailors, who had been repulsed in their assault on the bastion, rendered the best service they could by reinforcing Terry's northern line -thus enabling him to send a detachment to the assistance of Ames. The fleet kept up a continuous fire upon that part of the fort which was still occupied by the enemy. By means of signals they could be informed where to direct their shots.

During the succeeding nights the enemy blew up Fort Caswell on the opposite side of Cape Fear River, and abandoned two extensive works on Smith's Island in the river.

Our captures in all amounted to 169 guns, besides small-arms, with full supplies of ammunition, and 2,083 prisoners. In addition to these, there were about 700 dead and wounded left there. We had lost 110 killed and 536 wounded.

In this assault on Fort Fisher, Bell, one of the brigade commanders, was killed, and two, Curtis and Pennypacker, were badly wounded.

Secretary Stanton, who was on his way back from Savannah, arrived off Fort Fisher soon after it fell. When he heard the good news he promoted all the officers of any considerable rank for their conspicuous gallantry. Terry had been nominated for major-general, but had not been confirmed. This confirmed him; and soon after I recommended him for a brigadier-generalcy in the regular army, and it was given to him for this victory.

CHAPTER LXII

SHERMAN'S MARCH NORTH - SHERIDAN ORDERED TO LYNCHBURG - CANBY ORDERED TO MOVE AGAINST MOBILE - MOVEMENTS OF SCHOFIELD AND THOMAS - CAPTURE OF COLUMBIA, SOUTH CAROLINA - SHERMAN IN THE CAROLINAS

WHEN news of Sherman being in possession of Savannah reached the North, distinguished statesmen and visitors began to pour in to see him. Among others who went was the Secretary of War, who seemed much pleased at the result of his campaign. Mr. Draper, the collector of customs of New York, who was with Mr. Stanton's party, was put in charge of the public property that had been abandoned and captured. Savannah was then turned over to General Foster's command to hold, so that Sherman might have his own entire army free to operate as might be decided upon in the future. I sent the chief engineer of the Army of the Potomac (General Barnard) with letters to General Sherman. He remained some time with the general, and when he returned brought back letters, one of which contained suggestions from Sherman as to what ought to be done in cooperation with him, when he should have started upon his march northward.

I must not neglect to state here the fact that I had no idea originally of having Sherman march from Savannah to Richmond, or even to North Carolina. The season was bad, the roads impassable for anything except such an army as he had, and I should not have thought of ordering such a move. I had, therefore, made preparations to collect transports to carry Sherman and his army around to the James River by water, and so informed him. On receiving this letter he went to work immediately to prepare for the move, but seeing that it would require a long time to collect the transports, he suggested the idea then of marching up north through the Carolinas. I was only too happy to approve this; for if successful, it promised every advantage. His march through Georgia had thoroughly destroyed all lines of transportation in that State, and had completely cut the enemy off from all sources of supply to the west of it. If North and South Carolina were rendered helpless so far as capacity for feeding Lee's army was concerned, the Confederate garrison at Richmond would be reduced in territory, from which to draw supplies, to very narrow limits in the State of Virginia; and, although that section of the country was fertile, it was already well exhausted of both forage and food. I approved Sherman's suggestion therefore at once.

The work of preparation was tedious, because supplies, to load the wagons for the march, had to be brought from a long distance. Sherman would now have to march through a country furnishing fewer provisions than that he had previously been operating in during his march to the sea. Besides, he was confronting, or marching toward, a force of the enemy vastly superior to any his troops had encountered on their previous march; and the territory through which he had to pass had now become of such vast importance to the very existence of the Confederate army, that the most desperate efforts were to be expected in order to save it.

Sherman, therefore, while collecting the necessary supplies to start with, made arrangements with Admiral Dahlgren, who commanded that part of the navy on the South Carolina and Georgia coast, and General Foster, commanding the troops, to take positions, and hold a few points on the sea coast, which he (Sherman) designated, in the neighborhood of Charleston.

This provision was made to enable him to fall back upon the sea coast, in case he should encounter a force sufficient to stop his onward progress. He also wrote me a letter, making suggestions as to what he would like to have done in support of his movement farther north. This letter was brought to City Point by General Barnard at a time when I happened to be going to Washington City, where I arrived on the 21st of January. I cannot tell the provision I had already made to cooperate with Sherman, in anticipation of his expected movement, better than by giving my reply to this letter.

HEADQUARTERS ARMIES OF THE UNITED STATES, WASHINGTON, D.C.,
Jan. 21, 1865;

MAJOR-GENERAL W. T. SHERMAN,
    Commanding Mil. Div. of the Mississippi.

GENERAL :-Your letters brought by General Barnard were received at City Point, and read with interest. Not having them with me, however, I cannot say that in this I will be able to satisfy you on all points of recommendation. As I arrived here at one P.M, and must leave at six P.M., having in the meantime spent over three hours with the Secretary and General Halleck, I must be brief. Before your last request to have Thomas make a campaign into the heart of Alabama, I had ordered Schofield to Annapolis, Md., with his corps. The advance (six thousand) will reach the seaboard by the 23d, the remainder following as rapidly as railroad transportation can be procured from Cincinnati. The corps numbers over twenty-one thousand men. I was induced to do this because I did not believe Thomas could possibly be got off before spring. His pursuit of Hood indicated a sluggishness that satisfied me that he would never do to conduct one of your campaigns. The command of the advance of the pursuit was left to subordinates, whilst Thomas followed far behind. When Hood had crossed the Tennessee, and those in pursuit had reached it, Thomas had not much more than half crossed the State, from whence he returned to Nashville to take steamer for Eastport. He is possessed of excellent judgment, great coolness and honesty, but he is not good on a pursuit. He also reported his troops fagged, and that it was necessary to equip up. This report and a determination to give the enemy no rest determined me to use his surplus troops elsewhere.

Thomas is still left with a sufficient force surplus to go to Selma under an energetic leader. He has been telegraphed to, to know whether he could go, and, if so, which of the several routes he would select. No reply is yet received. Canby has been ordered to act offensively from the sea-coast to the interior, towards Montgomery and Selma. Thomas's forces will move from the north at an early day, or some of his troops will be sent to Canby. Without further reinforcements Canby will have a moving column of twenty thousand men.

Fort Fisher, you are aware, has been captured. We have a force there of eight thousand effective. At New Bern about half the number. It is rumored, through deserters, that Wilmington also has fallen. I am inclined to believe the rumor, because on the 17th we knew the enemy were blowing up their works about Fort Caswell, and that on the 18th Terry moved on Wilmington.

If Wilmington is captured, Schofield will go there. If not, he will be sent to New Bern. In either event, all the surplus forces at the two points will move to the interior toward Goldsboro in cooperation with your movements. From either point, railroad communications can be run out, there being here abundance of rolling-stock suited to the gauge of those roads.

There have been about sixteen thousand men sent from Lee's army south. Of these, you will have fourteen thousand against you, if Wilmington is not held by the enemy, casualties at Fort Fisher having overtaken about two thousand.

All these troops are subject to your orders as you come in communication with them. They will be so instructed. From about Richmond I will watch Lee closely, and if he detaches much more, or attempts to evacuate, will pitch in. In the meantime, should you be brought to a halt anywhere, I can send two corps of thirty thousand effective men to your support, from the troops about Richmond.

To resume: Ganby is ordered to operate to the interior from the Gulf. A. J. Smith may go from the north, but I think it doubtful. A force of twenty-eight or thirty thousand will co-operate with you from New Bern or Wilmington, or both. You can call for reinforcements.

This will be handed you by Captain Hudson, of my staff, who will return with any message you may have for me. If there is anything I can do for you in the way of having supplies on ship-board, at any point on the sea-coast, ready for you, let me know it.

Yours truly,
U.S. GRANT,
Liet.-General.

I had written on the 18th of January to General Sherman, giving him the news of the battle of Nashville. He was much pleased at the result, although, like myself, he had been very much disappointed at Thomas for permitting Hood to cross the Tennessee River and nearly the whole State of Tennessee, and come to Nashville to be attacked there. He, however, as I had done, sent Thomas a warm congratulatory letter.

On the 10th of January, 1865, the resolutions of thanks to Sherman and his army passed by Congress were approved.

Sherman, after the capture, at once had the debris in Savannah cleared up, commencing the work by removing the piling and torpedoes from the river, and taking up all other obstructions. He had then intrenched the city, so that it could be held by a small garrison. By the middle of January all his work was done, except the accumulation of supplies to commence his movements with.

He proposed to move in two columns, one from Savannah, going along by the river of the same name, and the other by roads farther east, threatening Charleston. He commenced the advance by moving his right wing to Beaufort, South Carolina, then to Pocotaligo by water. This column, in moving north, threatened Charleston, and, indeed, it was not determined at first that they would not have a force visit Charleston. South Carolina had done so much to prepare the public mind of the South for secession, and had been so active in precipitating the decision of the question before the South was fully prepared to meet it, that there was, at that time, a feeling throughout the North and also largely entertained by people of the South, that the State of South Carolina, and Charleston, the hot-bed of secession in particular, ought to have a heavy hand laid upon them. In fact, nothing but the decisive results that followed deterred the radical portion of the people from condemning the movement, because Charleston had been left out. To pass into the interior would, however, be to insure the evacuation of the city, and its possession by the navy and Foster's troops. It is so situated between two formidable rivers that a small garrison could have held it against all odds as long as their supplies would hold out. Sherman therefore passed it by.

By the first of February all preparations were completed for the final march, Columbia, South Carolina, being the first objective ; Fayetteville, North Carolina, the second ; and Goldsboro, or neighborhood, the final one, unless something further should be determined upon. The right wing went from Pocotaligo, and the left from about Hardeeville on the Savannah River, both columns taking a pretty direct route for Columbia. The cavalry, however, were to threaten Charleston on the right, and Augusta on the left.

On the 15th of January Fort Fisher had fallen, news of which Sherman had received before starting out on his march. We already had New Bern and had soon Wilmington, whose fall followed that of Fort Fisher; as did other points on the sea coast, where the National troops were now in readiness to cooperate with Sherman's advance when he had passed Fayetteville.

On the 18th of January I ordered Canby, in command at New Orleans, to move against Mobile, Montgomery and Selma, Alabama, for the purpose of destroying roads, machine shops, etc. On the 8th of February I ordered Sheridan, who was in the Valley of Virginia, to push forward as soon as the weather would permit and strike the canal west of Richmond at or about Lynchburg; and on the 20th I made the order to go to Lynchburg as soon as the roads would permit, saying "As soon as it is possible to travel, I think you will have no difficulty about reaching Lynchburg with a cavalry force alone. From there you could destroy the railroad and canal in every direction, so as to be of no further use to the rebellion. * * * This additional raid, with one starting from East Tennessee under Stoneman, numbering about four or five thousand cavalry; one from Eastport, Mississippi, ten thousand cavalry; Canby, from Mobile Bay, with about eighteen thousand mixed troops -these three latter pushing for Tuscaloosa, Selma and Montgomery; and Sherman with a large army eating out the vitals of South Carolina -is all that will be wanted to leave nothing for the rebellion to stand upon. I would advise you to overcome great obstacles to accomplish this. Charleston was evacuated on Tuesday last."

On the 27th of February, more than a month after Canby had received his orders, I again wrote to him, saying that I was extremely anxious to hear of his being in Alabama. I notified him, also, that I had sent Grierson to take command of his cavalry, he being a very efficient officer. I further suggested that Forrest was probably in Mississippi, and if he was there, he would find him an officer of great courage and capacity whom it would be difficult to get by. I still further informed him that Thomas had been ordered to start a cavalry force into

Mississippi on the 20th of February, or as soon as possible thereafter. This force did not get off however.

All these movements were designed to be in support of Sherman's march, the object being to keep the Confederate troops in the West from leaving there. But neither Canby nor Thomas could be got off in time. I had some time before depleted Thomas's army to reinforce Canby, for the reason that Thomas had failed to start an expedition which he had been ordered to send out, and to have the troops where they might do something. Canby seemed to be equally deliberate in all of his movements. I ordered him to go in person; but he prepared to send a detachment under another officer. General Granger had got down to New Orleans, in some way or other, and I wrote Canby that he must not put him in command of troops. In spite of this he asked the War Department to assign Granger to the command of a corps.

Almost in despair of having adequate service rendered to the cause in that quarter, I said to Canby: "I am in receipt of a dispatch * * * informing me that you have made requisitions for a construction corps and material to build seventy miles of railroad. I have directed that none be sent. Thomas's army has been depleted to send a force to you that they might be where they could act in winter, and at least detain the force the enemy had in the West. If there had been any idea of repairing railroads, it could have been done much better from the North, where we already had the troops. I expected your movements to be cooperative with Sherman's last. This has now entirely failed. I wrote to you long ago, urging you to push promptly and to live upon the country, and destroy railroads, machine shops, etc., not build them. Take Mobile and hold it, and push your forces to the interior -to Montgomery and to Selma. Destroy railroads, rolling stock, and everything useful for carrying on war, and, when you have done this, take such positions as can be supplied by water. By this means alone you can occupy positions from which the enemy's roads in the interior can be kept broken."

Most of these expeditions got off finally, but too late to render any service in the direction for which they were designed.

The enemy, ready to intercept his advance, consisted of Hardee's troops and Wheeler's cavalry, perhaps less than fifteen thousand men in all; but frantic efforts were being made in Richmond, as I was sure would be the case, to retard Sherman's movements. Everything possible was being done to raise troops in the South. Lee dispatched against Sherman the troops which had been sent to relieve Fort Fisher, which, including those of the other defences of the harbor and its neighborhood, amounted, after deducting the two thousand killed, wounded and captured, to fourteen thousand men. After Thomas's victory at Nashville what remained, of Hood's army were gathered together and forwarded as rapidly as possible to the east to cooperate with these forces; and, finally, General Joseph E. Johnston, one of the ablest commanders of the South though not in favor with the administration (or at least with Mr. Davis), was put in command of all the troops in North and South Carolina.

Schofield arrived at Annapolis in the latter part of January, but before sending his troops to North Carolina I went with him down the coast to see the situation of affairs, as I could give fuller directions after being on the ground than I could very well have given without. We soon returned, and the troops were sent by sea to Cape Fear River. Both New Bern and Wilmington are connected with Raleigh by railroads which unite at Goldsboro. Schofield was to land troops at Smithville, near the mouth of the Cape Fear River on the west side, and move up to secure the Wilmington and Charlotteville Railroad. This column took their pontoon bridges with them, to enable them to cross over to the island south of the city of Wilmington. A large body was sent by the north side to cooperate with them. They succeeded in taking the city on the 22d of February. I took the precaution to provide for Sherman's army, in case he should be forced to turn in toward the sea coast before reaching North Carolina, by forwarding supplies to every place where he was liable to have to make such a deflection from his projected march. I also sent railroad rolling stock, of which we had a great abundance, now that we were not operating the roads in Virginia. The gauge of the North Carolina railroads being the same as the Virginia railroads had been altered too ; these cars and locomotives were ready for use there without any change.

On the 31st of January I countermanded the orders given to Thomas to move south to Alabama and Georgia. (I had previously reduced his force by sending a portion of it to Terry.) I directed in lieu of this movement, that he should send Stoneman through East Tennessee, and push him well down toward Columbia, South Carolina, in support of Sherman. Thomas did not get Stoneman off in time, but, on the contrary, when I had supposed he was on his march in support of Sherman I heard of his being in Louisville, Kentucky. I immediately changed the order, and directed Thomas to send him toward Lynchburg. Finally, however, on the 12th of March, he did push down through the northwestern end of South Carolina, creating some consternation. I also ordered Thomas to send the 4th corps (Stanley's) to Bull Gap and to destroy no more roads east of that. I also directed him to concentrate supplies at Knoxville, with a view to a probable movement of his army through that way toward Lynchburg.

Goldsboro is four hundred and twenty-five miles from Savannah. Sherman's march was without much incident until he entered Columbia, on the 17th of February. He was detained in his progress by having to repair and corduroy the roads, and rebuild the bridges. There was constant skirmishing and fighting between the cavalry of the two armies, but this did not retard the advance of the infantry. Four days, also, were lost in making complete the destruction of the most important railroads south of Columbia; there was also some delay caused by the high water, and the destruction of the bridges on the line of the road. A formidable river had to be crossed near Columbia and that in the face of a small garrison under General Wade Hampton. There was but little delay, however, further than that caused by high water in the stream. Hampton left as Sherman approached, and the city was found to be on fire.

There has since been a great deal of acrimony displayed in discussions of the question as to who set Columbia on fire. Sherman denies it on the part of his troops, and Hampton denies it on the part of the Confederates. One thing is certain: as soon as our troops took possession, they at once proceeded to extinguish the flames to the best of their ability with the limited means at hand. In any case, the example set by the Confederates in burning the village of Chambersburg, Pa., a town which was not garrisoned, would seem to make a defence of the act of firing the seat of government of the State most responsible for the conflict then raging, not imperative.

The Confederate troops having vacated the city, the mayor took possession, and sallied forth to meet the commander of the National forces for the purpose of surrendering the town, making terms for the protection of property, etc. Sherman paid no attention at all to the overture, but pushed forward and took the town without making any conditions whatever with its citizens. He then, however, cooperated with the mayor in extinguishing the flames and providing for the people who were rendered destitute by this destruction of their homes. When he left there he even gave the mayor five hundred head of cattle to be distributed among the citizens, to tide them over until some arrangement could be made for their future supplies. He remained in Columbia until the roads, public buildings, workshops and everything that could be useful to the enemy were destroyed. While at Columbia, Sherman learned for the first time that what remained of Hood's army was confronting him, under the command of General Beauregard.

Charleston was evacuated on the 18th of February, and Foster garrisoned the place. Wilmington was captured on the 22d. Columbia and Cheraw farther north, were regarded as so secure from invasion that the wealthy people of Charleston and Augusta had sent much of their valuable property to these two points to be stored. Among the goods sent there were valuable carpets, tons of old Madeira, silverware, and furniture. I am afraid much of these goods fell into the hands of our troops. There was found at Columbia a large amount of powder, some artillery, small-arms and fixed ammunition. These, of course, were among the articles destroyed. While here, Sherman also learned of Johnston's restoration to command. The latter was given, as already stated, all troops in North and South Carolina. After the completion of the destruction of public property about Columbia, Sherman proceeded on his march and reached Cheraw without any special opposition and without incident to relate. The railroads, of course, were thoroughly destroyed on the way. Sherman remained a day or two at Cheraw; and, finally, on the 6th of March crossed his troops over the Pedee and advanced straight for Fayetteville. Hardee and Hampton were there, and barely escaped. Sherman reached Fayetteville on the 11th of March. He had dispatched scouts from Cheraw with letters to General Terry, at Wilmington, asking him to send a steamer with some supplies of bread, clothing and other articles which he enumerated. The scouts got through successfully, and a boat was sent with the mail and such articles for which Sherman had asked as were in store at Wilmington; unfortunately, however, those stores did not contain clothing.

Four days later, on the 15th, Sherman left Fayetteville for Goldsboro. The march, now, had to be made with great caution, for he was approaching Lee's army and nearing the country that still remained open to the enemy. Besides, he was confronting all that he had had to confront in his previous march up to that point, reinforced by the garrisons along the road and by what remained of Hood's army. Frantic appeals were made to the people to come in voluntarily and swell the ranks of our foe. I presume, however, that Johnston did not have in all over 35,000 or 40,000 men. The people had grown tired of the war, and desertions from the Confederate army were much more numerous than the voluntary accessions.

There was some fighting at Averysboro on the 16th between Johnston's troops and Sherman's, with some loss; and at Bentonville on the 19th and 21st of March, but Johnston withdrew from the contest before the morning of the 22d. Sherman's loss in these last engagements in killed, wounded, and missing, was about sixteen hundred. Sherman's troops at last reached Goldsboro on the 23d of the month and went into bivouac; and there his men were destined to have a long rest. Schofield was there to meet him with the troops which had been sent to Wilmington.

Sherman was no longer in danger. He had Johnston confronting him; but with an army much inferior to his own, both in numbers and morale. He had Lee to the north of him with a force largely superior ; but I was holding Lee with a still greater force, and had he made his escape and gotten down to reinforce Johnston, Sherman, with the reinforcements he now had from Schofield and Terry, would have been able to hold the Confederates at bay for an indefinite period. He was near the seashore with his back to it, and our navy occupied the harbors. He had a railroad to both Wilmington and New Bern, and his flanks were thoroughly protected by streams, which intersect that part of the country and deepen as they approach the sea. Then, too, Sherman knew that if Lee should escape me I would be on his heels, and he and Johnston together would be crushed in one blow if they attempted to make a stand. With the loss of their capital, it is doubtful whether Lee's army would have amounted to much as an army when it reached North Carolina. Johnston's army was demoralized by constant defeat and would hardly have made an offensive movement, even if they could have been induced to remain on duty. The men of both Lee's and Johnston's armies were, like their brethren of the North, as brave as men can be; but no man is so brave that he may not meet such defeats and disasters as to discourage him and dampen his ardor for any cause, no matter how just he deems it.

CHAPTER LXIII

ARRIVAL OF THE PEACE COMMISSIONERS - LINCOLN AND THE PEACE COMMISSIONERS - AN ANECDOTE OF LINCOLN - THE WINTER BEFORE PETERSBURG - SHERIDAN DESTROYS THE RAILROAD - GORDON CARRIES THE PICKET LINE - PARKE RECAPTURES THE LINE - THE BATTLE OF WHITE OAK ROAD

ON the last of January, 1865, peace commissioners from the so-called Confederate States presented themselves on our lines around Petersburg, and were immediately conducted to my headquarters at City Point. They proved to be Alexander H. Stephens, Vice-President of the Confederacy, Judge Campbell, Assistant-Secretary of War, and R. M. T. Hunter, formerly United States Senator and then a member of the Confederate Senate.

It was about dark when they reached my headquarters, and I at once conducted them to the steamer *Mary Martin*, a Hudson River boat which was very comfortably fitted up for the use of passengers. I at once communicated by telegraph with Washington and informed the Secretary of War and the President of the arrival of these commissioners and that their object was to negotiate terms of peace between the United States and, as they termed it, the Confederate Government. I was instructed to retain them at City Point, until the President, or some one whom he would designate, should come to meet them. They remained several days as guests on board the boat. I saw them quite frequently, though I have no recollection of having had any conversation whatever with them on the subject of their mission. It was something I had nothing to do with, and I therefore did not wish to express any views on the subject. For my own part I never had admitted, and never was ready to admit, that they were the representatives of a *government*. There had been too great a waste of blood and treasure to concede anything of the kind. As long as they remained there, however, our relations were pleasant and I found them all very agreeable gentlemen. I directed the captain to furnish them with the best the boat afforded, and to administer to their comfort in every way possible. No guard was placed over them and no restriction was put upon their movements; nor was there any pledge asked that they would not abuse the privileges extended to them. They were permitted to leave the boat when they felt like it, and did so, coming up on the bank and visiting me at my headquarters.

I had never met either of these gentlemen before the war, but knew them well by reputation and through their public services, and I had been a particular admirer of Mr. Stephens. I had always supposed that he was a very small man, but when I saw, him in the dusk of the evening I was very much surprised to find so large a man as he seemed to be. When he got down on to the boat I found that he was wearing a coarse gray woolen overcoat, a manufacture that had been introduced into the South during the rebellion. The cloth was thicker than anything of the kind I had ever seen, even in Canada. The overcoat extended nearly to his feet, and was so large that it gave him the appearance of being an average sized man. He took this off when he reached the cabin of the boat, and I was struck with the apparent change in size, in the coat and out of it.

After a few days, about the 2d of February, I received a dispatch from Washington, directing me to send the commissioners to Hampton Roads to meet the President and a member of the cabinet. Mr. Lincoln met them there and had an interview of short duration. It was not a great while after they met that the President visited me at City Point. He spoke of his having met the commissioners, and said he had told them that there would be no use in entering into any negotiations unless they would recognize, first: that the Union as a whole must be forever preserved, and second: that slavery must be abolished. If they were willing to concede these two points, then he was ready to enter into negotiations and was almost willing to hand them a blank sheet of paper with his signature attached for them to fill in the terms upon which they were willing to live with us in the Union and be one people. He always showed a generous and kindly spirit toward the Southern people, and I never heard him abuse an enemy. Some of the cruel things said about President Lincoln, particularly in the North, used to pierce him to the heart; but never in my presence did he evince a revengeful disposition and I saw a great deal of him at City Point, for he seemed glad to get away from the cares and anxieties of the capital.

Right here I might relate an anecdote of Mr. Lincoln. It was on the occasion of his visit to me just after he had talked with the peace commissioners at Hampton Roads. After a little conversation he asked me if I had seen that overcoat of Stephens's. I replied that I had. "Well," said he, "did you see him take it off?" I said yes. "Well," said he, "didn't you think it was the biggest shuck and the littlest ear that ever you did see?" Long afterwards I told this story to the Confederate General J.B. Gordon, at the time a member of the Senate. He repeated it to Stephens, and, as I heard afterwards, Stephens laughed immoderately at the simile of Mr. Lincoln.

The rest of the winter, after the departure of the peace commissioners, passed off quietly and uneventfully, except for two or three little incidents. On one occasion during this period, while I was visiting Washington City for the purpose of conferring with the administration, the enemy's cavalry under General Wade Hampton, passing our extreme left and then going to the south, got in east of us. Before their presence was known, they had driven off a large number of beef cattle that were grazing in that section. It was a fair capture, and they were sufficiently needed by the Confederates. It was only retaliating for what we had done, sometimes for many weeks at a time, when out of supplies -taking what the Confederate army otherwise would have gotten. As appears in this book, on one single occasion we captured five thousand head of cattle which were crossing the Mississippi River near Port Hudson on their way from Texas to supply the Confederate army in the East.

One of the most anxious periods of my experience during the rebellion was the last few weeks before Petersburg. I felt that the situation of the Confederate army was such that they would try to make an escape at the earliest practicable moment, and I was afraid, every morning, that I would awake from my sleep to hear that Lee had gone, and that nothing was left but a picket line. He had his railroad by the way of Danville south, and I was afraid that he was running off his men and all stores and ordnance except such as it would be necessary to carry with him for his immediate defence. I knew he could move much more lightly and more rapidly than I, and that, if he got the start, he would leave me behind so that we would have the same army to fight again farther south -and the war might be prolonged another year.

I was led to this fear by the fact that I could not see how it was possible for the Confederates to hold out much longer where they were. There is no doubt that Richmond would have been evacuated much sooner than it was, if it had not been that it was the capital of the so-called Confederacy, and the fact of evacuating the capital would, of course, have had a very demoralizing effect upon the Confederate army. When it was evacuated (as we shall see further on), the Confederacy at once began to crumble and fade away. Then, too, desertions were taking place, not only among those who were with General Lee in the neighborhood of their capital, but throughout the whole Confederacy. I remember that in a conversation with me on one occasion long prior to this, General Butler remarked that the Confederates would find great difficulty in getting more men for their army; possibly adding, though I am not certain as to this, "unless they should arm the slave."

The South, as we all knew, were conscripting every able-bodied man between the ages of eighteen and forty-five ; and now they had passed a law for the further conscription of boys from fourteen to eighteen, calling them the junior reserves, and men from forty-five to sixty to be called the senior reserves. The latter were to hold the necessary points not in immediate danger, and especially those in the rear. General Butler, in alluding to this conscription, remarked that they were thus "robbing both the cradle and the grave," an expression which I afterwards used in writing a letter to Mr. Washburn.

It was my belief that while the enemy could get no more recruits they were losing at least a regiment a day, taking it throughout the entire army, by desertions alone. Then by casualties of war, sickness, and other natural causes, their losses were much heavier. It was a mere question of arithmetic to calculate how long they could hold out while that rate of depletion was going on. Of course long before their army would be thus reduced to nothing the army which we had in the field would have been able to capture theirs. Then too I knew from the great number of desertions, that the men who had fought so bravely, so gallantly and so long for the cause which they believed in and as earnestly, I take it, as our men believed in the cause for which they were fighting -had lost hope and become despondent. Many of them were making application to be sent North where they might get employment until the war was over, when they could return to their Southern homes.

For these and other reasons I was naturally very impatient for the time to come when I could commence the spring campaign, which I thoroughly believed would close the war.

There were two considerations I had to observe, however, and which detained me. One was the fact that the winter had been one of heavy rains, and the roads were impassable for artillery and teams. It was necessary to wait until they had dried sufficiently to enable us to move the wagon trains and artillery necessary to the efficiency of an army operating in the enemy's country. The other consideration was that General Sheridan with the cavalry of the Army of the Potomac was operating on the north side of the James River, having come down from the Shenandoah. It was necessary that I should have his cavalry with me, and I was therefore obliged to wait until he could join me south of the James River.

Let us now take account of what he was doing.

On the 5th of March I had heard from Sheridan. He had met Early between Staunton and Charlottesville and defeated him, capturing nearly his entire command. Early and some of his officers escaped by finding refuge in the neighboring houses or in the woods.

On the 12th I heard from him again. He had turned east, to come to White House. He could not go to Lynchburg as ordered, because the rains had been so very heavy and the streams were so very much swollen. He had a pontoon train with him, but it would not reach half way across some of the streams, at their then stage of water, which he would have to get over in going south as first ordered.

I had supplies sent around to White House for him, and kept the depot there open until he arrived. We had intended to abandon it because the James River had now become our base of supplies.

Sheridan had about ten thousand cavalry with him, divided into two divisions commanded respectively by Custer and Devin. General Merritt was acting as chief of cavalry. Sheridan moved very light, carrying only four days' provisions with him, with a larger supply of coffee, salt and other small rations, and a very little else besides ammunition. They stopped at Charlottesville and commenced tearing up the railroad back toward Lynchburg. He also sent a division along the James River Canal to destroy locks, culverts, etc. All mills and factories along the lines of march of his troops were destroyed also.

Sheridan had in this way consumed so much time that his making a march to White House was now somewhat hazardous. He determined therefore to fight his way along the railroad and canal till he was as near to Richmond as it was possible to get, or until attacked. He did this, destroying the canal as far as Goochland, and the railroad to a point as near Richmond as he could get. On the 10th he was at Columbia. Negroes had joined his column to the number of two thousand or more, and they assisted considerably in the work of destroying the railroads and the canal. His cavalry was in as fine a condition as when he started, because he had been able to find plenty of forage. He had captured most of Early's horses and picked up a good many others on the road. When he reached Ashland he was assailed by the enemy in force. He resisted their assault with part of his command, moved quickly across the South and North Anna, going north, and reached White House safely on the 19th.

The time for Sherman to move had to be fixed with reference to the time he could get away from Goldsboro where he then was. Supplies had to be got up to him which would last him through a long march, as there would probably not be much to be obtained in the country through which he would pass. I had to arrange, therefore, that he should start from where he was, in the neighborhood of Goldsboro, on the 18th of April, the earliest day at which he supposed he could be ready.

Sherman was anxious that I should wait where I was until he could come up, and make a sure thing of it ; but I had determined to move as soon as the roads and weather would admit of my doing so. I had been tied down somewhat in the matter of fixing any time at my pleasure for starting, until Sheridan, who was on his way from the Shenandoah Valley to join me, should arrive, as both his presence and that of his cavalry were necessary to the execution of the plans which I had in mind. However, having arrived at White House on the 1.th of March, I was enabled to make my plans.

Prompted by my anxiety lest Lee should get away some night before I was aware of it, and having the lead of me, push into North Carolina to join with Johnston in attempting to crush out Sherman, I had, as early as the 1st of the month of March, given instructions to the troops around Petersburg to keep a sharp lookout to see that such a movement should not escape their notice, and to be ready to strike at once if it was undertaken.

It is now known that early in the month of March Mr. Davis and General Lee had a consultation about the situation of affairs in and about Richmond and Petersburg, and they both agreed that these places were no longer tenable for them, and that they must get away as soon as possible. They, too, were waiting for dry roads, or a condition of the roads which would make it possible to move.

General Lee, in aid of his plan of escape, and to secure a wider opening to enable them to reach the Danville Road with greater security than he would have in the way the two armies were situated, determined upon an assault upon the right of our lines around Petersburg. The night of the 24th of March was fixed upon for this assault, and General Gordon was assigned to the execution of the plan. The point between Fort Stedman and Battery No. 1, where our lines were closest together, was selected as the point of his attack. The attack was to be made at night, and the troops were to get possession of the higher ground in the rear where they supposed we had intrenchments, then sweep to the right and left, create a panic in the lines of our army, and force me to contract my lines. Lee hoped this would detain me a few days longer and give him an opportunity of escape. The plan was well conceived and the execution of it very well done indeed, up to the point of carrying a portion of our line.

Gordon assembled his troops under the cover of night, at the point at which they were to make their charge, and got possession of our picket-line, entirely without the knowledge of the troops inside of our main line of intrenchments; this reduced the distance he would have to charge over to not much more than fifty yards. For some time before the deserters had been coming in with great frequency, often bringing their arms with them, and this the Confederate general knew. Taking advantage of this knowledge he sent his pickets, with their arms, creeping through to ours as if to desert. When they got to our lines they at once took possession and sent our pickets to the rear as prisoners. In the main line our men were sleeping serenely, as if in great security. This plan was to have been executed and much damage done before daylight; but the troops that were to reinforce Gordon had to be brought from the north side of the James River and, by some accident on the railroad on their way over, they were detained for a considerable time; so that it got to be nearly daylight before they were ready to make the charge.

The charge, however, was successful and almost without loss, the enemy passing through our lines between Fort Stedman and Battery No. 10. Then turning to the right and left they captured the fort and the battery, with all the arms and troops in them. Continuing the charge, they also carried batteries Eleven and Twelve to our left, which they turned toward City Point.

Meade happened to be at City Point that night, and this break in his line cut him off from all communication with his headquarters. Parke, however, commanding the 9th corps when this breach took place, telegraphed the facts to Meade's headquarters, and learning that the general was away, assumed command himself and with commendable promptitude made all preparations to drive the enemy back. General Tidball gathered a large number of pieces of artillery and planted them in rear of the captured works so as to sweep the narrow space of ground between the lines very thoroughly. Hartranft was soon out with his division, as also was Willcox. Hartranft to the right of the breach headed the rebels off in that direction and rapidly drove them back into Fort Stedman. On the other side they were driven back into the intrenchments which they had captured, and batteries eleven and twelve were retaken by Willcox early in the morning.

Parke then threw a line around outside of the captured fort and batteries, and communication was once more established. The artillery fire was kept up so continuously that it was impossible for the Confederates to retreat, and equally impossible for reinforcements to join them. They all, therefore, fell captives into our hands. This effort of Lee's cost him about four thousand men, and resulted in their killing, wounding and capturing about two thousand of ours.

After the recapture of the batteries taken by the Confederates, our troops made a charge and carried the enemy's intrenched picket line, which they strengthened and held. This, in turn, gave us but a short distance to charge over when our attack came to be made a few days later.

The day that Gordon was making dispositions for this attack (24th of March) I issued my orders for the movement to commence on the 27th. Ord, with three divisions of infantry and Mackenzie's cavalry, was to move in advance on the night of the 27th, from the north side of the James River and take his place on our extreme left, thirty miles away.

He left Weitzel with the rest of the Army of the James to hold Bermuda Hundred and the north of the James River. The engineer brigade was to be left at City Point, and Parke's corps in the lines about Petersburg.

Ord was at his place promptly. Humphreys and Warren were then on our extreme left with the 2d and 5th corps. They were directed on the arrival of Ord, and on his getting into position in their places, to cross Hatcher's Run and extend out west toward Five Forks, the object being to get into a position from which we could strike the South Side Railroad and ultimately the Danville Railroad. There was considerable fighting in taking up these new positions for the 2d and 5th corps, in which the Army of the James had also to participate somewhat, and the losses were quite severe.

This was what was known as the battle of White Oak Road.

See orders to Major-Generals Meade, Ord, and Sheridan, March 24th, Appendix.

CHAPTER LXIV

INTERVIEW WITH SHERIDAN - GRAND MOVEMENT OF THE ARMY OF THE POTOMAC - SHERIDAN'S ADVANCE ON FIVE FORKS - BATTLE OF FIVE FORKS - PARKE AND WRIGHT STORM THE ENEMY'S LINE - BATTLES BEFORE PETERSBURG

SHERIDAN reached City Point on the 26th day of March. His horses, of course, were jaded and many of them had lost their shoes. A few days of rest were necessary to recuperate the animals and also to have them shod and put in condition for moving. Immediately on General Sheridan's arrival at City Point I prepared his instructions for the move which I had decided upon. The movement was to commence on the 29th of the month.

After reading the instructions I had given him, Sheridan walked out of my tent, and I followed to have some conversation with him by himself -not in the presence of anybody else, even of a member of my staff. In preparing his instructions I contemplated just what took place; that is to say, capturing Five Forks, driving the enemy from Petersburg and Richmond and terminating the contest before separating from the enemy. But the Nation had already become restless and discouraged at the prolongation of the war, and many believed that it would never terminate except by compromise. Knowing that unless my plan proved an entire success it would be interpreted as a disastrous defeat, I provided in these instructions that in a certain event he was to cut loose from the Army of the Potomac and his base of supplies, and living upon the country proceed south by the way of the Danville Railroad, or near it, across the Roanoke, get in the rear of Johnston, who was guarding that road, and cooperate with Sherman in destroying Johnston; then with these combined forces to help carry out the instructions which Sherman already had received, to act in cooperation with the armies around Petersburg and Richmond.

I saw that after Sheridan had read his instructions he seemed somewhat disappointed at the idea, possibly, of having to cut loose again from the Army of the Potomac, and place himself between the two main armies of the enemy. I said to him: "General, this portion of your instructions I have put in merely as a blind;" and gave him the reason for doing so, heretofore described. I told him that, as a matter of fact, I intended to close the war right here, with this movement, and that he should go no farther. His face at once brightened up, and slapping his hand on his leg he said: "I am glad to hear it, and we can do it."

Sheridan was not however to make his movement against Five Forks until he got further instructions from me.

One day, after the movement I am about to describe had commenced, and when his cavalry was on our extreme left and far to the rear, south, Sheridan rode up to where my headquarters were then established, at Dabney's Mills. He met some of my staff officers outside, and was highly jubilant over the prospects of success, giving reasons why he believed this would prove the final and successful effort. Although my chief-of-staff had urged very strongly that we return to our position about City Point and in the lines around Petersburg, he asked Sheridan to come in to see me and say to me what he had been saying to them. Sheridan felt a little modest about giving his advice where it had not been asked; so one of my staff came in and told me that Sheridan had what they considered important news, and suggested that I send for him. I did so, and was glad to see the spirit of confidence with which he was imbued. Knowing as I did from experience, of what great value that feeling of confidence by a commander was, I determined to make a movement at once, although on account of the rains which had fallen after I had started out the roads were still very heavy. Orders were given accordingly.

Finally the 29th of March came, and fortunately there having been a few days free from rain, the surface of the ground was dry, giving indications that the time had come when we could move. On that date I moved out with all the army available after leaving sufficient force to hold the line about Petersburg. It soon set in raining again however, and in a very short time the roads became practically impassable for teams, and almost so for cavalry. Sometimes a horse or mule would be standing apparently on firm ground, when all at once one foot would sink, and as he commenced scrambling to catch himself all his feet would sink and he would have to be drawn by hand out of the quicksands so common in that part of Virginia and other southern States. It became necessary therefore to build corduroy roads every foot of the way as we advanced, to move our artillery upon. The army had become so accustomed to this kind of work, and were so well prepared for it, that it was done very rapidly. The next day, March 30th, we had made sufficient progress to the southwest to warrant me in starting Sheridan with his cavalry over by Dinwiddie with instructions to then come up by the road leading northwest to Five Forks, thus menacing the right of Lee's line.

This movement was made for the purpose of extending our lines to the west as far as practicable towards the enemy's extreme right, or Five Forks. The column moving detached from the army still in the trenches was, excluding the cavalry, very small. The forces in the trenches were themselves extending to the left flank. Warren was on the extreme left when the extension began, but Humphreys was marched around later and thrown into line between him and Five Forks.

My hope was that Sheridan would be able to carry Five Forks, get on the enemy's right flank and rear, and force them to weaken their centre to protect their right so that an assault in the centre might be successfully made. General Wright's corps had been designated to make this assault, which I intended to order as soon as information reached me of Sheridan's success. He was to move under cover as close to the enemy as he could get.

It is natural to suppose that Lee would understand my design to be to get up to the South Side and ultimately to the Danville Railroad, as soon as he had heard of the movement commenced on the 29th. These roads were so important to his very existence while he remained in Richmond and Petersburg, and of such vital importance to him even in case of retreat, that naturally he would make most strenuous efforts to defend them. He did on the 30th send Pickett with five brigades to reinforce Five Forks. He also sent around to the right of his army some two or three other divisions, besides directing that other troops be held in readiness on the north side of the James River to come over on call. He came over himself to superintend in person the defence of his right flank.

Sheridan moved back to Dinwiddie Court House on the night of the 30th, and then took a road leading northwest to Five Forks. He had only his cavalry with him. Soon encountering the rebel cavalry he met with a very stout resistance. He gradually drove them back however until in the neighborhood of Five Forks. Here he had to encounter other troops besides those he had been contending with, and was forced to give way.

In this condition of affairs he notified me of what had taken place and stated that he was falling back toward Dinwiddie gradually and slowly, and asked me to send Wright's corps to his assistance. I relied to him that it was impossible to send Wright's corps because that corps was already in line close up to the enemy, where we should want to assault when the proper time came, and was besides a long distance from him; but the 2nd (Humphreys's) and 5th (Warren's) corps were on our extreme left and a little to the rear of it in a position to threaten the left flank of the enemy at Five Forks, and that I would send Warren.

Accordingly orders were sent to Warren to move at once that night (the 31st) to Dinwiddie Court House and put himself in communication with Sheridan as soon as possible, and report to him. He was very slow in moving, some of his troops not starting until after 5 o'clock next morning. When he did move it was done very deliberately, and on arriving at Gravelly Run he found the stream swollen from the recent rains so that he regarded it as not fordable. Sheridan of course knew of his coming, and being impatient to get the troops up as soon as possible, sent orders to him to hasten. He was also hastened or at least ordered to move up rapidly by General Meade. He now felt that he could not cross that creek without bridges, and his orders were changed to move so as to strike the pursuing enemy in flank or get in their rear; but he was so late in getting up that Sheridan determined to move forward without him. However, Ayres's division of Warren's corps reached him in time to be in the fight all day, most of the time separated from the remainder of the 5th corps and fighting directly under Sheridan.

Warren reported to Sheridan about 11 o'clock on the 1st, but the whole of his troops were not up so as to be much engaged until late in the afternoon. Griffin's division in backing to get out of the way of a severe cross fire of the enemy was found marching away from the fighting. This did not continue long, however; the division was brought back and with Ayres's division did most excellent service during the day. Crawford's division of the same corps had backed still farther off, and although orders were sent repeatedly to bring it up, it was late before it finally got to where it could be of material assistance. Once there it did very excellent service.

Sheridan succeeded by the middle of the afternoon or a little later, in advancing up to the point from which to make his designed assault upon Five Forks itself. He was very impatient to make the assault and have it all over before night, because the ground he occupied would be untenable for him in bivouac during the night. Unless the assault was made and was successful, he would be obliged to return to Dinwiddie Court House, or even further than that for the night.

It was at this junction of affairs that Sheridan wanted to get Crawford's division in hand, and he also wanted Warren. He sent staff officer after staff officer in search of Warren, directing that general to report to him, but they were unable to find him. At all events Sheridan was unable to get that officer to him. Finally he went himself. He issued an order relieving Warren and assigning Griffin to the command of the 5th corps. The troops were then brought up and the assault successfully made.

I was so much dissatisfied with Warren's dilatory movements in the battle of White Oak Road and in his failure to reach Sheridan in time, that I was very much afraid that at the last moment he would fail

Sheridan. He was a man of fine intelligence, great earnestness, quick perception, and could make his dispositions as quickly as any officer, under difficulties where he was forced to act. But I had before discovered a defect which was beyond his control that was very prejudicial to his usefulness in emergencies like the one just before us. He could see every danger at a glance before he had encountered it. He would not only make preparations to meet the danger which might occur, but he would inform his commanding officer what others should do while he was executing his move.

I had sent a staff officer to General Sheridan to call his attention to these defects, and to say that as much as I liked General Warren, now was not a time when we could let our personal feelings for any one stand in the way of success; and if his removal was necessary to success, not to hesitate. It was upon that authorization that Sheridan removed Warren. I was very sorry that it had been done, and regretted still more that I had not long before taken occasion to assign him to another field of duty.

It was dusk when our troops under Sheridan went over the parapets of the enemy. The two armies were mingled together there for a time in such manner that it was almost a question which one was going to demand the surrender of the other. Soon, however, the enemy broke and ran in every direction; some six thousand prisoners, besides artillery and small-arms in large quantities, falling into our hands. The flying troops were pursued in different directions, the cavalry and 5th corps under Sheridan pursuing the larger body which moved northwest.

This pursuit continued until about nine o'clock at night, when Sheridan halted his troops, and knowing the importance to him of the part of the enemy's line which had been captured, returned, sending the 5th corps across Hatcher's Run to just southwest of Petersburg, and facing them toward it. Merritt, with the cavalry, stopped and bivouacked west of Five Forks.

This was the condition which affairs were in on the night of the 1st of April. I then issued orders for an assault by Wright and Parke at four o'clock on the morning of the 2d. I also ordered the 2d corps, General

Humphreys, and General Ord with the Army of the James, on the left, to hold themselves in readiness to take any advantage that could be taken from weakening in their front.

I notified Mr. Lincoln at City Point of the success of the day; in fact I had reported to him during the day and evening as I got news, because he was so much interested in the movements taking place that I wanted to relieve his mind as much as I could. I notified Weitzel on the north side of the James River, directing him, also, to keep close up to the enemy, and take advantage of the withdrawal of troops from there to promptly enter the city of Richmond.

I was afraid that Lee would regard the possession of Five Forks as of so much importance that he would make a last desperate effort to retake it, risking everything upon the cast of a single die. It was for this reason that I had ordered the assault to take place at once, as soon as I had received the news of the capture of Five Forks. The corps commanders, however, reported that it was so dark that the men could not see to move, and it would he impossible to make the assault then. But we kept up a continuous artillery fire upon the enemy around the whole line including that north of the James River, until it was light enough to move, which was about a quarter to five in the morning.

At that hour Parke's and Wright's corps moved out as directed, brushed the abatis from their front as they advanced under a heavy fire of musketry and artillery, and went without flinching directly on till they mounted the parapets and threw themselves inside of the enemy's line. Parke, who was on the right, swept down to the right and captured a very considerable length of line in that direction, but at that point the outer was so near the inner line which closely enveloped the city of Petersburg that he could make no advance forward and, in fact, had a very serious task to turn the lines which he had captured to the defence of his own troops and to hold them; but he succeeded in this.

Wright swung around to his left and moved to Hatcher's Run, sweeping everything before him. The enemy had traverses in rear of his captured line, under cover of which he made something of a stand, from one to another, as Wright moved on ; but the latter met no serious obstacle. As you proceed to the left the outer line becomes gradually much farther from the inner one, and along about Hatcher's Run they must be nearly two miles apart. Both Parke and Wright captured a considerable amount of artillery and some prisoners -Wright about three thousand of them.

In the meantime Ord and Humphreys, in obedience to the instructions they had received, had succeeded by daylight, or very early in the morning, in capturing the intrenched picket-lines in their front; and before Wright got up to that point, Ord had also succeeded in getting inside of the enemy's intrenchments. The second corps soon followed; and the outer works of Petersburg were in the hands of the National troops, never to be wrenched from them again. When Wright reached Hatcher's Run, he sent a regiment to destroy the South Side Railroad just outside of the city.

My headquarters were still at Dabney's sawmills, As soon as I received the news of Wright's success, I sent dispatches announcing the fact to all points around the line, including the troops at Bermuda Hundred and those on the north side of the James, and to the President at City Point. Further dispatches kept coming in, and as they did I sent the additional news to these points. Finding at length' that they were all in, I mounted my horse to join the troops who were inside the works. When I arrived there I rode my horse over the parapet just as Wright's three thousand prisoners were coming out. I was soon joined inside by General Meade and his staff.

Lee made frantic efforts to recover at least part of the lost ground. Parke on our right was repeatedly assaulted, but repulsed every effort. Before noon Longstreet was ordered up from the north side of the James River thus bringing the bulk of Lee's army around to the support of his extreme right. As soon as I learned this I notified Weitzel and directed him to keep up close to the enemy and to have Hartsuff, commanding the Bermuda Hundred front, to do the same thing, and if they found any break to go in ; Hartsuff especially should do so, for this would separate Richmond and Petersburg.

Sheridan, after he had returned to Five Forks, swept down to Petersburg, coming in on our left. This gave us a continuous line from the Appomattox River below the city to the same river above. At eleven o'clock, not having heard from Sheridan, I reinforced Parke with two brigades from City Point. With this additional force he completed his captured works for better defence, and built back from his right, so as to protect his flank. He also carried in and made an abatis between himself and the enemy. Lee brought additional troops and artillery against Parke even after this was done, and made several assaults with very heavy losses.

The enemy had in addition to their intrenched line close up to Petersburg, two enclosed works outside of it, Fort Gregg and Fort Whitworth. We thought it had now become necessary to carry them by assault. About one o'clock in the day, Fort Gregg was assaulted by Foster's division of the 24th corps (Gibbon's), supported by two brigades from Ord's command. The battle was desperate and the National troops were repulsed several times; but it was finally carried, and immediately the troops in Fort Whitworth evacuated the place. The guns of Fort Gregg were turned upon the retreating enemy, and the commanding officer with some sixty of the men of Fort Whitworth surrendered.

I had ordered Miles in the morning to report to Sheridan. In moving to execute this order he came upon the enemy at the intersection of the White Oak Road and the Claiborne Road. The enemy fell back to Sutherland Station on the South Side Road and were followed by Miles. This position, naturally a strong and defensible one, was also strongly intrenched. Sheridan now came up and Miles asked permission from him to make the assault, which Sheridan gave. By this time Humphreys had got through the outer works in his front, and came up also and assumed command over Miles, who commanded a division in his corps. I had sent an order to Humphreys to turn to his right and move towards Petersburg. This order he now got, and started off, thus leaving Miles alone. The latter made two assaults, both of which failed, and he had to fall back a few hundred yards.

Hearing that Miles had been left in this position, I directed Humphreys to send a division back to his relief. He went himself.

Sheridan before starting to sweep down to Petersburg had sent Merritt with his cavalry to the west to attack some Confederate cavalry that had assembled there. Merritt drove them north to the Appomattox River. Sheridan then took the enemy at Sutherland Station on the reverse side from where Miles was, and the two together captured the place, with a large number of prisoners and some pieces of artillery, and put the remainder, portions of three Confederate corps, to flight. Sheridan followed, and drove them until night, when further pursuit was stopped. Miles bivouacked for the night on the ground which he with Sheridan had carried so handsomely by assault. I cannot explain the situation here better than by giving my dispatch to City Point that evening:

BOYDTON ROAD, NEAR PETERSBURG,
April 2, 1865-4.40 P.M.

COLONEL T.S. BOWERS,
   City Point.

We are now up and have a continuous line of troops, and in a few hours will be intrenched from the Appomattox below Petersburg to the river above. Heth's and Wilcox's divisions, such part of them as were not captured, were cut off from town, either designedly on their part or because they could not help it. Sheridan with the cavalry and 5th corps is above them. Miles's division, 2d corps, was sent from the White Oak Road to Sutherland Station on the South Side Railroad, where he met them, and at last accounts was engaged with them. Not knowing whether Sheridan would get up in time, General Humphreys was sent with another division from here. The whole captures since the army started out gunning will amount to not less than twelve thousand men, and probably fifty pieces of artillery. I do not know the number of men and guns accurately however. * * * I think the President might come out and pay us a visit tomorrow.

U. S. GRANT, Lieutenant-General.

During the night of April 2d our line was intrenched from the river above to the river below. I ordered a bombardment to be commenced the next morning at five A.M., to be followed by an assault at six o'clock; but the enemy evacuated Petersburg early in the morning.

CHAPTER LXV

THE CAPTURE OF PETERSBURG - MEETING PRESIDENT LINCOLN IN PETERSBURG - THE CAPTURE OF RICHMOND - PURSUING THE ENEMY - VISIT TO SHERIDAN AND MEADE

GENERAL MEADE and I entered Petersburg on the morning of the 3d and took a position under cover of a house which protected us from the enemy's musketry which was flying thick and fast there. As we would occasionally look around the corner we could see the streets and the Appomattox bottom, presumably near the bridge, packed with the Confederate army. I did not have artillery brought up, because I was sure Lee was trying to make his escape, and I wanted to push immediately in pursuit. At all events I had not the heart to turn the artillery upon such a mass of defeated and fleeing men, and I hoped to capture them soon.

Soon after the enemy had entirely evacuated Petersburg, a man came in who represented himself to be an engineer of the Army of Northern Virginia. He said that Lee had for some time been at work preparing a strong enclosed intrenchment, into which he would throw himself when forced out of Petersburg, and fight his final battle there ; that he was actually at that time drawing his troops from Richmond, and falling back into this prepared work. This statement was made to General Meade and myself when we were together. I had already given orders for the movement up the south side of the Appomattox for the purpose of heading off Lee; but Meade was so much impressed by this man's story that he thought we ought to cross the Appomattox there at once and move against Lee in his new position. I knew that Lee was no fool, as he would have been to have put himself and his army between two formidable streams like the James and Appomattox rivers, and between two such armies as those of the Potomac and the James. Then these streams coming together as they did to the east of him, it would be only necessary to close up in the west to have him thoroughly cut off from all supplies or possibility of reinforcement. It would only have been a question of days, and not many of them, if he had taken the position assigned to him by the so-called engineer, when he would have been obliged to surrender his army. Such is one of the ruses resorted to in war to deceive your antagonist. My judgment was that Lee would necessarily have to evacuate Richmond, and that the only course for him to pursue would be to follow the Danville Road. Accordingly my object was to secure a point on that road south of Lee, and I told Meade this. He suggested that if Lee was going that way we would follow him. My reply was that we did not want to follow him; we wanted to get ahead of him and cut him off, and if he would only stay in the position he (Meade) believed him to be in at that time, I wanted nothing better; that when we got in possession of the Danville Railroad, at its crossing of the Appomattox River, if we still found him between the two rivers, all we had to do was to move eastward and close him up. That we would then have all the advantage we could possibly have by moving directly against him from Petersburg, even if he remained in the position assigned him by the engineer officer.

I had held most of the command aloof from the intrenchments, so as to start them out on the Danville Road early in the morning, supposing that Lee would be gone during the night. During the night I strengthened Sheridan by sending him Humphreys's corps.

Lee, as we now know, had advised the authorities at Richmond, during the day, of the condition of affairs, and told them it would be impossible for him to hold out longer than night, if he could hold out that long. Davis was at church when he received Lee's dispatch. The congregation was dismissed with the notice that there would be no evening service. The rebel government left Richmond about two o'clock in the afternoon of the 2d.

At night Lee ordered his troops to assemble at Amelia Court House, his object being to get away, join Johnston if possible, and to try to crush Sherman before I could get there. As soon as I was sure of this I notified Sheridan and directed him to move out on the Danville Railroad to the south side of the Appomattox River as speedily as possible. He replied that he already had some of his command nine miles out. I then ordered the rest of the Army of the Potomac under Meade to follow the same road in the morning. Parke's corps followed by the same road, and the Army of the James was directed to follow the road which ran alongside of the South Side Railroad to Burke's Station, and to repair the railroad and telegraph as they proceeded. That road was a 5 feet gauge, while our rolling stock was all of the 4 feet 81 inches gauge; consequently the rail on one side of the track had to be taken up throughout the whole length and re-laid so as to conform to the gauge of our cars and locomotives.

Mr. Lincoln was at City Point at the time, and had been for some days. I would have let him know what I contemplated doing, only while I felt a strong conviction that the move was going to be successful, yet it might not prove so; and then I would have only added another to the many disappointments he had been suffering for the past three years. But when we started out he saw that we were moving for a purpose, and bidding us Godspeed, remained there to hear the result.

The next morning after the capture of Petersburg, I telegraphed Mr. Lincoln asking him to ride out there and see me, while I would await his arrival. I had started all the troops out early in the morning, so that after the National army left Petersburg there was not a soul to be seen, not even an animal in the streets. There was absolutely no one there, except my staff officers and, possibly, a small escort of cavalry. We had selected the piazza of a deserted house, and occupied it until the President arrived.

About the first thing that Mr. Lincoln said to me, after warm congratulations for the victory, and thanks both to myself and to the army which had accomplished it, was: "Do you know, general, that I have had a sort of a sneaking idea for some days that you intended to do something like this." Our movements having been successful up to this point, I no longer had any object in concealing from the President all my movements, and the objects I had in view. He remained for some days near City Point, and I communicated with him frequently and fully by telegraph.

Mr. Lincoln knew that it had been arranged for Sherman to join me at a fixed time, to co-operate in the destruction of Lee's army. I told him that I had been very anxious to have the Eastern armies vanquish their old enemy who had so long resisted all their repeated and gallant attempts to subdue them or drive them from their capital. The Western armies had been in the main successful until they had conquered all the territory from the Mississippi River to the State of North Carolina, and were now almost ready to knock at the back door of Richmond, asking admittance. I said to him that if the Western armies should be even upon the field, operating against Richmond and Lee, the credit would be given to them for the capture, by politicians and non-combatants from the section of country which those troops hailed from. It might lead to disagreeable bickerings between members of Congress of the East and those of the West in some of their debates. Western members might be throwing it up to the members of the East that in the suppression of the rebellion they were not able to capture an army, or to accomplish much in the way of contributing toward that end, but had to wait until the Western armies had conquered all the territory south and west of them, and then come on to help them capture the only army, they had been engaged with.

Mr. Lincoln said he saw that now, but had never thought of it before, because his anxiety was so great that he did not care where the aid came from so the work was done. The Army of the Potomac has every reason to be proud of its four year's record in the suppression of the rebellion. The army, it had to fight was the protection to the capital of a people which was attempting to found a nation upon the territory of the United States. Its loss would be the loss of the cause. Every energy, therefore, was put forth by the Confederacy to protect and maintain their capital. Everything else would go if it went. Lee's army had to be strengthened to enable it to maintain its position, no matter what territory was wrested from the South in another quarter.

I never expected any such bickering as I have indicated, between the soldiers of the two sections; and, fortunately, there has been none between the politicians. Possibly I am the only one who thought of the liability of such a state of things in advance.

When our conversation was at an end Mr. Lincoln mounted his horse and started on his return to City Point, while I and my staff started to join the army, now a good many miles in advance. Up to this time I had not received the report of the capture of Richmond.

Soon after I left President Lincoln I received a dispatch from General Weitzel which notified me that he had taken possession of Richmond at about 8.15 o'clock in the morning of that day, the 3d, and that he had found the city on fire in two places. The city was in the most utter confusion. The authorities had taken the precaution to empty all the liquor into the gutter, and to throw out the provisions which the Confederate government had left, for the people to gather up. The city had been deserted by the authorities, civil and military, without any notice whatever that they were about to leave. In fact, up to the very hour of the evacuation the people had been led to believe that Lee had gained an important victory somewhere around Petersburg.

Weitzel's command found evidence of great demoralization in Lee's army, there being still a great many men and even officers in the town. The city was on fire. Our troops were directed to extinguish the flames, which they finally succeeded in doing. The fire had been started by some one connected with the retreating army. All authorities deny that it was authorized, and I presume it was the work of excited men who were leaving what they regarded as their capital and may have felt that it was better to destroy it than have it fall into the hands of their enemy. Be that as it may, the National troops found the city in flames, and used every effort to extinguish them.

The troops that had formed Lee's right, a great many of them, were cut off from getting back into Petersburg, and were pursued by our cavalry so hotly and closely that they threw away caissons, ammunition, clothing, and almost everything to lighten their loads, and pushed along up the Appomattox River until finally they took water and crossed over.

I left Mr. Lincoln and started, as I have already said, to join the command, which halted at Sutherland Station, about nine miles out. We had still time to march as much farther, and time was an object; but the roads were bad and the trains belonging to the advance corps had blocked up the road so that it was impossible to get on. Then, again, our cavalry had struck some of the enemy and were pursuing them; and the orders were that the roads should be given up to the cavalry whenever they appeared. This caused further delay.

General Wright, who was in command of one of the corps which were left back, thought to gain time by letting his men go into bivouac and trying to get up some rations for them, and clearing out the road, so that when they did start they would be uninterrupted. Humphreys, who was far ahead, was also out of rations. They did not succeed in getting them up through the night; but the Army of the Potomac, officers and men, were so elated by the reflection that at last they were following up a victory to its end, that they preferred marching without rations to running a possible risk of letting the enemy elude them. So the march was resumed at three o'clock in the morning.

Merritt's cavalry had struck the enemy at Deep Creek, and driven them north to the Appomattox, where, I presume, most of them were forced to cross.

On the morning of the 4th I learned that Lee had ordered rations up from Danville for his famishing army, and that they were to meet him at Farmville. This showed that Lee had already abandoned the idea of following the railroad down to Danville, but had determined to go farther west, by the way of Farmville. I notified Sheridan of this and directed him to get possession of the road before the supplies could reach Lee. He responded that he had already sent Crook's division to get upon the road between Burkesville and Jetersville, then to face north and march along the road upon the latter place; and he thought Crook must be there now. The bulk of the army moved directly for Jetersville by two roads.

After I had received the dispatch from Sheridan saying that Crook was on the Danville Road, I immediately ordered Meade to make a forced march with the Army of the Potomac, and to send Parke's corps across from the road they were on to the South Side Railroad, to fall in the rear of the Army of the James and to protect the railroad which that army was repairing as it went along.

Our troops took possession of Jetersville and in the telegraph office, they found a dispatch from Lee, ordering two hundred thousand rations from Danville. The dispatch had not been sent, but Sheridan sent a special messenger with it to Burkesville and had it forwarded from there. In the meantime, however, dispatches from other sources had reached Danville, and they knew there that our army was on the line of the road; so that they sent no further supplies from that quarter.

At this time Merritt and Mackenzie, with the cavalry, were off between the road which the Army of the Potomac was marching on and the Appomattox River, and were attacking the enemy in flank. They picked up a great many prisoners and forced the abandonment of some property.

Lee intrenched himself at Amelia Court House, and also his advance north of Jetersville, and sent his troops out to collect forage. The country was very poor and afforded but very little. His foragers scattered a great deal; many of them were picked up by our men, and many others never returned to the Army of Northern Virginia.

Griffin's corps was intrenched across the railroad south of Jetersville, and Sheridan notified me of the situation. I again ordered Meade up with all dispatch, Sheridan having but the one corps of infantry with a little cavalry confronting Lee's entire army. Meade, always prompt in obeying orders, now pushed forward with great energy, although he was himself sick and hardly able to be out of bed. Humphreys moved at two, and Wright at three o'clock in the morning, without rations, as I have said, the wagons being far in the rear.

I stayed that night at Wilson's Station on the South Side Railroad. On the morning of the 5th I sent word to Sheridan of the progress Meade was making, and suggested that he might now attack Lee. We had now no other objective than the Confederate armies, and I was anxious to close the thing up at once.

On the 5th I marched again with Ord's command until within about ten miles of Burkesville, where I stopped to let his army pass. I then received from Sheridan the following dispatch:

"The whole of Lee's army is at or near Amelia Court House, and on this side of it. General Davies, whom I sent out to Painesville on their right flank, has just captured six pieces of artillery and some wagons. We can capture the Army of Northern Virginia if force enough can be thrown to this point, and then advance upon it. My cavalry was at Burkesville yesterday, and six miles beyond, on the Danville Road, last night. General Lee is at Amelia Court House in person. They are out of rations, or nearly so. They were advancing up the railroad towards Burkesville yesterday, when we intercepted them at this point."

It now became a life and death struggle with Lee to get south to his provisions.

Sheridan, thinking the enemy might turn off immediately towards Farmville, moved Davies's brigade of cavalry out to watch him. Davies found the movement had already commenced. He attacked and drove away their cavalry which was escorting wagons to the west, capturing and burning 180 wagons. He also captured five pieces of artillery. The Confederate infantry then moved against him and probably would have handled him very roughly, but Sheridan had sent two more brigades of cavalry to follow Davies, and they came to his relief in time. A sharp engagement took place between these three brigades of cavalry and the enemy's infantry, but the latter was repulsed.

Meade himself reached Jetersville about two o'clock in the afternoon, but in advance of all his troops. The head of Humphreys's corps followed in about an hour afterwards. Sheridan stationed the troops as they came up, at Meade's request, the latter still being very sick. He extended two divisions of this corps off to the west of the road to the left of Griffin's corps, and one division to the right. The cavalry by this time had also come up, and they were put still farther off to the left, Sheridan feeling certain that there lay the route by which the enemy intended to escape. He wanted to attack, feeling that if time was given, the enemy would get away; but Meade prevented this, preferring to wait till his troops were all up.

At this juncture Sheridan sent me a letter which had been handed to him by a colored man, with a note from himself saying that he wished I was there myself. The letter was dated Amelia Court House, April 5th, and signed by Colonel Taylor. It was to his mother, and showed the demoralization of the Confederate army. Sheridan's note also gave me the information as here related of the movements of that day. I received a second message from Sheridan on the 5th, in which he urged more emphatically the importance of my presence. This was brought to me by a scout in gray uniform. It was written on tissue paper, and wrapped up in tinfoil such as chewing tobacco is folded in. This was a precaution taken so that if the scout should be captured he could take this tinfoil out of his pocket and putting it into his mouth, chew it. It would cause no surprise at all to see a Confederate soldier chewing tobacco. It was nearly night when this letter was received. I gave Ord directions to continue his march to Burkesville and there intrench himself for the night, and in the morning to move west to cut off all the roads between there and Farmville.

I then started with a few of my staff and a very small escort of cavalry, going directly through the woods, to join Meade's army. The distance was about sixteen miles; but the night being dark our progress was slow through the woods in the absence of direct roads. However, we got to the outposts about ten o'clock in the evening, and after some little parley convinced the sentinels of our identity and were conducted in to where Sheridan was bivouacked. We talked over the situation for some little time, Sheridan explaining to me what he thought Lee was trying to do, and that Meade's orders, if carried out, moving to the right flank, would give him the coveted opportunity of escaping us and putting us in rear of him.

We then together visited Meade, reaching his headquarters about midnight. I explained to Meade that we did not want to follow the enemy ; we wanted to get ahead of him, and that his orders would allow the enemy to escape, and besides that, I had no doubt that Lee was moving right then. Meade changed his orders at once. They were now given for an advance on Amelia Court House, at an early hour in the morning, as the army then lay; that is, the infantry being across the railroad, most of it to the west of the road, with the cavalry swung out still farther to the left.

CHAPTER LXVI

BATTLE OF SAILOR'S CREEK - ENGAGEMENT AT FARM-VILLE - CORRESPONDENCE WITH GENERAL LEE - SHERIDAN INTERCEPTS THE ENEMY.

THE Appomattox, going westward, takes a long sweep to the southwest from the neighborhood of the Richmond and Danville Railroad bridge, and then trends northwesterly. Sailor's Creek, an insignificant stream, running northward, empties into the Appomattox between the High Bridge and Jetersville. Near the High Bridge the stage road from Petersburg to Lynchburg crosses the Appomattox River, also on a bridge. The railroad runs on the north side of the river to Farmville, a few miles west, and from there, re-crossing, continues on the south side of it. The roads coming up from the southeast to Farmville cross the Appomattox River there on a bridge and run on the north side, leaving the Lynchburg and Petersburg Railroad well to the left.

Lee, in pushing out from Amelia Court House, availed himself of all the roads between the Danville Road and Appomattox River to move upon, and never permitted the head of his columns to stop because of any fighting that might be going on in his rear. In this way he came very near succeeding in getting to his provision trains and eluding us with at least part of his army.

As expected, Lee's troops had moved during the night before, and our army in moving upon Amelia Court House soon encountered them. There was a good deal of fighting before Sailor's Creek was reached. Our cavalry charged in upon a body of theirs which was escorting a wagon train in order to get it past our left. A severe engagement ensued, in which we captured many prisoners, and many men also were killed and wounded. There was as much gallantry displayed by some of the Confederates in these little engagements as was displayed at any time during the war, notwithstanding the sad defeats of the past week.

The armies finally met on Sailor's Creek, when a heavy engagement took place, in which infantry, artillery and cavalry were all brought into action. Our men on the right, as they were brought in against the enemy, came in on higher ground, and upon his flank, giving us every advantage to be derived from the lay of the country. Our firing was also very much more rapid, because the enemy commenced his retreat westward and in firing as he retreated had to turn around every time he fired. The enemy's loss was very heavy, as well in killed and wounded as in captures. Some six general officers fell into our hands in this engagement, and seven thousand men were made prisoners. This engagement was commenced in the middle of the afternoon of the 6th, and the retreat and pursuit were continued until nightfall, when the armies bivouacked upon the ground where the night had overtaken them.

When the move towards Amelia Court House had commenced that morning, I ordered Wright's corps, which was on the extreme right, to be moved to the left past the whole army, to take the place of Griffin's, and ordered the latter at the same time to move by and place itself on the right. The object of this movement was to get the 6th corps, Wright's, next to the cavalry, with which they had formerly served so harmoniously and so efficiently in the valley of Virginia.

The 6th corps now remained with the cavalry and under Sheridan's direct command until after the surrender.

Ord had been directed to take possession of all the roads southward between Burkesville and the High Bridge. On the morning of the 6th he sent Colonel Washburn with two infantry regiments with instructions to destroy High Bridge and to return rapidly to Burkesville Station; and he prepared himself to resist the enemy there. Soon after Washburn had started Ord became a little alarmed as to his safety and sent Colonel Read, of his staff, with about eighty cavalrymen, to overtake him and bring him back. Very shortly after this he heard that the head of Lee's column had got up to the road between him and where Washburn now was, and attempted to send reinforcements, but the reinforcements could not get through. Read, however, had got through ahead of the enemy. He rode on to Farmville and was on his way back again when he found his return cut off, and Washburn confronting apparently the advance of Lee's army. Read drew his men up into line of battle, his force now consisting of less than six hundred men, infantry and cavalry, and rode along their front, making a speech to his men to inspire them with the same enthusiasm that he himself felt. He then gave the order to charge. This little band made several charges, of course unsuccessful ones, but inflicted a loss upon the enemy more than equal to their own entire number. Colonel Read fell mortally wounded, and then Washburn; and at the close of the conflict nearly every officer of the command and most of the rank and file had been either killed or wounded. The remainder then surrendered. The Confederates took this to be only the advance of a larger column which had headed them off, and so stopped to intrench; so that this gallant band of six hundred had checked the progress of a strong detachment of the Confederate army.

This stoppage of Lee's column no doubt saved to us the trains following. Lee himself pushed on and crossed the wagon road bridge near the High Bridge, and attempted to destroy it. He did set fire to it, but the flames had made but little headway when Humphreys came up with his corps and drove away the rear-guard which had been left to protect it while it was being burned up Humphreys forced his way across with some loss, and followed Lee to the intersection of the road crossing at Farmville with the one from Petersburg. Here Lee held a position which was very strong, naturally, besides being intrenched. Humphreys was alone, confronting him all through the day, and in a very hazardous position. He put on a bold face, however, and assaulted with some loss, but was not assaulted in return.

Our cavalry had gone farther south by the way of Prince Edward's Court House, along with the 5th corps (Griffin's), Ord falling in between Griffin and the Appomattox. Crook's division of cavalry and Wright's corps pushed on west of Farmville. When the cavalry reached Farmville they found that some of the Confederates were in ahead of them, and had already got their trains of provisions back to that point; but our troops were in time to prevent them from securing anything to eat, although they succeeded in again running the trains off, so that we did not get them for some time. These troops retreated to the north side of the Appomattox to join Lee, and succeeded in destroying the bridge after them. Considerable fighting ensued there between Wright's corps and a portion of our cavalry and the Confederates, but finally the cavalry forded the stream and drove them away. Wright built a footbridge for his men to march over on and then marched out to the junction of the roads to relieve Humphreys, arriving there that night. had stopped the night before at Burkesville Junction. Our troops were then pretty much all out of the place, but we had a field hospital there, and Ord's command was extended from that point towards Farmville.

Here I met Dr. Smith, a Virginian and an officer of the regular army, who told me that in a conversation with General Ewell, one of the prisoners and a relative of his, Ewell had said that when we had got across the James River he knew their cause was lost, and it was the duty of their authorities to make the best terms they could while they still had a right to claim concessions. The authorities thought differently, however. Now the cause was lost and they had no right to claim anything. He said further, that for every man that was killed after this in the war somebody is responsible, and it would be but very little better than murder. He was not sure that Lee would consent to surrender his army without being able to consult with the President, but he hoped he would.

I rode in to Farmville on the 7th, arriving there early in the day. Sheridan and Ord were pushing through, away to the south. Meade was back towards the High Bridge, and Humphreys confronting Lee as before stated. After having gone into bivouac at Prince Edward's Court House, Sheridan learned that seven trains of provisions and forage were at Appomattox, and determined to start at once and capture them; and a forced march was necessary in order to get there before Lee's army could secure them. He wrote me a note telling me this. This fact, together with the incident related the night before by Dr. Smith, gave me the idea of opening correspondence with General Lee on the subject of the surrender of his army. I therefore wrote to him on this day, as follows:

HEADQUARTERS ARMIES OF THE U. S.,
5 P.M., April 7, 1865.

GENERAL R.E. LEE,
 Commanding C. S. A.

The results of the last week must convince you of the hopelessness of further resistance on the part of the Army of Northern Virginia in this struggle. I feel that it is so, and regard it as my duty to shift from myself the responsibility of any further effusion of blood, by asking of you the surrender of that portion of the Confederate States army known as the Army of Northern Virginia.

U.S. GRANT,
Lieut.-General.

Lee replied on the evening of the same day as follows:

April 7, 1865.

GENERAL :--I have received your note of this day. Though not entertaining the opinion you express on the hopelessness of further resistance on the part of the Army of Northern Virginia, I reciprocate your desire to avoid useless effusion of blood, and therefore before considering your proposition, ask the terms you will offer on condition of its surrender.

RE. LEE, General.

LIEUT.-GENERAL U. S. GRANT,
 Commanding Armies of the U. S.

This was not satisfactory, but I regarded it as deserving another letter and wrote him as follows:

April 8, 1865.

GENERAL R.E. LEE,
      Commanding C. S. A.

Your note of last evening in reply to mine of same date, asking the condition on which I will accept the surrender of the Army of Northern Virginia is just received. In reply I would say that, peace being my great desire, there is but one condition I would insist upon, namely: that the men and officers surrendered shall be disqualified for taking up arms again against the Government of the United States until properly exchanged. I will meet you, or will designate officers to meet any officers you may name for the same purpose, at any point agreeable to you, for the purpose of arranging definitely the terms upon which the surrender of the Army of Northern Virginia will be received.

U.S. GRANT,
Lieut.-General.

Lee's army was rapidly crumbling. Many of his soldiers had enlisted from that part of the State where they now were, and were continually dropping out of the ranks and going to their homes. I know that I occupied a hotel almost destitute of furniture at Farmville, which had probably been used as a Confederate hospital. The next morning when I came out I found a Confederate colonel there, who reported to me and said that he was the proprietor of that house, and that he was a colonel of a regiment that had been raised in that neighborhood. He said that when he came along past home, he found that he was the only man of the regiment remaining with Lee's army, so he just dropped out, and now wanted to surrender himself. I told him to stay there and he would not be molested. That was one regiment which had been eliminated from Lee's force by this crumbling process.

Although Sheridan had been marching all day, his troops moved with alacrity and without any straggling. They began to see the end of what they had been fighting four years for. Nothing seemed to fatigue them. They were ready to move without rations and travel without rest until the end. Straggling had entirely ceased and every man was now a rival for the front. The infantry marched about as rapidly as the cavalry could.

Sheridan sent Custer with his division to move south of Appomattox Station, which is about five miles southwest of the Court House, to get west of the trains and destroy the roads to the rear. They got there the night of the 8th, and succeeded partially; but some of the train men had just discovered the movement of our troops and succeeded in running off three of the trains. The other four were held by Custer.

The head of Lee's column came marching up there on the morning of the 9th, not dreaming, I suppose, that there were any Union soldiers near. The Confederates were surprised to find our cavalry had possession of the trains. However, they were desperate and at once assaulted, hoping to recover them. In the melee that ensued they succeeded in burning one of the trains, but not in getting anything from it. Custer then ordered the other trains run back on the road towards Farmville, and the fight continued.

So far, only our cavalry and the advance of Lee's army were engaged. Soon, however, Lee's men were brought up from the rear, no doubt expecting they had nothing to meet but our cavalry. But our infantry had pushed forward so rapidly that by the time the enemy got up they found Griffin's corps and the Army of the James confronting them. A sharp engagement ensued, but Lee quickly set up a white flag.

CHAPTER LXVII

NEGOTIATIONS AT APPOMATTOX - INTERVIEW WITH LEE AT MCLEAN'S HOUSE - THE TERMS OF SURRENDER - LEE'S SURRENDER - INTERVIEW WITH LEE AFTER THE SURRENDER

ON the 8th I had followed the Army of the Potomac in rear of Lee. I was suffering very severely with a sick headache, and stopped at a farmhouse on the road some distance in rear of the main body of the army. I spent the night in bathing my feet in hot water and mustard, and putting mustard plasters on my wrists and the back part of my neck, hoping to be cured by morning. During the night I received Lee's answer to my letter of the 8th, inviting an interview between the lines on the following morning.* But it was for a different purpose from that of surrendering his army, and I answered him as follows:

HEADQUARTERS ARMIES OF THE U. S.,
April 9, 1865.

GENERAL R.E. LEE,
Commanding C. S. A.

Your note of yesterday is received. As I have no authority to treat on the subject of peace, the meeting proposed for ten A.M. today could lead to no good. I will state, however, General, that I am equally anxious for peace with yourself, and the whole North entertains the same feeling. The terms upon which peace can be had are well understood. By the South laying down their arms they will hasten that most desirable event, save thousands of human lives, and hundreds of millions of property not yet destroyed. Sincerely hoping that all our difficulties may be settled without the loss of another life, I subscribe myself, etc,

U.S. GRANT,
Lieutenant-General.

---

*See Appendix.

I proceeded at an early hour in the morning, still suffering with the headache, to get to the head of the column. I was not more than two or three miles from Appomattox Court House at the time, but to go direct I would have to pass through Lee's army, or a portion of it. I had therefore to move south in order to get upon a road coming up from another direction.

When the white flag was put out by Lee, as already described, I was in this way moving towards Appomattox Court Mouse, and consequently could not be communicated with immediately, and be informed of what Lee had done. Lee, therefore, sent a flag to the rear to advise Meade and one to the front to Sheridan, saying that he had sent a message to me for the purpose of having a meeting to consult about the surrender of his army, and asked for a suspension of hostilities until I could be communicated with. As they had heard nothing of this until the fighting had got to be severe and all going against Lee, both of these commanders hesitated very considerably about suspending hostilities at all. They were afraid it was not in good faith, and we had the Army of Northern Virginia where it could not escape except by some deception. They, however, finally consented to a suspension of hostilities for two hours to give an opportunity of communicating with me in that time, if possible. It was found that, from the route I had taken, they would probably not be able to communicate with me and get an answer back within the time fixed unless the messenger should pass through the rebel lines.

Lee, therefore, sent an escort with the officer bearing this message through his lines to me.

April 9, 1865.

GENERAL:-I received your note of this morning on the picket-line whither I had come to meet you and ascertain definitely what terms were embraced in your proposal of yesterday with reference to the surrender of this army. I now request an interview in accordance with the offer contained in your letter of yesterday for that purpose.

R.E. LEE, General.

LIEUTENANT - GENERAL U.S. GRANT,
Commanding U.S. Armies.

When the officer reached me I was still suffering with the sick headache; but the instant I saw the contents of the note I was cured. I wrote the following note in reply and hastened on:

April 9, 1865.

GENERAL R.E. LEE,
      Commanding C.S. Armies.

Your note of this date is but this moment (11.50 A.M.) received, in consequence of my having passed from the Richmond and Lynchburg road to the Farmville and Lynchburg road. I am at this writing about four miles west of Walker's Church and will push forward to the front for the purpose of meeting you. Notice sent to me on this road where you wish the interview to take place will meet me.

U.S. GRANT,
Lieutenant-General.

I was conducted at once to where Sheridan was located with his troops drawn up in line of battle facing the Confederate army near by. They were very much excited, and expressed their view that this was all a ruse employed to enable the Confederates to get away. They said they believed that Johnston was marching up from North Carolina now, and Lee was moving to join him; and they would whip the rebels where they now were in five minutes if I would only let them go in. But I had no doubt about the good faith of Lee, and pretty soon was conducted to where he was. I found him at the house of a Mr. McLean, at Appomattox Court House, with Colonel Marshall, one of his staff officers, awaiting my arrival. The head of his column was occupying a hill, on a portion of which was an apple orchard, beyond a little valley which separated it from that on the crest of which Sheridan's forces were drawn up in line of battle to the south.

Before stating what took place between General Lee and myself, I will give all there is of the story of the famous apple tree.

Wars produce many stories of fiction, some of which are told until they are believed to be true. The war of the rebellion was no exception to this rule, and the story of the apple tree is one of those fictions based on a slight foundation of fact. As I have said, there was an apple orchard on the side of the hill occupied by the Confederate forces. Running diagonally up the hill was a wagon road, which, at one point, ran very near one of the trees, so that the wheels of vehicles had, on that side, cut off the roots of this tree, leaving a little embankment. General Babcock, of my staff, reported to me that when he first met General Lee he was sitting upon this embankment with his feet in the road below and his back resting against the tree. The story had no other foundation than that. Like many other stories, it would be very good if it was only true.

I had known General Lee in the old army, and had served with him in the Mexican War; but did not suppose, owing to the difference in our age and rank, that he would remember me; while I would more naturally remember him distinctly, because he was the chief of staff of General Scott in the Mexican War.

When I had left camp that morning I had not expected so soon the result that was then taking place, and consequently was in rough garb. I was without a sword, as I usually was when on horseback on the field, and wore a soldier's blouse for a coat, with the shoulder straps of my rank to indicate to the army who I was. When I went into the house I found General Lee. We greeted each other, and after shaking hands took our seats. I had my staff with me, a good portion of whom were in the room during the whole of the interview.

What General Lee's feelings were I do not know. As he was a man of much dignity, with an impassible face, it was impossible to say whether he felt inwardly glad that the end had finally come, or felt sad over the result, and was too manly to show it. Whatever his feelings,

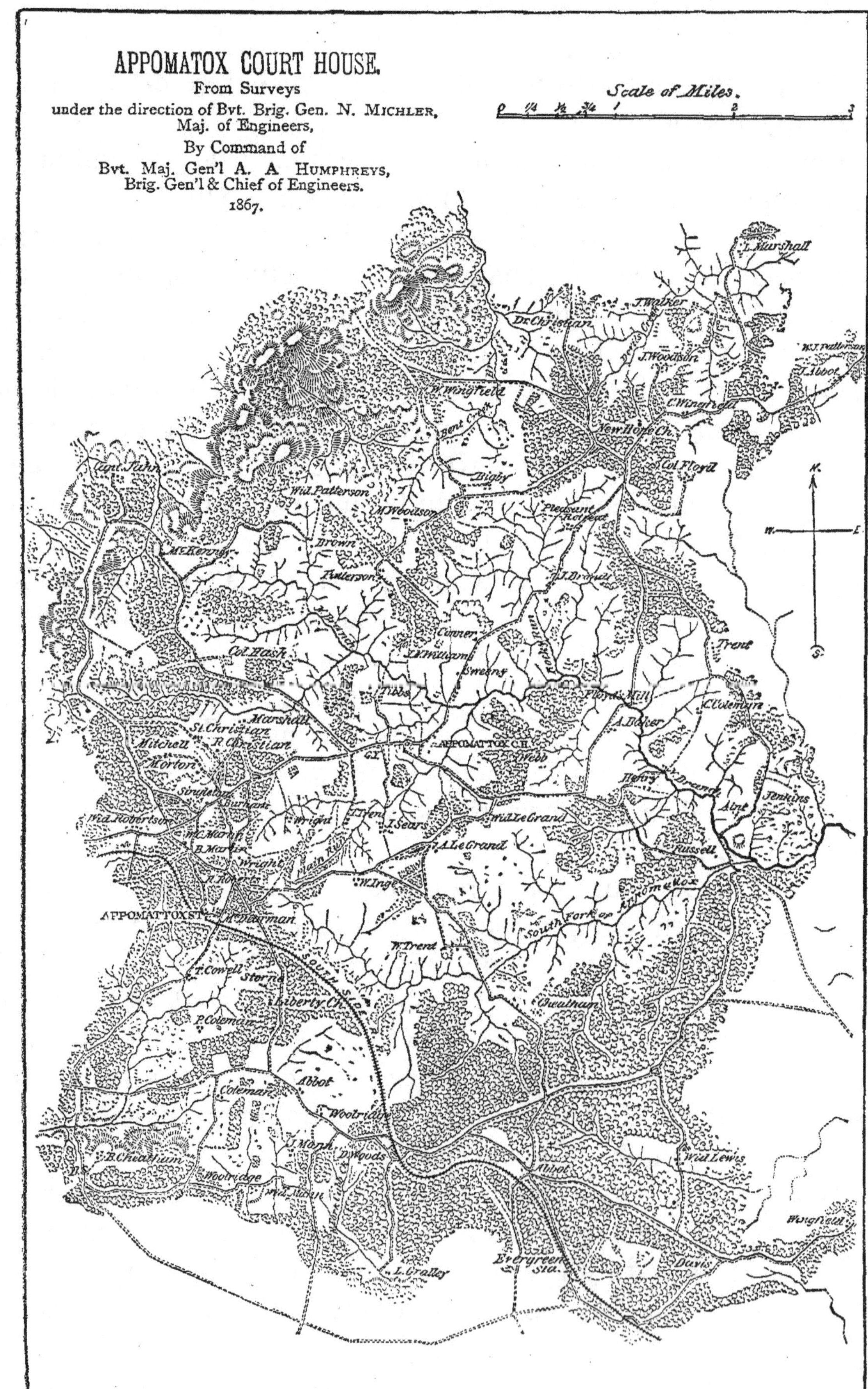
APPOMATOX COURT HOUSE.
From Surveys
under the direction of Bvt. Brig. Gen. N. Michler,
Maj. of Engineers,
By Command of
Bvt. Maj. Gen'l A. A. Humphreys,
Brig. Gen'l & Chief of Engineers.
1867.
Scale of Miles.
N.
W.
E.
S.
J. Marshall
Dr. Christian
J. Walker
J. Woodson
W.J. Patterson
J. Abbot
W. Wingfield
C. Wingfield
New Hope Ch.
Col. Floyd
Capt. John
Wid. Patterson
Bigby
M. Woodson
Pleasant Retreat
Brown
Patterson
J.J. Brown
M. Kenny
Conner
Col. Hash
J.W. William
Trent
Swear
Tibbs
Floyd's Mill
C. Coleman
Marshall
A. Baker
St. Christian
Mitchell
P. Christian
APPOMATTOX C.H.
Morton
Webb
Henry
Singleton
Burhart
Jenkins
Wid. Robertson
Wright
Trent
J. Sears
Wid. Le Grand
Russell
W.C. Morton
B. Morton
A. Le Grand
J. Horner
Wright
Main Rd.
W. Inge
APPOMATTOX ST.
M. Harman
W. Trent
South Fork or Appomattox
T. Cowell
Storne
Liberty Ch.
Cheatham
P. Coleman
Abbot
Coleman
Woolridge
J. Monk
D. Woods
Wid. Lewis
B. Cheatham
Abbot
Woolridge
Wid. Monk
Wingfield
L. Crater
Evergreen Sta.
Davis

they were entirely concealed from my observation; but my own feelings, which had been quite jubilant on the receipt of his letter, were sad and depressed. I felt like anything rather than rejoicing at the downfall of a foe who had fought so long and valiantly, and had suffered so much for a cause, though that cause was, I believe, one of the worst for which a people ever fought, and one for which there was the least excuse. I do not question, however, the sincerity of the great mass of those who were opposed to us.

General Lee was dressed in a full uniform which was entirely new, and was wearing a sword of considerable value, very likely the sword which had been presented by the State of Virginia ; at all events, it was an entirely different sword from the one that would ordinarily be worn in the field. In my rough traveling suit, the uniform of a private with the straps of a lieutenant-general, I must have contrasted very strangely with a man so handsomely dressed, six feet high and of faultless form. But this was not a matter that I thought of until afterwards.

We soon fell into a conversation about old army times. He remarked that he remembered me very well in the old army; and I told him that as a matter of course I remembered him perfectly, but from the difference in our rank and years (there being about sixteen years' difference in our ages), I had thought it very likely that I had not attracted his attention sufficiently to be remembered by him after such a long interval. Our conversation grew so pleasant that I almost forgot the object of our meeting. After the conversation had run on in this style for some time, General Lee called my attention to the object of our meeting, and said that he had asked for this interview for the purpose of getting from me the terms I proposed to give his army. I said that I meant merely that his army should lay down their arms, not to take them up again during the continuance of the war unless duly and properly exchanged. He said that he had so understood my letter.

Then we gradually fell off again into conversation about matters foreign to the subject which had brought us together. This continued for some little time, when General Lee again interrupted the course of the conversation by suggesting that the terms I proposed to give his army ought to be written out. I called to General Parker, secretary on my staff, for writing materials, and commenced writing out the following terms:

APPOMATTOX C.H., VA.,
April 9th, 1865.

GEN. R.E. LEE,
      Comd'g C.S.A.

      GEN: In accordance with the substance of my letter to you of the 8th inst., I propose to receive the surrender of the Army of N. Va. on the following terms, to wit: Rolls of all the officers and men to be made in duplicate. One copy to be given to an officer designated by me, the other to be retained by such officer or officers as you may designate. The officers to give their individual paroles not to take up arms against the Government of the United States until properly exchanged, and each company or regimental commander sign a like parole for the men of their commands. The arms, artillery and public property to be parked and stacked, and turned over to the officer appointed by me to receive them. This will not embrace the side-arms of the officers, nor their private horses or baggage. This done, each officer and man will be allowed to return to their homes, not to be disturbed by United States authority so long as they observe their paroles and the laws in force where they may reside.

Very respectfully,
U. S. GRANT,
Lt. Gen.

     When I put my pen to the paper I did not know the first word that I should make use of in writing the terms. I only knew what was in my mind, and I wished to express it clearly, so that there could be no mistaking it. As I wrote on, the thought occurred to me that the officers had their own private horses and effects, which were important to them, but of no value to us; also that it would be an unnecessary humiliation to call upon them to deliver their side arms.

     No conversation, not one word, passed between General Lee and myself, either about private property, side arms, or kindred subjects. He appeared to have no objections to the terms first proposed; or if he had a point to make against them he wished to wait until they were in writing to make it. When he read over that part of the terms about side arms, horses and private property of the officers, he remarked, with some feeling, I thought, that this would have a happy effect upon his army.

Then, after a little further conversation, General Lee remarked to me again that their army was organized a little differently from the army of the United States (still maintaining by implication that we were two countries) ; that in their army the cavalrymen and artillerists owned their own horses ; and he asked if he was to understand that the men who so owned their horses were to be permitted to retain them. I told him that as the terms were written they would not; that only the officers were permitted to take their private property. He then, after reading over the terms a second time, remarked that that was clear.

I then said to him that I thought this would be about the last battle of the war -I sincerely hoped so; and I said further I took it that most of the men in the ranks were small farmers. The whole country had been so raided by the two armies that it was doubtful whether they would be able to put in a crop to carry themselves and their families through the next winter without the aid of the horses they were then riding. The United States did not want them and I would, therefore, instruct the officers I left behind to receive the paroles of his troops to let every man of the Confederate army who claimed to own a horse or mule take the animal to his home. Lee remarked again that this would have a happy effect.

He then sat down and wrote out the following letter:

HEADQUARTERS ARMY OF NORTHERN VIRGINIA,
April 9, 1865.

GENERAL:-I received your letter of this date containing the terms of the surrender of the Army of Northern Virginia as proposed by you. As they are substantially the same as those expressed in your letter of the 8th inst., they are

Eng. by A. Dresher.

McLean's House at Appomatox in which General Lee Signed the Terms of Surrender

accepted. I will proceed to designate the proper officers to carry the stipulations into effect.

R.E. LEE, General.

LIEUT - GENERAL U.S. GRANT.

While duplicates of the two letters were being made, the Union generals present were severally presented to General Lee.

The much talked of surrendering of Lee's sword and my handing it back, this and much more that has been said about it is the purest romance. The word sword or sidearms was not mentioned by either of us until I wrote it in the terms. There was no premeditation, and it did not occur to me until the moment I wrote it down. If I had happened to omit it, and General Lee had called my attention to it, I should have put it in the terms precisely as I acceded to the provision about the soldiers retaining their horses.

General Lee, after all was completed and before taking his leave, remarked that his army was in a very bad condition for want of food, and that they were without forage; that his men had been living for some days on parched corn exclusively, and that he would have to ask me for rations and forage. I told him I certainly," and asked for how many men he wanted rations. His answer was I about twenty-five thousand : " and I authorized him to send his own commissary and quartermaster to Appomattox Station, two or three miles away, where he could have, out of the trains we had stopped, all the provisions wanted. As for forage, we had ourselves depended almost entirely upon the country for that.

Generals Gibbon, Griffin and Merritt were designated by me to carry into effect the paroling of Lee's troops before they should start for their homes -General Lee leaving Generals Longstreet, Gordon and Pendleton for them to confer with in order to facilitate this work. Lee and I then separated as cordially as we had met, he returning to his own lines, and all went into bivouac for the night at Appomattox.

(2)

Appomattox C.H. Va.
Apl. 9th 1865

Gen. R. E. Lee,
Comdg C.S.A.

Genl.

In accordance with the substance of my letter to you of the 8th inst I propose to receive the surrender of the Army of N. Va. on the following terms, to wit:

Rolls of all the officers and men to be made in duplicate, one copy to be given to an officer designated by me, the other to be retained by such officer or officers as you may designate. The officers to give their individual paroles not to take up arms against the

Government of the United States, and each Company or Regimental Commander sign a like parole for the men of their commands.

The Arms, Artillery and public property to be parked and stacked and turned over to the officer appointed by me to receive them. This will not embrace the side Arms of the Officers, nor their private horses or baggage. This done each officer and man will be allowed to return to their homes not to be disturbed by United States Authority so long as they observe their parole and the laws in force where they may reside.

Very respectfully
U S Grant Lt

Soon after Lee's departure I telegraphed to Washington as follows:

HEADQUARTERS APPOMATTOX C.H., VA.,
April 9th, 1865, 4.30 P.M.

HON. E.M. STANTON,
Secretary of War, Washington.

General Lee surrendered the Army of Northern Virginia this afternoon on terms proposed by myself. The accompanying additional correspondence will show the conditions fully.

U.S. GRANT,
Lieut. -General.

When news of the surrender first reached our lines our men commenced firing a salute of a hundred guns in honor of the victory. I at once sent word, however, to have it stopped. The Confederates were now our prisoners, and we did not want to exult over their downfall.

I determined to return to Washington at once, with a view to putting a stop to the purchase of supplies, and what I now deemed other useless outlay of money. Before leaving, however, I thought I would like to see General Lee again; so next morning I rode out beyond our lines towards his headquarters, preceded by a bugler and a staff-officer carrying a white flag. Lee soon mounted his horse, seeing who it was, and met me. We had there between the lines, sitting on horseback, a very pleasant conversation of over half an hour, in the course of which Lee said to me that the South was a big country and that we might have to march over it three or four times before the war entirely ended, but that we would now be able to do it as they could no longer resist us. He expressed it as his earnest hope, however, that we would not be called upon to cause more loss and sacrifice of life; but he could not foretell the result. I then suggested to General Lee that there was not a man in the Confederacy whose influence with the soldiery and the whole people was as great as his, and that if he would now advise the surrender of all the armies I had no doubt his advice would be followed with alacrity. But Lee said, that he could not do that without consulting the President first. I knew there was no use to urge him to do anything against his ideas of what was right.

I was accompanied by my staff and other officers, some of whom seemed to have a great desire to go inside the Confederate lines. They finally asked permission of Lee to do so for the purpose of seeing some of their old army friends, and the permission was granted. They went over, had a very pleasant time with their old friends, and brought some of them back with them when they returned.

When Lee and I separated he went back to his lines and I returned to the house of Mr. McLean. Here the officers of both armies came in great numbers, and seemed to enjoy the meeting as much as though they had been friends separated for a long time while fighting battles under the same flag. For the time being it looked very much as if all thought of the war had escaped their minds. After an hour pleasantly passed in this way I set out on horseback, accompanied by my staff and a small escort, for Burkesville Junction, up to which point the railroad had by this time been repaired.

NOTE. -The facsimile of the terms of Lee's surrender inserted at this place, was copied from the original document furnished the publishers through the courtesy of General Ely S. Parker, Military Secretary on General Grant's staff at the time of the surrender.

Three pages of paper were prepared in General Grant's manifold order book on which he wrote the terms, and the interlineations and erasures were added by General Parker at the suggestion of General Grant. After such alteration it was handed to General Lee, who put on his glasses, read it, and handed it back to General Grant. The original was then transcribed by General Parker upon official headed paper and a copy furnished General Lee.

The facsimile herewith shows the color of the paper of the original document and all interlineations and erasures.

There is a popular error to the effect that Generals Grant and Lee each signed the articles of surrender. The document in the form of a letter was signed only by General Grant, in the parlor of McLean's house while General Lee was

sitting in the room, and General Lee immediately wrote a letter accepting the terms and handed it to General Grant. This letter is copied on page 301.
PUBLISHERS .

CHAPTER LXVIII

MORALE OF THE TWO ARMIES - RELATIVE CONDITIONS OF THE NORTH AND SOUTH - PRESIDENT LINCOLN VISITS RICHMOND - ARRIVAL AT WASHINGTON - PRESIDENT LINCOLN'S ASSASSINATION - PRESIDENT JOHNSON'S POLICY

AFTER the fall of Petersburg, and when the armies of the Potomac and the James were in motion to head off Lee's army, the morale of the National troops had greatly improved. There was no more straggling, no more rear guards. The men who in former times had been falling back, were now, as I have already stated, striving to get to the front. For the first time in four weary years they felt that they were now nearing the time when they could return to their homes with their country saved. On the other hand, the Confederates were more than correspondingly depressed. Their despondency increased with each returning day, and especially after the battle of Sailor's Creek. They threw away their arms in constantly increasing numbers, dropping out of the ranks and betaking themselves to the woods in the hope of reaching their homes. I have already instanced the case of the entire disintegration of a regiment whose colonel I met at Farmville. As a result of these and other influences, when Lee finally surrendered at Appomattox, there were only 28,356 officers and men left to be paroled, and many of these were without arms. It was probably this latter fact which gave rise to the statement sometimes made, North and South, that Lee surrendered a smaller number of men than what the official figures show. As a matter of official record, and in addition to the number paroled as given above, we captured between March 29th and the date of surrender 19,132 Confederates, to say nothing of Lee's other losses, killed, wounded and missing, during the series of desperate conflicts which marked his headlong and determined flight. The same record shows the number of cannon, including those at Appomattox, to have been 689 between the dates named.

There has always been a great conflict of opinion as to the number of troops engaged in every battle, or all important battles, fought between the sections, the South magnifying the number of Union troops engaged and belittling their own. Northern writers have fallen, in many instances, into the same error. I have often heard gentlemen, who were thoroughly loyal to the Union, speak of what a splendid fight the South had made and successfully continued for four years before yielding, with their twelve million of people against our twenty, and of the twelve four being colored slaves, non-combatants. I will add to their argument. We had many regiments of brave and loyal men who volunteered under great difficulty from the twelve million belonging to the South.

But the South had rebelled against the National government. It was not bound by any constitutional restrictions. The whole South was a military camp. The occupation of the colored people was to furnish supplies for the army. Conscription was resorted to early, and embraced every male from the age of eighteen to forty-five, excluding only those physically unfit to serve in the field, and the necessary number of civil officers of State and intended National government. The old and physically disabled furnished a good portion of these. The slaves, the non-combatants, one-third of the whole, were required to work in the field without regard to sex, and almost without regard to age. Children from the age of eight years could and did handle the hoe; they were not much older when they began to hold the plough. The four million of colored non-combatants were equal to more than three times their number in the North, age for age and sex for sex, in supplying food from the soil to support armies. Women did not work in the fields in the North, and children attended school.

The arts of peace were carried on in the North. Towns and cities grew during the war. Inventions were made in all kinds of machinery to increase the products of a day's labor in the shop, and in the field. In the South no opposition was allowed to the government which had been set up and which would have become real and respected if the rebellion had been successful. No rear had to be protected. All the troops in service could be brought to the front to contest every inch of ground threatened with invasion. The press of the South, like the people who remained at home, were loyal to the Southern cause.

In the North, the country, the towns and the cities presented about the same appearance they do in time of peace. The furnace was in blast, the shops were filled with workmen, the fields were cultivated, not only to supply the population of the North and the troops invading the South, but to ship abroad to pay a part of the expense of the war. In the North the press was free up to the point of open treason.

The citizen could entertain his views and express them. Troops were necessary in the Northern States to prevent prisoners from the Southern army being released by outside force, armed and set at large to destroy by fire our Northern cities. Plans were formed by Northern and Southern citizens to burn our cities, to poison the water supplying them, to spread infection by importing clothing from infected regions, to blow up our river and lake steamers -regardless of the destruction of innocent lives. The copperhead disreputable portion of the press magnified rebel successes, and belittled those of the Union army. It was, with a large following, an auxiliary to the Confederate army. The North would have been much stronger with a hundred thousand of these men in the Confederate ranks and the rest of their kind thoroughly subdued, as the Union sentiment was in the South, than we were as the battle was fought.

As I have said, the whole South was a military camp. The colored people, four million in number, were submissive, and worked in the field and took care of the families while the able-bodied white men were at the front fighting for a cause destined to defeat. The cause was popular, and was enthusiastically supported by the young men. The conscription took all of them, Before the war was over, further conscriptions took those between fourteen and eighteen years of age as junior reserves, and those between forty-five and sixty as senior reserves. It would have been an offence, directly after the war, and perhaps it would be now, to ask any able-bodied man in the South, who was between the ages of fourteen and sixty at any time during the war, whether he had been in the Confederate army. He would assert that he had, or account for his absence from the ranks. Under such circumstances it is hard to conceive how the North showed such a superiority of force in every battle fought. I know they did not.

During 1862 and 33, John H. Morgan, a partisan officer, of no military education, but possessed of courage and endurance, operated in the rear of the Army of the Ohio in Kentucky and Tennessee. He had no base of supplies to protect, but was at home wherever he went. The army operating against the South, on the contrary, had to protect its lines of communication with the North, from which all supplies had to come to the front. Every foot of road had to be guarded by troops stationed at convenient distances apart. These guards could not render assistance beyond the points where stationed. Morgan was foot-loose and could operate where his information, always correct -led him to believe he could do the greatest damage. During the time he was operating in this way he killed, wounded and captured several times the number he ever had under his command at any one time. He destroyed many millions of property in addition. Places he did not attack had to be guarded as if threatened by him. Forrest, an abler soldier, operated farther west, and held from the National front quite as many men as could be spared for offensive operations. It is safe to say that more than half the National army was engaged in guarding lines of supplies, or were on leave, sick in hospital or on detail which prevented their bearing arms. Then, again, large forces were employed where no Confederate army confronted them. I deem it safe to say that there were no large engagements where the National numbers compensated for the advantage of position and intrenchment occupied by the enemy.

While I was in pursuit of General Lee, the President went to Richmond in company with Admiral Porter, and on board his flagship. He found the people of that city in great consternation. The leading citizens among the people who had remained at home surrounded him, anxious that something should be done to relieve them from suspense. General Weitzel was not then in the city, having taken offices in one of the neighboring villages after his troops had succeeded in subduing the conflagration which they had found in progress on entering the Confederate capital. The President sent for him, and, on his arrival, a short interview was had on board the vessel, Admiral Porter and a leading citizen of Virginia being also present. After this interview the President wrote an order in about these words: which I quote from memory: "General Weitzel is authorized to permit the body calling itself the Legislature of Virginia to meet for the purpose of recalling the Virginia troops from the Confederate armies."

Immediately some of the gentlemen composing that body wrote out a call for a meeting and had it published in their papers. This call, however, went very much further than Mr. Lincoln had contemplated, as he did not say the "Legislature of Virginia" but "the body which called itself the Legislature of Virginia." Mr. Stanton saw the call as published in the Northern papers the very next issue and took the liberty of countermanding the order authorizing any meeting of the Legislature, or any other body, and this notwithstanding the fact that the President was nearer the spot than he was.

This was characteristic of Mr. Stanton, He was a man who never questioned his own authority, and who always did in war time what he wanted to do. He was an able constitutional lawyer and jurist; but the Constitution was not an impediment to him while the war lasted. In this latter particular I entirely agree with the view he evidently held. The Constitution was not framed with a view to any such rebellion as that of 1861-5. While it did not authorize rebellion it made no provision against it. Yet the right to resist or suppress rebellion is as inherent as the right of self-defence, and as natural as the right of an individual to preserve his life when in jeopardy. The Constitution was therefore in abeyance for the time being, so far as it in any way affected the progress and termination of the war.

Those in rebellion against the government of the United States were not restricted by constitutional provisions, or any other, except the acts of their Congress, which was loyal and devoted to the cause for which the South was then fighting. It would be a hard case when one-third of a nation, united in rebellion against the national authority, is entirely untrammeled, that the other two-thirds, in their efforts to maintain the Union intact, should be restrained by a Constitution prepared by our ancestors for the express purpose of insuring the permanency of the confederation of the States.

After I left General Lee at Appomattox Station, I went with my staff and a few others directly to Burkesville Station on my way to Washington. The road from Burkesville back having been newly repaired and the ground being soft, the train got off the track frequently, and, as a result, it was after midnight of the second day when I reached City Point. As soon as possible I took a dispatch-boat thence to Washington City.

While in Washington I was very busy for a time in preparing the necessary orders for the new state of affairs; communicating with my different commanders of separate departments, bodies of troops, etc. But by the 14th I was pretty well through with this work, so as to be able to visit my children, who were then in Burlington, New Jersey, attending school. Mrs. Grant was with me in Washington at the time, and we were invited by President and Mrs. Lincoln to accompany them to the theatre on the evening of that day. I replied to the President's verbal invitation to the effect, that if we were in the city we would take great pleasure in accompanying them; but that I was very anxious to get away and visit my children, and if I could get through my work during the day I should do so. I did get through and started by the evening train on the 14th, sending Mr. Lincoln word, of course, that I would not be at the theatre.

At that time the railroad to New York entered Philadelphia on Broad Street; passengers were conveyed in ambulances to the Delaware River, and then ferried to Camden, at which point they took the cars again. When I reached the ferry, on the east side of the City of

Philadelphia, I found people awaiting my arrival there ; and also dispatches informing me of the assassination of the President and Mr. Seward, and of the probable assassination of the Vice-President, Mr. Johnson, and requesting my immediate return. It would be impossible for me to describe the feeling that overcame me at the news of these assassinations, more especially the assassination of the President. I knew his goodness of heart, his generosity, his yielding disposition, his desire to have everybody happy, and above all his desire to see all the people of the United States enter again upon the full privileges of citizenship with equality among all. I knew also the feeling that Mr. Johnson had expressed in speeches and conversation against the Southern people, and I feared that his course towards them would be such as to repel, and make them unwilling citizens ; and if they became such they would remain so for a long while. I felt that reconstruction had been set back, no telling how far.

I immediately arranged for getting a train to take me back to Washington City; but Mrs. Grant was with me; it was after midnight and Burlington was but an hour away. Finding that I could accompany her to our house and return about as soon as they would be ready to take me from the Philadelphia station, I went up with her and returned immediately by the same special train. The joy that I had witnessed among the people in the street and in public places in Washington when I left there, had been turned to grief; the city was in reality a city of mourning. I have stated what I believed then the effect of this would be, and my judgment now is that I was right. I believe the South would have been saved from very much of the hardness of feeling that was engendered by Mr. Johnson's course towards them during the first few months of his administration. Be this as it may, Mr. Lincoln's assassination was particularly unfortunate for the entire nation.

Mr. Johnson's course towards the South did engender bitterness of feeling. His denunciations of treason and his ever ready remark, "Treason is a crime and must be made odious," was repeated to all those men of the South who came to him to get some assurances of safety so that they might go to work at something with the feeling that what they obtained would be secure to them. He uttered his denunciations with great vehemence, and as they were accompanied with no assurances of safety, many Southerners were driven to a point almost beyond endurance.

The President of the United States is, in a large degree, or ought to be, a representative of the feeling, wishes and judgment of those over whom he presides; and the Southerners who read the denunciations of themselves and their people must have come to the conclusion that he uttered the sentiments of the Northern people; whereas, as a matter of fact, but for the assassination of Mr. Lincoln, I believe the great majority of the Northern people, and the soldiers unanimously, would have been in favor of a speedy reconstruction on terms that would be the least humiliating to the people who had rebelled against their government. They believed, I have no doubt, as I did, that besides being the mildest, it was also the wisest, policy.

The people who had been in rebellion must necessarily come back into the Union, and be incorporated as an integral part of the nation. Naturally the nearer they were placed to an equality with the people who had not rebelled, the more reconciled they would feel with their old antagonists, and the better citizens they would be from the beginning. They surely would not make good citizens if they felt that they had a yoke around their necks.

I do not believe that the majority of the Northern people at that time were in favor of negro suffrage. They supposed that it would naturally follow the freedom of the negro, but that there would be a time of probation, in which the ex-slaves could prepare themselves for the privileges of citizenship before the full right would be conferred; but Mr. Johnson, after a complete revolution of sentiment, seemed to regard the South not only as an oppressed people, but as the people best entitled to consideration of any of our citizens. This was more than the people who had secured to us the perpetuation of the Union were prepared for, and they became more radical in their views. The Southerners had the most power in the executive branch, Mr. Johnson having gone to their side; and with a compact South, and such sympathy and support as they could get from the North, they felt that they would be able to control the nation at once, and already many of them acted as if they thought they were entitled to do so.

Thus Mr. Johnson, fighting Congress on the one hand, and receiving the support of the South on the other, drove Congress, which was overwhelmingly republican, to the passing of first one measure and then another to restrict his power. There being a solid South on one side that was in accord with the political party in the North which had sympathized with the rebellion, it finally, in the judgment of Congress and of the majority of the legislatures of the States, became necessary to enfranchise the Negro, in all his ignorance. In this work, I shall not discuss the question of how far the policy of Congress in this particular proved a wise one, It became an absolute necessity, however, because of the foolhardiness of the President and the blindness of the Southern people to their own interest. As to myself, while strongly favoring the course that would be the least humiliating to the people who had been in rebellion, I had gradually worked up to the point where, with the majority of the people, I favored immediate enfranchisement.

CHAPTER LXIX

SHERMAN AND JOHNSTON -JOHNSTON'S SURRENDER TO SHERMAN - CAPTURE OF MOBILE - WILSON'S EXPEDITION - CAPTURE OF JEFFERSON DAVIS - GENERAL THOMAS'S QUALITIES - ESTIMATE OF GENERAL CANBY.

WHEN I left Appomattox I ordered General Meade to proceed leisurely back to Burkesville Station with the Army of the Potomac and the Army of the James, and to go into camp there until further orders from me. General Johnston, as has been stated before, was in North Carolina confronting General Sherman. It could not be known positively, of course, whether Johnston would surrender on the news of Lee's surrender, though I supposed he would; and if he did not, Burkesville Station was the natural point from which to move to attack him. The army which I could have sent against him was superior to his, and that with which Sherman confronted him was also superior; and between the two he would necessarily have been crushed, or driven away. With the loss of their capital and the Army of Northern Virginia it was doubtful whether Johnston's men would have had the spirit to stand. My belief was that he would make no such attempt; but I adopted this course as a precaution against what might happen, however improbable.

Simultaneously with my starting from City Point, I sent a messenger to North Carolina by boat with dispatches to General Sherman, informing him of the surrender of Lee and his army; also of the terms which I had given him; and I authorized Sherman to give the same terms to Johnston if the latter chose to accept them. The country is familiar with the terms that Sherman agreed to conditionally, because they embraced a political question as well as a military one and he would therefore have to confer with the government before agreeing to them definitely.

General Sherman had met Mr. Lincoln at City Point while visiting there to confer with me about our final movement, and knew what Mr. Lincoln had said to the peace commissioners when he met them at Hampton Roads, viz. : that before he could enter into negotiations with them they would have to agree to two points : one being that the Union should be preserved, and the other that slavery should be abolished ; and if they were ready to concede these two points he was almost ready to sign his name to a blank piece of paper and permit them to fill out the balance of the terms upon which we would live together. He had also seen notices in the newspapers of Mr. Lincoln's visit to Richmond, and had read in the same papers that while there he had authorized the convening of the Legislature of Virginia.

Sherman thought, no doubt, in adding to the terms that I had made with General Lee, that he was but carrying out the wishes of the President of the United States. But seeing that he was going beyond his authority, he made it a point that the terms were only conditional. They signed them with this understanding, and agreed to a truce until the terms could be sent to Washington for approval; if approved by the proper authorities there, they would then be final; if not approved, then he would give due notice, before resuming hostilities. As the world knows, Sherman, from being one of the most popular generals of the land (Congress having even gone so far as to propose a bill providing for a second lieutenant-general for the purpose of advancing him to that grade), was denounced by the President and Secretary of War in very bitter terms. Some people went so far as to denounce him as a traitor -a most preposterous term to apply to a man who had rendered so much service as he had, even supposing he had made a mistake in granting such terms as he did to Johnston and his army. If Sherman had taken authority to send Johnston with his army home, with their arms to be put in the arsenals of their own States, without submitting the question to the authorities at Washington, the suspicions against him might have some foundation. But the feeling against Sherman died out very rapidly, and it was not many weeks before he was restored to the fullest confidence of the American people.

When, some days after my return to Washington, President Johnson and the Secretary of War received the terms which General Sherman had forwarded for approval, a cabinet meeting was immediately called and I was sent for. There seemed to be the greatest consternation, lest Sherman would commit the government to terms which they were not willing to accede to and which he had no right to grant. A message went out directing the troops in the South not to obey General Sherman. I was ordered to proceed at once to North Carolina and take charge of matters there myself. Of course I started without delay, and reached there as soon as possible. I repaired to Raleigh, where Sherman was, as quietly as possible, hoping to see him without even his army learning of my presence.

When I arrived I went to Sherman's headquarters, and we were at once closeted together. I showed him the instructions and orders under which I visited him. I told him that I wanted him to notify General Johnston that the terms which they had conditionally agreed upon had not been approved in Washington, and that he was authorized to offer the same terms I had given General Lee. I sent Sherman to do this himself. I did not wish the knowledge of my presence to be known to the army generally ; so I left it to Sherman to negotiate the terms of the surrender solely by himself, and without the enemy knowing that I was anywhere near the field. As soon as possible I started to get away, to leave Sherman quite free and untrammeled.

At Goldsboro', on my way back, I met a mail, containing the last newspapers, and I found in them indications of great excitement in the North over the terms Sherman had given Johnston ; and harsh orders that had been promulgated by the President and Secretary of War. I knew that Sherman must see these papers, and I fully realized what great indignation they would cause him, though I do not think his feelings could have been more excited than were my own. But like the true and loyal soldier that he was, he carried out the instructions I had given him,

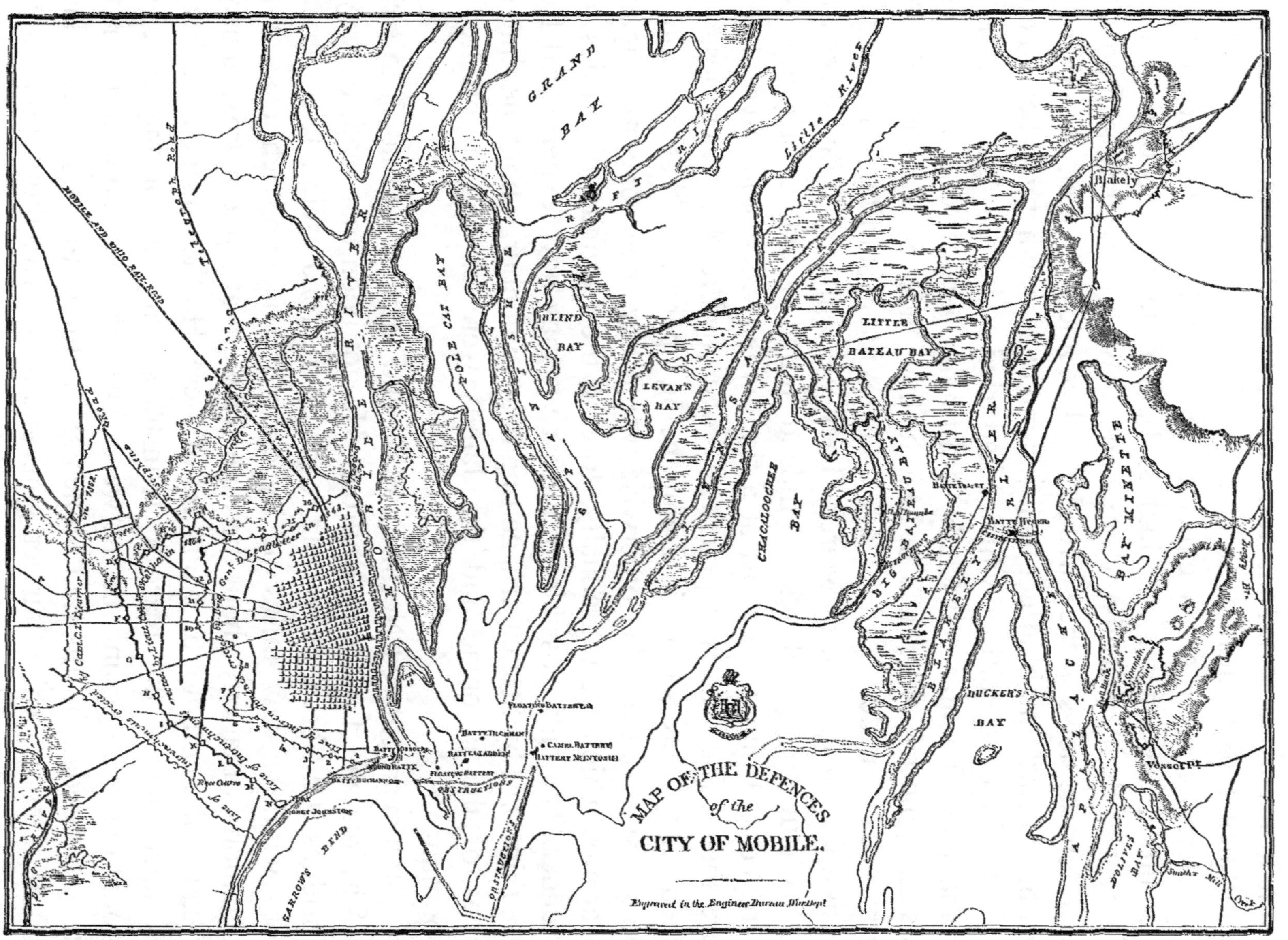
MAP OF THE DEFENCES
of the
CITY OF MOBILE.
Engraved in the Engineer Bureau Missispt
GRAND BAY
Little River
Blakely
BLIND BAY
LEVAN'S BAY
LITTLE BATEAU BAY
POLE CAT BAY
CHACALOOCHEE BAY
BIG BATEAU BAY
DUCKER'S BAY
D'OLIVE BAY
BAY MINETTE
MOBILE AND OHIO RAIL-ROAD
PASCAGOULA ROAD
FLOATING BATTERY
BATTY TILGHMAN
CANAL BATTERY
BATTERY McINTOSH
BATTY LADDEN
FLOATING BATTERY
OBSTRUCTIONS
BATTY McINTOSH
GUN BATTY
BATTY BUCHANAN
SIDNEY JOHNSTON
SARROW'S BEND
FORT SIDNEY JOHNSON
Smith Mill Creek

obtained the surrender of Johnston's army, and settled down in his camp about Raleigh, to await final orders.

There were still a few expeditions out in the South that could not be communicated with, and had to be left to act -according to the judgment of their respective commanders. With these it was impossible to tell how the news of the surrender of Lee and Johnston, of which they must have heard, might affect their judgment as to what was best to do.

The three expeditions which I had tried so hard to get off from the commands of Thomas and Canby did finally get off: one under Canby himself, against Mobile, late in March; that under Stoneman from East Tennessee on the 20th; and the one under Wilson, starting from Eastport, Mississippi, on the 22d of March. They were all eminently successful, but without any good result. Indeed much valuable property was destroyed and many lives lost at a time when we would have liked to spare them. The war was practically over before their victories were gained. They were so late in commencing operations, that they did not hold any troops away that otherwise would have been operating against the armies which were gradually, forcing the Confederate armies to a surrender. The only possible good that we may have experienced from these raids was by Stoneman's getting near Lynchburg about the time the armies of the Potomac and the James were closing in on Lee at Appomattox.

Stoneman entered North Carolina and then pushed north to strike the Virginia and Tennessee Railroad. He got upon that road, destroyed its bridges at different places and rendered the road useless to the enemy up to within a few miles of Lynchburg. His approach caused the evacuation of that city about the time we were at Appomattox, and was the cause of a commotion we heard of there. He then pushed south, and was operating in the rear of Johnston's army about the time the negotiations were going on between Sherman and Johnston for the latter's surrender. In this raid Stoneman captured and destroyed a large amount of stores, while fourteen guns and nearly two thousand prisoners were the trophies of his success.

Canby appeared before Mobile on the 27th of March. The city of Mobile was protected by two forts, besides other intrenchments -Spanish Fort, on the east side of the bay, and Fort Blakely, north of the city. These forts were invested. On the night of the 8th of April, the National troops having carried the enemy's works at one point, Spanish Fort was evacuated; and on the 9th, the very day of Lee's surrender, Blakely was carried by assault, with a considerable loss to us. On the 11th the city was evacuated.

I had tried for more than two years to have an expedition sent against Mobile when its possession by us would have been of great advantage. It finally cost lives to take it when its possession was of no importance, and when, if left alone, it would within a few days have fallen into our hands without any bloodshed whatever.

Wilson moved out with full 12,000 men, well equipped and well armed. He was an energetic officer and accomplished his work rapidly. Forrest was in his front, but with neither his old-time army nor his old-time prestige. He now had principally conscripts. His conscripts were generally old men and boys. He had a few thousand regular cavalry left, but not enough to even retard materially the progress of Wilson's cavalry. Selma fell on the 2d of April, with a large number of prisoners and a large quantity of war material, machine shops, etc., to be disposed of by the victors. Tuscaloosa, Montgomery and West Point fell in quick succession. These were all important points to the enemy by reason of their railroad connections, as depots of supplies, and because of their manufactories of war material. They were fortified or intrenched, and there was considerable fighting before they were captured. Macon surrendered on the 21st of April. Here news was received of the negotiations for the surrender of Johnston's army. Wilson belonged to the military division commanded by Sherman, and of course was bound by his terms. This stopped all fighting.

General Richard Taylor had now become the senior Confederate officer still at liberty east of the Mississippi River, and on the 4th of May he surrendered everything within the limits of this extensive command.

General E. Kirby Smith surrendered the trans-Mississippi department on the 26th of May, leaving no other Confederate army at liberty to continue the war.

Wilson's raid resulted in the capture of the fugitive president of the defunct confederacy before he got out of the country. This occurred at Irwinsville, Georgia, on the 11th of May. For myself, and I believe Mr. Lincoln shared the feeling, I would have been very glad to have seen Mr. Davis succeed in escaping, but for one reason : I feared that if not captured, he might get into the trans-Mississippi region and there set up a more contracted confederacy. The young men now out of homes and out of employment might have rallied under his standard and protracted the war yet another year. The Northern people were tired of the war, they were tired of piling up a debt which would be a further mortgage upon their homes.

Mr. Lincoln, I believe, wanted Mr. Davis to escape, because he did not wish to deal with the matter of his punishment. He knew there would be people clamoring for the punishment of the ex-Confederate president, for high treason. He thought blood enough had already been spilled to atone for our wickedness as a nation. At all events he did not wish to be the judge to decide whether more should be shed or not. But his own life was sacrificed at the hands of an assassin before the ex-President of the Confederacy was a prisoner in the hands of the government which he had lent all his talent and all his energies to destroy.

All things are said to be wisely directed, and for the best interest of all concerned. This reflection does not, however, abate in the slightest our sense of bereavement in the untimely loss of so good and great a man as Abraham Lincoln.

He would have proven the best friend the South could have had, and saved much of the wrangling and bitterness of feeling brought out by reconstruction under a President who at first wished to revenge himself upon Southern men of better social standing than himself, but who still sought their recognition, and in a short time conceived the idea and advanced the proposition to become their Moses to lead them triumphantly out of all their difficulties.

The story of the legislation enacted during the reconstruction period to stay the hands of the President is too fresh in the minds of the people to be told now. Much of it, no doubt, was unconstitutional; but it was hoped that the laws enacted would serve their purpose before the question of constitutionality could be submitted to the judiciary and a decision obtained. These laws did serve their purpose, and now remain .a dead letter upon the statute books of the United States, no one taking interest enough in them to give them a passing thought.

Much was said at the time about the garb Mr. Davis was wearing when he was captured. I cannot settle this question from personal knowledge of the facts; but I have been under the belief, from information given to me by General Wilson shortly after the event, that when Mr. Davis learned that he was surrounded by our cavalry he was in his tent dressed in a gentleman's dressing gown. Naturally enough, Mr. Davis wanted to escape, and would not reflect much how this should be accomplished provided it might be done successfully. If captured, he would be no ordinary prisoner. He represented all there was of that hostility to the government which had caused four years of the bloodiest war -and the most costly in other respects of which history makes any record. Every one supposed he would be tried for treason if captured, and that he would be executed. Had he succeeded in making his escape in any disguise it would have been adjudged a good thing afterwards by his admirers.

As my official letters on file in the War Department, as well as my remarks in this book, reflect upon General Thomas by dwelling somewhat upon his tardiness, it is due to myself, as well as to him, that I give my estimate of him as a soldier. The same remark will apply also in the case of General Canby. I had been at West Point with Thomas one year, and had known him later in the old army. He was a man of commanding appearance, slow and deliberate in speech and action; sensible, honest and brave. He possessed valuable soldierly qualities in an eminent degree. He gained the confidence of all who served under him, and almost their love. This implies a very valuable quality. It is a quality which calls out the most efficient services of the troops serving under the commander possessing it.

Thomas's dispositions were deliberately made, and always good. He could not be driven from a point he was given to hold. He was not as good, however, in pursuit as he was in action. I do not believe that he could ever have conducted Sherman's army from Chattanooga to Atlanta against the defences and the commander guarding that line in 1864. On the other hand, if it had been given him to hold the line which Johnston tried to hold, neither that general nor Sherman, nor any other officer could have done it better.

Thomas was a valuable officer, who richly deserved, as he has received, the plaudits of his countrymen for the part he played in the great tragedy of 1861-5.

General Canby was an officer of great merit. He was naturally studious, and inclined to the law. There have been in the army but very few, if any, officers who took as much interest in reading and digesting every act of Congress and every regulation for the government of the army as he. His knowledge gained in this way made him a most valuable staff officer, a capacity in which almost all his army services were rendered up to the time of his being assigned to the Military Division of the Gulf. He was an exceedingly modest officer, though of great talent and learning. I presume his feelings when first called upon to command a large army against a fortified city, were somewhat like my own when marching a regiment against General Thomas Harris in Missouri in 1861.Neither of us would have felt the slightest trepidation in going into battle with some one else commanding. Had Canby been in other engagements afterwards, he would, I have no doubt, have advanced without any fear arising from a sense of the responsibility. He was afterwards killed in the lava beds of Southern Oregon, while in pursuit of the hostile Modoc Indians. His character was as pure as his talent and learning were great. His services were valuable during the war, but principally as a bureau officer. I have no idea that it was from choice that his services were rendered in an office, but because of his superior efficiency there.

CHAPTER LXX

THE END OF THE WAR - THE MARCH TO WASHINGTON - ONE OF LINCOLN'S ANECDOTES - GRAND REVIEW AT WASHINGTON - CHARACTERISTICS OF LINCOLN AND STANTON - ESTIMATE OF THE DIFFERENT CORPS COMMANDERS

THINGS began to quiet down, and as the certainty that there would be no more armed resistance became clearer, the troops in North Carolina and Virginia were ordered to march immediately to the capital, and go into camp there until mustered out. Suitable garrisons were left at the prominent places throughout the South to insure obedience to the laws that might be enacted for the government of the several States, and to insure security to the lives and property of all classes. I do not know how far this was necessary, but I deemed it necessary, at that time, that such a course should be pursued. think now that these garrisons were continued after they ceased to be absolutely required; but it is not to be expected that such a rebellion as was fought between the sections from 1861 to 1865 could terminate without leaving many serious apprehensions in the mind of the people as to what should be done.

Sherman marched his troops from Goldsboro, up to Manchester, on the south side of the James River, opposite Richmond, and there put them in camp, while he went back to Savannah to see what the situation was there.

It was during this trip that the last outrage was committed upon him. Halleck had been sent to Richmond to command Virginia, and had issued orders prohibiting even Sherman's own troops from obeying his, Sherman's, orders. Sherman met the papers on his return, containing this order of Halleck, and very justly felt indignant at the outrage. On his arrival at Fortress Monroe returning from Savannah, Sherman received an invitation from Halleck to come to Richmond and be his guest. This he indignantly refused, and informed Halleck, furthermore, that he had seen his order. He also stated that he was coming up to take command of his troops, and as he marched through it would probably be as well for Halleck not to show himself, because he (Sherman) would not be responsible for what some rash person might do through indignation for the treatment he had received. Very soon after that, Sherman received orders from me to proceed to Washington City, and to go into camp on the south side of the city pending the mustering out of the troops.

There was no incident worth noting in the march northward from Goldsboro, to Richmond, or in that from Richmond to Washington City. The army, however, commanded by Sherman, which had been engaged in all the battles of the West and had marched from the Mississippi through the Southern States to the sea, from there to Goldsboro, and thence to Washington City, had passed over many of the battlefields of the Army of the Potomac, thus having seen, to a greater extent than any other body of troops, the entire theatre of the four years' war for the preservation of the Union.

The march of Sherman's army from Atlanta to the sea and north to Goldsboro, while it was not accompanied with the danger that was anticipated, yet was magnificent in its results, and equally magnificent in the way it was conducted. It had an important bearing, in various ways, upon the great object we had in view, that of closing the war. All the States east of the Mississippi River up to the State of Georgia, had felt the hardships of the war. Georgia, and South Carolina, and almost all of North Carolina, up to this time, had been exempt from invasion by the Northern armies, except upon their immediate sea coasts. Their newspapers had given such an account of Confederate success, that the people who remained at home had been convinced that the Yankees had been whipped from first to last, and driven from pillar to post, and that now they could hardly be holding out for any other purpose than to find a way out of the war with honor to themselves.

Even during this march of Sherman's the newspapers in his front were proclaiming daily that his army was nothing better than a mob of men who were frightened out of their wits and hastening, panic-stricken, to try to get under the cover of our navy for protection against the Southern people. As the army was seen marching on triumphantly, however the minds of the people became disabused and they saw the true state of affairs. In turn they became disheartened, and would have been glad to submit without compromise.

Another great advantage resulting from this march, and which was calculated to hasten the end, was the fact that the great storehouse of Georgia was entirely cut off from the Confederate armies. As the troops advanced north from Savannah, the destruction of the railroads in South Carolina and the southern part of North Carolina, further cut off their resources and left the armies still in Virginia and North Carolina dependent for supplies upon a very small area of country, already very much exhausted of food and forage.

In due time the two armies, one from Burkesville Junction and the other from the neighborhood of Raleigh, North Carolina, arrived and went into camp near the Capital, as directed. The troops were hardy, being inured to fatigue, and they appeared in their respective camps as ready and fit for duty as they had ever been in their lives. I doubt whether an equal body of men of any nation, take them man for man, officer for officer, was ever gotten together that would have proved their equal in a great battle.

The armies of Europe are machines: the men are brave and the officers capable; but the majority of the soldiers in most of the nations of Europe are taken from a class of people who are not very intelligent and who have very little interest in the contest in which they are called upon to take part. Our armies were composed of men who were able to read, men who knew what they were fighting for, and could not be induced to serve as soldiers, except in an emergency when the safety of the nation was involved, and so necessarily must have been more than equal to men who fought merely because they were brave and because they were thoroughly drilled and inured to hardships.

There was nothing of particular importance occurred during the time these troops were in camp before starting north.

I remember one little incident which I will relate as an anecdote characteristic of Mr. Lincoln. It occurred a day after I reached Washington, and about the time General Meade reached Burkesville with the army. Governor Smith of Virginia had left Richmond with the Confederate States government, and had gone to Danville. Supposing I was necessarily with the army at Burkesville, he addressed a letter to me there informing me that, as governor of the Commonwealth of the State of Virginia, he had temporarily removed the State capital from Richmond to Danville, and asking if he would be permitted to perform the functions of his office there without molestation by the Federal authorities. I give this letter only in substance. He also inquired of me whether in case he was not allowed to perform the duties of his office, he with a few others might not be permitted to leave the country and go abroad without interference. General Meade being informed that a flag of truce was outside his pickets with a letter to me, at once sent out and had the letter brought in without informing the officer who brought it that I was not present. He read the letter and telegraphed me its contents. Meeting Mr. Lincoln shortly after receiving this dispatch, I repeated its contents to him. Mr. Lincoln, supposing I was asking for instructions, said, in reply to that part of Governor Smith's letter which inquired whether he with a few friends would be permitted to leave the country unmolested, that his position was like that of a certain Irishman (giving the name) he knew in Springfield who was very popular with the people, a man of considerable promise, and very much liked. Unfortunately he had acquired the habit of drinking, and his friends could see that the habit was growing on him. These friends determined to make an effort to save him, and to do this they drew up a pledge to abstain from all alcoholic drinks. They asked Pat to join them in signing the pledge, and he consented. He had been so long out of the habit of using plain water as a beverage that he resorted to soda water as a substitute. After a few days this began to grow distasteful to him. So holding the glass behind him, he said: "Doctor, couldn't you drop a bit of brandy in that unbeknownst to myself."

I do not remember what the instructions were the President gave me, but I know that Governor Smith was not permitted to perform the duties of his office. I also know that if Mr. Lincoln had been spared, there would have been no efforts made to prevent any one from leaving the country who desired to do so. He would have been equally willing to permit the return of the same expatriated citizens after they had time to repent of their choice.

On the 18th of May orders were issued by the adjutant-general for a grand review by the President and his cabinet of Sherman's and Meade's armies. The review commenced on the 23d and lasted two days. Meade's army occupied over six hours of the first day in passing the grand stand which had been erected in front of the President's house. Sherman witnessed this review from the grand stand which was occupied by the President and his cabinet. Here he showed his resentment for the cruel and harsh treatment that had unnecessarily been inflicted upon him by the Secretary of War, by refusing to take his extended hand.

Sherman's troops had been in camp on the south side of the Potomac. During the night of the 23d he crossed over and bivouacked not far from the Capitol. Promptly at ten o'clock on the morning of the 24th, his troops commenced to pass in review. Sherman's army made a different appearance from that of the Army of the Potomac. The latter had been operating where they received directly from the North full supplies of food and clothing regularly: the review of this army therefore was the review of a body of 65,000 well-drilled, well-disciplined and orderly soldiers inured to hardship and fit for any duty, but without the experience of gathering their own food and supplies in an enemy's country, and of being ever on the watch. Sherman's army was not so well-dressed as the Army of the Potomac, but their marching could not be excelled; they gave the appearance of men who had been thoroughly drilled to endure hardships, either by long and continuous marches or through exposure to any climate, without the ordinary shelter of a camp. They exhibited also some of the order of march through Georgia where the "sweet potatoes sprung up from the ground" as Sherman's army went marching through. In the rear of a company there would be a captured horse or mule loaded with small cooking utensils, captured chickens and other food picked up for the use of the men. Negro families who had followed the army would sometimes come along in the rear of a company, with three or four children packed upon a single mule, and the mother leading it.

The sight was varied and grand: nearly all day for two successive days, from the Capitol to the Treasury Building, could be seen a mass of orderly soldiers marching in columns of companies. The National flag was flying from almost every house and store; the windows were filled with spectators; the doorsteps and sidewalks were crowded with colored people and poor whites who did not succeed in securing better quarters from which to get a view of the grand armies. The city was about as full of strangers who had come to see the sights as it usually is on inauguration day when a new President takes his seat.

It may not be out of place to again allude to President Lincoln and the Secretary of War, Mr. Stanton, who were the great conspicuous figures in the executive branch of the government. There is no great difference of opinion now, in the public mind, as to the characteristics of the President. With Mr. Stanton the case is different. They were the very opposite of each other in almost every particular, except that each possessed great ability. Mr. Lincoln gained influence over men by making them feel that it was a pleasure to serve him. He preferred yielding his own wish to gratify others, rather than to insist upon having his own way. It distressed him to disappoint others. In matters of public duty, however, he had what he wished, but in the least offensive way. Mr. Stanton never questioned his own authority to command, unless resisted. He cared nothing for the feeling of others. In fact it seemed to be pleasanter to him to disappoint than to gratify. He felt no hesitation in assuming the functions of the executive, or in acting without advising with him. If his act was not sustained, he would change it -if he saw the matter would be followed up until he did so.

It was generally supposed that these two officials formed the complement of each other. The Secretary was required to prevent the President's being imposed upon. The President was required in the more responsible place of seeing that injustice was not done to others. I do not know that this view of these two men is still entertained by the majority of the people. It is not a correct view, however, in my estimation. Mr. Lincoln did not require a guardian to aid him in the fulfillment of a public trust.

Mr. Lincoln was not timid, and he was willing to trust his generals in making and executing their plans. The Secretary was very timid, and it was impossible for him to avoid interfering with the armies covering the capital when it was sought to defend it by an offensive movement against the army guarding the Confederate capital. He could see our weakness, but he could not see that the enemy was in danger. The enemy would not have been in danger if Mr. Stanton had been in the field. These characteristics of the two officials were clearly shown shortly after Early came so near getting into the capital.

Among the army and corps commanders who served with me during the war between the States, and who attracted much public attention, but of whose ability as soldiers I have not yet given any estimate, are Meade, Hancock, Sedgwick, Burnside, Terry and Hooker. There were others of great merit, such as Griffin, Humphreys, Wright and Mackenzie. Of those first named, Burnside at one time had command of the Army of the Potomac, and later of the Army of the Ohio. Hooker also commanded the Army of the Potomac for a short time.

General Meade was an officer of great merit, with drawbacks to his usefulness that were beyond his control. He had been an officer of the engineer corps before the war, and consequently had never served with troops until he was over forty-six years of age. He never had, I believe, a command of less than a brigade. He saw clearly and distinctly the position of the enemy, and the topography of the country in front of his own position. His first idea was to take advantage of the lay of the ground, sometimes without reference to the direction we wanted to move afterwards. He was subordinate to his superiors in rank to the extent that he could execute an order which changed his own plans with the same zeal he would have displayed if the plan had been his own. He was brave and conscientious, and commanded the respect of all who knew him. He was unfortunately of a temper that would get beyond his control, at times, and make him speak to officers of high rank in the most offensive manner. No one saw this fault more plainly than he himself, and no one regretted it more. This made it unpleasant at times, even in battle, for those around him to approach him even with information. In spite of this defect he was a most valuable officer and deserves a high place in the annals of his country.

General Burnside was an officer who was generally liked and respected. He was not, however, fitted to command an army. No one knew this better than himself. He always admitted his blunders, and extenuated those of officers under him beyond what they were entitled to. It was hardly his fault that he was ever assigned to a separate command.

Of Hooker I saw but little during the war. I had known him very well before, however. Where I did see him, at Chattanooga, his achievement in bringing his command around the point of Lookout Mountain and into Chattanooga Valley was brilliant. I nevertheless regarded him as a dangerous man. He was not subordinate to his superiors. He was ambitious to the extent of caring nothing for the rights of others. His disposition was, when engaged in battle, to get detached from the main body of the army and exercise a separate command, gathering to his standard all he could of his juniors.

Hancock stands the most conspicuous figure of all the general officers who did not exercise a separate command. He commanded a corps longer than any other one, and his name was never mentioned as having committed in battle a blunder for which he was responsible. He was a man of very conspicuous personal appearance. Tall, well formed and, at the time of which I now write, young and fresh looking, he presented an appearance that would attract the attention of an army as he passed. His genial disposition made him friends, and his personal courage and his presence with his command in the thickest of the fight won for him the confidence of troops serving under him. No matter how hard the fight, the 2d corps always felt that their commander was looking after them.

Sedgwick was killed at Spottsylvania before I had an opportunity of forming an estimate of his qualifications as a soldier from personal observation. I had known him in Mexico when both of us were lieutenants, and when our service gave no indication that either of us would ever be equal to the command of a brigade. He stood very high in the army, however, as an officer and a man. He was brave and conscientious. His ambition was not great, and he seemed to dread responsibility. He was willing to do any amount of battling, but always wanted some one else to direct. He declined the command of the Army of the Potomac once, if not oftener.

General Alfred H. Terry came into the army as a volunteer without a military education. His way was won without political influence up to an important separate command --the expedition against Fort Fisher, in January, 1865. His success there was, most brilliant, and won for him the rank of brigadier-general in the regular army and of major-general of volunteers. He is a man who makes friends of those under him by his consideration of their wants and their dues. As a commander, he won their confidence by his coolness in action and by his clearness of perception in taking in the situation under which he was placed at any given time.

Griffin, Humphreys, and Mackenzie were good corps commanders, but came into that position so near to the close of the war as not to attract public attention. All three served as such, in the last campaign of the armies of the Potomac and the James, which culminated at Appomattox Court House, on the 9th of April, 1865. The sudden collapse of the rebellion monopolized attention to the exclusion of almost everything else. I regarded Mackenzie as the most promising young officer in the army. Graduating at West Point, as he did, during the second year of the war, he had won his way up to the command of a corps before its close. This he did upon his own merit and without influence.

CONCLUSION

THE cause of the great War of the Rebellion against the United States will have to be attributed to slavery. For some years before the war began it was a trite saying among some politicians that "A state half slave and half free cannot exist." All must become slave or all free, or the state will go down. I took no part myself in any such view of the case at the time, but since the war is over, reviewing the whole question, I have come to the conclusion that the saying is quite true.

Slavery was an institution that required unusual guarantees for its security wherever it existed; and in a country like ours where the larger portion of it was free territory inhabited by an intelligent and well-to-do population, the people would naturally have but little sympathy with demands upon them for its protection. Hence the people of the South were dependent upon keeping control of the general government to secure the perpetuation of their favorite institution. They were enabled to maintain this control long after the States where slavery existed had ceased to have the controlling power, through the assistance they received from odd men here and there throughout the Northern States. They saw their power waning, and this led them to encroach upon the prerogatives and independence of the Northern States by enacting such laws as the Fugitive Slave Law. By this law every Northern man was obliged, when properly summoned, to turn out and help apprehend the runaway slave of a Southern man. Northern marshals became slave-catchers, and Northern courts had to contribute to the support and protection of the institution.

This was a degradation which the North would not permit any longer than until they could get the power to expunge such laws from the statute books. Prior to the time of these encroachments the great majority of the people of the North had no particular quarrel with slavery, so long as they were not forced to have it themselves. But they were not willing to play the role of police for the South in the protection of this particular institution.

In the early days of the country, before we had railroads, telegraphs and steamboats, in a word, rapid transit of any sort the States were each almost a separate nationality. At that time the subject of slavery caused but little or no disturbance to the public mind. But the country grew, rapid transit was established, and trade and commerce between the States got to be so much greater than before, that the power of the National government became more felt and recognized and, therefore, had to be enlisted in the cause of this institution.

It is probably well that we had the war when we did. We are better off now than we would have been without it, and have made more rapid progress than we otherwise should have made. The civilized nations of Europe have been stimulated into unusual activity, so that commerce, trade, travel, and thorough acquaintance among people of different nationalities, has become common ; whereas, before, it was but the few who had ever had the privilege of going beyond the limits of their own country or who knew anything about other people. Then, too, our republican institutions were regarded as experiments up to the breaking out of the rebellion, and monarchical Europe generally believed that our republic was a rope of sand that would part the moment the slightest strain was brought upon it. Now it has shown itself capable of dealing with one of the greatest wars that was ever made, and our people have proven themselves to be the most formidable in war of any nationality.

But this war was a fearful lesson, and should teach us the necessity of avoiding wars in the future.

The conduct of some of the European states during our troubles shows the lack of conscience of communities where the responsibility does not come upon a single individual. Seeing a nation that extended from ocean to ocean, embracing the better part of a continent, growing as we were growing in population, wealth and intelligence, the European nations thought it would be well to give us a check. We might, possibly, after a while threaten their peace, or, at least, the perpetuity of their institutions. Hence, England was constantly finding fault with the administration at Washington because we were not able to keep up an effective blockade. She also joined, at first, with France and Spain in setting up an Austrian prince upon the throne in Mexico, totally disregarding any rights or claims that Mexico had of being treated as an independent power. It is true they trumped up grievances as a pretext, but they were only pretexts which can always be found when wanted.

Mexico, in her various revolutions, had been unable to give that protection to the subjects of foreign nations which she would have liked to give, and some of her revolutionary leaders had forced loans from them. Under pretence of protecting their citizens, these nations seized upon Mexico as a foothold for establishing a European monarchy upon our continent, thus threatening our peace at home. I, myself, regarded this as a direct act of war against the United States by the powers engaged, and supposed as a matter of course that the United States would treat it as such when their hands were free to strike. I often spoke of the matter to Mr. Lincoln and the Secretary of War, but never heard any special views from them to enable me to judge what they thought or felt about it. I inferred that they felt a good deal as I did, but were unwilling to commit themselves while we had our own troubles upon our hands.

All of the powers except France very soon withdrew from the armed intervention for the establishment of an Austrian prince upon the throne of Mexico; but the governing people of these countries continued to the close of the war to throw obstacles in our way. After the surrender of Lee, therefore, entertaining the opinion here expressed, I sent Sheridan with a corps to the Rio Grande to have him where he might aid Juarez in expelling the French from Mexico. These troops got off before they could be stopped; and went to the Rio Grande, where Sheridan distributed them up and down the river, much to the consternation of the troops in the quarter of Mexico bordering on that stream. This soon led to a request from France that we should withdraw our troops from the

Rio Grande and to negotiations for the withdrawal of theirs. Finally Bazaine was withdrawn from Mexico by order of the French Government. From that day the empire began to totter. Mexico was then able to maintain her independence without aid from us.

France is the traditional ally and friend of the United States. I did not blame France for her part in the scheme to erect a monarchy upon the ruins of the Mexican Republic. That was the scheme of one man, an imitator without genius or merit. He had succeeded in stealing the government of his country, and made a change in its form against the wishes and instincts of his people. He tried to play the part of the first Napoleon, without the ability to sustain that role. He sought by new conquests to add to his empire and his glory; but the signal failure of his scheme of conquest was the precursor of his own overthrow.

Like our own war between the States, the Franco Prussian war was an expensive one; but it was worth to France all it cost her people. It was the completion of the downfall of Napoleon III. The beginning was when he landed troops on this continent. Failing here, the prestige of his name all the prestige he ever had was gone. He must achieve a success or fall. He tried to strike down his neighbor, Prussia and fell.

I never admired the character of the first Napoleon; but I recognize his great genius. His work, too, has left its impress for good on the face of Europe. The third Napoleon could have no claim to having done a good or just act.

To maintain peace in the future it is necessary to be prepared for war. There can scarcely be a possible chance of a conflict, such as the last one, occurring among our own people again; but, growing as we are, in population, wealth and military power, we may become the envy of nations which led us in all these particulars only a few years ago; and unless we are prepared for it we may be in danger of a combined movement being some day made to crush us out. Now, scarcely twenty years after the war, we seem to have forgotten the lessons it taught, and are going on as if in the greatest security, without the power to resist an invasion by the fleets of fourth-rate European powers for a time until we could prepare for them.

We should have a good navy, and our sea-coast defences should be put in the finest possible condition. Neither of these cost much when it is considered where the money goes, and what we get in return. Money expended in a fine navy, not only adds to our security and tends to prevent war in the future, but is very material aid to our commerce with foreign nations in the meantime. Money spent upon sea-coast defences is spent among our own people, and all goes back again among the people. The work accomplished, too, like that of the navy, gives us a feeling of security.

England's course towards the United States during the rebellion exasperated the people of this country very much against the mother country. I regretted it. England and the United States are natural allies, and should be the best of friends. They speak one language, and are related by blood and other ties. We together, or even either separately, are better qualified than any other people to establish commerce between all the nationalities of the world.

England governs her own colonies, and particularly those embracing the people of different races from her own, better than any other nation. She is just to the conquered, but rigid. She makes them self supporting, but gives the benefit of labor to the laborer. She does not seem to look upon the colonies as outside possessions which she is at liberty to work for the support and aggrandizement of the home government.

The hostility of England to the United States during our rebellion was not so much real as it was apparent. It was the hostility of the leaders of one political party. I am told that there was no time during the civil war when they were able to get up in England a demonstration in favor of secession, while these were constantly being gotten up in favor of the Union, or, as they called it, in favor of the North. Even in Manchester, which suffered so fearfully by having the cotton cut off from her mills, they had a monster demonstration in favor of the North at the very time when their workmen were almost famishing.

It is possible that the question of a conflict between races may come up in the future, as did that between freedom and slavery before. The condition of the colored man within our borders may become a source of anxiety, to say the least. But he was brought to our shores by compulsion, and he now should be considered as having as good a right to remain here as any other class of our citizens. It was looking to a settlement of this question that led me to urge the annexation of Santo Domingo during the time I was President of the United States.

Santo Domingo was freely offered to us, not only by the administration, but by all the people, almost without price. The island is upon our shores, is very fertile, and is capable of supporting fifteen millions of people. The products of the soil are so valuable that labor in her fields would be so compensated as to enable those who wished to go there to quickly repay the cost of their passage. I took it that the colored people would go there in great numbers, so as to have independent states governed by their own race. They would still be States of the Union, and under the protection of the General Government; but the citizens would be almost wholly colored.

By the war with Mexico, we had acquired, as we have seen, territory almost equal in extent to that we already possessed. It was seen that the volunteers of the Mexican war largely composed the pioneers to settle up the Pacific coast country. Their numbers, however, were scarcely sufficient to be a nucleus for the population of the important points of the territory acquired by that war. After our rebellion, when so many young men were at liberty to return to their homes, they found they were not, satisfied with the farm, the store, or the work-shop of the villages, but wanted larger fields. The mines of the mountains first attracted them; but afterwards they found that rich valleys and productive grazing and farming lands were there. This territory, the geography of which was not known to us at the close of the rebellion, is now as well mapped as any portion of our country. Railroads traverse it in every direction, north, south, east, and west. The mines are worked. The high lands are used for grazing purposes, and rich agricultural lands are found in many of the valleys. This is the work of the volunteer. It is probable that the Indians would have had control of these lands for a century yet but for the war. We must conclude, therefore, that wars are not always evils unmixed with some good.

Prior to the rebellion the great mass of the people were satisfied to remain near the scenes of their birth. In fact an immense majority of the whole people did not feel secure against coming to want should they move among entire strangers. So much was the country divided into small communities that localized idioms had grown up, so that you could almost tell what section a person was from by hearing him speak. Before, new territories were settled by a "class"; people who shunned contact with others; people who, when the country began to settle up around them, would push out farther from civilization. Their guns furnished meat, and the cultivation of a very limited amount of the soil, their bread and vegetables. All the streams abounded with fish. Trapping would furnish pelts to be brought into the States once a year, to pay for necessary articles which they could not raise -powder, lead, whiskey, tobacco and some store goods. Occasionally some little articles of luxury would enter into these purchases -a quarter of a pound of tea, two or three pounds of coffee, more of sugar, some playing cards, and if anything was left over of the proceeds of the sale, more whiskey.

Little was known of the topography of the country beyond the settlements of these frontiers-men. This is all changed now. The war begot a spirit of independence and enterprise. The feeling now is, that a youth must cut loose from his old surroundings to enable him to get up in the world. There is now such a commingling of the people that particular idioms and pronunciation are no longer localized to any great extent; the country has filled up I from the centre all around to the sea"; railroads connect the two oceans and ail parts of the interior; maps, nearly perfect, of every part of the country are now furnished the student of geography.

The war has made us a nation of great power and intelligence. We have but little to do to preserve peace, happiness and prosperity at home, and the respect of other nations. Our experience ought to teach us the necessity of the first; our power secures the latter.

I feel that we are on the eve of a new era, when there is to be great harmony between the Federal and Confederate. I cannot stay to be a living witness to the correctness of this prophecy; but I feel it within me that it is to be so. The universally kind feeling expressed for me at a time when it was supposed that each day would prove my last, seemed to me the beginning of the answer to I Let us have peace."

The expressions of these kindly feelings were not restricted to a section of the country, nor to a division of the people. They came from individual citizens of all nationalities; from all denominations -the Protestant, the Catholic, and the Jew; and from the various societies of the land -scientific, educational, religious, or otherwise. Politics did not enter into the matter at all.

I am not egotist enough to suppose all this significance should be given because I was the object of it. But the war between the States was a very bloody and a very costly war. One side or the other had to yield principles they deemed dearer than life before it could be brought to an end. I commanded the whole of the mighty host engaged on the victorious side. I was, no matter whether deservedly so or not, a representative of that side of the controversy. It is a significant and gratifying fact that Confederates should have joined heartily in this spontaneous move. I hope the good feeling inaugurated may continue to the end.

APPENDIX.

REPORT OF LIEUTENANT - GENERAL U. S. GRANT,

OF THE

UNITED STATES ARMIES - 1864 - l65.

HEADQUARTERS ARMIES OF THE UNITED STATES, WASHINGTON, D.C.
July 22, 1865.

HON. E.M. STANTON, Secretary of War.

SIR :-I have the honor to submit the following report of the operations of the Armies of the United States from the date of my appointment to command the same.

From an early period in the rebellion I had been impressed with the idea that active and continuous operations of all the troops that could be brought into the field, regardless of season and weather, were necessary to a speedy termination of the war. The resources of the enemy and his numerical strength were far inferior to ours: but as an offset to this, we had a vast territory, with a population hostile to the government, to garrison, and long lines of river and railroad communications to protect, to enable us to supply the operating armies.

The armies in the East and West acted independently and without concert, like a balky team, no two ever pulling together, enabling the enemy to use to great advantage his interior lines of communication for transporting troops from East to West, reinforcing the army most vigorously pressed, and to furlough large numbers, during seasons of inactivity on our part, to go to their homes and do the work of producing, for the support of their armies. it was a question whether our numerical strength and resources were not more than balanced by these disadvantages and the enemy's superior position.

From the first, I was firm in the conviction that no peace could be had that would be stable and conducive to the happiness of the people, both North and South, until the military power of the rebellion was entirely broken.

I therefore determined, first, to use the greatest number of troops practicable against the armed force of the enemy ; preventing him from using the same force at different seasons against first one and then another of our armies, and the possibility of repose for refitting and producing necessary supplies for carrying on resistance. Second, to hammer continuously against the armed force of the enemy and his resources, until by mere attrition, if in no other way, there should be nothing left to him but an equal submission with the loyal section of our common country to the constitution and lams of the land.

These views have been kept constantly in mind, and orders given and campaigns made to carry them out. Whether they might have been better in conception and execution is for the people, who mourn the loss of friends fallen, and who have to pay the pecuniary cost, to say. All I can say is, that what I have done has been done conscientiously, to the best of my ability, and in what I conceived to be for the best interests of the whole country.

At the date when this report begins, the situation of the contending forces was about as follows: The Mississippi River was strongly garrisoned by Federal troops, from St. Louis, Missouri, to its mouth. The line of the Arkansas was also held, thus giving us armed possession of all west of the Mississippi, north of that stream. A few points in Southern Louisiana, not remote from the river, were held by us, together with a small garrison at and near the mouth of the Rio Grande. All the balance of the vast territory of Arkansas, Louisiana, and Texas was in the almost undisputed possession of the enemy, with an army of probably not less than eighty thousand effective men, that could have been brought into the field had there been sufficient opposition to have brought them out. The let-alone policy had demoralized this force so that probably but little more than one-half of it was ever present in garrison at any one time. But the one-half, or forty thousand men, with the bands of guerillas scattered through Missouri, Arkansas, and along the Mississippi River, and the disloyal character of much of the population, compelled the use of a large number of troops to keep navigation open on the river, and to protect the loyal people to the west of it. To the east of the Mississippi we held substantially with the line of the Tennessee and Holston rivers, running eastward to include nearly all of the State of Tennessee. South of Chattanooga, a small foothold had been obtained in Georgia, sufficient to protect East Tennessee from incursions from the enemy's force at Dalton, Georgia. West Virginia was substantially within our lines. Virginia, with the exception of the northern border, the Potomac River, a small area about the mouth of James River, covered by the troops at Norfolk and Fort Monroe, and the territory covered by the Army of the Potomac lying along the Rapidan, was in the possession of the enemy. Along the sea coast footholds had been obtained at Plymouth, Washington, and New Bern, in North Carolina; Beaufort, Folly and Morris Islands, Hilton Head, Fort Pulaski, and Port Royal, in South Carolina ; Fernandina and St. Augustine, in Florida. Key West and Pensacola were also in our possession, while all the important ports were blockaded by the navy. The accompanying map, a copy of which was sent to General Sherman and other commanders in March, 1864, shows by red lines the territory occupied by us at the beginning of the rebellion, and at the opening of the campaign of 1864, while those in blue are the lines which it was proposed to occupy.

Behind the Union lines there were many bands of guerillas and a large population disloyal to the government, making it necessary to guard every foot of road or river used in supplying our armies. In the South, a reign of military despotism prevailed, which made every man and boy capable of bearing arms a soldier; and those who could not bear arms in the field acted as provosts for collecting deserters and returning them. This enabled the enemy to bring almost his entire strength into the field.

The enemy had concentrated the bulk of his forces east of the Mississippi into two armies, commanded by Generals R. E. Lee and J. E. Johnston, his ablest and best generals. The army commanded by Lee occupied the south bank of the Rapidan, extending from Mine Run westward, strongly intrenched, covering and defending Richmond, the rebel capital, against the Army of the Potomac. The army under Johnston occupied a strongly intrenched position at Dalton, Georgia, covering and defending Atlanta, Georgia, a place of great importance as a railroad centre, against the armies under Major-General W.T. Sherman. In addition to these armies he had a large cavalry force under Forrest, in Northeast Mississippi; a considerable force, of all arms, in the Shenandoah Valley, and in the western part of Virginia and extreme eastern part of Tennessee ; and also confronting our sea coast garrisons, and holding blockaded ports where we had no foothold upon land.

These two armies, and the cities covered and defended by them, were the main objective points of the campaign.

Major-General W.T. Sherman, who was appointed to the command of the Military Division of the Mississippi, embracing all the armies and territory east of the Mississippi River to the Alleghanies and the Department of Arkansas, west of the Mississippi, had the immediate command of the armies operating against Johnston.

Major-General George G. Meade had the immediate command of the Army of the Potomac, from where I exercised general supervision of the movements of all our armies.
General Sherman was instructed to move against Johnston's army, to break it up, and to go into the interior of the enemy's country as far as he could, inflicting all the damage he could upon their war resources. If the enemy in his front showed signs of joining Lee, to follow him up to the full extent of his ability, while I would prevent the concentration of Lee upon him, if it was in the power of the Army of the Potomac to do so. More specific written instructions were not given, for the reason that I had talked over with him the plans of the campaign, and was satisfied that he understood them and would execute them to the fullest extent possible.

Major-General N.P. Banks, then on an expedition up Red River against Shreveport, Louisiana (which had been organized previous to my appointment to command), was notified by me on the 15th of March, of the importance it was that Shreveport should be taken at the earliest possible day, and that if he found that the taking of it would occupy from ten to fifteen days' more time than General Sherman had given his troops to be absent from their command, he would send them back at the time specified by General Sherman, even if it led to the abandonment of the main object of the Red River expedition, for this force was necessary to movements east of the Mississippi ; that should his expedition prove successful, he would hold Shreveport and the Red River with such force as he might deem necessary, and return the balance of his troops to the neighborhood of New Orleans, commencing no move for the further acquisition of territory, unless it was to make that then held by him more easily held ; that it might be a part of the spring campaign to move against Mobile ; that it certainly would be, if troops enough could be obtained to make it without embarrassing other movements ; that New Orleans would be the point of departure for such an expedition ; also, that I had directed General Steele to make a real move from Arkansas, as suggested by him (General Banks), instead of a demonstration, as
Steele thought advisable.

On the 31st of March, in addition to the foregoing notification and directions, he was instructed as follows:

" 1st. If successful in your expedition against Shreveport, that you turn over the defence of the Red River to General Steele and the navy.

" 2d. That you abandon Texas entirely, with the exception of your hold upon the Rio Grande. This can be held with four thousand men, if they will turn their attention immediately to fortifying their positions. At least one-half of the force required for this service might be taken from the colored troops.

" 3d. By properly fortifying on the Mississippi River, the force to guard it from Port Hudson to New Orleans can be reduced to ten thousand men, if not to a less number. Six thousand more would then hold all the rest of the territory necessary to hold until active operations can again be resumed west of the river. According to your last return, this would give you a force of over thirty thousand effective men with which to move against Mobile. To this I expect to add five thousand men from Missouri. If, however, you think the force here stated too small to hold the territory regarded as necessary to hold possession of, I would say concentrate at least twenty-five thousand men of your present command for operations against Mobile. With these and such additions as I can give you from elsewhere, lose no time in making a demonstration, to be followed by an attack upon Mobile. Two Or more ironclads will be ordered to report to Admiral Farragut. This gives him a strong naval fleet with which to co-operate. You can make your own arrangements with the admiral for his cooperation, and select your own line of approach. My own idea of the matter is that Pascagoula should be your base; but, from your long service in the Gulf Department, you will know best about the matter. It is intended that your movements shall be co-operative with movements elsewhere, and you cannot now start too soon. All I would now add is, that you commence the concentration of your forces at once. Preserve a profound secrecy of what you intend doing, and start at the earliest possible moment.

" U.S. GRANT, Lieutenant-General."

" MAJOR-GENERAL N.P. BANKS."

Major-General Meade was instructed that Lee's army would be his objective point; that wherever Lee went he would go also. For his movement two plans presented themselves: One to cross the Rapidan below Lee, moving by his right flank; the other above, moving by his left. Each presented advantages over the other, with corresponding objections. By crossing above, Lee would be cut off from all chance of ignoring Richmond or going north on a raid. But if we took this route, all we did would have to be done whilst the rations we started with held out ; besides, it separated us from Butler, so that he could not be directed how to co-operate. If we took the other route, Brandy Station could be used as a base of supplies until another was secured on the York or James rivers. Of these, however, it was decided to take the lower route. The following letter of instruction was addressed to Major-General B.F. Butler:

" FORT MONROE, VIRGINIA, April 2, 1864.

" GENERAL :--In the spring campaign, which it is desirable shall commence at as early a day as practicable, it is proposed to have co-operative action of all the armies in the field, as far as this object can be accomplished.

" It will not be possible to unite our armies into two or three large ones to act as so many units, owing to the absolute necessity of holding on to the territory already taken from the enemy. But, generally speaking, concentration can be practically effected by armies moving to the interior of the enemy's country from the territory they have to guard. By such movement, they interpose themselves between the enemy and the country to be guarded, thereby reducing the number necessary to guard important points, or at least occupy the attention of a part of the enemy 's force, if no greater object is gained. Lee 's army and Richmond being the greater objects towards which our attention must be directed in the next campaign, it is desirable to unite all the force we can against them. The necessity of covering Washington with the Army of the Potomac, and of covering your department with your army, makes it impossible to unite these forces at the beginning of any move. I propose, therefore, what comes nearest this of anything that seems practicable: The Army of the Potomac will act from its present base, Lee's army being the objective point. You will collect all the forces from your command that can be spared from garrison duty -I should say not less than twenty thousand effective men- to operate on the south side of James River, Richmond being your objective point. To the force you already have will be added about ten thousand men
from South Carolina, under Major-General Gillmore, who will command them in person. Major-General W.F. Smith is ordered to report to you, to command the troops sent into the field from your own department.

"General Gillmore will be ordered to report to you at Fortress Monroe, with all the troops on transports, by the 18th instant, or as soon thereafter as practicable. Should you not receive notice by that time to move, you will make such disposition of them and your other forces as you may deem best calculated to deceive the enemy as to the real move to be made.

344

"When you are notified to move, take City Point with as much force as possible. Fortify, or rather intrench, at once, and concentrate all your troops for the field there as rapidly as you ran. From City Point directions cannot be given at this time for your further movements.

" The fact that has already been stated -that is, that Richmond is to be your objective point, and that there is to b e co-operation between your force and the Army of the Potomac must be your guide. This indicates the necessity of your holding close to the south bank of the James River as you advance. Then, should the enemy be forced into his intrenchments in Richmond, the Army of the Potomac would follow, and by means of transports the two armies would become a unit.

"All the minor details of your advance are left entirely to your direction. If, however, you think it practicable to use your cavalry south of you, so as to cut the railroad about Hicksford, about the time of the general advance, it would be of immense advantage.

"You will please forward for my information, at the earliest practicable day, all orders, details, and instructions you may give for the execution of this order.

" U.S. GRANT, Lientenant-General.
"MAJOR-GENERAL B. F. BUTLER."

On the 16th these instructions were substantially reiterated. On the 19th, in order to secure full co-operation between his army and that of General Meade, he was informed that I expected him to move from Fort Monroe the same day that General Meade moved from Culpeper. The exact time I was to telegraph him as soon as it was fixed, and that it would not be earlier than the 27th of April; that it was my intention to fight Lee between Culpeper and Richmond, if he would stand. Should he, however, fall back into Richmond, I would follow up and make a junction with his (General Butler's) army on the James River ; that, could I be certain he would be able to invest Richmond on the south side, so as to have his left resting on the James? above the city, I would form the junction there ; that circumstances might make this course advisable anyhow ; that he should use every exertion to secure footing as far up the south side of the river as he could, and as soon as possible after the receipt of orders to move ; that if he could not carry the city, he should at least detain as large a force there as possible.

In co-operation with the main movements against Lee and Johnston, I was desirous of using all other troops necessarily kept in departments remote from the fields of immediate operations, and also those kept in the background for the protection of our extended lines between the loyal States and the armies operating against them.

A very considerable force, under command of Major-General Sigel, was so held for the protection of West Virginia, and the frontiers of Maryland and Pennsylvania. Whilst these troops could not be withdrawn to distant fields without exposing the North to invasion by comparatively small bodies of the enemy, they could act directly to their front, and give better protection than if lying idle in garrison. By such a movement they would either compel the enemy to detach largely for the protection of his supplies and lines of communication, or he would lose them. General Sigel was therefore directed to organize all his available force into two expeditions, to move from Beverly and Charleston, under command of Generals Ord and Crook, against the East Tennessee and Virginia Railroad. Subsequently, General Ord having been relieved at his own request, General Sigel was instructed, at his own suggestion, to give up the expedition by Beverly, and to form two columns, one under General Crook, on the Kanawha, numbering about ten thousand men, and one on the Shenandoah, numbering about seven thousand men. The one on the Shenandoah to assemble between Cumberland and the Shenandoah, and the infantry and artillery advanced to Cedar Creek with such cavalry as could be made available at the moment, to threaten the enemy in the Shenandoah Valley, and advance as far as possible; while General Crook would take possession of Lewisburg with part of his force and move down the Tennessee Railroad, doing as much damage as he could, destroying the New River Bridge and the salt works, at Saltville, Va.

Owing to the weather and bad condition of the roads, operations were delayed until the 1st of May, when, everything being in readiness and the roads favorable, orders were given for a general movement of all the armies not later than the 4th of May.

My first object being to break the military power of the rebellion, and capture the enemy's important strongholds, made me desirous that General Butler should succeed in his movement against Richmond, as that would tend more than anything else, unless it mere the capture of Lee's army, to accomplish this desired result in the East. If he failed, it was my determination, by hard fighting, either to compel Lee to retreat, or to so cripple him that he could not detach a large force to go north, and still retain enough for the defence of Richmond. It was well understood, by both Generals Butler and Meade, before starting on the campaign, that it was my intention to put both their armies south of the James River, in case of failure to destroy Lee without it.

Before giving General Butler his instructions, I visited him at Fort Monroe, and in conversation pointed out the apparent importance of getting possession of Petersburg, and destroying railroad communication as far south as possible. Believing, however, in the practicability of capturing Richmond unless it was reinforced, I made that the objective point of his operations. As the Army of the Potomac was to move simultaneously with him, Lee could not detach from his army with safety, and the enemy did not have troops elsewhere to bring to the defence of the city in time to meet a rapid movement from the north of James River.

I may here state that, commanding all the armies as I did, I tried, as far as possible, to leave General Meade in independent command of the Army of the Potomac. My instructions for that army were all through him, and were general in their nature, leaving all the details and the execution to him. The campaigns that followed proved him to be the right man in the right place. His commanding always in the presence of an officer superior to him in rank has drawn from him much of that public attention that his zeal and ability entitle him to, and which he would otherwise have received.

The movement of the Army of the Potomac commenced early on the morning of the 4th of May, under the immediate direction and orders of Major-General Meade, pursuant to instructions. Before night, the whole army was across the Rapidan (the fifth and sixth corps crossing at Germania Ford, and the second corps at Ely's Ford, the cavalry, under Major-General Sheridan, moving in advance,) with the greater part of its trains, numbering about four thousand wagons, meeting with but slight opposition. The average distance traveled by the troops that day was about twelve miles. This I regarded as a great success, and it removed from my mind the most serious apprehensions I had entertained, that of crossing the river in the face of an active, large, well appointed, and ably commanded army, and how so large a train was to be carried through a hostile country, and protected. Early on the 5th, the advance corps (the fifth, Major-General G.K. Warren commanding,) met and engaged the enemy outside his intrenchments near Mine Run. The battle raged furiously all day, the whole army being brought into the fight as fast as the corps could be get upon the field, which, considering the density of the forest and narrowness of the roads, was done with commendable promptness.

General Burnside, with the ninth corps, was, at the time the Army of the Potomac moved, left with the bulk of his corps at the crossing of the Rappahannock River and Alexandria Railroad, holding the road back to Bull Run, with instructions not to move until he received notice that a crossing of the Rapidan was secured, but to move promptly as soon as such notice was received. This crossing he was apprised of on the afternoon of the 4th. By six o'clock of the morning of the 6th he was leading his corps into action near the Wilderness Tavern, some of his troops having marched a distance of over thirty miles, crossing both the Rappahannock and Rapidan rivers. Considering that a large proportion, probably two-thirds of his command, was composed of new troops, unaccustomed to marches, and carrying the accoutrements of a soldier, this was a remarkable march.

The battle of the Wilderness was renewed by us at five o 'clock on the morning of the 6th, and continued with unabated fury until darkness set in, each army holding substantially the same position that they had on the evening of the 5th. After dark, the enemy made a feeble attempt to turn our right flank, capturing several hundred prisoners and creating considerable confusion. But the promptness of General Sedgwick, who was personally present and commanded that part of our line, soon reformed it and restored order. On the morning of the 7th, reconnaissance's showed that the enemy had fallen behind his intrenched lines, with pickets to the front, covering a part of the battlefield. From this it was evident to my mind that the two days' fighting had satisfied him of his inability to further maintain the contest in the open field, notwithstanding his advantage of position, and that he would wait an attack behind his works. I therefore determined to push on and put my whole force between him and Richmond; and orders were at once issued for a movement by his right flank. On the night of the 7th, the march was commenced towards Spottsylvania Court House, the fifth corps moving on the most direct road. But the enemy having become apprised of our movement, and having the shorter line, was enabled to reach there first. On the 8th, General Warren met a force of the enemy, which had been sent out to oppose and delay his advance, to gain time to fortify the line taken up at Spottsylvania. This force was steadily driven back on the main force, within the recently constructed works, after considerable fighting, resulting in severe loss to both sides. On the morning of the 9th, General Sheridan started on a raid against the enemy's lines of communication with Richmond. The 9th, 10th, and 11th were spent in maneuvering and fighting, without decisive results. Among the killed on the 9th was that able and distinguished soldier Major-General John Sedgwick, commanding the sixth army corps. Major-General H.G. Wright succeeded him in command. Early on the morning of the 12th a general attack was made on the enemy in position. The second corps, Major-General Hancock commanding, carried a salient of his line, capturing most of Johnson's division of Ewell's corps and twenty pieces of artillery. But the resistance was so obstinate that the advantage gained did not prove decisive. The 13th, 14th, 15th, 16th, 17th, and 18th, were consumed in maneuvering and awaiting the arrival of reinforcements from Washington. Deeming it impracticable to make any further attack upon the enemy at Spottsylvania Court House, orders were issued on the 18th with a view to a movement to the North Anna, to commence at twelve o'clock on the night of the 19th. Late in the afternoon of the 19th, Ewell's corps came out of its works on our extreme right flank; but the attack was promptly repulsed, with heavy loss. This delayed the movement to the North Anna until the night of the 21st, when it was commenced. But the enemy again, having the shorter line, and being in possession of the main roads, was enabled to reach the North Anna in advance of us, and took position behind it. The fifth corps reached the North Anna on the afternoon of the 23d, closely followed by the sixth corps. The second and ninth corps got up about the same time, the second holding the railroad bridge, and the ninth lying between that and Jericho Ford. General Warren effected a crossing the same afternoon, and got a position without much opposition. Soon after getting into position he was violently attacked, but repulsed the enemy with great slaughter. On the 25th, General Sheridan rejoined the Army of the Potomac from the raid on which he started from Spottsylvania, having destroyed the depots at Beaver Dam and Ashland stations, four trains of cars, large supplies of rations, and many miles of railroad track ; recaptured about four hundred of our men on their way to Richmond as prisoners of war; met and defeated the enemy's cavalry at Yellow Tavern; carried the first line of works around Richmond (but finding the second line too strong to be carried by assault), re-crossed to the north bank of the Chickahominy at Meadow Bridge under heavy fire, and moved by a detour to Haxall's Landing, on the James River, where he communicated with General Butler. This raid had the effect of drawing off the whole of the enemy's cavalry force, making it comparatively easy to guard our trains.

General Butler moved his main force up the James River, in pursuance of instructions, on the 4th of May, General Gillmore having joined him with the tenth corps. At the same time he sent a force of one thousand eight hundred cavalry, by way of West Point, to form a junction with him wherever he might get a foothold, and a force of three thousand cavalry, under General Kautz, from Suffolk, to operate against the road south of Petersburg and Richmond. On the 5th, he occupied, without opposition, both City Point and Bermuda Hundred, his movement being a complete surprise. On the 6th, he was in position with his main army, and commenced intrenching. On the 7th he made a reconnaissance against the Petersburg and Richmond Railroad, destroying a portion of it after some fighting. On the 9th he telegraphed as follows:

" HEADQUARTERS , NEAR BERMUDA LANDING ,
May 9, 1864.

"HON. E.M. STANTON , Secretary of War.

"Our operations may be summed up in a few words. With one thousand seven hundred cavalry we have advanced up the Peninsula, forced the Chickahominy, and have safely brought them to their present position. These were colored cavalry, and are now holding our advance pickets towards Richmond.

"General Kautz, with three thousand cavalry from Suffolk, on the same day with our movement up James River, forced the black Water, burned the railroad bridge at Stony Creek, below Petersburg, cutting into Beauregard 's force at that point.

"We have landed here, intrenched ourselves, destroyed many miles of railroad, and got a position which, with proper supplies, we can hold out against the whole of Lee's army. I have ordered up the supplies.

" Beauregard, with a large portion of his force, was left south by the cutting of the railroads by Kautz. That portion which reached Petersburg under Hill I have whipped today, killing and wounding many and taking many prisoners, after a severe and well contested fight.

"General Grant will not be troubled with any further reinforcements to Lee from Beauregard's force.

" BENJ. F. BUTLER, Major-General. "

On the evening of the 13th and morning of the 14th he carried a portion of the enemy's first line of defences at Drury's Bluff, or Fort Darling, with small loss. The time thus consumed from the 6th lost to us the benefit of the surprise and capture of Richmond and Petersburg, enabling, as it did, Beauregard to collect his loose forces in North and South Carolina, and bring them to the defence of those places. On the 16th, the enemy attacked General Butler in his position in front of Drury's Bluff. He was forced back, or drew back, into his intrenchments between the forks of the James and Appomattox rivers, the enemy intrenching strongly in his front, thus covering his railroads, the city, and all that was valuable to him. His army, therefore, though in a position of great security, was as completely shut off from further operations directly against Richmond as if it had been in a bottle strongly corked. It required but a comparatively small force of the enemy to hold it there.

On the 12th, General Kautz, with his cavalry, was started on a raid against the Danville Railroad, which he struck at Coalfield, Powhatan, and Chula Stations, destroying them, the railroad track, two freight trains, and one locomotive, together with large quantities of commissary and other stores; thence, crossing to the South Side Road, struck it at Wilson's, Wellsville, and Black's and White's Stations, destroying the road and station-houses; thence he proceeded to City Point, which he reached on the 18th.

On the 19th of April, and prior to the movement of General Butler, the enemy, with a land force under General Hoke and an iron-clad ram, attacked Plymouth, N.C., commanded by General H.W. Wessells, and our gunboats there; and, after severe fighting, the place was carried by assault, and the entire garrison and armament captured. The gunboat Smithfield was sunk, and the Miami disabled. The army sent to operate against Richmond having hermetically sealed itself up at Bermuda hundred, the enemy was enabled to bring the most, if not all, the reinforcements brought from the south by Beauregard against the Army of the Potomac. In addition to this reinforcement, a very considerable one, probably not less than fifteen thousand men, was obtained by calling in the scattered troops under Breckinridge from the western part of Virginia.

The position of Bermuda Hundred was as easy to defend as it was difficult to operate from against the enemy. I determined, therefore, to bring from it all available forces, leaving enough only to secure what had been gained ; and accordingly, on the 22d, I directed that they be sent forward, under command of Major-General W. F. Smith, to join the Army of the Potomac.

On the 24th of May, the 9th army corps, commanded b y Major-General A. E. Burnside, was assigned to the Army of the Potomac, and from this time forward constituted a portion of Major-General Meade's command.

Finding the enemy's position on the North Anna stronger than either of his previous ones, I withdrew on the night of the 26th to the north bank of the North Anna, and moved via Hanover Town to turn the enemy's position by his right.

Generals Torbert's and Merritt's divisions of cavalry, under Sheridan, and the 6th corps, led the advance ; crossed the Pamunkey River at Hanover Town, after considerable fighting, and on the 26th the two divisions of cavalry had a severe, but successful engagement with the enemy at Hawes's Shop. On the 29th and 30th we advanced, with heavy skirmishing, to the Hanover Court House and Cold Harbor Road, and developed the enemy 's position north of the Chickahominy. Late on the evening of the last day the enemy came out and attacked our left, but was repulsed with very considerable loss. An attack was immediately ordered by General Meade, along his whole line, which resulted in driving the enemy from a part of his intrenched skirmish line.

On the 31st, General Wilson's division of cavalry destroyed the railroad bridges over the South Anna River, after defeating the enemy's cavalry. General Sheridan, on the same day, reached Cold Harbor, and held it until relieved by the 6th corps and General Smith's command, which had just arrived, via White House, from General Butler's army.

On the 1st day of June an attack was made at five P.M. by the 6th corps and the troops under General Smith, the other corps being held in readiness to advance on the receipt of orders. This resulted in our carrying and holding the enemy's first line of works in front of the right of the 6th corps, and in front of General Smith. During the attack the enemy made repeated assaults on each of the corps not engaged in the main attack, but was repulsed with heavy loss in every instance, That night he made several assaults to regain what he had lost in the day, but failed. The 2nd was spent in getting troops into position for an attack on the 3rd. On the 3rd of June we again assaulted the enemy's works, in the hope of driving him from his position. In this attempt our loss was heavy, while that of the enemy, I have reason to believe, was comparatively light. It was the only general attack made from the Rapidan to the James which did not inflict upon the enemy losses to compensate for our own losses. I would not be understood as saying that all previous attacks resulted in victories to our arms, or accomplished as much as I had hoped from them; but they inflicted upon the enemy severe losses, which tended, in the end, to the complete overthrow of the rebellion.

From the proximity of the enemy to his defences around Richmond, it was impossible, by any flank movement, to interpose between him and the city. I was still in a condition to either move by his left flank, and invest Richmond from the north side, or continue my move by his right flank to the south side of the James. While the former might have been better as a covering for Washington, yet a full survey of all the ground satisfied me that it would be impracticable to hold a line north and east of Richmond that would protect the Fredericksburg Railroad, a long, vulnerable line, which would exhaust much of our strength to guard, and that would have to be protected to supply the army, and would leave open to the enemy all his lines of communication on the south side of the James. My idea, from the start, had been to beat Lee's army north of Richmond, if possible. Then, after destroying his lines of communication north of the James River, to transfer the army to the south side, and besiege Lee in Richmond, or follow him south if he should retreat. After the battle of the Wilderness, it was evident that the enemy deemed it of the first importance to run no risks with the army he then had. He acted purely on the defensive, behind breastworks, or feebly on the offensive immediately in front of them, and where, in case of repulse, he could easily retire behind them. Without a greater sacrifice of life than I was willing to make, all could not be accomplished that I had designed north of Richmond. I therefore determined to continue to hold substantially the ground we then occupied, taking advantage of any favorable circumstances that might present themselves, until the cavalry could be sent to Charlottesville and Gordonsville to effectually break up the railroad connection between Richmond and the Shenandoah Valley and Lynchburg ; and when the cavalry got well off, to move the army to the south side of the James River, by the enemy's right flank, where I felt I could cut off all his sources of supply, except by the canal.

On the 7th, two divisions of cavalry, under General Sheridan, got off on the expedition against the Virginia Central Railroad, with instructions to Hunter, whom I hoped he would meet near Charlottesville, to join his forces to Sheridan's, and after the work laid out for them was thoroughly done, to join the Army of the Potomac by the route laid down in Sheridan's instructions.

On the 10th of June, General Butler sent a force of infantry, under General Gillmore, and of cavalry under General Kautz, to capture Petersburg, if possible, and destroy the railroad and common bridges across the Appomattox. The cavalry carried the works on the south side, and penetrated well in towards the town, but were forced to retire. General Gillmore, finding the works which he approached very strong, and deeming an assault impracticable, returned to Bermuda Hundred without attempting one.

Attaching great importance to the possession of Petersburg, I sent back to Bermuda Hundred and City Point, General Smith's command by water, via the White House, to reach there in advance of the Army of the Potomac. This was for the express purpose of securing Petersburg before the enemy, becoming aware of our intention, could reinforce the place.

The movement from Cold Harbor commenced after dark on the evening of the 12th. One division of cavalry, under General Wilson, and the 5th corps, crossed the Chickahominy at Long Bridge, and moved out to White Oak Swamp, to cover the crossings of the other corps. The advance corps reached James River, at Wilcox's Landing and Charles City Court House, on the night of the 13th.

During three long years the Armies of the Potomac and Northern Virginia had been confronting each other. In that time they had fought more desperate battles than it probably ever before fell to the lot of two armies to fight, without materially changing the vantage ground of either. The Southern press and people, with more shrewdness than was displayed in the North, finding that they had failed to capture Washington and march on to New York, as they had boasted they would do, assumed that they only defended their Capital and Southern territory. Hence, Antietam, Gettysburg, and all the other battles that had been fought, were by them set down as failures on our part, and victories for them. Their army believed this. It produced a morale which could only be overcome by desperate and continuous hard fighting. The battles of the Wilderness, Spottsylvania, North Anna and Cold Harbor, bloody and terrible as they were on our side, were even more damaging to the enemy, and so crippled him as to make him wary ever after of taking the offensive. His losses in men were probably not so great, owing to the fact that we were, save in the Wilderness, almost invariably the attacking party; and when he did attack, it was in the open field. The details of these battles, which for endurance and bravery on the part of the soldiery, have rarely been surpassed, are given in the report of Major-General Meade, and the subordinate reports accompanying it.

During the campaign of forty-three days, from the Rapidan to the James River, the army had to be supplied from an ever shifting base, by wagons, over narrow roads, through a densely wooded country, with a lack of wharves at each new base from which to conveniently discharge vessels. Too much credit cannot, therefore, be awarded to the quartermaster and commissary departments for the zeal and efficiency displayed by them. Under the general supervision of the chief quartermaster, Brigadier-General R. Ingalls, the trains were made to occupy all the available roads between the army and our water base, and but little difficulty was experienced in protecting them.

The movement in the Kanawha and Shenandoah valleys, under General Sigel, commenced on the 1st of May. General Crook, who had the immediate command of the Kanawha expedition, divided his forces into two columns, giving one, composed of cavalry, to General Averell. They crossed the mountains by separate routes. Averell struck the Tennessee and Virginia Railroad, near Wytheville, on the 10th, and proceeding to New River and Christiansburg, destroyed the road, several important bridges and depots, including New River Bridge, forming a junction with Crook at Union on the 15th. General Sigel moved up the Shenandoah Valley, met the enemy at New Market on the 15th, and, after a severe engagement, was defeated with heavy loss, and re-fired behind Cedar Creek. Not regarding the operations of General Sigel as satisfactory, I asked his removal from command, and Major-General Hunter was appointed to supersede him. His instructions were embraced in the following dispatches to Major-General H. W. Halleck, chief of staff of the army:

"NEAR SPOTTSYLVANIA COURT HOUSE, VA.,
May 20, 1864.

* * * * * * *

"The enemy are evidently relying for supplies greatly on such as are brought over the branch road running through Staunton. On the whole, therefore, I think it would be better for General Hunter to move in that direction ; reach Staunton and Gordonsville or Charlottesville, if he does not meet too much opposition. If he can hold at bay a force equal to his own, he will be doing good service. * * *

"U.S. GRANT, Lieutenant-General.

"MAJOR-GENERAL H.W. HALLECK ."

JERICHO FORD, VA., May 25, 1864.

"If Hunter can possibly get to Charlottesville and Lynchburg, he should do so, living on the country. The railroads and canal should be destroyed beyond possibility of repairs for weeks. Completing this, he could find his way back to his original base, or from about Gordonsville join this army.

"U.S. GRANT, Lieutenant-General.

"MAJOR-GENERAL H.W. HALLECK ."

General Hunter immediately took up the offensive, and, moving up the Shenandoah Valley, met the enemy on the 5th of June at Piedmont, and, after a battle of ten hours, routed and defeated him, capturing on the field of battle one thousand five hundred men, three pieces of artillery, and three hundred stand of small arms. On the 8th of the same month he formed a junction with Crook and Averell at Staunton, from which place he moved direct on Lynchburg, via Lexington, which place he reached and invested on the 16th day of June. Up to this time he was very successful ; and but for the difficulty of taking with him sufficient ordnance stores over so long a march, through a hostile country, he would, no doubt, have captured that, to the enemy important, point. The destruction of the enemy's supplies and manufactories was very great. To meet this movement under General Hunter, General Lee sent a force, perhaps equal to a corps, a part of which reached Lynchburg a short time before Hunter. After some skirmishing on the 17th and 18th, General Hunter, owing to a want of ammunition to give battle, retired from before the place. Unfortunately, this want of ammunition left him no choice of route for his return but by way of Kanawha. This lost to us the use of his troops for several weeks from the defence
of the North.

Had General Hunter moved by way of Charlottesville, instead of Lexington, as his instructions contemplated, he would have been in a position to have covered the Shenandoah Valley against the enemy, should the force he met have seemed to endanger it. If it did not, he would have been within easy distance of the James River Canal, on the main line of communication between Lynchburg and the force sent for its defence. I have never taken exception to the operations of General Hunter, and am not now disposed to find fault with him, for I have no doubt he acted within what he conceived to be the spirit of his instructions and the interests of the service. The promptitude of his movements and his gallantry should entitle him to the commendation of his country.

To return to the Army of the Potomac: The 2d corps commenced crossing the James River on the morning of the 14th by ferryboats at Wilcox's Landing. The laying of the pontoon bridge was completed about midnight of the 14th, and the crossing of the balance of the army was rapidly pushed forward by both bridge and ferry.

After the crossing had commenced, I proceeded by steamer to Bermuda Hundred to give the necessary orders for the immediate capture of Petersburg.

The instructions to General Butler were verbal, and were for him to send General Smith immediately, that night, with all the troops he could give him without sacrificing the position he then held. I told him that I would return at once to the Army of the Potomac, hasten its crossing, and throw it forward to Petersburg by divisions as rapidly as it could be done; that we could reinforce our armies more rapidly there than the enemy could bring troops against us. General Smith got off as directed, and confronted the enemy's pickets near Petersburg before daylight next morning, but for some reason that I have never been able to satisfactorily understand, did not get ready to assault his main lines until near sundown. Then, with a part of his command only, he made the assault, and carried the lines northeast of Petersburg from the Appomattox River, for a distance of over two and a half miles, capturing fifteen pieces of artillery and three hundred prisoners. This was about seven P.M. Between the line thus captured and Petersburg there were no other works, and there was no evidence that the enemy had reinforced Petersburg with a single brigade from any source. The night was clear -the moon shining brightly- and favorable to further operations. General Hancock, with two divisions of the 2nd corps, reached General Smith just after dark, and offered the service of these troops as he (Smith) might wish, waiving rank to the named commander, who he naturally supposed knew best the position of affairs, and what to do with the troops. But instead of taking these troops and pushing at once into Petersburg, he requested General Hancock to relieve a part of his line in the captured works, which was done before midnight.

By the time I arrived the next morning the enemy was in force. An attack was ordered to be made at six o'clock that evening by the troops under Smith and the ad and 9th corps. It required until that time for the 9th corps to get up and into position. The attack was made as ordered, and the fighting continued with but little intermission until six o'clock the next morning, and resulted in our carrying the advance and some of the main works of the enemy to the right (our left) of those previously captured by General Smith, several pieces of artillery, and over four hundred prisoners.

The 5th corps having got up, the attacks were renewed and persisted in with great vigor on the 17th and 18th, but only resulted in forcing the enemy into an interior line, from which he could not be dislodged. The advantages of position gained by us were very great. The army then proceeded to envelop Petersburg towards the South Side Railroad, as far as possible without attacking fortifications.

On the 16th the enemy, to reinforce Petersburg, withdrew from a part of his intrenchment in front of Bermuda Hundred, expecting, no doubt, to get troops from north of the James to take the place of those withdrawn before we could discover it. General Butler, taking advantage of this, at once moved a force on the railroad between Petersburg and Richmond. As soon as I was apprised of the advantage thus gained, to retain it I ordered two divisions of the 6th corps, General Wright commanding, that were embarking at Wilcox's Landing, under orders for City Point, to report to General Butler at Bermuda Hundred, of which

General Butler was notified, and the importance of holding a position in advance of his present line urged upon him.

About two o'clock in the afternoon General Butler was forced back to the line the enemy had withdrawn from in the morning. General Wright, with his two divisions, joined General Butler on the forenoon of the 17th, the latter still holding with a strong picket line the enemy's works. But instead of putting these divisions into the enemy's works to hold them, he permitted them to halt and rest some distance in the rear of his own line. Between four and five o'clock in the afternoon the enemy attacked and drove in his pickets and reoccupied his old line.

On the night of the 20th and morning of the 21st a lodgment was effected by General Butler, with one brigade of infantry, on the north bank of the James, at Deep Bottom, and connected by pontoon bridge with Bermuda Hundred.

On the 19th, General Sheridan, on his return from his expedition against the Virginia Central Railroad, arrived at the White House just as the enemy's cavalry was about to attack it, and compelled it to retire. The result of this expedition was, that General Sheridan met the enemy's cavalry near Trevilian Station, on the morning of the 11th of June, whom he attacked, and after an obstinate contest drove from the field in complete rout. He left his dead and nearly all his wounded in our hands, and about four hundred prisoners and several hundred horses. On the 12th he destroyed the railroad from Trevilian Station to Louisa Court House. This occupied until three o'clock P.M., when he advanced in the direction of Gordonsville. He found the enemy reinforced by infantry, behind well constructed rifle pits, about five miles from the latter place, and too strong to successfully assault. On the extreme right, however, his reserve brigade carried the enemy's works twice, and was twice driven there from by infantry. Night closed the contest. Not having sufficient ammunition to continue the engagement, and his animals being without forage (the country furnishing but inferior grazing), and hearing nothing from General Hunter, he withdrew his command to the north side of the North Anna, and commenced his return march, reaching White House at the time before stated. After breaking up the depot at that place, he moved to the James River, which he reached safely after heavy fighting. He commenced crossing on the 25th, near Fort Powhatan, without further molestation, and rejoined the Army of the Potomac.

On the 22d, General Wilson, with his own division of cavalry of the Army of the Potomac, and General Kautz's division of cavalry of the Army of the James, moved against the enemy's railroads south of Richmond. Striking the Weldon Railroad at Reams's Station, destroying the depot and several miles of the road, and the South Side road about fifteen miles from Petersburg, to near Nottoway Station, where he met and defeated a force of the enemy's cavalry. He reached Burkesville Station on the afternoon of the 23rd, and from there destroyed the Danville Railroad to Roanoke Bridge, a distance of twenty-five miles, where he found the enemy in force, and in a position from which he could not dislodge him. He then commenced his return march, and on the 28th met the enemy's cavalry in force at the Weldon Railroad crossing of Stony Creek, where he had a severe but not decisive engagement. Thence he made a detour from his left with a view of reaching Reams's Station (supposing it to be in our possession). At this place he was met by the enemy's cavalry, supported by infantry, and forced to retire, with the loss of his artillery and trains. In this last encounter, General Kautz, with a part of his command, became separated, and made his way into our lines. General Wilson, with the remainder of his force, succeeded in crossing the Nottoway River and coming in safely on our left and rear. The damage to the enemy in this expedition more than compensated for the losses we sustained. It severed all connection by railroad with Richmond for several weeks.

With a view of cutting the enemy's railroad from near Richmond to the Anna rivers, and making him wary of the situation of his army in the Shenandoah, and, in the event of failure in this, to take advantage of his necessary withdrawal of troops from Petersburg, to explode a mine that had been prepared in front of the 9th corps and assault the enemy's lines at that place, on the night of the 26th of July the 2nd corps and two divisions of the cavalry corps and Kautz's cavalry were crossed to the north bank of the James River and joined the force General Butler had there. On the 27th the enemy was driven from his intrenched position, with the loss of four pieces of artillery. On the 28th our lines were extended from Deep Bottom to New Market Road, but in getting this position were attacked by the enemy in heavy force. The fighting lasted for several hours, resulting in considerable loss to both sides. The first object of this move having failed, by reason of the very large force thrown there by the enemy, I determined to take advantage of the diversion made, by assaulting Petersburg before he could get his force back there. One division of the 2d corps was withdrawn on the night of the 28th, and moved during the night to the rear of the 18th corps, to relieve that corps in the line, that it might be foot loose in the assault to be made. The other two divisions of the 2d corps .and Sheridan's cavalry were crossed over on the night of the 29th and moved in front of Petersburg. On the morning of the 30th, between four and five o'clock, the mine was sprung, blowing up a battery and most of a regiment, and the advance of the assaulting column, formed of the 9th corps, immediately took possession of the crater made by the explosion, and the line for some distance to the right and left of it, and a detached line in front of it, but for some cause failed to advance promptly to the ridge beyond. Had they done this, I have every reason to believe that Petersburg would have fallen. Other troops were immediately pushed forward, but the time consumed in getting them up enabled the enemy to rally from his surprise (which had been complete), and get forces to this point for its defence. The captured line thus held being untenable, and of no advantage to us, the troops were withdrawn, but not without heavy loss. Thus terminated in disaster what promised to be the most successful assault of the campaign.

Immediately upon the enemy's ascertaining that General Hunter was retreating from Lynchburg by way of the Kanawha River, thus laying the Shenandoah Valley open for raids into Maryland and

Pennsylvania, he returned northward and moved down that valley. As soon as this movement of the enemy was ascertained, General Hunter, who had reached the Kanawha River, was directed to move his troops without delay, by river and railroad, to Harper's Ferry; but owing to the difficulty of navigation by reason of low water and breaks in the railroad, great delay was experienced in getting there. It became necessary, therefore, to find other troops to check this movement of the enemy. For this purpose the 6th corps was taken from the armies operating against Richmond, to which was added the 19th corps, then fortunately beginning to arrive in Hampton Roads from the Gulf Department, under orders issued immediately after the ascertainment of the result of the Red River expedition. The garrisons of Baltimore and Washington were at this time made up of heavy artillery regiments, hundred days' men, and detachments from the invalid corps. One division under command of General Ricketts, of the 6th corps, was sent to Baltimore, and the remaining two divisions of the 6th corps, under General Wright, were subsequently sent to Washington. On the 3d of July the enemy approached Martinsburg. General Sigel, who was in command of our forces there, retreated across the Potomac at Shepherdstown ; and General Weber, commanding at Harper's Ferry, crossed the river and occupied Maryland Heights. On the 6th the enemy occupied Hagerstown, moving a strong column towards Frederick City. General Wallace, with Pickett's division and his own command, the latter mostly new and undisciplined troops, pushed out from Baltimore with great promptness, and met the enemy in force on the Monocacy, near the crossing of the railroad bridge. His force was not sufficient to insure success, but he fought the enemy nevertheless, and although it resulted in a defeat to our arms, yet it detained the enemy, and thereby served to enable General Wright to reach Washington with two divisions of the 6th corps, and the advance of the 19th corps, before him. From Monocacy the enemy moved on Washington, his cavalry advance reaching Rockville on the evening of the 10th. On the 12th a reconnaissance was thrown out in front of Fort Stevens, to ascertain the enemy's position and force. A severe skirmish ensued, in which we lost about two hundred and eighty in killed and wounded. The enemy's loss was probably greater. He commenced retreating during the night. Learning the exact condition of affairs at Washington, I requested by telegraph, at forty-five minutes past eleven P.M., on the 12th, the assignment of Major-General H.G. Wright to the command of all the troops that could be made available to operate in the field against the enemy, and directed that he should get outside of the trenches with all the force he could, and push Early to the last moment. General Wright commenced the pursuit on the 13th; on the 18th the enemy was overtaken at Snicker's Ferry, on the Shenandoah, when a sharp skirmish occurred; and on the 20th, General Averell encountered and defeated a portion of the rebel army at Winchester, capturing four pieces of artillery and several hundred prisoners.

Learning that Early was retreating south towards Lynchburg or Richmond, I directed that the 6th and 19th corps be got back to the armies operating against Richmond, so that they might be used in a movement against Lee before the return of the troops sent by him into the valley ; and that Hunter should remain in the Shenandoah Valley, keeping between any force of the enemy and Washington, acting on the defensive as much as possible. I felt that if the enemy had any notion of returning, the fact would be developed before the 6th and 19th corps could leave Washington. Subsequently, the 19th corps was excepted from the order to return to the James.

About the 25th it became evident that the enemy was again advancing upon Maryland and Pennsylvania, and the 6th corps, then at Washington, was ordered back to the vicinity of Harper's Ferry. The rebel force moved down the valley, and sent a raiding party into Pennsylvania which on the 30th burned Chambersburg, and then retreated, pursued by our cavalry, towards Cumberland. They were met and defeated by General Kelley, and with diminished numbers escaped into the mountains of West Virginia. From the time of the first raid the telegraph wires were frequently down between Washington and City Point, making it necessary to transmit messages a part of the way by boat. It took from twenty-four to thirty-six hours to get dispatches through and return answers back; so that often orders would be given, and then information would be received showing a different state of facts from those on which they were based, causing a confusion and apparent contradiction of orders that must have considerably embarrassed those who had to execute them, and rendered operations against the enemy less effective than they otherwise would have been. To remedy this evil, it was evident to my mind that some person should have the supreme command of all the forces in the Departments of West Virginia, Washington, Susquehanna, and the Middle Department, and I so recommended.

On the 2d of August, I ordered General Sheridan to report in person to Major-General Halleck, chief of staff, at Washington, with a view to his assignment to the command of all the forces against Early. At this time the enemy was concentrated in the neighborhood of Winchester, while our forces, under General Hunter, were concentrated on the Monocacy, at the crossing of the Baltimore and Ohio Railroad, leaving open to the enemy Western Maryland and Southern Pennsylvania. From where I was, I hesitated to give positive orders for the movement of our forces at Monocacy, lest by so doing I should expose Washington. Therefore, on the 4th, I left City Point to visit Hunter 's command, and determine for myself what was best to be done. On arrival there, and after consultation with General Hunter, I issued to him the following instructions:

MONOCACY BRIDGE, MARYLAND,
August 5, 1864-8 P.M.

" GENERAL :-Concentrate all your available force without delay in the vicinity of Harper's Ferry, leaving only such railroad guards and garrisons for public property as may be necessary. Use, in this concentrating, the railroad, if by so doing time can be saved. From Harper's Ferry, if it is found that the enemy has moved north of the Potomac in large force, push north, following him and attacking him wherever found; follow him, if driven south of the Potomac, as long as it is safe to do so. If it is ascertained that the enemy has but a small force north of the Potomac, then push south with the main force, detaching under a competent commander a sufficient force to look after the raiders, and drive them to their homes. In detaching such a force, the brigade of cavalry now *en route* from Washington via Rockville may be taken into account.

"There are now on their way to join you three other brigades of the best cavalry, numbering at least five thousand men and horses. These will be instructed, in the absence of further orders, to join you by the south side of the Potomac. One brigade will probably start tomorrow. In pushing up the Shenandoah Valley, where it is expected you will have to go first or last, it is desirable that nothing should be left to invite the enemy to return. Take all provisions, forage, and stock wanted for the use of your command; such as cannot be consumed, destroy. It is not desirable that the buildings should be destroyed, they should rather be protected; but the people should be informed that, so long as an army can subsist among them, recurrences of these raids must be expected, and we are determined to stop them at all hazards.

"Bear in mind, the object is to drive the enemy south ; and to do this, you want to keep him always in sight. Be guided in your course by the course he takes.

"Make your own arrangements for supplies of all kinds, giving regular vouchers for such as may be taken from loyal citizens in the country through which you march.

"U. S. GRANT, Lieutenant-General.

"MAJOR-GENERAL D. HUNTER."

The troops were immediately put in motion, and the advance reached Halltown that night.

General Hunter having, in our conversation, expressed a willingness to be relieved from command, I telegraphed to have Gen-eral Sheridan, then at Washington, sent to Harper's Ferry by the morning train, with orders to take general command of all the troops in the field, and to call on General Hunter at Monocacy, who would turn over to him my letter of instructions. I remained at Monocacy until General Sheridan arrived, on the morning of the 6th, and, after a conference with him in relation to military affairs in that vicinity, I returned to City Point by way of Washington.

On the 7th of August, the Middle Department, and the Departments of West Virginia, Washington, and Susquehanna, were constituted into the "Middle Military Division," and Major-General Sheridan was assigned to temporary command of the same.

Two divisions of cavalry, commanded by Generals Torbert and Wilson, were sent to Sheridan from the Army of the Potomac. The first reached him at Harper's Ferry about the 11th of August.

His operations during the month of August and the fore part of September were both of an offensive and defensive character, resulting in many severe skirmishes, principally by the cavalry, in which we were generally successful, but no general engagement took place. The two armies lay in such a position -the enemy on the west bank of the Opequon Creek covering Winchester, and our forces in front of Berryville -that either could bring on a battle at any time. Defeat to us would lay open to the enemy the States of Maryland and Pennsylvania for long distances before another army could be interposed to check him. Under these circumstances I hesitated about allowing the initiative to be taken. Finally, the use of the Baltimore and Ohio Railroad, and the Chesapeake and Ohio Canal, which were both obstructed by the enemy, became so indispensably necessary to us, and the importance of relieving Pennsylvania and Maryland from continuously threatened invasion so great, that I determined the risk should be taken. But fearing to telegraph the order for an attack without knowing more than I did of General Sheridan 's feelings as to what would be the probable result, I left City Point on the 15th of September to visit him at his headquarters, to decide, after conference with him, what should be done. I met him at Charlestown, and he pointed out so distinctly how each army lay ; what he could do the moment he was authorized, and expressed such confidence of success, that I saw there were but two words of instructions necessary -Go in ! For the conveniences of forage, the teams for supplying the army were kept at Harper's Ferry. I asked him if he could get out his teams and supplies in time to make an attack on the ensuing Tuesday morning. His reply was, that he could before daylight on Monday. He was off promptly to time, and I may here add, that the result was such that I have never since deemed it necessary to visit General Sheridan before giving him orders.

Early on the morning of the 19th, General Sheridan attacked General Early at the crossing on the Opequon Creek, and after a most sanguinary and bloody battle, lasting until five o 'clock in the evening, defeated him with heavy loss, carrying his entire position from Opequon Creek to Winchester, capturing several thousand prisoners and five pieces of artillery. The enemy rallied, and made a stand in a strong position at Fisher 's Hill, where he was attacked, and again defeated with heavy loss on the 20th [22d]. Sheridan pursued him with great energy through Harrisonburg, Staunton, and the gaps of the Blue Ridge. After stripping the upper valley of most of the supplies and provisions for the rebel army, he returned to Strasburg, and took position on the north side of Cedar Creek.

Having received considerable reinforcements, General Early again returned to the valley, and, on the 9th of October, his cavalry encountered ours near Strasburg, where the rebels were defeated, with the loss of eleven pieces of artillery and three hundred and fifty prisoners. On the night of the 18th, the enemy crossed the mountains which separate the branches of the Shenandoah, forded the North Fork, and early on the morning of the 19th, under cover of the darkness and the fog, surprised and turned our left flank, and captured the batteries which enfiladed our whole line. Our troops fell back with heavy loss and in much confusion, but were finally rallied between Middletown and Newtown. At this juncture, General Sheridan, who was at Winchester when the battle commenced, arrived on the field, arranged his lines just in time to repulse a heavy attack of the enemy, and immediately assuming the offensive, he attacked in turn with great vigor. The enemy was defeated with great slaughter, and the loss of most of his artillery and trains, and the trophies he had captured in the morning. The wreck of his army escaped during the night, and fled in the direction of Staunton and Lynchburg. Pursuit was made to Mount Jackson. Thus ended this, the enemy's last attempt to invade the North via the Shenandoah Valley. I was now enabled to return the 6th corps to the Army of the Potomac, and to send one division from Sheridan's army to the Army of the James, and another to Savannah, Georgia, to hold Sherman's new acquisitions on the sea coast, and thus enable him to move without detaching from his force for that purpose.

Reports from various sources led me to believe that the enemy had detached three divisions from Petersburg to reinforce Early in the Shenandoah Valley. I therefore sent the 2d corps and Gregg's division of cavalry, of the Army of the Potomac, and a force of General Butler's army, on the night of the 13th of August, to threaten Richmond from the north side of the James, to prevent him from sending troops away, and, if possible, to draw back those sent. In this move we captured six pieces of artillery and several hundred prisoners, detained troops that were under marching orders, and ascertained that but one division (Kershaw's), of the three reputed detached, had gone.

The enemy having withdrawn heavily from Petersburg to resist this movement, the 5th corps, General Warren commanding, was moved out on the 18th, and took possession of the Weldon Railroad. During the day he had considerable fighting. To regain possession of the road, the enemy made repeated and desperate assaults, but was each time repulsed with great loss. On the night of the 20th, the troops on the north side of the James were withdrawn, and Hancock and Gregg returned to the front at Petersburg. On the 25th, the 2d corps and Gregg's division of cavalry, while at Reams's Station destroying the railroad, were attacked, and after desperate fighting, a part of our line gave way, and five pieces of artillery fell into the hands of the enemy.

By the 12th of September, a branch railroad was completed from the City Point and Petersburg Railroad to the Weldon Railroad, enabling us to supply, without difficulty, in all weather, the army in front of Petersburg.

The extension of our lines across the Weldon Railroad compelled the enemy to so extend his, that it seemed he could have but few troops north of the James for the defence of Richmond. On the night of the 28th, the 10th corps, Major-General Birney, and the 18th corps, Major-General Ord commanding, of General Butler's army, were crossed to the north side of the James, and advanced on the morning of the 29th, carrying the very strong fortifications and intrenchments below Chaffin's Farm, known as Fort Harrison, capturing fifteen pieces of artillery, and the New Market Road and intrenchments. This success was followed up by a gallant assault upon Fort Gilmer, immediately in front of the Chaffin Farm fortifications, in which we were repulsed with heavy loss. Kautz's cavalry was pushed forward on the road to the right of this, supported by infantry, and reached the enemy's inner line, but was unable to get further. The position captured from the enemy was so threatening to Richmond, that I determined to hold it. The enemy made several desperate attempts to dislodge us, all of which were unsuccessful, and for which he paid dearly.

On the morning of the 30th, General Meade sent out a reconnaissance, with a view to attacking the enemy's line, if it was found sufficiently weakened by withdrawal of troops to the north side. In this reconnaissance we captured and held the enemy's works near Poplar Spring Church. In the afternoon, troops moving to get to the left of the point gained were attacked by the enemy in heavy force, and compelled to fall back until supported by the forces holding the captured works. Our cavalry under Gregg was also attacked, but repulsed the enemy with great loss.

On the 7th of October, the enemy attacked Kautz 's cavalry north of the James, and drove it back with heavy loss in killed, wounded, and prisoners, and the loss of all the artillery, eight or nine pieces. This he followed up by an attack on our intrenched infantry line, but was repulsed with severe slaughter. On the 13th, a reconnaissance was sent out by General Butler, with a view to drive the enemy from some new works he was constructing, which resulted in very heavy loss to us.

On the 27th, the Army of the Potomac, leaving only sufficient men to hold its fortified line, moved by the enemy's right flank. The 2nd corps followed by two divisions of the 5th corps, with the cavalry in advance and covering our left flank, forced a passage of Hatcher's Run, and moved up the south side of it towards the South Side Railroad, until the 2nd corps and part of the cavalry reached the Boydton Plank Road where it crosses Hatcher's Run. At this point we were six miles distant from the South Side Railroad, which I had hoped by this movement to reach and hold. But finding that we had not reached the end of the enemy 's fortifications, and no place presenting itself for a successful assault by which he might be doubled up and shortened, I determined to withdraw to within our fortified line, Orders were given accordingly. Immediately upon receiving a report that General Warren had connected with General Hancock, I returned to my headquarters. Soon after I left the enemy moved out across Hatcher's Run, in the gap between Generals Hancock and Warren, which was not closed as reported, and made a desperate attack on General Hancock's right and rear. General Hancock immediately faced his corps to meet it, and after a bloody combat drove the enemy within his works, and withdrew that night to his old position.

In support of this movement, General Butler made a demonstration on the north side of the James, and attacked the enemy on the Williamsburg Road, and also on the York River Railroad. In the former he was unsuccessful ; in the latter he succeeded in carrying a work which was afterwards abandoned, and his forces withdrawn to their former positions.

From this time forward the operations in front of Petersburg and Richmond, until the spring campaign of 1865, were confined to the defence and extension of our lines, and to offensive movements for crippling the enemy's lines of communication, and to prevent his detaching any considerable force to send south. By the 7th of February, our lines were extended to Hatcher's Run, and the Weldon Railroad had been destroyed to Hicksford.

General Sherman moved from Chattanooga on the 6th of May, with the Armies of the Cumberland, Tennessee, and Ohio, commanded, respectively, by Generals Thomas, McPherson, and Schofield, upon

Johnston's army at Dalton; but finding the enemy's position at Buzzard's Roost, covering Dalton, too strong to be assaulted, General McPherson was sent through Snake Gap to turn it, while Generals Thomas and Schofield threatened it in front and on the north. This movement was successful. Johnston, finding his retreat likely to be cut off, fell back to his fortified position at Resaca, where he was attacked on the afternoon of May 15th. A heavy battle ensued. During the night the enemy retreated south. Late on the 17th, his rear-guard was overtaken near Adairsville, and heavy skirmishing followed. The next morning, however, he had again disappeared. He was vigorously pursued, and was overtaken at Cassville on the 19th, but during the ensuing night retreated across the Etowah. While these operations were going on, General Jefferson C. Davis's division of Thomas's army was sent to Rome, capturing it with its forts and artillery, and its valuable mills and foundries. General Sherman, having given his army a few days' rest at this point, again put it in motion on the 23d, for Dallas, with a view of turning the difficult pass at Allatoona. On the afternoon of the 25th, the advance, under General Hooker, had a severe battle with the enemy, driving him back to New Hope Church, near Dallas. Several sharp encounters occurred at this point. The most important was on the 28th, when the enemy assaulted General McPherson at Dallas, but received a terrible and bloody repulse.

On the 4th of June, Johnston abandoned his intrenched position at New Hope Church, and retreated to the strong positions of Kennesaw, Pine, and Lost mountains. He was forced to yield the two last named places, and concentrate his army on Kenesaw, where, on the 27th, Generals Thomas and McPherson made a determined but unsuccessful assault. On the night of the 2d of July, Sherman commenced moving his army by the right flank, and on the morning of the 3d, found that the enemy, in consequence of this movement, had abandoned Kenesaw and retreated across the Chattahoochee.

General Sherman remained on the Chattahoochee to give his men rest and get up stores until the 17th of July, when he resumed his operations, crossed the Chattahoochee, destroyed a large portion of the railroad to Augusta, and drove the enemy back to Atlanta. At this place General Hood succeeded General Johnston in command of the rebel army, and assuming the offensive-defensive policy, made several severe attacks upon Sherman in the vicinity of Atlanta, the most desperate and determined of which was on the 22d of July. About one P.M. of this day the brave, accomplished, and noble hearted McPherson was killed. General Logan succeeded him, and commanded the Army of the Tennessee through this desperate battle, and until he was superseded by Major-General Howard, on the 26th, with the same success and ability that had characterized him in the command of a corps or division.

In all these attacks the enemy was repulsed with great loss. Finding it impossible to entirely invest the place, General Sherman, after securing his line of communications across the Chattahoochee, moved his main force round by the enemy's left flank upon the Montgomery and Macon roads, to draw the enemy from his fortifications. In this he succeeded, and after defeating the enemy near Rough-and-Ready, Jonesboro, and Lovejoy's, forcing him to retreat to the south, on the 2nd of September occupied Atlanta, the objective point of his campaign.

About the time of this move, the rebel cavalry, under Wheeler, attempted to cut his communications in the rear, but was repulsed at Dalton, and driven into East Tennessee, whence it proceeded west to McMinnville, Murfreesboro', and Franklin, and was finally driven south of the Tennessee. The damage done by this raid was repaired in a few days.

During the partial investment of Atlanta, General Rousseau joined General Sherman with a force of cavalry from Decatur, having made a successful raid upon the Atlanta and Montgomery Railroad, and its branches near Opelika. Cavalry raids were also made by Generals McCook, Garrard, and Stoneman, to cut the remaining railroad communication with Atlanta. The first two were successful the latter, disastrous.

General Sherman's movement from Chattanooga to Atlanta was prompt, skilful, and brilliant. The history of his flank movements and battles during that memorable campaign will ever be read with an interest unsurpassed by anything in history.

His own report, and those of his subordinate commanders, accompanying it, gave the details of that most successful campaign.

He was dependent for the supply of his armies upon a single track railroad from Nashville to the point where he was operating. This passed the entire distance through a hostile country, and every foot of it had to be protected by troops. The cavalry force of the enemy under Forrest, in Northern Mississippi, was evidently waiting for Sherman to advance far enough into the mountains of Georgia, to make a retreat disastrous, to get upon this line and destroy it beyond the possibility of further use. To guard against this danger, Sherman left what he supposed to be a sufficient force to operate against Forrest in West Tennessee. He directed General Washburn, who commanded there, to send Brigadier-General S.D. Sturgis in command of this force to attack him. On the morning of the 10th of June, General Sturgis met the enemy near Guntown, Mississippi, was badly beaten, and driven back in utter rout and confusion to Memphis, a distance of about one hundred miles, hotly pursued by the enemy. By this, however, the enemy was defeated in his designs upon Sherman's line of communications. The persistency with which he followed up this success exhausted him, and made a season for rest and repairs necessary. In the meantime, Major-General A.J. Smith, with the troops of the Army of the Tennessee that had been sent by General Sherman to General Banks, arrived at Memphis on their return from Red River, where they had done most excellent service. He was directed by General Sherman to immediately take the offensive against Forrest. This he did with the promptness and effect which has characterized his whole military career. On the 4th of July, he met the enemy at Tupelo, Mississippi, and whipped him badly. The fighting continued through three days. Our loss was small compared with that of the enemy. Having accomplished the object of his expedition, General Smith returned to Memphis.

During the months of March and April this same force under Forrest annoyed us considerably. On the 24th of March it captured Union City, Kentucky, and its garrison, and on the 24th attacked Paducah, commanded by Colonel S.G. Hicks, 40th Illinois Volunteers. Colonel H., having but a small force, withdrew to the forts near the river, from where he repulsed the enemy and drove him from the place.

On the 13th of April, part of this force, under the rebel General Buford, summoned the garrison of Columbus, Kentucky, to surrender, but received for reply from Colonel Lawrence, 34th New Jersey Volunteers, that being placed there by his Government with adequate force to hold his post and repel all enemies from it, surrender was out of the question.

On the morning of the same day Forrest attacked Fort Pillow, Tennessee, garrisoned by a detachment of Tennessee cavalry and the 1st Regiment Alabama colored troops, commanded by Major Booth. The garrison fought bravely until about three o'clock in the afternoon, when the enemy carried the works by assault; and, after our men threw down their arms, proceeded to an inhuman and merciless massacre of the garrison.

On the 14th, General Buford, having failed at Columbus, appeared before Paducah, but was again driven off.

Guerillas and raiders, seemingly emboldened by Forrest's operations, were also very active in Kentucky. The most noted of these was Morgan. With a force of from two to three thousand cavalry, he entered the State through Pound Gap in the latter part of May. On the 11th of June they attacked and captured Cynthiana, with its entire garrison. On the 12th he was overtaken by General Burbridge, and completely routed with heavy loss, and was finally driven out of the State. This notorious guerilla was afterwards surprised and killed near Greenville, Tennessee, and his command captured and dispersed by General Gillem.

In the absence of official reports of the commencement of the Red River expedition, except so far as relates to the movements of the troops sent by General Sherman under General A. J. Smith, I am unable to give the date of its starting. The troops under General Smith, comprising two divisions of the 16th and a detachment of the 17th army corps, left Vicksburg on the 10th of March, and reached the designated point on Red River one day earlier than that appointed by General Banks. The rebel forces at Fort de Russy, thinking to defeat him, left the fort on the 14th to give him battle in the open field; but, while occupying the enemy with skirmishing and demonstrations, Smith pushed forward to Fort de Russy, which had been left with a weak garrison, and captured it with its garrison, about three hundred and fifty men, eleven pieces of artillery, and many small-arms. Our loss was but slight. On the 15th he pushed forward to Alexandria, which place he reached on the 18th. On the 21st he had an engagement with the enemy at Henderson's Hill, in which he defeated him, capturing two hundred and ten prisoners and four pieces of artillery.

On the 28th, he again attacked and defeated the enemy under the rebel General Taylor, at Cane River. By the 26th, General Banks had assembled his whole army at Alexandria, and pushed forward to Grand Ecore. On the morning of April 6th he moved from Grand Ecore. On the afternoon of the 7th, he advanced and met the enemy near Pleasant Hill, and drove him from the field. On the same afternoon the enemy made a stand eight miles beyond Pleasant Hill, but was again compelled to retreat. On the 8th, at Sabine Cross Roads and Peach Hill, the enemy attacked and defeated his advance, capturing nineteen pieces of artillery and an immense amount of transportation and stores. During the night, General Banks fell back to Pleasant Hill, where another battle was fought on the 9th, and the enemy repulsed with great loss. During the night, General Banks continued his retrograde movement to Grand Ecore, and thence to Alexandria, which he reached on the 27th of April. Here a serious difficulty arose in getting Admiral Porter's fleet which accompanied the expedition, over the rapids, the water having fallen so much since they passed up as to prevent their return. At the suggestion of Colonel (now Brigadier-General) Bailey, and under his superintendence, wing-dams were constructed, by which the channel was contracted so that the fleet passed down the rapids in safety.

The army evacuated Alexandria on the 14th of May, after considerable skirmishing with the enemy's advance, and reached Morganzia and Point Coupee near the end of the month. The disastrous termination of this expedition, and the lateness of the season, rendered impracticable the carrying out of my plans of a movement in force sufficient to insure the capture of Mobile.

On the 23d of March, Major-General Steele left Little Rock with the 7th army corps, to co-operate with General Banks's expedition on the Red River, and reached Arkadelphia on the 28th. On the 16th of April, after driving the enemy before him, he was joined, near Elkin's Ferry, in Washita County, by General Thayer, who had marched from Fort Smith. After several severe skirmishes, in which the enemy was defeated, General Steele reached Camden, which he occupied about the middle of April.

On learning the defeat and consequent retreat of General Banks on Red River, and the loss of one of his own trains at Mark's Mill, in Dallas County, General Steele determined to fall back to the Arkansas River. He left Camden on the 26th of April, and reached Little Rock on the 2d of May. On the 30th of April, the enemy attacked him while crossing Saline River at Jenkins's Ferry, but was repulsed with considerable loss. Our loss was about six hundred in killed, wounded and prisoners.

Major-General Canby, who had been assigned to the command of the "Military Division of the West Mississippi," was therefore directed to send the 19th army corps to join the armies operating against Richmond, and to limit the remainder of his command to such operations as might be necessary to hold the positions and lines of communications he then occupied.

Before starting General A.J. Smith's troops back to Sherman, General Canby sent a part of it to disperse a force of the enemy that was collecting near the Mississippi River. General Smith met and defeated this force near Lake Chicot on the 5th of June. Our loss was about forty killed and seventy wounded.

In the latter part of July, General Canby sent Major-General Gordon Granger, with such forces as he could collect, to cooperate with Admiral Farragut against the defences of Mobile Bay. On the 8th of August, Fort Gaines surrendered to the combined naval and land forces. Fort Powell was blown up and abandoned.

On the 9th, Fort Morgan was invested, and, after a severe bombardment, surrendered on the 23d. The total captures amounted to one thousand four hundred and sixty-four prisoners, and one hundred and four pieces of artillery.

About the last of August, it being reported that the rebel General Price, with a force of about ten thousand men, had reached Jacksonport, on his way to invade Missouri, General A.J. Smith's command, then en route from Memphis to join Sherman, was ordered to Missouri. A cavalry force was also, at the same time, sent from Memphis, under command of Colonel Winslow. This made General Rosecrans's forces superior to those of Price, and no doubt was entertained he would be able to check Price and drive him back; while the forces under General Steele, in Arkansas, would cut off his retreat. On the 26th day of September, Price attacked Pilot Knob and forced the garrison to retreat, and thence moved north to the Missouri River, and continued up that river towards Kansas. General Curtis, commanding Department of Kansas, immediately collected such forces as he could to repel the invasion of Kansas, while General Rosecrans's cavalry was operating in his rear.

The enemy was brought to battle on the Big Blue and defeated, with the loss of nearly all his artillery and trains and a large number of prisoners. He made a precipitate retreat to Northern Arkansas. The impunity with which Price was enabled to roam over the State of Missouri for a long time, and the incalculable mischief done by him, shows to how little purpose a superior force may be used. There is no reason why General Rosecrans should not have concentrated his forces, and beaten and driven Price before the latter reached Pilot Knob.

September 20th, the enemy's cavalry, under Forrest, crossed the Tennessee near Waterloo, Alabama, and on the 23d attacked the garrison at Athens, consisting of six hundred men, which capitulated on the 24th. Soon after the surrender two regiments of reinforcements arrived, and after a severe fight were compelled to surrender. Forrest destroyed the railroad westward, captured the garrison at Sulphur Branch trestle, skirmished with the garrison at Pulaski on the 27th, and on the same day cut the Nashville and Chattanooga Railroad near Tullahoma and Dechard. On the morning of the 30th, one column of Forrest's command, under Buford, appeared before Huntsville, and summoned the surrender of the garrison. Receiving an answer in the negative, he remained in the vicinity of the place until next morning, when he again summoned its surrender, and received the same reply as on the night before. He withdrew in the direction of Athens, which place had been re-garrisoned, and attacked it on the afternoon of the 1st of October, but without success. On the morning of the 2d he renewed his attack, but was handsomely repulsed.

Another column under Forrest appeared before Columbia on the morning of the 1st, but did not make an attack. On the morning of the 3d he moved towards Mount Pleasant. While these operations were going on, every exertion was made by General Thomas to destroy the forces under Forrest before he could re-cross the Tennessee, but was unable to prevent his escape to Corinth, Mississippi.

In September, an expedition under General Burbridge was sent to destroy the salt works at Saltville, Virginia. He met the enemy on the 2d of October, about three miles and a half from Saltville, and drove him into his strongly intrenched position around the salt works, from which he was unable to dislodge him. During the night he withdrew his command and returned to Kentucky.

General Sherman, immediately after the fall of Atlanta, put his armies in camp in and about the place, and made all preparations for refitting and supplying them for future service. The great length of road from Atlanta to the Cumberland River, however, which had to be guarded, allowed the troops but little rest.

During this time Jefferson Davis made a speech in Macon, Georgia, which was reported in the papers of the South, and soon became known to the whole country, disclosing the plans of the enemy, thus enabling General Sherman to fully meet them. He exhibited the weakness of supposing that an army that had been beaten and fearfully decimated in a vain attempt at the defensive, could successfully undertake the offensive against the army that had so often defeated it.

In execution of this plan, Hood, with this army, was soon reported to the southwest of Atlanta. Moving far to Sherman's right, he succeeded in reaching the railroad about Big Shanty, and moved north on it.

General Sherman, leaving a force to hold Atlanta, with the remainder of his army fell upon him and drove him to Gadsden, Alabama. Seeing the constant annoyance he would have with the roads to his rear if he attempted to hold Atlanta, General Sherman proposed the abandonment and destruction of that place, with all the railroads leading to it, and telegraphed me as follows:

" CENTREVILLE, GEORGIA,
October 10-noon.

" Dispatch about Wilson just received. Hood is now crossing Coosa River, twelve miles below Rome, bound west. If he passes over the Mobile and Ohio road, had I not better execute the plan of my letter sent by Colonel Porter, and leave General Thomas with the troops now in Tennessee, to defend the Stat ? He will have an ample force when the reinforcements ordered reach Nashville.

"W.T. SHERMAN, Major-General.
"LIEUTENANT-GENERAL GRANT."

For a full understanding of the plan referred to in this dispatch, I quote from the letter sent by Colonel Porter : " I will therefore give my opinion, that your army and Canby 's should be reinforced to the maximum ; that after you get Wilmington, you strike for Savannah and the river ; that Canby be instructed to hold the Mississippi River, and send a force to get Columbus, Georgia, either by the way of the Alabama or the Appalachicola, and that I keep Hood employed and put my army in final order for a march on Augusta, Columbia, and Charleston, to be ready as soon as Wilmington is sealed as to commerce, and the city of Savannah is in our possession." This was in reply to a letter of mine of date September l2th, in answer to a dispatch of his containing substantially the same proposition, and in which I informed him of a proposed movement against Wilmington, and of the situation in Virginia, etc.

" CITY POINT, VIRGINIA,
October 11, 1864-11 A.M.

"Your dispatch of October 10th received. Does it not look as if Hood was going to attempt the invasion of Middle Tennessee, using the Mobile and Ohio and Memphis and Charleston roads to supply his base on the Tennessee River, about Florence Or Decatur ? If he does this, he ought to be met and prevented from getting north of the Tennessee River. If you were to cut loose, I do not believe you would meet Hood's army, but would be bushwhacked by all the old men and little boys, and such railroad guards as are still left at home. Hood would probably strike for Nashville, thinking that by going north he could inflict greater damage upon us than we could upon the rebels by going south. If there is any way of getting at Hood's army, I would prefer that, but I must trust to your own judgement. I find I shall not be able to send a force from here to act with you on Savannah. Your movements, therefore, will be independent of mine ; at least until the fall of Richmond takes place. I am afraid Thomas, with such lines of road as he has to protect, could not prevent Hood from going north. With Wilson turned loose, with all your cavalry, you will find the rebels put much more on the defensive than heretofore.

"U.S. GRANT, Lieutenant-General.

"MAJOR-GENERAL W.T. SHERMAN."

" KINGSTON, GEORGIA,
October 11-11 A.M.

"Hood moved his army from Palmetto Station across by Dallas and Cedartown, and is now on the Coosa River, south of Rome. He threw one corps on my road at Acworth and I was forced to follow. I hold Atlanta with the 2Oth corps, and have strong detachments along my line. This reduces my active force to a comparatively small army. We cannot remain here on the defensive. With the twenty-five thousand men, and the bold cavalry he has, he can constantly break my roads. I would infinitely prefer to make a wreck of the road, and of the country from Chattanooga to Atlanta, including the latter city -send back all my wounded and worthless, and with my effective army, move through Georgia, smashing things, to the sea. Hood may turn into Tennessee and Kentucky, but I believe he will be forced to follow me. Instead of my being on the defensive, I would be on the offensive; instead of guessing at what he means to do, he would have to guess at my plans. The difference in war is full twenty-five per cent. I can make Savannah, Charleston, or the mouth of the Chattahoochee.

"Answer quick, as I know we will not have the telegraph long.

"W.T. SHERMAN, Major-General.

"LIEUTENANT -GENERAL GRANT."

"CITY POINT, VIRGINIA,
October 11, 1864-11:30 P.M

"Your dispatch of today received. If you are satisfied the trip to the sea coast can be made, holding the line of the Tennessee River firmly, you may make it, destroying all the railroad south of Dalton or Chattanooga, as you think best.

"U.S. GRANT, Lieutenant-General.

"MAJOR-GENERAL W.T. SHERMAN."

It was the original design to hold Atlanta, and by getting through to the coast, with a garrison left on the southern railroads, leading east and west, through Georgia, to effectually sever the east from the west. In other words, cut the would be Confederacy in two again, as it had been cut once by our gaining possession of the Mississippi River. General Sherman's plan virtually effected this object.

General Sherman commenced at once his preparations for his proposed movement keeping his army in position in the meantime to watch Hood. Becoming satisfied that Hood had moved westward from Gadsden across Sand Mountain, General Sherman sent the 4th corps, Major-General Stanley commanding, and the 23d corps, Major-General Schofield commanding, back to Chattanooga to report to Major-General Thomas, at Nashville, whom he had placed in command of all the troops of his military division, save the four army corps and cavalry division he designed to move with through Georgia. With the troops thus left at his disposal, there was little doubt that General Thomas could hold the line of the Tennessee, or, in the event Hood should force it, would be able to concentrate and beat him in battle. It was therefore readily consented to that Sherman should start for the sea coast.

Having concentrated his troops at Atlanta by the 14th of November, he commenced his march, threatening both Augusta and Macon. His coming out point could not be definitely fixed. Having to gather his subsistence as he marched through the country, it was not impossible that a force inferior to his own might compel him to head for such point as he could reach, instead of such as he might prefer. The blindness of the enemy, however, in ignoring his movement, and sending Hood's army, the only considerable force he had west of Richmond and east of the Mississippi River, northward on an offensive campaign, left the whole country open, and Sherman's route to his own choice.

How that campaign was conducted, how little opposition was met with, the condition of the country through which the armies passed, the capture of Fort McAllister, on the Savannah River, and the occupation of Savannah on the 21st of December, are all clearly set forth in General Sherman's admirable report.

Soon after General Sherman commenced his march from Atlanta, two expeditions, one from Baton Rouge, Louisiana, and one from Vicksburg, Mississippi, were started by General Canby to cut the enemy's lines of communication with Mobile and detain troops in that field. General Foster, commanding Department of the South, also sent an expedition, via Broad River, to destroy the railroad between Charleston and Savannah. The expedition from Vicksburg, under command of Brevet Brigadier-General E.D. Osband (colonel 3d United States colored cavalry), captured, on the 27th of November, and destroyed the Mississippi Central Railroad bridge and trestle work over Big Black River, near Canton, thirty miles of the road, and two locomotives, besides large amounts of stores. The expedition from Baton Rouge was without favorable results. The expedition from the Department of the South, under the immediate command of Brigadier-General John P. Hatch, consisting of about five thousand men of all arms, including a brigade from the navy, proceeded up Broad River and debarked at Boyd's Neck on the 29th of November, from where it moved to strike the railroad at Grahamsville. At Honey Hill, about three miles from Grahamsville, the enemy was found and attacked in a strongly fortified position, which resulted, after severe fighting, in our repulse with a loss of seven hundred and forty-six in killed, wounded, and missing. During the night General Hatch withdrew. On the 6th of December General Foster obtained a position covering the Charleston and Savannah Railroad, between the Coosawhatchie and Tulifinny rivers.

Hood, instead of following Sherman, continued his move northward, which seemed to me to be leading to his certain doom. At all events, had I had the power to command both armies, I should not have changed the orders under which he seemed to be acting. On the 26th of October, the advance of Hood's army attacked the garrison at Decatur, Alabama, but failing to carry the place, withdrew towards Courtland, and succeeded, in the face of our cavalry, in effecting a lodgment on the north side of the Tennessee River, near Florence. On the 28th, Forrest reached the Tennessee, at Fort Heiman, and captured a gunboat and three transports. On the 2d of November he planted batteries above and below Johnsonville, on the opposite side of the river, isolating three gunboats and eight transports. On the 4th the enemy opened his batteries upon the place, and was replied to from the gunboats and the garrison. The gunboats becoming disabled were set on fire, as also were the transports, to prevent their falling into the hands of the enemy. About a million and a half dollars' worth of stores and property on the levee and in storehouses was consumed by fire. On the 5th the enemy disappeared and crossed to the north side of the Tennessee River, above Johnsonville, moving towards Clifton, and subsequently joined Hood. On the night of the 5th, General Schofield, with the advance of the 23d corps, reached Johnsonville, but finding the enemy gone, was ordered to Pulaski, and put in command of all the troops there, with instructions to watch the movements of Hood and retard his advance, but not to risk a general engagement until the arrival of General A.J. Smith's command from Missouri, and until General Wilson could get his cavalry remounted.

On the 19th, General Hood continued his advance. General Thomas, retarding him as much as possible, fell back towards Nashville for the purpose of concentrating his command and gaining time for the arrival of reinforcements. The enemy coming up with our main force, commanded by General Schofield, at Franklin, on the 30th, assaulted our works repeatedly during the afternoon until late at night, but were in every instance repulsed. His loss in this battle was one thousand seven hundred and fifty killed, seven hundred and two prisoners, and three thousand eight hundred wounded. Among his losses were six general officers killed, six wounded, and one captured. Our entire loss was two thousand three hundred. This was the first serious opposition the enemy met with, and I am satisfied was the fatal blow to all his expectations. During the night, General Schofield fell back towards Nashville. This left the field to the enemy, not lost by battle, but voluntarily abandoned so that General Thomas's whole force might be brought together. The enemy followed up and commenced the establishment of his line in front of Nashville on the 2d of December.

As soon as it was ascertained that Hood was crossing the Tennessee River, and that Price was going out of Missouri, General Rosecrans was ordered to send to General Thomas the troops of General

A. J. Smith's command, and such other troops as he could spare. The advance of this reinforcement reached Nashville on the 3Oth of November.

On the morning of the l5th December, General Thomas attacked Hood in position, and, in a battle lasting two days, defeated and drove him from the field in the utmost confusion, leaving in our hands most of his artillery and many thousand prisoners, including four general officers.

Before the battle of Nashville I grew very impatient over, as it appeared to me, the unnecessary delay. This impatience was increased upon learning that the enemy had sent a force of cavalry across the Cumberland into Kentucky. I feared Hood would cross his whole army and give us great trouble there. After urging upon General Thomas the necessity of immediately assuming the offensive, I started West to superintend matters there in person. Reaching Washington City, I received General Thomas's dispatch announcing his attack upon the enemy, and the result as far as the battle had progressed. I was delighted. All fears and apprehensions were dispelled. I am not yet satisfied but that General Thomas, immediately upon the appearance of Hood before Nashville, and before he had time to Fortify, should have moved out with his whole force and given him battle, instead of waiting to remount his cavalry, which delayed him until the inclemency of the weather made it impracticable to attack earlier than he did. But his final defeat of Hood was so complete, that it will be accepted as a vindication of that distinguished officer's judgment.

After Hood's defeat at Nashville he retreated, closely pursued by cavalry and infantry, to the Tennessee River, being forced to abandon many pieces of artillery and most of his transportation. On the 28th of December our advanced forces ascertained that he had made good his escape to the south side of the river.

About this time, the rains having set in heavily in Tennessee and North Alabama, making it difficult to move army transportation and artillery, General Thomas stopped the pursuit by his main force at the Tennessee River. A small force of cavalry, under Colonel W.J. Palmer,

15th Pennsylvania Volunteers, continued to follow Hood for some distance, capturing considerable transportation and the enemy's pontoon bridge. The details of these operations will be found clearly set forth in General Thomas's report.

A cavalry expedition, under Brevet Major-General Grierson, started from Memphis on the 21st of December. On the 25th he surprised and captured Forrest's dismounted camp at Verona, Mississippi, on the Mobile and Ohio Railroad, destroyed the railroad, sixteen cars loaded with wagons and pontoons for Hood's army, four thousand new English carbines, and large amounts of public stores. On the morning of the 28th he attacked and captured a force of the enemy at Egypt, and destroyed a train of fourteen cars; thence turning to the southwest, he struck the Mississippi Central Railroad at Winona, destroyed the factories and large amounts of stores at Bankston, and the machine shops and public property at Grenada, arriving at Vicksburg January 5th.

During these operations in Middle Tennessee, the enemy, with a force under General Breckinridge, entered East Tennessee. On the 13th of November he attacked General Gillem, near Morristown, capturing his artillery and several hundred prisoners. Gillem, with what was left of his command, retreated to Knoxville. Following up his success, Breckinridge moved to near Knoxville, but withdrew on the 18th, followed by General Ammen. Under the directions of General Thomas, General Stoneman concentrated the commands of Generals Burbridge and Gillem near Bean's Station, to operate against Breckinridge, and destroy or drive him into Virginia, destroy the salt works at Saltville, and the railroad into Virginia as far as he could go without endangering his command. On the 12th of December he commenced his movement, capturing and dispersing the enemy's forces wherever he met them. On the 16th he struck the enemy, under Vaughn, at Marion, completely routing and pursuing him to Wytheville, capturing all his artillery, trains, and one hundred and ninety-eight prisoners; and destroyed Wytheville, with its stores and supplies, and the extensive lead works near there.

Returning to Marion, he met a force under Breckinridge, consisting, among other troops, of the garrison of Saltville that had started in pursuit. He at once made arrangements to attack it the next morning; but morning found Breckinridge gone. He then moved directly to Saltville, and destroyed the extensive salt works at that place, a large amount of stores, and captured eight pieces of artillery. Having thus successfully executed his instructions, he returned General Burbridge to Lexington and General Gillem to Knoxville.

Wilmington, North Carolina, was the most important seacoast port left to the enemy through which to get supplies from abroad, and send cotton and other products out by blockade runners, besides being a place of great strategic value. The navy had been making strenuous exertions to seal the harbor of Wilmington, but with only partial effect. The nature of the outlet of Cape Fear River was such, that it required matching for so great a distance that, without possession of the land north of New Inlet, or Fort Fisher, it was impossible for the navy to entirely close the harbor against the entrance of blockade runners.

To secure the possession of this land required the cooperation of a land force, which I agreed to furnish. Immediately commenced the assemblage in Hampton Roads, under Admiral D.D. Porter, of the most formidable armada ever collected for concentration upon one given point. This necessarily attracted the attention of the enemy, as well as that of the loyal North; and through the imprudence of the public press, and very likely of officers of both branches of service, the exact object of the expedition became a subject of common discussion in the newspapers both North and South. The enemy, thus warned, prepared to meet it. This caused a postponement of the expedition until the later part of November, when, being again called upon by Hon. G.V. Fox, Assistant Secretary of the Navy, I agreed to furnish the men required at once, and went myself, in company with Major-General Butler, to Hampton Roads, where we had a conference with Admiral Porter as to the force required and the time of starting. A force of six thousand five hundred men was regarded as sufficient. The time of starting was not definitely arranged, but it was thought all would be ready by the 6th of December, if not before. Learning, on the 30th of November, that Bragg had gone to Georgia, taking with him most of the forces about Wilmington, I deemed it of the utmost importance that the expedition should reach its destination before the return of Bragg, and directed General Butler to make all arrangements for the departure of Major-General Weitzel, who had been designated to command the land forces, so that the navy might not be detained one moment.

On the 6th of December, the following instructions were given:

"CITY POINT, VIRGINIA,
December 6, 1864.

" GENERAL :-The first object of the expedition under General Weitzel is to close to the enemy the port of Wilmington. If successful in this, the second will be to capture Wilmington itself. There are reasonable grounds to hope for success, if advantage can be taken of the absence of the greater part of the enemy's forces now looking after Sherman in Georgia. The directions you have given for the numbers and equipment of the expedition are all right, except in the unimportant matter of where they embark and the amount of intrenching tools to be taken. The object of the expedition will be gained by effecting a landing on the main land between Cape Fear River and the Atlantic, north of the north entrance to the river. Should such landing be effected while the enemy still holds Fort Fisher and the batteries guarding the entrance to the river, then the troops should intrench themselves, and, by cooperating with the navy, effect the reduction and capture of those places. These in our hands, the navy could enter the harbor, and the port of Wilmington would be sealed. Should Fort Fisher and the point of land on which it is built fall into the hands of our troops immediately on landing, then it will be worth the attempt to capture Wilmington by a forced march and surprise. If time is consumed in gaining the first object of the expedition, the second will become a matter of after consideration.

The details for execution are intrusted to you and the officer immediately in command of the troops.

"Should the troops under General Weitzel fail to effect a landing at or near Fort Fisher, they will be returned to the armies operating against Richmond without delay.

"U. S. GRANT, Lieutenant-General.

"MAJOR GENERAL B. F. BUTLER."

General Butler commanding the army from which the troops were taken for this enterprise, and the territory within which they were to operate, military courtesy required that all orders and instructions should go through him. They were so sent; but General Weitzel has since officially informed me that he never received the foregoing instructions, nor was he aware of their existence, until he read General Butler's published official report of the Fort Fisher failure, with my indorsement and papers accompanying it. I had no idea of General Butler's accompanying the expedition until the evening before it got off from Bermuda Hundred, and then did not dream but that General Weitzel had received all the instructions, and would be in command. I rather formed the idea that General Butler was actuated by a desire to witness the effect of the explosion of the powder boat. The expedition was detained several days at Hampton Roads, awaiting the loading of the powder boat.

The importance of getting the Wilmington expedition off without any delay, with or without the powder boat, had been urged upon General Butler, and he advised to so notify Admiral Porter.

The expedition finally got off on the 13th of December, and arrived at the place of rendezvous, off New Inlet, near Fort Fisher; on the evening of the 15th. Admiral Porter arrived on the evening of the 18th, having put in at Beaufort to get ammunition for the monitors. The sea becoming rough, making it difficult to land troops, and the supply of water and coal being about exhausted, the transport fleet put back to Beaufort to replenish ; this, with the state of the weather, delayed the return to the place of rendezvous until the 24th. The powder boat was exploded on the morning of the 24th, before the return of General Butler from Beaufort ; but it would seem, from the notice taken of it in the

Southern newspapers, that the enemy were never enlightened as to the object of the explosion until they mere informed by the Northern press.

On the 25th a landing was effected without opposition, and a reconnaissance, under Brevet Brigadier-General Curtis, pushed up towards the fort. But before receiving a full report of the result of this reconnaissance, General Butler, in direct violation of the instructions given, ordered the re-embarkation of the troops and the return of the expedition. The re-embarkation was accomplished by the morning of the 27th.

On the return of the expedition, officers and men among them Brevet Major-General (then Brevet Brigadier-General) N.M. Curtis, First Lieutenant G. W. Ross, 117th Regiment New York Volunteers, First Lieutenant William H. Walling, and Second Lieutenant George Simpson, 142nd New York Volunteers, voluntarily reported to me that when recalled they were nearly into the fort, and, in their opinion, it could have been taken without much loss.

Soon after the return of the expedition, I received a dispatch from the Secretary of the Navy, and a letter from Admiral Porter, informing me that the fleet was still off Fort Fisher, and expressing the conviction that, under a proper leader, the place could be taken. The natural supposition with me was, that when the troops abandoned the expedition, the navy would do so also. Finding it had not, however, I answered on the 30th of December, advising Admiral Porter to hold on, and that I would send a force and make another attempt to take the place. This time I selected Brevet Major-General (now Major-General) A. H. Terry to command the expedition. The troops composing it consisted of the same that composed the former, with the addition of a small brigade, numbering about one thousand five hundred, and a small siege train. The latter it was never found necessary to land. I communicated direct to the commander of the expedition the following instructions:

"GENERAL :-The expedition intrusted to your command has been fitted out to renew the attempt to capture Fort Fisher, N.C., and Wilmington ultimately, if the fort falls. You will then proceed with as little delay as possible to the naval fleet lying off Cape Fear River, and report the arrival of yourself and command to Admiral D.D. Porter, commanding North Atlantic Blockading Squadron.

"It is exceedingly desirable that the most complete understanding should exist between yourself and the naval commander. I suggest, therefore, that you consult with Admiral Porter freely, and get from him the part to be performed by each branch of the public service, so that there may be unity of action. It would be well to have the whole programme laid down in writing. I hare served with Admiral Porter, and know that you can rely on his judgment and his nerve to undertake what he proposes. I would, therefore, defer to him as much as is consistent with your own responsibilities. The first object to be attained is to get a firm position on the spit of land on which Fort Fisher is built, from which you can operate against that fort. You want to look to the practicability of receiving your supplies, and to defending yourself against superior forces sent against you by any of the avenues left open to the enemy. If such a position call be obtained, the siege of Fort Fisher will not be abandoned until its reduction is accomplished, or another plan of campaign is ordered from these headquarters.

"My own views are, that if you effect a landing, the navy ought to run a portion of their fleet into Cape Fear River, while the balance of it operates on the outside. Land forces cannot invest Fort Fisher, or cut it off from supplies or reinforcements, while the river is in possession of the enemy.

"A siege train will be loaded on vessels and sent to Fort Monroe, in readiness to be sent to you if required. All other supplies can be drawn from Beaufort as you need them.

"Keep the fleet of vessels with you until your position is assured. When you find they can be spared, order them back, or such of them as you can spare, to Fort Monroe to report for orders.

"In case of failure to effect a landing, bring your command back to Beaufort, and report to these headquarters for further instructions. You will not debark at Beaufort until so directed.

"General Sheridan has been ordered to send a division of troops to Baltimore and place them on sea going vessels. These troops will be brought to Fort Monroe and kept there on the vessels until you are heard from. Should you require them, they will be sent to you.

"U.S. GRANT, Lieutenant-General.

"BREVET MAJOR-GENERAL A. H. TERRY."

Lieutenant Colonel C.B. Comstock, aide-de-camp (now brevet brigadier-general), who accompanied the former expedition, was assigned, in orders, as chief engineer to this.

It will be seen that these instructions did not differ materially from those given for the first expedition; and that in neither instance was there an order to assault Fort Fisher. This was a matter left entirely to the discretion of the commanding officer.

The expedition sailed from Fort Monroe on the morning of the 6th, arriving at the rendezvous, off Beaufort, on the 8th, where, owing to the difficulties of the weather; it lay until the morning of the 12th, when it got under way and reached its destination that evening. Under cover of the fleet, the disembarkation of the troops commenced on the morning of the 13th, and by three o'clock P.M. was completed without loss. On the 14th a reconnaissance was pushed to within five hundred yards of Fort Fisher, and a small advance work taken possession of and turned into a defensive line against any attempt that might be made from the fort. This reconnaissance disclosed the fact that the front of the work had been seriously injured by the navy fire. In the afternoon of the 15th the fort was assaulted, and after most desperate fighting was captured, with its entire garrison and armament. Thus was secured, by the combined efforts of the navy and army, one of the most important successes of the war. Our loss was: killed, one hundred and ten, wounded five hundred and thirty-six. On the 16th and 17th the enemy abandoned and blew up Fort Caswell and the works on Smith's Island, which mere immediately occupied by us. This gave us entire control of the mouth of the Cape Fear River.

At my request, Major-General B.F. Butler was relieved, and Major-General E. O.C. Ord assigned to the Department of Virginia and North Carolina.

The defence of the line of the Tennessee no longer requiring the force which had beaten and nearly destroyed the only army now threatening it, I determined to find other fields of operation for General Thomas's surplus troops, fields from which they would cooperate with other movements. General Thomas was therefore directed to collect all troops, not essential to hold his communications at Eastport, in readiness for orders. On the 7th of January, General Thomas was directed, if he was assured of the departure of Hood south from Corinth, to send General Schofield with his corps east with as little delay as possible. This direction was promptly complied with, and the advance of the corps reached Washington on the 23d of the same month, whence it was sent to Fort Fisher and New Bern. On the 26th he was directed to send General A. J. Smith's command and a division of cavalry to report to General Canby. By the 7th of February the whole force was *en route* for its destination.

The State of north Carolina was constituted into a military department, and Genera: Schofield assigned to command, and placed under the orders of Major-General Sherman. The following instructions mere given him:

"CITY POINT VA., January 31, 1865.

" GENERAL :-* * * Your movements are intended as cooperative with Sherman's through the States of South and North Carolina. The first point to be attained is to secure Wilmington.. Goldsboro' will then be your objective point, moving either from Wilmington or New Bern, or both, as you deem best. Should you not be able to reach Goldsboro', you will advance on the line or lines of railway connecting that place with the sea coast, as near to it as you can, building the road behind you. The enterprise under you has two objects: the first is to give General Sherman material aid, if needed, in his march north; the second, to open a base of supplies for him on his line of march. As soon, therefore, as you can determine which of the two points, Wilmington or New Bern, you can best use for throwing supplies from, to the interior, you will commence the accumulation of twenty days' rations and forage for sixty thousand men and twenty thousand animals. You will get of these as many as you can house and protect to such point in the interior as you may be able to occupy. I believe General Palmer has received some instructions direct from General Sherman on the subject of securing supplies for his army. You mill learn what steps he has taken, and be governed in your requisitions accordingly. A supply of ordnance stores will also be necessary.

"Make all requisitions upon the chiefs of their respective departments in the field with me at City Point. Communicate with me by every opportunity, and should you deem it necessary at any time, send a special boat to Fortress Monroe, from which point you can communicate by telegraph.

"The supplies referred to in these instructions are exclusive of those required for your own command.

"The movements of the enemy may justify, or even make it your imperative duty, to cut loose from your base, and strike for the interior to aid Sherman. In such case you will act on your own judgment without waiting for instructions. You will report, however, what you purpose doing. The details for carrying out these instructions are necessarily left to you. I would urge, however, if I did not know that you are already fully alive to the importance of it, prompt action. Sherman may be looked for in the neighborhood of Goldsboro' any time from the 22nd to the 26th of February; this limits your time very materially.

"If rolling-stock is not secured in the capture of Wilmington, it can be supplied from Washington. A large force of railroad men have already been sent to Beaufort, and other mechanics will go to Fort Fisher in a day or two.
On this point I have informed you by telegraph.

" U.S. GRANT, Lieutenant-General.
"MAJOR-GENERAL J.M. SCHOFIELD"

Previous to giving these instructions I had visited Fort Fisher, accompanied by General Schofield, for the purpose of seeing for myself the condition of things, and personally conferring with General Terry and Admiral Porter as to what was best to be done.

Anticipating the arrival of General Sherman at Savannah, his army entirely foot-loose, Hood being then before Nashville, Tennessee, the Southern railroads destroyed, so that it would take several months to reestablish a through line from west to east, and regarding the capture of Lee's army as the most important operation towards closing the rebellion, I sent orders to General Sherman on the 6th of December, that after establishing a base on the sea coast, with necessary garrison, to include all his artillery and cavalry, to come by water to City Point with the balance of his command.

On the 18th of December, having received information of the defeat and utter rout of Hood's army by General Thomas, and that, owing to the great difficulty of procuring ocean transportation, it would take over two months to transport Sherman's army, and doubting whether he might not contribute as much towards the desired result by operating from where he was, I wrote to him to that effect, and asked him for his views as to what would be best to do. A few days after this I received a communication from General Sherman, of date 16th December, acknowledging the receipt of my order of the 6th, and informing me of his preparations to carry it into effect as soon as he could get transportation. Also that he had expected, upon reducing Savannah, instantly to march to Columbia, South Carolina, thence to Raleigh, and thence to report to me ; but that this would consume about six weeks ' time after the fall of Savannah, whereas by sea he could probably reach me by the middle of January. The confidence he manifested in this letter of being able to march up and join me pleased me, and, without waiting for a reply to my letter of the 18th, I directed him, on the 28th of December, to make preparations to start, as he proposed, without delay; to break up the railroads in North and South Carolina, and join the armies operating against Richmond as soon as he could.

On the 21st of January I informed General Sherman that I had ordered the 23d corps, Major-General Schofield commanding, east ; that it numbered about twenty-one thousand men ; that we had at Fort Fisher, about eight thousand men ; at New Bern, about four thousand ; that if Wilmington was captured, General Schofield would go there ; if not, he would be sent to New Bern ; that, in either event, all the surplus force at both points would move to the interior towards Goldsboro', in cooperation with his movement ; that from either point railroad communication could be run out ; and that all these troops would be subject to his orders as he came into communication with them.

In obedience to his instructions, General Schofield proceeded to reduce Wilmington, North Carolina, in cooperation with the navy under Admiral Porter, moving his forces up both sides of the Cape Fear River. Fort Anderson, the enemy's main defence on the west bank of the river, was occupied on the morning of the 19th, the enemy having evacuated it after our appearance before it.

After fighting on 20th and 21st, our troops entered Wilmington on the morning of the 22nd, the enemy having retreated towards Goldsboro' during the night. Preparations were at once made for a movement on Goldsboro' in two columns, one from Wilmington, and the other from New Bernand to repair the railroad leading there from each place, as well as to supply General Sherman by Cape Fear River, towards Fayetteville, if it became necessary. The column from New Bern was attacked on the 8th of March, at Wise's Forks, and driven back with the loss of several hundred prisoners. On the 11th the enemy renewed his attack upon our intrenched position, but was repulsed with severe loss, and fell back during the night. On the 13th the Neuse River was crossed and Kinston occupied, and on the 21st Goldsboro' was entered. The column from Wilmington reached Cox's Bridge, on the Neuse River, ten miles above Goldsboro', on the 22nd.

By the 1st of February, General Sherman's whole army was in motion from Savannah. We captured Columbia, South Carolina, on the 17th; thence moved on Goldsboro', North Carolina, via Fayetteville, reaching the latter place on the 12th of March, opening up communication with General Schofield by way of Cape Fear River. On the 15th he resumed his march on Goldsboro'. He met a force of the enemy at Averysboro', and after a severe fight defeated and compelled it to retreat. Our loss in this engagement was about six hundred. The enemy's loss was much greater. On the 18th the combined forces of the enemy, under Joe Johnston, attacked his advance at Bentonville, capturing three guns and driving it back upon the main body. General Slocum, who was in the advance, ascertaining that the whole of Johnston's army was in the front, arranged his troops on the defensive, intrenched himself and awaited reinforcements, which were pushed forward. On the night of the 21st the enemy retreated to Smithfield, leaving his dead and wounded in our hands. From there Sherman continued to Goldsboro', which place had been occupied by General Schofield on the 21st (crossing the Neuse River ten miles above there, at Cox's Bridge, where General Terry had got possession and thrown a pontoon bridge on the 22nd), thus forming a junction with the columns from New Bern and Wilmington.

Among the important fruits of this campaign was the fall of Charleston, South Carolina. It was evacuated by the enemy on the night of the 17th of February, and occupied by our forces on the 18th.

On the morning of the 31st of January, General Thomas was directed to send a cavalry expedition, under General Stoneman, from East Tennessee, to penetrate South Carolina well down towards Columbia, to destroy the railroads and military resources of the country, and return, if he was able, to East Tennessee by way of Salisbury, North Carolina, releasing our prisoners there, if possible. Of the feasibility of this latter, however, General Stoneman was to judge. Sherman's movements, I had no doubt, would attract the attention of all the force the enemy could collect, and facilitate the execution of this. General Stoneman was so late in making his start on this expedition (and Sherman having passed out of the State of South Carolina), on the 27th of February I directed General Thomas to change his course, and order him to repeat his raid of last fall, destroying the railroad towards Lynchburg as far as he could. This would keep him between our garrisons in East Tennessee and the enemy. I regarded it not impossible that in the event of the enemy being driven from Richmond, he might fall back to Lynchburg and attempt a raid north through East Tennessee. On the 14th of February the following communication was sent to General Thomas:

"CITY POINT, VA., February 14, 1865.

"General Canby is preparing a movement from Mobile Bay against Mobile and the interior of Alabama. His force will consist of about twenty thousand men, besides A. J. Smith's command. The cavalry you have sent to Canby will be debarked at Vicksburg. It, with the available cavalry already in that section, will move from there eastward, in cooperation. Hood's army has been terribly reduced by the severe punishment you save it in Tennessee, by desertion consequent upon their defeat, and now by the withdrawal of many of them to oppose Sherman. (I take it a large portion of the infantry has been so withdrawn. It is so asserted in the Richmond papers, and a member of the rebel Congress said a few days since in a speech, that one-half of it had been brought to South Carolina to oppose Sherman) this being true, or even if it is not true. Canby's movement will attract all the attention of the enemy, and leave the advance from your standpoint easy. I think it advisable, therefore, that you prepare as much of a cavalry force as you can spare, and hold it in readiness to go south. The object would be threefold: first, to attract as much of the enemy's force as possible, to insure success to Canby; second, to destroy the enemy's line of communications and military resources; third, to destroy or capture their forces brought into the field. Tuscaloosa and Selma would probably be the points to direct the expedition against. This, however, would not be so important as the mere fact of penetrating deep into Alabama. Discretion should be left to the officer commanding the expedition to go where, according to the information he may receive; he will best secure the objects named above.

"Now that your force has been so much depleted, I do not know what number of men you can put into the field. If not more than five thousand men, however, all cavalry, I think it will be sufficient. It is not desirable that you should start this expedition until the one leaving Vicksburg has been three or four days out, or even a week. I do not know when it will start, but will inform you by telegraph as soon as I learn. If you should hear through other sources before hearing from me, you can act on the information received.

"To insure success your cavalry should go with as little wagon train as possible, relying upon the country for supplies. I would also reduce the number of guns to a battery, or the number of batteries, and put the extra teams to the guns taken. No guns or caissons should be taken with less than eight horses.

"Please inform me by telegraph, on receipt of this, what force you think you will be able to send under these directions.

"U.S. GRANT, Lieutenant-General.

"MAJOR-GENERAL G.H. THOMAS."

On the 15th, he was directed to start the expedition as soon after the 20th as he could get it off. I deemed it of the utmost importance, before a general movement of the armies operating against Richmond, that all communications with the city, north of James River, should be cut off. The enemy having withdrawn the bulk of his force from the Shenandoah Valley and sent it south, or replaced troops sent from Richmond, and desiring to reinforce Sherman, if practicable, whose cavalry was greatly inferior in numbers to that of the enemy, I determined to make a move from the Shenandoah, which, if successful, would accomplish the first at least, and possibly the latter of these objects. I therefore telegraphed General Sheridan as follows:

"CITY POINT, VA., February 20, 1865-1 P.M.

"GENERAL :-As soon as it is possible to travel, I think you will have no difficulty about reaching Lynchburg with a cavalry force alone. From there you could destroy the railroad and canal in every direction, so as to be of no further use to the rebellion. Sufficient cavalry should be left behind to look after Mosby's gang. From Lynchburg, if information you might get there would justify it, you will strike south, heading the streams in Virginia to the westward of Danville, and push on and join General Sherman. This additional raid, with one now about starting from East Tennessee under Stoneman, numbering four or five thousand cavalry, one from Vicksburg, numbering seven or eight thousand cavalry, one from Eastport, Mississippi, ten thousand cavalry, Canby from Mobile Bay, with about thirty-eight thousand mixed troops, these three latter pushing for Tuscaloosa, Selma, and Montgomery, and Sherman with a large army eating out the vitals of South Carolina, is all that will be wanted to leave nothing for the rebellion to stand upon. I would advise you to overcome great obstacles to accomplish this. Charleston was evacuated on Tuesday last.

"U. S. GRANT, Lieutenant-General.
"MAJOR-GENERAL P. H. SHERIDAN.

On the 25th I received a dispatch from General Sheridan, inquiring where Sherman was aiming for, and if I could give him definite information as to the points he might be expected to move on, this side of Charlotte, North Carolina. In answer, the following telegram was sent him:

"CITY POINT, VA., January 25, 1865.

"GENERAL:-Sherman's movements will depend on the amount of opposition he meets with from the enemy. If strongly opposed, he may possibly have to fall back to Georgetown, S.C., and fit out for a new start. I think, however, all danger for the necessity of going to that point has passed. I believe he has passed Charlotte. He may take Fayetteville on his way to Goldsboro'. If you reach Lynchburg, you will have to be guided in your after movements by the information you obtain. Before you could possibly reach Sherman, I think you would find him moving from Goldsboro ' towards Raleigh, or engaging the enemy strongly posted at one or the other of these places, with railroad communications opened from his army to Wilmington or New Bern.

"U.S. GRANT, Lieutenant-General.

"MAJOR-GENERAL P.H. SHERIDAN..

General Sheridan moved from Winchester on the 27th of February, with two divisions of cavalry, numbering about five thousand each. On the 1st of March he secured the bridge, which the enemy attempted to destroy, across the middle fork of the Shenandoah, at Mount Crawford, and entered Staunton on the 2d, the enemy having retreated on Waynesboro '. Thence he pushed on to Waynesboro', where he found the enemy in force in an intrenched position, under General Early. Without stopping to make a reconnaissance, an immediate attack was made, the position was carried, and sixteen hundred prisoners, eleven pieces of artillery, with horses and caissons complete, two hundred wagons and teams loaded with subsistence, and seventeen battle flags, were captured. The prisoners, under an escort of fifteen hundred men, were sent back to Winchester. Thence he marched on Charlottesville, destroying effectually the railroad and bridges as he went which place he reached on the 3rd. Here he remained two days, destroying the railroad towards Richmond and Lynchburg, including the large iron bridges over the north and south forks of the Rivanna River and awaited the arrival of his trains. This necessary delay caused him to abandon the idea of capturing Lynchburg. On the morning of the 6th, dividing his force into two columns, he sent one to Scottsville, whence it marched up the James River Canal to New Market, destroying every lock, and in many places the bank of the canal. From here a force was pushed out from this column to Duiguidsville, to obtain possession of the bridge across the James River at that place, but failed. The enemy burned it on our approach. The enemy also burned the bridge across the river at Hardwicksville. The other column moved down the railroad towards Lynchburg, destroying it as far as Amherst Court House, sixteen miles from Lynchburg; thence across the country, uniting with the column at New Market. The river being very high, his pontoons would not reach across it; and the enemy having destroyed the bridges by which he had hoped to cross the river and get on the South Side Railroad about Farmville, and destroy it to Appomattox Court House, the only thing left for him was to return to Winchester or strike a base at the White House. Fortunately, he chose the latter. From New Market he took up his line of march, following the canal towards Richmond, destroying every lock upon it and cutting the banks wherever practicable, to a point eight miles east of Goochland, concentrating the whole force at Columbia on the 10th. Here he rested one day, and sent through by scouts information of his whereabouts and purposes, and a request for supplies to meet him at White House, which reached me on the night of the 12th. An infantry force was immediately sent to get possession of White House, and supplies were forwarded. Moving from Columbia in a direction to threaten Richmond, to near Ashland Station, he crossed the Annas, and after having destroyed all the bridges and many miles of the railroad, proceeded down the north bank of the Pamunkey to White House, which place he reached on the 19th.

Previous to this the following communication was sent to General Thomas:

"CITY POINT, VIRGINIA, March 7, 1865-9:30 A.M.

" GENERAL :-I think it will be advisable nom for you to repair the railroad in East Tennessee, and throw a good force up to Bull 's Gap and fortify there. Supplies at Knoxville could always be got forward as required. With Bull's Gap fortified, you can occupy as outposts about all of East Tennessee, and be prepared, if it should be required of you in the spring, to make a campaign towards Lynchburg, or into North Carolina. I do not think Stoneman should break the road until he gets into Virginia, unless it should be to cut off rolling stock that may be caught west of that.

"U.S. GRANT, Lieutenant-General.

"MAJOR GENERAL G. H. THOMAS."

Thus it will be seen that in March, 1865, General Canby was moving an adequate force against Mobile and the army defending it under General Dick Taylor; Thomas was pushing out two large and well appointed cavalry expeditions, one from Middle Tennessee under Brevet Major-General Wilson against the enemy's vital points in Alabama, the other from East Tennessee, under Major-General Stoneman, towards Lynchburg and assembling the remainder of his available forces, preparatory to commence offensive operations from East Tennessee ; General Sheridan's cavalry was at White House; the armies of the Potomac and James were confronting the enemy, under Lee, in his defences of Richmond and Petersburg; General Sherman with his armies, reinforced by that of General Schofield, was at Goldsboro'; General Pope was making preparations for a spring campaign against the enemy under Kirby Smith and Price, west of the Mississippi; and General Hancock was concentrating a force in the vicinity of Winchester, Virginia, to guard against invasion or to operate offensively, as might prove necessary.

After the long march by General Sheridan's cavalry over winter roads, it was necessary to rest and refit at White House. At this time the greatest source of uneasiness to me was the fear that the enemy would leave his strong lines about Petersburg and Richmond for the purpose of uniting with Johnston, before he was driven from them by battle, or I was prepared to make an effectual pursuit. On the 24th of March,

404

General Sheridan moved from White House, crossed the James River at Jones's Landing, and formed a junction with the Army of the Potomac in front of Petersburg on the 27th. During this move, General Ord sent forces to cover the crossings of the Chickahominy.

On the 24th of March the following instructions for a general movement of the armies operating against Richmond were issued:

"CITY POINT, VIRGINIA, March 24, 1865.

"GENERAL :--On the 29th instant the armies operating against Richmond will be moved by our left, for the double purpose of turning the enemy out of his present position around Petersburg, and to insure the success of the cavalry under General Sheridan, which will start at the same time, in its efforts to reach and destroy the South Side and Danville railroads. Two corps of the Army of the Potomac will be moved at first in two columns, taking the two roads crossing Hatcher's Run, nearest where the present line held by us strikes that stream, both moving towards Dinwiddie Court House.

"The cavalry under General Sheridan, joined by the division now under General Davies, will move at the same time by the Weldon Road and the Jerusalem Plank Road, turning west from the latter before crossing the Nottoway, and west with the whole column before reaching Stony Creek. General Sheridan will then move independently, under other instructions which will be given him. All dismounted cavalry belonging to the Army of the Potomac, and the dismounted cavalry from the Middle Military Division not required for guarding property belonging to their arm of service, will report to Brigadier-General Benham, to be added to the defences of City Point. Major-General Parke will be left in command of all the army left for holding the lines about Petersburg and City Point, subject of course to orders from the commander of the Army of the Potomac. The 9th army corps will be left intact, to hold the present line of works so long as the whole line now occupied by us is held. If, however, the troops to the left of the 9th corps are withdrawn, then the left of the corps may be thrown back so as to occupy the position held by the army prior to the capture of the Weldon Road. All troops to the left of the 9th corps will be held in readiness to move at the shortest notice by such route as may be designated when the order is given.

"General Ord will detach three divisions, two white and one colored, or so much of them as he can, and hold his present lines, and march for the present left of the Army of the Potomac. In the absence of further orders, or until further orders are given, the white divisions will follow the left column of the Army of the Potomac, and the colored division the right column. During the movement Major-General Weitzel will be left in command of all the forces remaining behind from the Army of the James.

"The movement of troops from the Army of the James will commence on the night of the 27th instant. General Ord will leave behind the minimum number of cavalry necessary for picket duty, in the absence of the main army. A cavalry expedition, from General Ord's command, will also be started from Suffolk, to leave there on Saturday, the 1st of April, under Colonel Sumner, for the purpose of cutting the railroad about Hicksford. This, if accomplished, will have to be a surprise, and therefore from three to five hundred men will be sufficient. They should, however, be supported by all the infantry that can be spared from Norfolk and Portsmouth, as far out as to where the cavalry crosses the Blackwater. The crossing should probably be at Uniten. Should Colonel Sumner succeed in reaching the Weldon Road, he will be instructed to do all the damage possible to the triangle of roads between Hicksford, Weldon, and Gaston. The railroad bridge at Weldon being fitted up for the passage of carnages, it might be practicable to destroy any accumulation of supplies the enemy may have collected south of the Roanoke. All the troops will move with four days' rations in haversacks and eight days' in wagons. To avoid as much hauling as possible, and to give the Army of the James the same number of days' supplies with the Army of the Potomac, General Ord will direct his commissary and quartermaster to have sufficient supplies delivered at the terminus of the road to fill up in passing. Sixty rounds of ammunition per man will be taken in wagons, and as much grain as the transportation on hand will carry, after taking the specified amount of other supplies. The densely wooded country in which the army has to operate making the use of much artillery impracticable, the amount taken with the army will be reduced to six or eight guns to each division, at the option of the army commanders.

"All necessary preparations for carrying these directions into operation may be commenced at once. The reserves of the 9th corps should be massed as much as possible. While I would not now order an unconditional attack on the enemy's line by them, they should be ready and should make the attack if the enemy weakens his line in their front, without waiting for orders. In case they carry the line, then the whole of the 9th corps could follow up so as to join or cooperate with the balance of the army. To prepare for this, the 9th corps will have rations issued to them, same as the balance of the army. General Weitzel will keep vigilant watch upon his front, and if found at all practicable to break through at any point, he will do so. A success north of the James should be followed up with great promptness.

An attack will not be feasible unless it is found that the enemy has detached largely. In that case it may be regarded as evident that the enemy are relying upon their local reserves principally for the defence of Richmond. Preparations may be made for abandoning all the line north of the James, except enclosed works only to be abandoned, however, after a break is made in the lines of the enemy.

"By these instructions a large part of the armies operating against Richmond is left behind. The enemy, knowing this, may, as an only chance, strip their lines to the merest skeleton, in the hope of advantage not being taken of it, while they hurl everything against the moving column, and return. It cannot be impressed too strongly upon commanders of troops left in the trenches not to allow this to occur without taking advantage of it. The very fact of the enemy coming out to attack, if he does so, might be regarded as almost conclusive evidence of such a weakening of his lines. I would have it particularly enjoined upon corps commanders that, in case of an attack from the enemy, those not attacked are not to wait for orders from the commanding officer of the army to which they belong, but that they will move promptly, and notify the commander of their action. I would also enjoin the same action on the part of division commanders when other parts of their corps are engaged. In like manner, I would urge the importance of following up a repulse of the enemy.

"U.S. GRANT, Lieutenant-General.

"MAJOR-GENERALS MEADE, ORD, and SHERIDAN."

Early on the morning of the 25th the enemy assaulted our lines in front of the 9th corps (which held from the Appomattox River towards our left), and carried Fort Stedman, and a part of the line to the right and left of it, established themselves and turned the guns of the fort against us; but our troops on either flank held their ground until the reserves were brought up, when the enemy was driven back with a heavy loss in killed and wounded, and one thousand nine hundred prisoners. Our loss was sixty-eight killed, three hundred and thirty-seven wounded, and five hundred and six missing. General Meade at once ordered the other corps to advance and feel the enemy in their respective fronts. Pushing forward, they captured and held the enemy's strongly intrenched picket line in front of the 2d and 6th corps, and eight hundred and thirty-four prisoners. The enemy made desperate attempts to retake this line, but without success. Our loss in front of these was fifty-two killed, eight hundred and sixty-four wounded, and two hundred and seven missing. The enemy's loss in killed and wounded was far greater.

General Sherman having got his troops all quietly in camp about Goldsboro', and his preparations for furnishing supplies to them perfected, visited me at City Point on the 27th of March, and stated that he would be ready to move, as he had previously written me, by the 10th of April, fully equipped and rationed for twenty days, if it should become necessary to bring his command to bear against Lee's army, in cooperation with our forces in front of Richmond and Petersburg. General Sherman proposed in this movement to threaten Raleigh, and then, by turning suddenly to the right, reach the Roanoke at Gaston or thereabouts, whence he could move on to the Richmond and Danville Railroad, striking it in the vicinity of Burkesville, or join the armies operating against Richmond, as might be deemed best This plan he was directed to carry into execution, if he received no further directions in the meantime. I explained to him the movement I had ordered to commence on the 29th of March. That if it should not prove as entirely successful as I hoped, I would cut the cavalry loose to destroy the Danville and South Side railroads, and thus deprive the enemy of further supplies, and also to prevent the rapid concentration of Lee's and Johnston's armies.

I had spent days of anxiety lest each morning should bring the report that the enemy had retreated the night before. I was firmly convinced that Sherman's crossing the Roanoke would be the signal for Lee to leave. With Johnston and him combined, a long, tedious, and expensive campaign, consuming most of the summer, might become necessary. By moving out I would put the army in better condition for pursuit, and would at least, by the destruction of the Danville Road, retard the concentration of the two armies of Lee and Johnston, and cause the enemy to abandon much material that he might otherwise save. I therefore determined not to delay the movement ordered.

On the night of the 27th, Major-General Ord, with two divisions of the 24th corps, Major-General Gibbon commanding, and one division of the 25th corps, Brigadier-General Birney commanding, and Mackenzie's cavalry, took up his line of march in pursuance of the foregoing instructions, and reached the position assigned him near Hatcher's Run on the morning of the 29th. On the 28th the following instructions were given to General Sheridan:

"CITY POINT, VA., March 28, 1865.

"GENERAL :-The 5th army corps will move by the Vaughn Road at three A.M. tomorrow morning. The 2nd moves at about nine A.M., having but about three miles to march to reach the point designated for it to take on the right of the 5th corps, after the later reaching Dinwiddle Court House. Move your cavalry at as early an hour as you can, and without being confined to any particular road or roads. You may go out by the nearest roads in rear of the 5th corps, pass by its left, and passing near to or through Dinwiddie, reach the right and rear of the enemy as soon as you can. It is not the intention to attack the enemy in his intrenched position, but to force him out, if possible. Should he come out and attack us, or get himself where he can be attacked, move in with your entire force in your own way, and with the full reliance that the army will engage or follow, as circumstances will dictate. I shall be on the field, and will probably be able to communicate with you. Should I not do so, and you find that the enemy keeps within his main intrenched line, you may cut loose and push for the Danville Road. If you find it practicable, I would like you to cross the South Side Road, between Petersburg and Burkesville, and destroy it to some extent. I would not advise much detention, however, until you reach the Danville Road, which I would like you to strike as near to the Appomattox as possible. Make your destruction on that road as complete as possible. You can then pass on to the South Side Road, west of Burkesville, and destroy that in like manner.

"After having accomplished the destruction of the two railroads, which are now the only avenues of supply to Lee 's army, you may return to this army, selecting your road further south, or you ma y go on into North Carolina and join General Sherman. Should you select the latter course, get the information to me as early as possible, so that I may send orders to meet you at Goldsboro'.

"U. S. GRANT, Lieutenant-General.

"MAJOR-GENERAL, P.H.. SHERIDAN."

On the morning of the 29th the movement commenced. At night the cavalry was at Dinwiddie Court House, and the left of our infantry line extended to the Quaker Road, near its intersection with the Boydton Plank Road. The position of the troops from left to right was as follows : Sheridan, Warren, Humphreys, Ord, Wright, Parke.

Everything looked favorable to the defeat of the enemy and the capture of Petersburg and Richmond, if the proper effort was made. I therefore addressed the following communication to General Sheridan, having previously informed him verbally not to cut loose for the raid contemplated in his orders until he received notice from me to do so:

"GRAVELLY CREEK, March 29, 1865

"GENERAL, :-Our line is now unbroken from the Appomattox to Dinwiddie. We are all ready, however, to give up all, from the Jerusalem Plank Road to Hatcher's Run, whenever the forces can be used advantageously. After getting into line south of Hatcher's, we pushed forward to find the enemy's position. General Griffin was attacked near where the Quaker Road intersects the Boydton Road, but repulsed it easily, capturing about one hundred men. Humphreys reached Dabney's Mill, and was pushing on when last heard from.

"I now feel like ending the matter, if it is possible to do so, before going back. I do not want you, therefore, to cut loose and go after the enemy's roads at present. In the morning push around the enemy, if you can, and get on to his right rear. The movements of the enemy's cavalry may, of course, modify your action. We will act all together as one army here, until it is seen what can be done with the enemy. The signal officer at Cobb's Hill reported, at half past eleven A.M, that a cavalry column had passed that point from Richmond towards Petersburg, taking forty minutes to pass.

"U.S. GRANT, Lieutenant-General.

"MAJOR-GENERAL P. H. SHERIDAN."

From the night of the 29th to the morning of the 31st the rain fell in such torrents as to make it impossible to move a wheeled vehicle, except as corduroy roads were laid in front of them. During the 30th, Sheridan advanced from Dinwiddie Court House towards Five Forks, where he found the enemy in full force. General Warren advanced and extended his line across the Boydton Plank Road to near the White Oak Road, with a, view of getting across the latter; but, finding the enemy strong in his front and extending beyond his left, was directed to hold on where he was, and fortify. General Humphreys drove the enemy from his front into his main line on the Hatcher, near Burgess's Mills. Generals Ord, Wright, and Parke made examinations in their fronts to determine the feasibility of an assault on the enemy's lines. The two latter reported favorably. The enemy confronting us as he did, at every point from Richmond to our extreme left, I conceived his lines must be weakly held, and could be penetrated if my estimate of his forces was correct. I determined, therefore, to extend our line no farther, but to reinforce General Sheridan with a corps of infantry, and thus enable him to cut loose and turn the enemy's right flank, and with the other corps assault the enemy's lines. The result of the offensive effort of the enemy the week before, when he assaulted Fort Stedman, particularly favored this. The enemy's intrenched picket line captured by us at that time threw the lines occupied by the belligerents so close together at some points that it was but a moment's run from one to the other. Preparations mere at once made to relieve General Humphrey's corps, to report to General Sheridan; but the condition of the roads prevented immediate movement. On the morning of the 31st, General Warren reported favorably to getting possessions of the White Oak Road, and was directed to do so. To accomplish this, he moved with one division, instead of his whole corps, which was attacked by the enemy in superior force and driven back on the 2d division before it had time to form, and it, in turn, forced back upon the 3d division, when the enemy was checked, A division of the 2d corps was immediately sent to his support, the enemy driven back with heavy loss, and possession of the White Oak Road gained. Sheridan advanced, and with a portion of his cavalry got possession of the Five Forks ; but the enemy, after the affair with the 5th corps, reinforced the rebel cavalry, defending that point with infantry, and forced him back towards Dinwiddie Court House. Here General Sheridan displayed great generalship. Instead of retreating with his whole command on the main army, to tell the story of superior forces encountered, he deployed his cavalry on foot, leaving only mounted men enough to take charge of the horses. This compelled the enemy to deploy over a vast extent of wooded and broken country, and made his progress slow. At this juncture he dispatched to me what had taken place, and that he was dropping back slowly on Dinwiddie Court House. General Mackenzie's cavalry and one division of the 5th corps were immediately ordered to his assistance. Soon after receiving a report from General Meade that Humphreys could hold our position on the Boydton Road, and that the other two divisions of the 5th corps could go to Sheridan, they were so ordered at once. Thus the operations of the day necessitated the sending of Warren, because of his accessibility, instead of Humphreys, as was intended and precipitated intended movements. On the morning of the 1st of April, General Sheridan, reinforced by General Warren, drove the enemy back on Five Forks, where, late in the evening, he assaulted and carried his strongly fortified position, capturing all his artillery and between five and six thousand prisoners.

About the close of this battle, Brevet Major-General Charles Griffin relieved Major-General Warren in command of the 5th corps. The report of this reached me after nightfall. Some apprehensions filled my mind lest the enemy might desert his lines during the night, and by falling upon General Sheridan before assistance could reach him, drive him from his position and open the way for retreat. To guard against this, General Miles's division of Humphreys's corps was sent to reinforce him, and a bombardment was commenced and kept up until four o 'clock in the morning (April 2), when an assault was ordered on the enemy's lines. General Wright penetrated the lines with his whole corps, sweeping everything before him, and to his left towards Hatcher's Run, capturing many guns and several thousand prisoners. He was closely followed by two divisions of General Ord's command, until he met the other division of General Ord's that had succeeded in forcing the enemy's lines near Hatcher's Run. Generals Wright and Ord immediately swung to the right, and closed all of the enemy on that side of them in Petersburg, while General Humphreys pushed forward with two divisions and joined General Wright on the left. General Parke succeeded in carrying the enemy's main line, capturing guns and prisoners, but was unable to carry his inner line. General Sheridan being advised of the condition of affairs, returned General Miles to his proper command. On reaching the enemy's lines immediately surrounding Petersburg, a portion of General Gibbon's corps, by a most gallant charge, captured two strong inclosed works, the most salient and commanding south of Petersburg, thus materially shortening the line of investment necessary for taking in the city. The enemy south of Hatcher's Run retreated westward to Sutherland's Station, where they were overtaken by Miles's division. A severe engagement ensued, and lasted until both his right and left flanks were threatened by the approach of General Sheridan, who was moving from Ford's Station towards Petersburg, and a division sent by General Meade from the front of Petersburg, when he broke in the utmost confusion, leaving in our hands his guns and many prisoners. This force retreated by the main road along the Appomattox River. During the night of the 2nd the enemy evacuated Petersburg and Richmond, and retreated towards Danville. On the morning of the 3d pursuit was commenced. General Sheridan pushed for the Danville Road, keeping near the Appomattox, followed by General Meade with the 2nd and 6th corps, while General Ord moved for Burkesville, along the South Side Road ; the 9th corps stretched along that road behind him. On the 4th, General Sheridan struck the Danville Road near Jetersville, where he learned that Lee was at Amelia Court House. He immediately intrenched himself and awaited the arrival of General Meade, who reached there the next day. General Ord reached Burkesville on the evening of the 5th.

On the morning of the 5th, I addressed Major-General Sherman the following communication:

"WILSON'S STATION, April 5, 1865.

"GENERAL:-All indications now are that Lee will attempt to reach Danville with the remnant of his force . Sheridan, who was up with him last night, reports all that is left, horse, foot, and dragoons, at twenty thousand, much demoralized. We hope to reduce this number one-half. I shall push on to Burkesville, and if a stand is made at Danville, will in a very few days go there. If you can possibly do so, push on from where you are, and let us see if we cannot finish the job with Lee's and Johnston's armies. Whether it will be better for you to strike for Greensboro', or nearer to Danville, you will be better able to judge when you receive this. Rebel armies now are the only strategic points to strike at.

"U.S. GRANT, Lieutenant-General.

"MAJOR-GENERAL W.T. SHERMAN."

On the morning of the 6th, it was found that General Lee was moving west of Jetersville, towards Danville. General Sheridan moved with his cavalry (the 5th corps having been returned to General Meade on his reaching Jetersville) to strike his flank, followed by the 6th corps, while the 2d and 5th corps pressed hard after, forcing him to abandon several hundred wagons and several pieces of artillery. General Ord advanced from Burkesville towards Farmville, sending two regiments of infantry and a squadron of cavalry, under Brevet Brigadier-General Theodore Read, to reach and destroy the bridges. This advance met the head of Lee's column near Farmville, which it heroically attacked and detained until General Read was killed and his small force overpowered. This caused a delay in the enemy's movements, and enabled General Ord to get well up with the remainder of his force, on meeting which, the enemy immediately intrenched himself. In the afternoon, General Sheridan struck the enemy south of Sailors' Creek, captured sixteen pieces of artillery and about four hundred wagons, and detained him until the 6th corps got up, when a general attack of infantry and cavalry was made, which resulted in the capture of six or seven thousand prisoners, among whom were many general officers. The movements of the 2d corps and General Ord's command contributed greatly to the day's success.

On the morning of the 7th the pursuit was renewed, the cavalry, except one division, and the 5th corps moving by Prince Edward's Court House; the 6th corps, General Ord's command, and one division of cavalry, on Farmville; and the 2nd corps by the High Bridge Road. It was soon found that the enemy had crossed to the north side of the Appomattox; but so close was the pursuit, that the 2nd corps got possession of the common bridge at High Bridge before the enemy could destroy it, and immediately crossed over. The 6th corps and a division of cavalry crossed at Farmville to its support.

Feeling now that General Lee's chance of escape was utterly hopeless, I addressed him the following communication from Farmville:

"April 7, 1865.

"GENERAL: -The result of the last week must convince you of the hopelessness of further resistance on the part of the Army of Northern Virginia in this struggle. I feel that it is so, and regard it as my duty to shift from myself the responsibility of any further effusion of blood, by asking of you the surrender of that portion of the Confederate States army known as the Army of Northern Virginia.

"U.S. GRANT, Lieutenant-General.
"GENERAL R. E. LEE."

Early on the morning of the 8th, before leaving, I received at Farmville the following:

"April 7, 1865.

"GENERAL:-I have received your note of this date. Though not entertaining the opinion you express on the hopelessness of further resistance on the part of the Army of Northern Virginia, I reciprocate your desire to avoid useless effusion of blood, and therefore, before considering your proposition, ask the terms you will offer on condition of its surrender.

"R.E. LEE, General

"LIEUTENANT-GENERAL U.S. GRANT."

To this I immediately replied:

"April 8, 1865

"GENERAL: --Your note of last evening, in reply to mine of same date, asking the condition on which I will accept the surrender of the Army of Northern Virginia, is just received. In reply, I would say, that peace being my great desire, there is but one condition I would insist upon namely, That the men and officers surrendered shall be disqualified for taking up arms again against the Government of the United States until properly exchanged. I will meet you, or will designate officers to meet any officers you may name for the same purpose, at any point agreeable to you, for the purpose of arranging definitely the terms upon which the surrender of the Army of Northern Virginia will be received.

"U.S. GRANT, Lieutenant-General.

"GENERAL R.E. LEE."

Early on the morning of the 8th the pursuit was resumed. General Meade followed north of the Appomattox, and General Sheridan, with all the cavalry, pushed straight for Appomattox Station, followed by General Ord's command and the 5th corps. During the day General Meade's advance had considerable fighting with the enemy's rear guard, but was unable to bring on a general engagement. Late in the evening General Sheridan struck the railroad at Appomattox Station, drove the enemy from there, and captured twenty-five pieces of artillery, a hospital train, and four trains of cars loaded with supplies for Lee's army. During this day I accompanied General Meade's column, and about midnight received the following communication from General Lee:

"April 8, 1865.

"GENERAL: -I received, at a late hour, your note of today. In mine of yesterday I did not intend to propose the surrender of the Army of Northern

416

Virginia, but to ask the terms of your proposition. To be frank, I do not think the emergency has arisen to call for the surrender of this army; but as the restoration of peace should be the sole object of all, I desired to know whether your proposals would lead to that end. I cannot, therefore, meet you with a view to surrender the Army of Northern Virginia: but as far as your proposal may affect the Confederates States forces under my command, and tend to the restoration of peace, I should be pleased to meet you at ten A.M. tomorrow on the old stage road to Richmond, between the picket lines of the two armies.

"R.E. LEE, General.

"LIEUTENANT -GENERAL U. S. GRANT."

Early on the morning of the 9th I returned him an answer as follows, and immediately started to join the column south of the Appomattox:

"April 9, 1865.

" GENERAL :-Your note of yesterday is received. I have no authority to treat on the subject of peace; the meeting proposed for ten A.M. today could lead to no good. I will state, however, general, that I am equally anxious for peace with yourself, and the whole North entertains the same feeling. The terms upon which peace can be had are well understood. By the South laying down their arms they will hasten that most desirable event, save thousands of human lives, and hundreds of millions of property not yet destroyed. Seriously hoping that all our difficulties may be settled without the loss of another life, I subscribe myself, etc.

"U. S. GRANT, Lieutenant-General.

"GENERAL R.E. LEE."

On the morning of the 9th, General Ord's command and the 5th corps reached Appomattox Station just as the enemy was making a desperate effort to break through our cavalry. The infantry was at once thrown in. Soon after a white flag was received, requesting a suspension of hostilities pending negotiations for a surrender. Before reaching General Sheridan 's headquarters, I received the following from General Lee:

"APRIL 9, 1865.

417

"GENERAL: -I received your note of this morning on the picket line, whither I had come to meet you, and ascertain definitely what terms were embraced in your proposal of yesterday with reference to the surrender of this army. I now ask an interview, in accordance with the offer contained in your letter of yesterday, for that purpose.

"R.E LEE, General.

"LIEUTENANT -GENERAL U.S. GRANT."

The interview was held at Appomattox Courthouse, the result of which is set forth in the following correspondence:

APPOMATTOX COURT-HOUSE, Virginia, April 9, 1865.

"GENERAL: -In accordance with the substance of my letter to you of the 8th instant, I propose to receive the surrender of the Army of Northern Virginia on the following terms, to wit : Rolls of all the officers and men to be made in duplicate, one copy to be given to an officer to be designated by me, the other to be retained by such officer or officers as you may designate. The officers to give their individual paroles not to take up arms against the Government of the United States until properly exchanged ; and each company or regimental commander sign a like parole for the men of their commands. The arms, artillery, and public property to be parked and stacked, and turned over to the officers appointed by me to receive them. This will not embrace the side arms of the officers, nor their private horses or baggage. This done, each officer and man will be allowed to return to his home, not to be disturbed by United States authority so long as they observe their paroles and the laws in force where they may reside.

"U.S. GRANT, Lieutenant-General.

"GENERAL R. E. LEE."

"HEADQUARTERS ARMY OF NORTHERN VIRGINIA, April 9, 1865

"GENERAL: -I have received your letter of this date containing the terms of surrender of the Army of Northern Virginia as proposed by you. As they are substantially the same as those expressed in your letter of the 8th instant, they are accepted. I will proceed to designate the proper officers to carry the stipulations into effect.

"R.E. LEE, General.

"LIEUTENANT-GENERAL U.S. GRANT."

The command of Major-General Gibbon, the 5th army corps under Griffin, and Mackenzie's cavalry, were designated to remain at Appomattox Court-House until the paroling of the surrendered army was completed, and to take charge of the public property. The remainder of the army immediately returned to the vicinity of Burkesville.

General Lee's great influence throughout the whole South caused his example to be followed, and today the result is that the armies lately under his leadership are at their homes, desiring peace and quiet, and their arms are in the hands of our ordnance officers.

On the receipt of my letter of the 5th, General Sherman moved directly against Joe Johnston, who retreated rapidly on and through Raleigh, which place General Sherman occupied on the morning of the 13th. The day preceding, news of the surrender of General Lee reached him at Smithfield.

On the 14th a correspondence was opened between General Sherman and General Johnston, which resulted on the 18th in an agreement for a suspension of hostilities, and a memorandum or basis for peace, subject to the approval of the President. This agreement was disapproved by the President on the 21st, which disapproval, together with your instructions, was communicated to General Sherman by me in person on the morning of the 24th, at Raleigh, North Carolina, in obedience to your orders. Notice was at once given by him to General Johnston for the termination of the truce that had been entered into. On the 25th another meeting between them was agreed upon, to take place on the 25th, which terminated in the surrender and disbandment of Johnston's army upon substantially the same terms as were given to General Lee.

The expedition under General Stoneman from East Tennessee got off on the 20th of March, moving by way of Boone, North Carolina, and struck the railroad at Wytheville, Chambersburg, and Big Lick. The force striking it at Big Lick pushed on to within a few miles of Lynchburg, destroying the important bridges, while with the main force he effectually destroyed it between New River and Big Lick, and then turned for Greensboro', on the North Carolina Railroad; struck that road and destroyed the bridges between Danville and Greensboro', and between Greensboro' and the Yadkin, together with the depots of supplies along it, and captured four hundred prisoners. At Salisbury he attacked and defeated a force of the enemy under General Gardiner, capturing fourteen pieces of artillery and one thousand three hundred and sixty-four prisoners, and destroyed large amounts of army stores. At this place he destroyed fifteen miles of railroad and the bridges towards Charlotte. Thence he moved to Slatersville.

General Canby, who had been directed in January to make preparations for a movement from Mobile Bay against Mobile and the interior of Alabama, commenced his movement on the 20th of March. The 16th corps, Major-General A.J. Smith commanding, moved from Fort Gaines by water to Fish River; the 13th corps, under Major-General Gordon Granger, moved from Fort Morgan and joined the 16th corps on Fish River, both moving thence on Spanish Fort and investing it on the 27th; while Major-General Steele's command moved from Pensacola, cut the railroad leading from Tensas to Montgomery, effected a junction with them, and partially invested Fort Blakely. After a severe bombardment of Spanish Fort, a part of its line was carried on the 8th of April. During the night the enemy evacuated the fort. Fort Blakely was carried by assault on the 9th, and many prisoners captured; our loss was considerable. These successes practically opened to us the Alabama River, and enabled us to approach Mobile from the north. On the night of the 11th the city was evacuated, and was taken possession of by our forces on the morning of the 12th.

The expedition under command of Brevet Major-General Wilson, consisting of twelve thousand five hundred mounted men, was delayed by rains until March 22d, when it moved from Chickasaw, Alabama. On the 1st of April, General Wilson encountered the enemy in force under Forrest near Ebenezer Church, drove him in confusion, captured three hundred prisoners and three guns, and destroyed the central bridge over the Cahawba River. On the 2d he attacked and captured the fortified city of Selma, defended by Forrest, with seven thousand men and thirty-two guns, destroyed the arsenal, armory, naval foundry, machine shops, vast quantities of stores, and captured three thousand prisoners. On the 4th he captured and destroyed Tuscaloosa. On the 10th he crossed the Alabama River, and after sending information of his operations to General Canby, marched on Montgomery, which place he occupied on the 14th, the enemy having abandoned it. At this place many stores and five steamboats fell into our hands. Thence a force marched direct on Columbus, and another on West Point, both of which places were assaulted and captured on the 16th. At the former place we got one thousand five hundred prisoners and fifty-two field guns, destroyed two gunboats, the navy yard, foundries, arsenal, many factories, and much other public property. At the latter place we got three hundred prisoners, four guns, and destroyed nineteen locomotives and three hundred cars. On the 20th he took possession of Macon, Georgia, with sixty field guns, one thousand two hundred militia, and five generals, surrendered by General Howell Cobb. General Wilson, hearing that Jeff Davis was trying to make his escape, sent forces in pursuit and succeeded in capturing him on the morning of May 11th.

On the 4th day of May, General Dick Taylor surrendered to General Canby all the remaining rebel forces east of the Mississippi.

A force sufficient to insure an easy triumph over the enemy under Kirby Smith, west of the Mississippi, was immediately put in motion for Texas, and Major-General Sheridan designated for its immediate command ; but on the 26th day of May, and before they reached their destination, General Kirby Smith surrendered his entire command to Major-General Canby. This surrender did not take place, however, until after the capture of the rebel President and Vice President; and the bad faith was exhibited of first disbanding most of his army and permitting an indiscriminate plunder of public property.

Owing to the report that many of those lately in arms against the government had taken refuge upon the soil of Mexico, carrying with them arms rightfully belonging to the United States, which had been surrendered to us by agreement among them some of the leaders who had surrendered in person and the disturbed condition of affairs on the Rio Grande, the orders for troops to proceed to Texas were not changed.

There have been severe combats, raids, expeditions, and movements to defeat the designs and purposes of the enemy, most of them reflecting great credit on our arms, and which contributed greatly to our final triumph, that I have not mentioned. Many of these will be found clearly set forth in the reports herewith submitted; some in the telegrams and brief dispatches announcing them, and others, I regret to say, have not as yet been officially reported.

For information touching our Indian difficulties, I would respectfully refer to the reports of the commanders of departments in which they have occurred.

It has been my fortune to see the armies of both the West and the East fight battles, and from what I have seen I know there is no difference in their fighting qualities. All that it was possible for men to do in battle they have done. The Western armies commenced their battles in the Mississippi Valley, and received the final surrender of the remnant of the principal army opposed to them in North Carolina. The armies of the East commenced their battles on the river from which the Army of the Potomac derived its name, and received the final surrender of their old antagonists at Appomattox Court House, Virginia. The splendid achievements of each have nationalized our victories, removed all sectional jealousies (of which we have unfortunately experienced too much), and the cause of crimination and recrimination that might have followed had either section failed in its duty. All have a proud record, and all sections can well congratulate themselves and each other for having done their full share in restoring the supremacy of law over every foot of territory belonging to the United States. Let them hope for perpetual peace and harmony with that enemy, whose manhood, however mistaken the cause, drew forth such herculean deeds of valor. I have the honor to be,

Very respectfully, your obedient servant,
U.S. GRANT, Lieutenant-General.

THE END

9 781582 188942